I B M
S P S S
FOR INTERMEDIATE
STATISTICS

Use and Interpretation

Fourth Edition

IBM SPSS

FOR INTERMEDIATE STATISTICS

Use and Interpretation

Fourth Edition

Nancy L. Leech
University of Colorado Denver

Karen C. Barrett
Colorado State University

George A. Morgan
Colorado State University

Routledge
Taylor & Francis Group
New York   London

Routledge
Taylor & Francis Group
711 Third Avenue
New York, NY 10017

Routledge
Taylor & Francis Group
27 Church Road
Hove, East Sussex BN3 2FA

© 2011 by Taylor and Francis Group, LLC
Routledge is an imprint of Taylor & Francis Group, an Informa business

Printed in the United States of America on acid-free paper
10 9 8 7 6 5 4 3 2 1

International Standard Book Number: 978-0-415-88047-3 (Paperback)

Visit the Taylor & Francis Web site at
http://www.taylorandfrancis.com

and the Psychology Press Web site at
http://www.psypress.com

Table of Contents

PREFACE

This book is designed to help students learn how to analyze and interpret research data with intermediate statistics. It is intended to be a supplemental text in an intermediate statistics course in the behavioral sciences, social sciences, or education and it can be used in conjunction with any mainstream text. We have found that the book makes IBM SPSS easy to use so that it is not necessary to have a formal, instructional computer lab; you should be able to learn how to use SPSS on your own with this book. Access to the SPSS program and some familiarity with Windows® is all that is required. Although SPSS is quite easy to use, there is such a wide variety of options and statistics that knowing which ones to use and how to interpret the printouts can be difficult. This book is intended to help with these challenges.

SPSS 19 and Earlier Versions

We use SPSS 19 from IBM SPSS in this book; except for enhanced tables and graphics, there are only minor differences from version 10 to 18. In October 2009, IBM bought the SPSS Corporation and changed the name of the program used in this book from *SPSS for Windows* to *IBM SPSS Statistics*. We expect future Windows and Mac versions to be similar. Our students have used this book, or earlier editions of it, with all of the versions of SPSS for Windows; most of the procedures and outputs are quite similar. We point out some of the changes at various points in the text.

In addition to various SPSS modules that may be available at your university, there are versions available to students that you can rent for 6 or 12 months online. You can get information about available products for graduate students by visiting http://www-01.ibm.com/software/analytics/spss/products/statistics/gradpack/. *IBM SPSS Statistics Standard GradPack* enables you to do all the statistics in this book, those in our *IBM SPSS for Introductory Statistics,* 4th edition book (Morgan, Leech, Gloeckner, & Barrett, 2011), and many others.

Goals of This Book

This book demonstrates how to produce a variety of statistics that are usually included in intermediate statistics courses, plus some (e.g., reliability measures, canonical correlation, and multilevel models) that are unusual in intermediate statistics books but may be useful in your research. Our goal is to describe the use and interpretation of these statistics as much as possible in nontechnical, jargon-free language.

Helping you learn how to choose the appropriate statistics, interpret the outputs, and develop skills in writing about the meaning of the results are the main goals of this book. Thus, we have included material on:

      1. How the appropriate **choice of a statistic** is based on the design of the research.
      2. How to use SPSS to **help answer research questions**.
      3. How to **interpret SPSS outputs**.
      4. How to **write about the outputs** in the Results section of a paper.

This information will help you develop skills that cover all steps in the research process: design, data collection, data entry, data analysis, interpretation of outputs, and writing results. The modified high school and beyond data set (HSB) used in this book is similar to one you might have for a thesis, dissertation, or research project. Therefore, we think it can serve as a model for your analysis. The Web site, http://www.researchmethodsarena.com/9780415880473, contains the HSB data file and several other data sets that are used for the extra statistics problems at the end of chapters. However, **you will need to have access to or purchase the SPSS program.**

PREFACE

To make the text more readable, we have chosen not to cite many references in the text; however, we have provided a short bibliography, "For Further Reading," of some of the books and articles that we have found useful. We assume that most students will use this book in conjunction with a class that has a statistics textbook; it will help you to read more about each statistic before doing the assignments.

Our companion book, Morgan et al. (2011), *IBM SPSS for Introductory Statistics: Use and Interpretation* (4th ed.), also published by Routledge/Taylor & Francis, is on the "For Further Reading" list at the end of this book. To learn more about that book feel free to visit www.psypress.com/ibm-spss-intro-stats. Our introductory book provides an extended discussion of how to interpret and write about introductory statistics, including ones such as *t* tests, chi-square, and correlation. A brief review of such basic statistics is provided in Appendix B of this book.

Instructional Features

Several user-friendly features of this book include
1. The **key SPSS windows** that you see when performing the statistical analyses. This has been helpful to "visual learners."
2. The **complete outputs** for the analyses that we have done so you can see what you will get, after some editing in SPSS to make the outputs fit better on the pages.
3. **Callout boxes** on the outputs that point out parts of the output to focus on and indicate what they mean.
4. For each output, a boxed **interpretation section** that will help you understand the output.
5. Specially developed flow charts and tables to help you **select an appropriate inferential statistic** and tell you how to **interpret statistical significance and effect sizes** (in Chapter 5). This chapter also provides an extended example of how to identify and write a research problem, several research questions, and a results paragraph for a *t* test and bivariate regression.
6. For the statistics in Chapters 3, 4, and 6–11, an example of **how to write about the output** and make a table for a thesis, dissertation, or research paper.
7. **Interpretation questions** that stimulate you to think about the information in the chapter and outputs.
8. Several **extra SPSS problems** at the end of each chapter, except Chapters 1 and 5, for you to run with SPSS and discuss.
9. Information (in Appendix A) on how to **get started with SPSS** and some other useful commands.
10. A brief review (Appendix B) of **basic statistics**.
11. **Answers** to the odd-numbered interpretation questions (Appendix C).
12. **Several data sets are available on the book Web site** http://www.researchmethods arena.com/ 9780415880473. These realistic data sets provide you with data to be used to solve the chapter problems and the extra SPSS problems at the end of each chapter. Also on the website are three other files: (a) a **Quick Reference Guide (QRG)** to commonly used SPSS procedures, (b) a document, **Making APA Tables and Figures**, describing how to make tables in APA format, and (c) a file to use with the syntax for Canonical Correlation in Chapter 10.
13. An **Instructor Resource Web site** is available to course instructors who request access from the publisher. To request access, please visit the book page or the Textbook Resource tabs at www.psypress.com. It contains aids for teaching the course, including PowerPoint® slides, the answers to the even–numbered interpretation questions, and extra SPSS problems. Students will benefit from the chapter outlines and study guides. The study guide portion includes a list of key concepts to remember and define after reading each chapter.

PREFACE

Researchers who purchase copies for their personal use can access the data files by visiting http://www.researchmethodsarena.com/9780415880473.

Overview of the Chapters

Our approach in this book is to present how to use and interpret IBM SPSS in the context of proceeding as if the HSB data were the actual data from your research project. However, before starting the SPSS assignments, we have two introductory chapters. The first chapter is an introduction and review of research design and how it would apply to analyzing the HSB data. In addition, this chapter includes a review of measurement and descriptive statistics. Chapter 2 discusses rules for coding data, exploratory data analysis (EDA), and assumptions. Much of what is done in this chapter involves preliminary analyses to get ready to answer the research questions that you might investigate in a report.

Chapters 3 and 4 present methods for assessing the reliability and validity of your data. Chapter 3 covers how to compute Cronbach's alpha, test–retest, and interobserver reliability. Chapter 4 presents one method of assessing validity; it includes exploratory factor analysis and principal components analysis.

Chapter 5 provides a brief overview of research designs (between groups and within subjects). This chapter provides flow charts and tables useful for selecting an appropriate statistic. Also included is an overview of how to interpret and write about the results of two basic inferential statistics. This section includes not only testing for statistical significance but also discussions of power and effect size measures, including guidelines for interpretation.

Chapters 6–11 are designed to help you answer several research questions. Solving the problems in these chapters should give you a good idea of some of the intermediate statistics that can be computed with IBM SPSS. Hopefully, seeing how the research questions and design lead naturally to the choice of statistics will become apparent after using this book. In addition, it is our hope that interpreting what you get back from the computer will become clearer after doing these assignments, studying the outputs, answering the interpretation questions, and doing the extra SPSS problems.

Our Approach to Research Questions, Measurement, and Selection of Statistics

In Chapters 1 and 5, our approach is somewhat nontraditional because we have found that students have a great deal of difficulty with some aspects of research and statistics but not others. Most can learn formulas and "crunch" the numbers quite easily and accurately with a calculator or with a computer. However, many have trouble knowing what statistics to use and how to interpret the results. They do not seem to have a "big picture" or see how research design and measurement influence data analysis. Part of the problem is inconsistent terminology. For these reasons, we have tried to present a semantically consistent and coherent picture of how research design leads to three basic kinds of research questions (difference, associational, and descriptive) which, in turn, lead to three kinds or groups of statistics with the same names. We realize that these and other attempts to develop and utilize a consistent framework are both nontraditional and somewhat of an oversimplification. However, we think the framework and consistency pay off in terms of student understanding and the ability to actually use statistics to answer the research questions. Instructors who are not persuaded that this framework is useful can skip Chapter 1 and the first part of Chapter 5 and still have a book that helps their students use and interpret SPSS.

Major Changes and Additions to This Edition

The major change in this edition is updating the windows and text to IBM SPSS 19. We have also attempted to correct any typos in the 3rd edition and clarify some passages. In Chapter 2, we added research questions and directions for conducting each statistic to assist the reader in conducting exploratory data analysis. In the chapter on reliability (Chapter 3) we included an "example of how to write about" each problem. Chapter 5 includes an expanded discussion on effect sizes to include information on confidence intervals of effect sizes. Chapter 6 includes new information on part and partial correlations and how they are interpreted. We included write-ups for each example in Chapter 8, as well as how to do post-hocs with ANCOVAs. Chapter 11 is revised and now includes how to do polynomials for multilevel models. We expanded the appendix about Getting Started with IBM SPSS (Appendix A) to include several useful procedures that were not discussed in the body of the text.

In addition, we have modified the format of the examples of how to write about the outputs to meet the changes in APA format in the 6th edition (2010) of the *Publication Manual of the American Psychological Association*. Although this edition was written using version 19, the program is sufficiently similar to prior versions of this software that we feel you should be able to use this book with earlier and later versions as well.

Bullets, Arrows, Bold, and Italics

To help you do the problems with SPSS, we have developed some conventions. We use bullets to indicate actions in SPSS Windows that you will take. For example:

- Highlight *gender* and *math achievement*.
- Click on the arrow to move the variables into the right-hand box.
- Click on **Options** to get Fig. 2.16.
- Check **Mean, Std Deviation, Minimum,** and **Maximum**.
- Click on **Continue**.

Note that the words in italics are variable names and words in bold are words that you will see in the SPSS Windows and utilize to produce the desired output. In the text they are spelled and capitalized as you see them in the Windows. Bold also is used to identify key terms when they are introduced, defined, or important to understanding.

The words you will see in the pull-down menus are given in bold with arrows between them. For example:

- Select **Analyze → Descriptive Statistics → Frequencies**

(This means pull down the Analyze menu, then slide your cursor down to Descriptive Statistics, over to Frequencies, and click.)

Occasionally, we have used underlines to emphasize critical points or commands.

We have tried hard to make this book accurate and clear so that it could be used by students and professionals to learn to compute and interpret statistics without the benefit of a class. However, we find that there are always some errors and places that are not totally clear. Thus, we would like for you to help us identify any grammatical or statistical errors and to point out places that need to be clarified. Please send suggestions to *nancy.leech@ucdenver.edu*.

PREFACE

Acknowledgments

This SPSS book is consistent with and could be used as a supplement for Gliner, Morgan, and Leech (2009), *Research Methods in Applied Settings: An Integrated Approach to Design and Analysis,* or Morgan, Gliner, and Harmon (2006), *Understanding and Evaluating Research in Applied and Clinical Settings*. Information about both books can be found at www.psypress.com. In fact, some sections of Chapters 1 and 5 have been only slightly modified from these texts. For this we thank Jeff Gliner, coauthor of those books. Orlando Griego was an author on our first edition of this SPSS book; this revision still shows the imprint of his student-friendly writing style.

We would like to acknowledge the assistance of the many students in our education and human development classes who have used earlier versions of this book and provided helpful suggestions for improvement. We could not have completed the task or made it look so good without our technology consultants, Don Quick and Ian Gordon, and our word processor, Sophie Nelson. Linda White, Catherine Lamana, Alana Stewart, and several other student workers were key to creating figures in earlier versions. Jikyeong Kang, Bill Sears, LaVon Blaesi, Mei-Huei Tsay, and Sheridan Green assisted with classes and the development of materials for the DOS and earlier Windows versions of the assignments. Laura Jensen, Lisa Vogel, Andrea Fritz, James Lyall, Joan Anderson, Pam Cress, Joan Clay, and Yasmine Andrews helped with writing or editing parts of this or earlier editions. Jeff Gliner, Jerry Vaske, Jim zumBrunnen, Laura Goodwin, David MacPhee, Gene Gloeckner, James O. Benedict, Barry Cohen, John Ruscio, Tim Urdan, and Steve Knotek provided reviews of earlier editions and/or suggestions for improving the text. Carolyn Springer, Jay Parkes, Joshua Watson, and John Rugutt provided helpful reviews for the 3rd edition. Don Quick, Sophie Nelson, and John Cumming wrote helpful appendixes for this edition. Bob Fetch and Ray Yang provided helpful feedback on the readability and user friendliness of the text. Finally, the patience of our spouses (Grant, Terry, and Hildy) and families enabled us to complete the task, without too much family strain.

Nancy L. Leech
University of Colorado Denver

Karen Caplovitz Barrett
Colorado State University

George A. Morgan
Colorado State University

CHAPTER 1

Introduction

This chapter will review important information about measurement and descriptive statistics and provide an overview of the expanded high school and beyond (HSB) data set, which will be used in this chapter and throughout the book to demonstrate the use and interpretation of the several statistics that are presented. First, we provide a brief review of some key terms, as we will use them in this book.

Research Problems and Variables

Research Problems

The research process begins with an issue or problem of interest to the researcher. This **research problem** is a statement that <u>asks about the relationships between two or more variables</u>. Almost all research studies have *more* than two variables.

Variables

Variables are key elements in research. A **variable** is defined as a characteristic of the participants or situation for a given study that has several values in that study. <u>A variable must be able to vary or have different values or levels in the study.</u>[1] For example, *gender* is a variable because it has two levels, female or male. *Age* is a variable that has a large number of values. *Type of treatment/intervention* (or *type of curriculum*) is a variable if there is more than one treatment or a treatment and a control group. *Number of days to learn something or to recover from an ailment* are common measures of the effect of a treatment and, thus, are also variables. Similarly, *amount of mathematics knowledge* is a variable because it can vary from none to a lot. If a concept <u>has only one value</u> in a particular study, it is not a variable; <u>it is a constant</u>. Thus, ethnic group is not a variable if all participants are European-American. Gender is not a variable if all participants in a study are female.

In quantitative research, variables are defined operationally and are commonly divided into **independent variables** (active or attribute), **dependent variables**, and **extraneous variables**. Each of these topics will be dealt with briefly in the following sections.

Operational definitions of variables. An operational definition describes or <u>defines a variable in terms of the operations or techniques used to make it happen or measure it</u>. When quantitative researchers describe the variables in their study, they specify what they mean by demonstrating how they measured the variable. Demographic variables like age, gender, or ethnic group are usually measured simply by asking the participant to choose the appropriate category from a list. Types of treatment (or curriculum) are usually operationally defined much more extensively by describing what was done during the treatment or new curriculum. Likewise, abstract concepts like mathematics knowledge, self-concept, or mathematics anxiety need to be defined operationally by spelling out in some detail how they were measured in a particular study. To do this, the investigator may provide sample questions, append the actual instrument, or provide a reference where more information can be found.

---

[1] To help you, we have identified the SPSS variable names and labels using italics (e.g., *gender* and *ethnic*). Sometimes italics are also used to emphasize a word. We have put in bold the terms used in the SPSS windows and outputs (e.g., **SPSS Data Editor**) and other key terms when they are introduced, defined, or are important to understanding. Underlines are used to emphasize critical points. Bullets precede instructions about SPSS actions (e.g., click, highlight).

Independent Variables

We refer to two types of independent variables: **active** and **attribute.** It is important to distinguish between these types when we discuss the results of a study.

Active or manipulated independent variables. An active independent variable is a variable, such as a workshop, new curriculum, or intervention, at least one level of which <u>is given to a group of participants,</u> ideally within a specified period of time during the study. For example, a researcher might investigate a new kind of therapy compared to the traditional treatment. A second example might be to study the effect of a new teaching method, such as cooperative learning, on student performance. In these two examples, the variable of interest was something that was *given to* the participants. Thus, active independent variables are *given* to the participants during the study but are <u>not necessarily given or manipulated by the experimenter.</u> The independent variable may be given by a clinic, school, or someone other than the investigator, but from the participants' point of view the situation was manipulated. Ideally, the <u>treatment is given *after* the study was planned</u> so that there can be a pretest and so participants can be randomly assigned to receive it or not. If there is no pretest, or no random assignment, internal validity of the study will be in jeopardy. Other writers have similar but, perhaps, slightly different definitions of active independent variables. **Randomized experimental** and **quasi-experimental** studies have an active independent variable. An active independent variable is a necessary but not sufficient condition to make cause-and-effect conclusions; the clearest causal conclusions can be drawn from well-controlled randomized experiments when participants are *assigned randomly* to *one of two or more* groups, at least one of which will receive the intervention.

Attribute or measured independent variables. A variable that cannot be manipulated, yet is a major focus of the study viewed by the researchers as a predictor of or influence on one or more dependent variables, can be called an attribute independent variable. For attribute independent variables, the values of the independent variables are <u>preexisting attributes of the persons or their ongoing environment</u> that are not systematically changed during the study. For example, gender, age, ethnic group, IQ, and self-esteem can be used as attribute independent variables. Studies with only attribute independent variables are called **nonexperimental** studies.

In keeping with SPSS, but unlike authors of some research methods books, we do not restrict the term independent variable to those variables that are manipulated or active. We define an independent variable more broadly to include any predictors, antecedents, or *presumed* causes or influences under investigation in the study. Attributes of the participants, as well as active independent variables, fit within this definition. For the social sciences and education, attribute independent variables are especially important. Type of disability or level of disability may be the major focus of a study. Disability certainly qualifies as a variable since it can take on different values even though they are not *given during* the study. For example, cerebral palsy is different from Down syndrome, which is different from spina bifida, yet all are disabilities. Also, there are different levels of the same disability. People already have defining characteristics or attributes that place them into one of two or more categories. The different disabilities are already present when we begin our study. Thus, we might also be interested in studying variables that are not given or manipulated during the study, even by other persons, schools, or clinics.

Other labels for the independent variable. SPSS uses a variety of terms in addition to independent variable, for example, **factor** (Chapters 8, 9, 10, and 11), and **covariate** (Chapters 7 and 11). In other cases, (Chapters 3 and 4) SPSS and statisticians do not make a distinction between the independent and dependent variable; they just label them **variables.** For example, there is no independent variable for a correlation or chi-square. However, even for chi-square, we think it is sometimes educationally useful to think of one variable as the independent variable and the other as the outcome (dependent variable), as is the case in analysis of variance (ANOVA) or multivariate analysis of variance (MANOVA).

Values of the independent variable. SPSS uses the term **values** to describe the several options or values of a variable. These values are *not* necessarily ordered, and several other terms — **categories, levels, groups,** or **samples** — are sometimes used interchangeably with the term values, especially in statistics books. Suppose that an investigator is performing a study to investigate the effect of a treatment. One group of participants is assigned to the treatment group. A second group does not receive the treatment. The study could be conceptualized as having one independent variable (*treatment type)*, with two values or levels (*treatment* and *no treatment*). The independent variable in this example would be classified as an active independent variable. Now, suppose instead that the investigator was primarily interested in comparing two different treatments but decided to include a third no-treatment group as a control group in the study. The study still would be conceptualized as having one active independent variable (*treatment type*) but with three values or levels (the two treatment conditions and the control condition). As an additional example, consider *gender*, which is an attribute independent variable with two values, *male* and *female*.

Note that in SPSS each variable is given a **variable label** that assists the researcher in understanding the variable. Moreover, each value or level is assigned a number used by SPSS to compute statistics, and these numbers can be assigned **value labels** that indicate what the numbers stand for (e.g., *male* and *female*). It is especially important to use value labels when the variable is **nominal** (i.e., when the values of the variable are just names and, thus, are not ordered), so that you can know the category to which each of the numbers refers.

Dependent Variables

The **dependent variable** is assumed to <u>measure or assess the effect of the independent variable</u>. It is thought of as the <u>presumed outcome or criterion</u>. Dependent variables are often test scores, ratings on questionnaires, readings from instruments (e.g., electrocardiogram, galvanic skin response), or measures of physical performance. Dependent variables, like independent variables, must have at least two values; <u>most dependent variables have many values, varying from low to high</u>.

SPSS also uses a number of other terms in addition to dependent variable. **Dependent list** is used in cases where you can do the same statistic several times, for a list of dependent variables (e.g., see one-way ANOVA). **Grouping variable** is used in Chapter 7 for discriminant analysis.

Extraneous Variables

These are variables (also called nuisance variables or, in some designs, covariates) that are <u>not of primary interest in a particular study but could influence the dependent variable</u>. Environmental factors (e.g., temperature or distractions), time of day, and characteristics of the experimenter, teacher, or therapist are some possible extraneous variables that need to be controlled. SPSS does not use the term extraneous variable. However, sometimes such variables are controlled using statistics that are available in SPSS.

Research Hypotheses and Research Questions

Research hypotheses <u>are predictive statements about the relationship between variables.</u> **Research questions** <u>are similar to hypotheses, except that they do not entail specific predictions</u> and are phrased in question format. For example, one might have the following research question: "Is there a difference in students' scores on a standardized test if they took two tests in one day versus taking only one test on each of two days?" A research hypothesis regarding the same issue might be: "Students who take only one test per day will score *better* on standardized tests than will students who take two tests in one day."

We divide research questions into three broad types: **difference, associational,** and **descriptive** as shown in the middle of Fig 1.1. The figure also shows the general and specific purposes and the general types of statistics for each of these three types of research question.

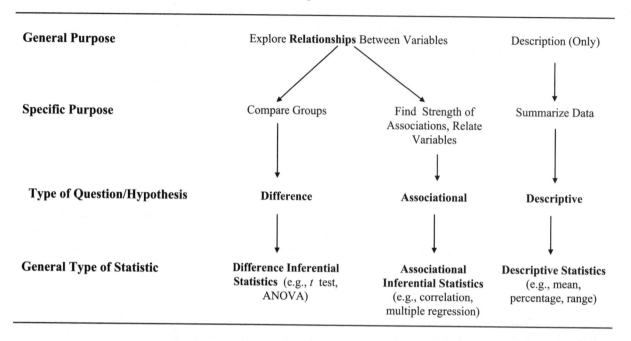

Fig. 1.1. Schematic diagram showing how the purpose and type of research question correspond to the general type of statistic used in a study.

Difference research questions. For these questions, we compare scores (on the dependent variable) of two or more groups (e.g., males and females). Each group is composed of individuals who have the same value or level of the independent variable and who potentially (and hopefully!) have a different level of the dependent variable than do individuals in the other groups. This type of question attempts to demonstrate that groups are not the same on the dependent variable.

Associational research questions are those in which two or more variables are associated or related. This approach usually involves an attempt to see how two or more variables covary or how one or more variables enable one to predict another variable. When two variables covary positively, individuals who have high scores on one variable also tend to have high scores on the other variable; other individuals have relatively low scores on both variables or middling scores on both variables.

Descriptive research questions are not answered with inferential statistics. They merely describe or summarize data without trying to generalize to a larger population of individuals.

Figure 1.1 shows that both <u>difference and associational questions</u> or hypotheses <u>are similar in that they explore the relationships between variables.</u>[2] Note that difference and associational questions differ in specific purpose and the kinds of statistics they use to answer the question.

---

[2]This similarity is in agreement with the statement by statisticians that all common parametric inferential statistics are relational. We use the term associational for the second type of research question rather than relational or correlational to distinguish it from the *general purpose* of both difference and associational questions/hypotheses, which is to study relationships. Also we wanted to distinguish between correlation, as a specific statistical technique, and the broader type of associational question and that group of statistics.

Remember that research questions are similar to hypotheses, but they are stated in question format. We think it is advisable to use the question format when one does not have a clear directional prediction and also for the descriptive approach. As implied by Fig. 1.1, it is acceptable to phrase any research question that involves two or more variables as whether there is a relationship between the variables (e.g., "Is there a relationship between *gender* and *math achievement*?" or "Is there a relationship between *anxiety* and *GPA*?"). However, we think that phrasing the question as a difference or association is desirable because it helps one choose an appropriate statistic and interpret the result. For more information on how to write research questions, please see the Appendix on writing research questions.

Complex Research Questions

Most research questions posed in this book involve more than two variables at a time. We call such questions and the appropriate statistics **complex**. Some of these statistics are called **multivariate** in other texts, but there is not a consistent definition of multivariate in the literature. We provide examples of how to write complex research questions in the chapter pertaining to each complex statistic.

In a factorial ANOVA, there are two (or more) independent variables and one dependent variable. We will see, in Chapter 8, that when you do one factorial ANOVA there are actually three (or more) research questions. This *set* of three questions can be considered a complex difference question because the study has two independent variables. Likewise, complex associational questions are used in studies with more than one independent variable considered together.

Table 1.1 expands our overview of research questions to include both basic and complex questions of each of the three types: **descriptive**, **difference**, and **associational**. The table also includes references to other chapters in this book and examples of the types of statistics that we include under each of the six types of questions.

A Sample Research Problem:
The Modified High School and Beyond (HSB) Study

The SPSS file name of the data set used with this book is *hsbdataB.sav*; it stands for high school and beyond data. It is based on a national sample of data from more than 28,000 high school students. Our data set includes a sample of 75 students drawn randomly from the larger population. The data that we have for this sample include school outcomes such as grades and the number of mathematics courses of different types that the students took in high school. Also, there are several kinds of standardized test data and demographic data such as gender and mother's and father's education. To provide an example of questionnaire data, we have included 14 questions about mathematics attitudes. These data were developed for this book and, thus, are not really the math[3] attitudes of the 75 students in this sample; however, they are based on real data gathered by one of the authors to study motivation. Also, we made up data for *religion*, *ethnic group*, and *SAT-math*, which are somewhat realistic overall. These inclusions enable us to do some additional statistical analyses.

The Research Problem

Imagine that you are interested in the general problem of <u>what factors seem to influence mathematics achievement</u> at the end of high school. You might have some hunches or hypotheses about such factors based on your experience and your reading of the research and popular literature. Some factors that might influence mathematics achievement are commonly called demographics: for example, *gender, ethnic*

---

[3] We have decided to use the short version of mathematics (i.e., math) throughout the book to save space and because it is used in common language.

group, and *mother's* and *father's education.* A probable influence would be the mathematics courses that the student has taken. We might speculate that *grades in mathematics* and in other subjects could have an impact on *math achievement.* However, other variables, such as *students' IQs* or *parents' encouragement and assistance,* could be the actual causes of both high grades and math achievement. Such variables could influence what courses one took and the grades one received and might be correlates of the demographic variables. We might wonder how spatial performance scores, such as *mosaic pattern test* scores and *visualization scores,* might enable a more complete understanding of the problem and whether these skills seem to be influenced by the same factors as *math achievement.*

Table 1.1. *Summary of Six Types of Research Questions and Appropriate Statistics*

Type of Research Question – Number of Variables	Statistics (Example)
1) **Basic Descriptive Questions** – One variable	Table 1.5, Ch. 1 (e.g., mean, standard deviation, frequency distribution)
2) **Complex Descriptive Questions** – Two or more variables, but no use of inferential statistics	Ch. 2, 3, 4 (e.g., mean & SD for a variable after forming groups based on another variable, principal components analysis, measures of reliability)
3) **Basic/Single Factor Difference Questions** – One independent and one dependent variable. Independent variable usually has a few levels (ordered or not).	Table 5.1, Appendix B (*t* test, one-way ANOVA)
4) **Complex/Multifactor Difference Question** – Three or more variables. Usually two or a few independent variables and one (or more) dependent variables.	Table 5.3, Ch. 7. 8, 9, 10, 11 (discriminant analysis, factorial ANOVA, MANOVA, HLM)
5) **Basic Associational Questions** – One independent variable and one dependent variable. Usually at least five *ordered* levels for both variables. Often they are continuous.	Table 5.2, Appendix B (bivariate regression, correlation tested for significance)
6) **Complex/Multivariate Associational Questions** – Two or more independent variables and one (or more) dependent variable. Often five or more ordered levels for all variables but some or all can be dichotomous variables.	Table 5.4, Ch. 6, 7, 10, 11 (multiple or logistic regression, discriminant analysis, canonical correlation, HLM)

Note: Many studies have more than one dependent variable. It is common to treat each one separately (i.e., to do several *t* tests, ANOVAs, correlations, or multiple regressions). However, there are complex statistics (e.g., MANOVA and canonical correlation) used to treat several dependent variables together in one analysis.

The HSB Variables

Before we state the research problem and questions in more formal ways, we need to step back and discuss the types of variables and the approaches that might be used to study the above problem. We need to identify the independent/antecedent (presumed causes) variables, the dependent/outcome variable(s), and any extraneous variables.

The primary dependent variable. Given the above research problem, which focuses on mathematics achievement at the end of the senior year, the primary dependent variable is *math achievement.*

Independent and extraneous variables. The *number of math courses taken* is best considered to be an **input** (the SPSS term), antecedent, or independent variable in this study. What about *father's* and *mother's education* and *gender*? How would you classify *gender* and *parents' education* in terms of the type of variable? What about *grades*? Like the *number of math courses*, these variables would usually be considered independent variables because they occurred before the math achievement test. However, some of these variables, specifically parental education, might be viewed as extraneous variables that need to be "controlled." *Visualization* and *mosaic pattern test* scores probably could be either independent or dependent variables depending upon the specific research question, because they were measured at approximately the same time as math achievement, at the end of the senior year. We have labeled them **Both** under **Role**. Note that student's class is a constant and is not a variable in this study because all the participants are high school seniors (i.e., it does not vary; it is the population of interest).

Types of independent variables. As we discussed previously, independent variables can be **active** (given to the participant during the study or manipulated by the investigator) or **attributes** of the participants or their environments. Are there any **active** independent variables in this study? No! There is no intervention, new curriculum, or similar treatment. All the independent variables, then, are attribute variables because they are attributes or characteristics of these high school students. Because all the independent variables are attributes, the research approach cannot be experimental. This means that we will *not* be able to draw definite conclusions about cause and effect (i.e., we will find out what is related to math achievement, but we will not know for sure what causes or influences math achievement).

Now we will examine the *hsbdataB.sav* file that you will use to study this complex research problem. On the companion website, we have provided a file that contains the data for each of the 75 participants on 45 variables. The variables in the *hsbdataB.sav* file have already been labeled (see Fig 1.2) and entered (see Fig 1.3) to enable you to get started on analyses quickly. The website contains several SPSS data files for you to use, but it does not include the actual SPSS program, which you will have to have access to in order to open the files and to do the assignments.

The SPSS Variable View
Figure 1.2 is a piece of what SPSS calls the **variable view** in the **SPSS Data Editor** for the hsbdataB.sav file. Figure 1.2 shows information about each of the first five variables. When you open this file and click on **Variable View** at the bottom left corner of the screen, this is what you will see. What is included in the variable view screen is described in more detail in Appendix A, Getting Started with SPSS. Here, focus on the Name, Label, Values, and Missing columns. **Name** is a short name for each variable (e.g., *faed* or *alg1*).[4] **Label** is a longer label for the variable (e.g., *father's education* or *Algebra 1 in h.s.*). The **Values** column contains the **value labels,** but you can see the label for only one value at a time (e.g., 0 = male). That is, you cannot see that 1 = female unless you click on the row for that variable under the value column. The **Missing** column indicates whether there are any special, user-identified missing values. **None** means that there are no special missing values, just the usual *SPSS* **system missing** value, which is a blank.

---

[4] In SPSS 7–11, the variable name had to be eight characters or less. In SPSS 12–19, it can be longer, but we recommend that you keep it short. If a longer name is used with SPSS 7–11, the name will be truncated. SPSS names must start with a letter and must not contain blank spaces or certain special characters (e.g., !, ?, ', or *).

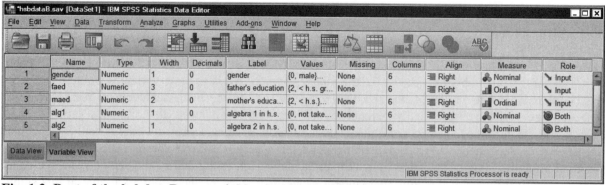

Fig. 1.2. Part of the hsbdataB.sav variable view in the SPSS data editor.

Variables in the Modified HSB Data Set

The 45 variables shown in Table 1.2 (with the values/levels or range of their values in parentheses) are found in the *hsbdataB.sav* file. Note that variables 33–38 and 42–44 were computed from the *math attitude* variables (19–32).

Table 1.2. *HSB Variable Descriptions*

	Name	Label (and Values)
		Demographic School and Test Variables
1.	gender	*gender* (0 = male, 1 = female).
2.	faed	*father's education* (2 = less than h.s. to 10 = PhD/MD).
3.	maed	*mother's eduction* (2 = less than h.s. grad to 10 = PhD/MD).
4.	alg1	*algebra 1 in h.s.* (1 = taken, 0 = not taken)
5.	alg2	*algebra 2 in h.s.* (1 = taken, 0 = not taken)
6.	geo	*geometry in h.s.* (1 = taken, 0 = not taken)
7.	trig	*trigonometry in h.s.* (1 = taken, 0 = not taken)
8.	calc	*calculus in h.s.* (1 = taken, 0 = not taken)
9.	mathgr	*math grades* (0 = low, 1 = high)
10.	grades	*grades in h.s.* (1 = less than a D average to 8 = mostly an A average)
11.	mathach	*math achievement score* (−8.33 to 25).[5] This is a test something like the ACT math.
12.	mosaic	*mosaic, pattern test* score (−4 to 56). This is a test of pattern recognition ability involving the detection of relationships in patterns of tiles.
13.	visual	*visualization score* (−4 to 16). This is a 16-item test that assesses visualization in three dimensions (i.e., how a three-dimensional object would look if its spatial position were changed).
14.	visual2	*visualization retest* – the visualization test score students obtained when they retook the test a month or so later.
15.	satm	*scholastic aptitude test – math* (200 = lowest, 800 = highest possible)
16.	ethnic	*ethnicity in student records* (1 = Euro-American, 2 = African-American, 3 = Latino-American, 4 = Asian-American, 98 = other or multiethnic, chose 2 or more, 99 = missing, left blank)
17.	religion	*religion* (1 = protestant, 2 = catholic, 3 = no religion, 98 = chose one of several other religions, 99 = left blank)
18.	ethnic2	*ethnicity reported by student* (same as values for ethnic)

[5]Negative test scores result from a penalty for guessing.

Math Attitude Questions 1–14 (Rated from 1 = very atypical to 4 = very typical)

19.	item01	*motivation* – "I practice math skills until I can do them well."
20.	item02	*pleasure* – "I feel happy after solving a hard problem."
21.	item03	*competence* – "I solve math problems quickly."
22.	item04	*(low) motiv* – "I give up easily instead of persisting if a math problem is difficult."
23.	item05	*(low)comp* – "I am a little slow catching on to new topics in math."
24.	item06	*(low)pleas* – "I do not get much pleasure out of math problems."
25.	item07	*motivation* – "I prefer to figure out how to solve problems without asking for help."
26.	item08	*(low)motiv* – "I do not keep at it very long when a math problem is challenging."
27.	item09	*competence* – "I am very competent at math."
28.	item10	*(low)pleas* – "I smile only a little (or not at all) when I solve a math problem."
29.	item11	*(low)comp* – "I have some difficulties doing math as well as other kids my age."
30.	item12	*motivation* – "I try to complete my math problems even if it takes a long time to finish."
31.	item13	*motivation* – "I explore all possible solutions of a complex problem before going on to another one."
32.	item14	*pleasure* – "I really enjoy doing math problems."

Variables Computed From the Above Variables

33.	item04r	*item04 reversed* (4 now = high motivation)
34.	item05r	*item05 reversed* (4 now = high competence)
35.	item08r	*item08 reversed* (4 now = high motivation)
36.	item11r	*item11 reversed* (4 now = high competence)
37.	competence	*competence scale*. An average computed as follows: (item03 + item05r + item09 + item11r)/4
38.	motivation	*motivation scale* (item01 + item04r + item07 + item08r + item12 + item13)/6
39.	mathcrs	*math courses taken* (0 = none, 5 = all five)
40.	faedRevis	*father's educ revised* (1 = HS grad or less, 2 = some college, 3 = BS or more)
41.	maedRevis	*mother's educ revised* (1 = HS grad or less, 2 = some college, 3 = BS or more)
42.	item06r	*item06 reversed* (4 now = high pleasure)
43.	item10r	*item10 reversed* (4 now = high pleasure)
44.	pleasure	*pleasure scale* (item02 + item06r + item 10r + item14)/4
45.	parEduc	*parents' education* (average of the <u>unrevised</u> mother's and father's educations)

The variables of *ethnic* and *religion* were added to the original HSB data set to provide true nominal (unordered) variables with a few (4 and 3) levels or values. In addition, for *ethnic* and *religion*, we have made two missing value codes to illustrate this possibility. All other variables use blanks, the SPSS system missing value, for missing data. For *ethnicity*, 98 indicates *multiethnic* and other. For *religion*, all the high school students who were not *Protestant* or *Catholic* but who did indicate some religion were coded 98 and considered to be missing because none of the other religions had enough members to make a reasonably sized group. Those who left the ethnicity or religion questions blank were coded as 99, also missing.

The Raw HSB Data and Data Editor

Figure 1.3 is a piece of the *hsbdataB.sav* file showing the first 10 student participants for variables 1 through 17 (*gender* through *religion*). Notice the short variable names (e.g., *faed*, *alg1*) at the top of the *hsbdataB.sav* file. Be aware that the participants are listed down the left side of the page, and the variables are always listed across the top. <u>You will usually enter data this way</u>. If a variable is measured more than once, such as *visual* and *visual2* (see Fig 1.3), it will be entered as two variables with slightly different names. The one exception to this rule that will be covered in this book is when you want to analyze repeated-measures using **Linear Mixed Models**. In that case, you enter a separate line for each occasion on which the individual has data (see Chapter 11).

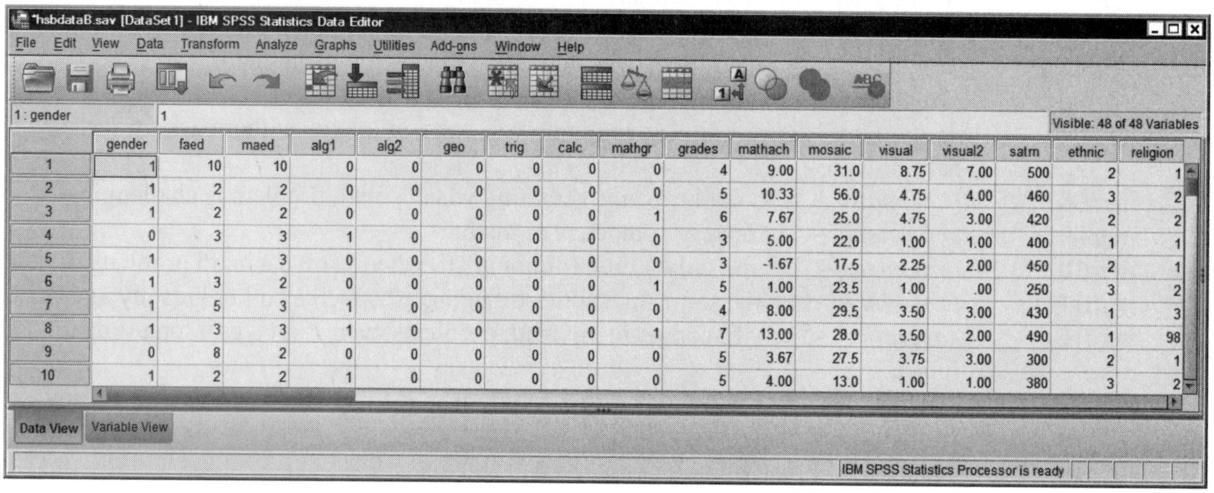

	gender	faed	maed	alg1	alg2	geo	trig	calc	mathgr	grades	mathach	mosaic	visual	visual2	satm	ethnic	religion
1	1	10	10	0	0	0	0	0	0	4	9.00	31.0	8.75	7.00	500	2	1
2	1	2	2	0	0	0	0	0	0	5	10.33	56.0	4.75	4.00	460	3	2
3	1	2	2	0	0	0	0	0	1	6	7.67	25.0	4.75	3.00	420	2	2
4	0	3	3	1	0	0	0	0	0	3	5.00	22.0	1.00	1.00	400	1	1
5	1	.	3	0	0	0	0	0	0	3	-1.67	17.5	2.25	2.00	450	2	1
6	1	3	2	0	0	0	0	0	1	5	1.00	23.5	1.00	.00	250	3	2
7	1	5	3	1	0	0	0	0	0	4	8.00	29.5	3.50	3.00	430	1	3
8	1	3	3	1	0	0	0	0	1	7	13.00	28.0	3.50	2.00	490	1	98
9	0	8	2	0	0	0	0	0	0	5	3.67	27.5	3.75	3.00	300	2	1
10	1	2	2	1	0	0	0	0	0	5	4.00	13.0	1.00	1.00	380	3	2

Fig. 1.3. Part of the hsbdataB data view in the SPSS Data Editor. [6]

Note that in Fig. 1.3, most of the values are single digits, but *mathach, mosaic,* and *visual* include some decimals and even negative numbers. Notice also that some cells, like *father's education* for participant 5, are blank because a datum is missing. Perhaps participant 5 did not know her father's education. Blank is the system missing value that can be used for any missing data in an SPSS data file. We suggest that you leave missing data blank under most circumstances; however, you may run across "user defined" missing data codes like −1, 9, 98, or 99 in other researchers' data, or you may choose to distinguish more than one type of missing data by using such codes so that you can include one or more types in certain analyses (For example, one might wish to distinguish individuals who indicated a religion other than Catholic or Protestant from those who indicated "no religion" or left the question blank; see *religion,* subject 9).

Research Questions for the Modified HSB Study[7]

In this book, we will generate a large number of research questions from the modified HSB data set. In this section, we list some of the possible questions you might ask in order to give you an idea of the range of types of questions that one might have in a typical research project. For review, we start with basic **descriptive questions** and some questions about assumptions. Also for review, we list some simple **difference** and **associational questions** that can be answered with basic (two-variable) inferential statistics such as a *t* test or correlation. These statistics are not discussed in this book, but how to compute them can be found in Appendix B. For more in-depth discussion of how to use SPSS to compute these

[6] If the values for *gender* are shown as *female* or *male*, the **value labels** rather than the numerals are being displayed. In that case, click on the circled symbol to change the format to show only the numeric values for each variable.

[7] The High School and Beyond (HSB) study was conducted by the National Opinion Research Center (1980). The example discussed here and throughout the book is based on 13 variables obtained from a random sample of 75 of 28,240 high school seniors. These variables include achievement scores, grades, and demographics. The raw data for the 13 variables were slightly modified from data in an Appendix in Hinkle, Wiersma, and Jurs (1994). That file had no missing data, which is unusual in behavioral science research, so we made some.

statistics, see Morgan, Leech, Gloeckner, and Barrett (2011). Finally, we pose a number of complex questions that can be answered with the statistics discussed in this book.

(1) Often, we start with **basic descriptive questions** about the demographics of the sample. Thus, we could answer, with the outputs in Chapter 2, the following basic descriptive questions: "What is the average educational level of the fathers of the students in this sample?" "What percentage of the students is male, and what percentage is female?"

(2) In Chapter 2, we also examine whether the variables with five or more ordered levels are distributed normally, an **assumption** of many statistics. One question is, "Are the frequency distributions of the math achievement scores markedly **skewed**, that is, different from the **normal curve distribution**?"

(3) How to make a table cross-tabulating two categorical variables (ones with a few values or categories) is described in Appendix B. Cross-tabulation and the **chi-square** statistic can answer research questions such as, "Is there a relationship between *gender* and *math grades* (high or low)?

(4) In Appendix B, we will also describe how to answer **basic associational research questions** (using **Pearson product-moment correlation coefficients**) such as, "Is there a positive association/relationship between *grades in high school* and *math achievement*?" A **correlation matrix** of all the correlations among several key variables will provide the basis for computing **factor analysis** in Chapter 4 and **multiple regression** in Chapter 6. In Chapter 3, correlation is also used to assess **reliability**.

(5) **Basic difference questions** such as, "Do males and females differ on *math achievement*?" and "Are there differences among the three *father's education* groups in regard to average scores on *math achievement*?" can be answered with a *t* **test** or **one-way ANOVA**, as described in Appendix B.

(6) **Complex difference questions** will be answered with **factorial ANOVA** in Chapter 8, **repeated or mixed ANOVA** in Chapter 9, **MANOVA** in Chapter 10, or **multilevel linear modeling** in Chapter 11. One *set* of three questions that could be answered using **factorial ANOVA** is as follows: (1) "Is there a difference between students who have fathers with no college, some college, or a BS or more with respect to the student's *math achievement*?" (2) "Is there a difference between students who had a B or better *math grade* average and those with less than a B average on a *math achievement* test at the end of high school?" and (3) "Is there an **interaction** between *father's education* and *math grades* with respect to *math achievement*?"

(7) How well can you predict *math achievement* from a combination of four variables: *motivation scale, grades in high school, parents' education,* and *gender*? This *complex associational question* can be answered with **multiple regression,** as discussed in Chapter 6. If the dependent variable, *math achievement,* were dichotomous (high vs. low achievement), **logistic regression** or possibly **discriminant** analysis, discussed in Chapter 7, would be appropriate to answer this question.

(8) Are there differences among the three *father's education* groups on a linear combination of *grades in high school, math achievement, and visualization test*? This complex difference question can be answered with a **single-factor MANOVA**, as discussed in Chapter 10.

(9) Are differences in students' *math achievement* related to the school they attend, and are these differences among schools related to the *Mean Socioeconomic Status* of the school they attend?

This complex, multilevel question is addressed in Chapter 11 using **multilevel linear modeling or hierarchical linear modeling (HLM)**.

More complex questions can be found in Chapters 3–11 under each of the several "problems" in those chapters.

This introduction to the research problem and questions raised by the HSB data set should help make the assignments meaningful, and it should provide a guide and examples for your own research.

Frequency Distributions

Frequency distributions are critical to understanding our use of measurement terms. We begin this section with a discussion of frequency distributions and two examples. Frequency tables and distributions can be used whether the variable involved has ordered or unordered levels (SPSS calls them **values**). In this section, we will consider only variables with many ordered values, ranging from low to high.

A **frequency distribution** is a tally or count of the <u>number of times each score on a single variable occurs</u>. For example, the frequency distribution of final grades in a class of 50 students might be 7 *A*s, 20 *B*s, 18 *C*s, and 5 *D*s. Note that in this frequency distribution most students have *B*s or *C*s (grades in the middle) and similar smaller numbers have *A*s and *D*s (high and low grades). When there are small numbers of scores for the low and high values and most scores are for the middle values, the distribution is said to be **approximately normally distributed.** We will discuss the normal curve in more detail later in this chapter.

When the variable is **continuous** or has many ordered levels (or values), the frequency distribution usually is based on ranges of values for the variable. For example, the frequencies (number of students), shown by the bars in Fig 1.4, are for a range of points (in this case, SPSS selected a range of 50, 250–299, 300–349, 350–399, etc.).

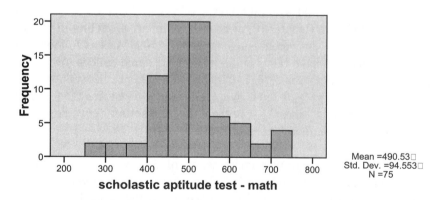

Mean =490.53
Std. Dev. =94.553
N =75

Fig. 1.4. A grouped frequency distribution for *SAT math* scores.
 Notice that the largest number of students (about 20) has scores in the middle two bars of the range (450–550). Similar small numbers of students have very low and very high scores. The bars in the histogram form a distribution (pattern or curve) that is quite similar to the normal, bell-shaped curve shown later in Fig. 1.7. Thus, the frequency distribution of the *SAT math* scores is said to be **approximately normal**.

Figure 1.5 shows the frequency distribution for the *competence scale*. Notice that the bars form a pattern very different from the normal curve. This distribution can be said to be **not normally distributed**. As we will see later in the chapter, the distribution is **negatively skewed**. That is, the tail of the curve or the extreme scores are on the low end or left side. Note how much this differs from the *SAT math* score frequency distribution. As you will see in the Measurement section (below), we call the *competence scale* variable **ordinal.**

You can create these figures yourself using the *hsbdataB.sav* file. Select:
- **Graphs → Legacy Dialogs → Histogram.**
- Then move *scholastic aptitude test – math* (or *competence scale*) into the **Variable** box.
- Click **OK.** The program can superimpose a normal curve on the histogram if you request it, but we have found this curve more confusing than helpful to our students.

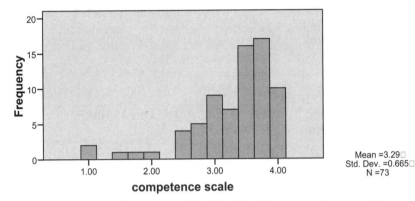

Fig. 1.5. A grouped frequency distribution for competence scale.

Levels of Measurement

Measurement is the assignment of numbers to different characteristics according to rules. The way these numbers are assigned differs across variables, and these differences can affect which statistical tests are appropriate for the data. These differences in the way numbers are assigned can be classified according to the "levels of measurement" that they represent. Depending on the level of measurement of a variable, the data can mean different things. For example, the number 2 might indicate a score of two; it might indicate that the subject was a Catholic; or it might indicate that the subject was ranked second in the class. To help understand these differences, types, or levels of variables, have been identified. It is common and traditional to discuss four levels or scales of measurement: **nominal**, **ordinal**, **interval**, and **ratio**, which vary from the unordered (nominal) to the highest level (ratio).[8] These four traditional terms are not the same as those used in SPSS, and we think that they are not always the most useful for determining what statistics to use.

SPSS uses three terms (**nominal**, **ordinal**, and **scale**) for the levels or types of measurement. How these correspond to the traditional terms is shown in Table 1.3. When you name and label variables in SPSS, you have the opportunity to select one of these three types of measurement (see Fig 1.2). Although what you choose does *not* affect what SPSS does in most cases, an appropriate choice both indicates that you understand your data and may help guide your selection of statistics.

---

[8] Unfortunately, the terms "level" and "scale" are used several ways in research. Levels refer to the categories or values of a variable (e.g., male or female or 1, 2, or 3); level can also refer to the three or four different types of measurement (nominal, ordinal, etc). These several types of measurement have also been called "scales of measurement," but SPSS/PASW uses scale specifically for the highest type or level of measurement. Other researchers use scale to describe to describe questionnaire items that are rated from strongly disagree to strongly agree (Likert scale) and for the sum of such items (summated scale). We wish there weren't so many uses of these terms; the best we can do is try to be clear about our usage.

We believe that the terms **nominal, dichotomous, ordinal**, and **approximately normal** (or normally distributed) are usually more useful than the traditional or SPSS measurement terms for the selection and interpretation of statistics. In part, this is because statisticians disagree about the usefulness of the traditional levels of measurement in determining the appropriate selection of statistics. Furthermore, our experience is that the traditional terms are frequently misunderstood and applied inappropriately by students. The main problem with the SPSS terms is that the term scale is not commonly used as a measurement level, and it has other meanings (see footnote 8) that make its use here confusing. Hopefully, our terms, as discussed below, are clear and useful.

Table 1.3 compares the three sets of terms and provides a summary description of our definitions of them. Professors differ in the terminology they prefer and on how much importance to place on levels or scales of measurement, so you will see all of these terms, and the others mentioned below, in textbooks and articles.

Table 1.3. *Similar Traditional, SPSS, and Our Measurement Terms*

Traditional Term	Traditional Definition	SPSS Term	Our Term	Our Definition
Nominal	Two or more <u>unordered</u> categories	Nominal	Nominal	Three or more <u>unordered</u> categories.
-----	-----	-----	Dichotomous	Two categories, either ordered or unordered.
Ordinal	<u>Ordered</u> levels, in which the difference in magnitude between levels is not equal	Ordinal	Ordinal	Three or more <u>ordered</u> levels, in which the difference in magnitude between pairs of adjacent levels (e.g., scores such as 1 and 2, or 2 and 3) is unequal, and/or the frequency distribution deviates markedly from the normal distribution.
Interval & Ratio	**Interval:** <u>ordered</u> levels, in which the difference between levels is equal, but there is no true zero. **Ratio:** <u>ordered</u> levels; the difference between levels is equal, and there is a true zero.	Scale	Approximately Normal	Many (at least five) <u>ordered</u> levels or scores, with the frequency distribution of the scores being approximately normally distributed.

Nominal Variables

This is the most basic or lowest level of measurement, in which the numerals assigned to each category stand for the <u>name</u> of the category, but they have no implied order or value. For example, in the HSB data, the values for the *religion* variable are 1= *Protestant*, 2 = *Catholic*, 3 = *no religion*. This does not mean that that two Protestants equal one Catholic or any of the typical mathematical uses of the numerals. The same reasoning applies to many other true nominal variables, such as ethnic group, type of disability, or section number in a class schedule. In each of these cases, the categories are distinct and nonoverlapping but not ordered. Each category or group in the modified HSB variable *ethnicity* is different from each other, but there is no necessary order to the categories. Thus, the categories could be numbered 1 for *Asian American*, 2 for *Latino American*, 3 for *African American*, and 4 for *European American* or the reverse or any combination of assigning one number to each category.

What this implies is that you must *not* treat the numbers used for identifying nominal categories as if they were numbers that could be used in a formula, added together, subtracted from one another, or used to compute an average. Average *ethnicity* makes no sense. However, if you ask SPSS to compute the mean *ethnicity*, it will do so and give you meaningless information. The important aspect of nominal measurement is to have clearly defined, non-overlapping or mutually exclusive categories that can be coded reliably by observers or by self-report.

Using nominal measurement does dramatically limit the statistics that can be used with your data, but it does not altogether eliminate the possible use of statistics to summarize your data and make inferences. Therefore, even when the data are unordered or nominal categories, your research may benefit from the use of appropriate statistics. Later we will discuss the types of statistics, both descriptive and inferential, that are appropriate for nominal data.

Other terms for nominal variables. Unfortunately, the literature is full of different terms that describe similar, but not identical, measurement aspects of variables. **Categorical, qualitative,** and **discrete** are terms sometimes used interchangeably with nominal, but we think that nominal is better because it is possible to have ordered, discrete categories (e.g., remedial, average, and accelerated "tracks" of math classes, which we and other researchers would consider an ordinal variable). "Qualitative" is also used to discuss a different approach to doing research, with important differences in philosophy, assumptions, and methods for conducting research.

Dichotomous Variables

Dichotomous variables always <u>have only two levels or categories</u>. In some cases, they may have an implied order (e.g., *math grades* in high school are coded 0 for *less than an A or B* average and 1 for *mostly A or B*). Other dichotomous variables do not have any order to the categories (e.g., *male* or *female*). For many purposes, it is best to use the same statistics for dichotomous and nominal variables. However, a statistic such as the mean or average, which would be meaningless for a three or more category nominal variable (e.g., *ethnicity*), does have meaning when there are only two categories and when coded as dummy variables (0, 1) is especially easily interpretable. For example, in the HSB data, the average *gender* is .55 (with *males* = 0 and *females* = 1). This means that 55% of the participants were *females*, the higher code. Furthermore, we will see with multiple regression that dichotomous variables, especially when coded as *dummy variables*, can be used as independent variables along with other variables that are normally distributed.

Other terms for dichotomous variables. In the SPSS **Variable View** (e.g., see Fig 1.2), we label dichotomous variables **nominal**, and this is common in textbooks. However, please <u>remember that dichotomous variables are really a special case</u>, and for some purposes they can be treated as if they were normally distributed. Note that dichotomous data have two discrete categories, so these variables are sometimes called **discrete variables, categorical variables,** or **dummy variables**.

Ordinal Variables

In ordinal measurement, not only are there mutually exclusive categories as in nominal scales, but also the categories are <u>ordered</u> from low to high, such that ranks could be assigned (e.g., 1st, 2nd, 3rd). Thus, in an ordinal scale one knows which participant is highest or most preferred on a dimension, but the intervals between the various categories are not equal. Often, whether the intervals between categories can be viewed as equal is a matter of judgment. Our definition of **ordinal** focuses on whether the frequency counts for each category or value are distributed like the bell-shaped, normal curve with more responses in the middle categories and fewer in the lowest and highest categories. If not approximately normal, we would call the variable ordinal. Ordered variables with only three or four categories would also be called ordinal. As indicated in Table 1.3, however, the traditional definition of ordinal focuses on whether the differences between pairs of levels are equal. This can be important, for example if one will be creating summed or averaged scores (as in subscales of a questionnaire that involve aggregating a set of questionnaire items). If differences between levels are *meaningfully* unequal, then averaging a score of 5 (e.g., indicating the participants' age is 65+) and a score of 2 (e.g., indicating that the participants' age is 20 – 25) may not make sense. Averaging the *ranks* of the scores may be more meaningful if it is clear that they are ordered but that the differences between adjacent scores differs across levels of the variable. However, sometimes even if the differences between levels is not literally equal (e.g., the difference between a level indicating infancy and a level indicating preschool is not equal in years to the difference between a level of "young adulthood" and "older adulthood") it may be reasonable to treat the levels as interval level data if the levels comprise the most meaningful distinctions and data are <u>normally distributed</u>.

Other terms for ordinal variables. Some authors use the term **ranks** interchangeably with ordinal. However, most analyses that are designed for use with ordinal data (i.e., nonparametric tests) rank the data as a part of the procedure, assuming that the data you are entering are not already ranked. Moreover, the process of ranking changes the distribution of data such that the data can be used in many analyses ordinarily requiring normally distributed data. Ordinal data are often **categorical** (e.g., good, better, best are three ordered categories), so that term is sometimes used to include both nominal and ordinal data, and the categories may be **discrete** (e.g., number of children in a family is a discrete number, 1, 2. It does not make sense to have a number of children in between 1 and 2).

Approximately Normal (or Scale) Variables

Not only do approximately normally distributed variables have levels or scores that are *ordered* from low to high, but also, as stated in Table 1.3, the frequencies of the scores are approximately normally distributed. That is, most scores are somewhere in the middle with similar smaller numbers of low and high scores. Thus, a 5-point Likert scale, such as strongly agree to strongly disagree, would be considered normal if the frequency distribution was approximately normal. We think normality, because it is an assumption of many statistics, should be the focus of this highest level of measurement. Many normal variables are continuous (i.e., they have an infinite number of possible values within some range). If not continuous, we suggest that there be at least five ordered values or levels that have an implicit, underlying continuous nature. For example, a 5-point Likert scale has only five response categories but, in theory, a person's rating could fall anywhere between 1 and 5 (e.g., halfway between 3 and 4).

Other terms for approximately normal variables. Continuous, dimensional, and **quantitative** are some terms that you will see in the literature for variables that vary from low to high and are assumed to be normally distributed. SPSS uses **scale** as previously noted. Traditional measurement terminology uses the terms **interval** and **ratio.** SPSS does not use these terms, but because they are common in the literature and overlap with the term **scale**, we will describe them briefly. **Interval** variables have ordered categories that are equally spaced (i.e., have equal intervals between them). Most physical measurements (e.g., *length, weight, temperature*) have equal intervals between them. Many physical measurements (*length* and *weight*), in fact, have not only equal intervals between the levels or scores but also a true zero, which means in the above examples, zero length or weight. Such variables are called **ratio** variables. Our Fahrenheit temperature scale and almost all psychological scales do <u>not</u> have a true zero, and, thus, even if they are very well-constructed equal-interval scales, it is not possible to say that zero degrees Fahrenheit involves the absence of something or that one has no intelligence or no extroversion or no attitude of a certain type. The differences between interval scales and ratio scales are not important for us because we can do all of the types of statistics that we have available with interval data. SPSS terminology supports this nondistinction by using the term **scale** for both interval and ratio data. In fact because it is an assumption of most parametric statistics, <u>it may be more important for statistical purposes that the variables be approximately normally distributed than whether they have equal intervals.</u>

Labeling Levels of Measurement in SPSS

When you label variables in SPSS, the **Measure** column (see Fig. 1.2) provides only three choices: nominal, ordinal, or scale. How do you decide which to use?

Labeling variables as nominal. If the variable has only two levels (e.g., Yes or No, Pass or Fail), most researchers and we would label it **nominal** in the SPSS variable view because that is traditional and it is often best to use the same statistics with dichotomous variables that you would with a nominal variable. As mentioned earlier, there are times when dichotomous variables can be treated as if they were ordered; however, as long as you use numbers to code them, SPSS will still allow you to use them in such analyses. If there are three or more categories or values, you need to determine whether the categories are ordered (vary from low to high). If the categories are just different names and not ordered, label the variable as **nominal** in the SPSS variable view. Especially if there are more than two categories, this <u>distinction between nominal and ordered variables makes a lot of difference</u> in choosing and interpreting appropriate statistics.

Labeling variables as ordinal. If the categories or values of a variable vary from low to high (i.e., are ordered) and there are only three or four such values (e.g., good, better, best, or strongly disagree, disagree, agree, strongly agree), we recommend that you label the variable **ordinal**. Also, if there are five or more ordered levels or values of a variable <u>and</u> you suspect that the frequency distribution of the variable is substantially nonnormal, label the variable **ordinal**. That is, if you <u>do not</u> think that the distribution is approximately symmetrical and that most of the participants had scores somewhere in the middle of the distribution, call the variable ordinal. If most of the participants are thought to be either quite high or low or you suspect that the distribution will be some shape other than bell-shaped, label the variable ordinal.

Labeling variables as scale. If the variable has five or more <u>ordered</u> categories or values and you have no reason to suspect that the distribution is nonnormal, label the variable **scale** in the SPSS variable view **measure** column. If the variable is essentially continuous (e.g., is measured to one or more decimal places or is the average of several items), it is likely to be at least approximately normally distributed, so call it **scale**. As you see in Chapter 2, we recommend that you check the skewness of your variables with five or more ordered levels and then adjust what you initially called a variable's measurement, if necessary. That is, you might want to change it from ordinal to scale, if it turns out to be approximately normal or change from scale to ordinal[9] if it turns out to be too skewed.

.

Why We Prefer Our Four Levels of Measurement: A Review

As shown in Table 1.3 and Table 1.4, we distinguish between four levels of measurement: nominal, dichotomous, ordinal, and normal. Even though you cannot label variables as dichotomous or normal in the SPSS variable view, we think that these four levels are conceptually and practically useful. Remember that because dichotomous variables form a special case they can be used and interpreted much like normally distributed variables, which is why we think it is good to distinguish between nominal and dichotomous even though SPSS does not.

---

[9] Another alternative would be to transform the variable to normalize the distribution.

Likewise, we think that normally distributed or normal is a better label than the SPSS term scale because the latter could easily be confused with other uses of the term scale (see footnote 8) and because whether the variable is approximately normally distributed is what for us distinguishes it from an ordinal variable. Furthermore, what is important for most of the inferential statistics that you will compute with SPSS is the assumption that the dependent variable must be at least approximately normally distributed.

Table 1.4. *Characteristics and Examples of the Four Types of Measurement*

	Nominal	**Dichotomous**	**Ordinal**	**Normal**

Characteristics	3+ levels
	Not ordered
	True categories
	Names, labels
		2 levels
		Ordered or not
			3+ levels
			Ordered levels
			Unequal intervals
			   between levels
			Not normally distributed
				5+ levels
				Ordered levels
				Approximately
				   normally
				   distributed
				Equal intervals
				   between levels

Examples	Ethnicity Religion Curriculum type Hair color	Gender Math grades (high vs. low)	Competence scale Mother's education	SAT math Math achievement Height

Remember that in SPSS there are only three measurement types or levels, and you are the one who determines if the variable is called nominal, ordinal, or scale (see Fig. 1.2). We called dichotomous variables nominal, and we labeled approximately normal variables as scale in our *hsbdataB.sav* file.

Descriptive Statistics

In Chapter 2, we will obtain descriptive statistics to summarize data and check assumptions; we will also produce plots that visually display distributions of variables. Here we provide a brief review of descriptive statistics and their appropriate use given the level of measurement of the variable.

Measures of Central Tendency
The three measures of the center of a distribution are: **mean, median,** and **mode**.

Mean. The arithmetic average or mean takes into account all of the available information. Thus, it is usually the statistic of choice if the data are normally distributed. The mean is computed by adding up all the scores and dividing by the number of scores ($M = \Sigma X/N$). For normally distributed data, the raw scores should be used in this calculation; for ordinal scores, it is sometimes useful to calculate a mean of the <u>ranked</u> scores.

Median. The middle score or median is the appropriate measure of central tendency for ordinal level raw data. The median is a better measure of central tendency than the mean when the frequency distribution is skewed. For example, the median income of 100 midlevel workers and one millionaire reflects the central tendency of the group better (and is substantially lower) than the mean income. The average or mean would be inflated in this example by the income of the one millionaire. For normally distributed data, the median is the same (or approximately the same) as the mean.

Mode. The most common category, or mode, can be used with any kind of data but generally provides the least precise information about central tendency. Moreover, if one's data are continuous, there often are multiple modes, none of which truly represents the "typical" score. In fact if there are multiple modes, SPSS provides only the lowest one. One would use the mode as the measure of central tendency if the variable is nominal or if you want a quick noncalculated measure. The mode is the tallest bar in a bar graph or histogram.

You can compute the **Mean, Median,** and **Mode**, plus other descriptive statistics, with SPSS by using the Frequencies command.

To get Fig 1.6, select:
- **Analyze** → **Descriptive Statistics** → **Frequencies** → *scholastic aptitude test – math* → **Statistics** → **Mean, Median, and Mode** → **Continue** → **OK**.

Note in Fig. 1.6 that the mean and median are very similar, which is in agreement with our conclusion from Fig. 1.4 that *SATM* is approximately normally distributed. Note that the mode is 500, as shown in Fig. 1.4 by the tallest bars.

Statistics

scholastic aptitude test - math

N	Valid	75
	Missing	0
Mean		490.53
Median		490.00
Mode		500

Fig. 1.6. Central tendency measures using the SPSS frequencies command.

Measures of Variability

Variability tells us about the spread or dispersion of the scores. At one extreme, if all of the scores in a distribution are the same, there is no variability. If the scores are all different and widely spaced, the variability will be high. The **range** (highest minus lowest score) is the crudest measure of variability but does give an indication of the spread in scores if they are ordered.

Standard Deviation. This common measure of variability is most appropriate when one has normally distributed data, although the standard deviation of <u>ranked</u> ordinal data may be useful in some cases. The standard deviation is based on the deviation of each score (x) from the mean of all the scores (M). Those deviation scores are squared and then summed ($\Sigma(x - M)^2$). This sum is divided by $n - 1$, and, finally, the square root is taken

$$s = \sqrt{\frac{\Sigma(X-M)^2}{n-1}}$$

Interquartile range. For ordinal data, the interquartile range, the distance between the 25th and 75th percentiles, is a useful measure of variability.

With nominal data, none of the above variability measures (range, standard deviation, or interquartile range) are appropriate. Instead, one might ask how many different categories there are (if categories are not predefined) and what the percentages or frequency counts are in each category to get some idea of variability. Minimum and maximum frequencies in the different categories, especially relative to the total number of individuals and number of categories, also may provide information about variability for nominal data.

Conclusions About Measurement and the Use of Statistics

Statistics based on means and standard deviations are valid for normally distributed or **normal** data. Typically, these data are used in the most powerful tests called **parametric** statistics. However, if the data are ordered but grossly nonnormal (i.e., **ordinal**), means and standard deviations may not give meaningful answers. Then the median and a **nonparametric** test would be preferred. Nonparametric tests typically have somewhat less **power** than parametric tests (they are less able to demonstrate significance even when true effects exist in the population), but the sacrifice in power for nonparametric tests based on ranks usually is relatively minor. If the data are **nominal**, one would have to use the mode and information about the distribution of individuals in categories to describe the distribution. Usually, there would be a major sacrifice in power if one reduced continuous data to a categorical variable (e.g., by doing a median split) and then analyzed the resulting variable using nonparametric statistics designed for categorical data.

Table 1.5 summarizes much of the above information about the appropriate use of various kinds of descriptive statistics given nominal, dichotomous, ordinal, or normal data.

Table 1.5. *Selection of Appropriate Descriptive Statistics and Plots for Levels of Measurement*

Plots	Nominal	Dichotomous	Ordinal	Normal
Frequency distribution	Yes[a]	Yes	Yes	OK[b]
Bar chart	Yes	Yes	Yes	OK
Histogram	No[c]	No	OK	Yes
Frequency polygon	No	No	OK	Yes
Box and whiskers plot	No	No	Yes	Yes
Central Tendency				
Mean	No	OK	Of ranks, OK	Yes
Median	No	OK = Mode	Yes	OK
Mode	Yes	Yes	OK	OK
Variability				
Range	No	Always 1	Yes	Yes
Standard deviation	No	No	Of ranks, OK	Yes
Interquartile range	No	No	OK	OK
How many categories	Yes	Always 2	OK	Not if truly continuous
Shape				
Skewness	No	No	Yes	Yes

[a]Yes means a good choice with this level of measurement.
[b]OK means OK to use, but not the best choice at this level of measurement.
[c]No means not appropriate at this level of measurement.

The Normal Curve

Figure 1.7 is an example of a normal curve. The frequencies of many of the variables used in the behavioral sciences are distributed approximately as a normal curve. Examples of such variables that approximately fit a normal curve are height, weight, intelligence, and many personality variables. Notice that for each of these examples most people would fall toward the middle of the distribution, with fewer people at the extremes. If the average height of men in the United States is 5'10", then this height will be in the middle of the curve. The heights of men who are taller than 5'10" will be to the right of the middle on the curve, and those of men who are shorter than 5'10" will be to the left of the middle on the curve, with only a few men being 7 feet or 5 feet tall.

The normal curve can be thought of as derived from a frequency distribution. It is theoretically formed from counting an "infinite" number of occurrences of a variable. Usually when the normal curve is depicted, only the X axis (horizontal) is shown. To determine how a frequency distribution is obtained, you could take a fair coin, flip it 10 times, and record the number of heads on this first set or trial. Then flip it another 10 times, and record the number of heads. If you had nothing better to do, you could do 100 trials. After performing this task, you could plot the number of times that the coin turned up heads out of each trial of 10. What would you expect? Of course, the largest number of trials probably would show 5 heads out of 10. There would be very few, if any trials, where 0, 1, 9, or 10 heads occur. It could happen, but the probability is quite low, which brings us to a probability distribution. If we performed this experiment 100 times, or 1,000 times, or 1,000,000 times, the frequency distribution would "fill in" and look more and more like a normal curve.

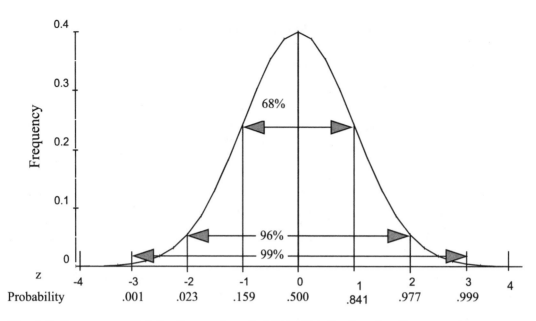

Fig. 1.7. Frequency distribution and probability distribution for the normal curve.

Properties of the Normal Curve

The normal curve has five properties that are always present.

1. The normal curve is unimodal. It has one "hump," and this hump is in the middle of the distribution. The most frequent value is in the middle of the curve.
2. The mean, median, and mode are equal.
3. The curve is symmetric. If you fold the normal curve in half, the right side would fit perfectly with the left side; that is, it is not **skewed**.
4. The range is infinite. This means that the extremes approach but never touch the X axis.
5. The curve is neither too peaked nor too flat, and its tails are neither too short nor too long; it has no **kurtosis.**

Nonnormally Shaped Distributions

Skewness. If one tail of a frequency distribution is longer than the other and if the mean and median are different, the curve is skewed. Because most common inferential statistics (e.g., *t* test) assume that the dependent variable is normally distributed, it is important that we know if our variables are highly skewed.

Figure 1.5 showed a frequency distribution that is skewed to the left. This is called a negative skew. A perfectly normal curve has a skewness of zero (0.0). The curve in Fig. 1.5, for the *competence* scale, has a skewness statistic of −1.63, which indicates that the curve is quite different from a normal curve. We will use a somewhat arbitrary guideline that if the skewness is more than +1.0 or less than −1.0 the distribution is markedly skewed and it would be prudent to either transform the data or use a nonparametric (ordinal type) statistic. However, some parametric statistics, such as the two-tailed *t* test and ANOVA, are quite robust so even a skewness of more than +/−1 may not change the results much. We will provide more examples and discuss this more in Chapter 2.

Kurtosis. If a frequency distribution is more peaked than the normal curve, it is said to have positive kurtosis and is called leptokurtic. Note in Fig. 1.4 that the *SAT-math* histogram is peaked (i.e., the bar for 500 would extend above the normal curve line), and thus there is some positive kurtosis. If a frequency distribution is relatively flat with heavy tails, it has negative kurtosis and is called platykurtic. Although

SPSS can easily compute a kurtosis value for any variable using an option in the **Frequencies** command, usually we will not do so because kurtosis does not seem to affect the results of most statistical analyses very much.

Areas Under the Normal Curve

The normal curve is also a probability distribution. Visualize that the area under the normal curve is equal to 1.0. Therefore, portions of this curve could be expressed as fractions of 1.0. For example, if we assume that 5'10" is the average height of men in the United States, then the probability of a man being 5'10" or taller is .5. The probability of a man being over 6'3" or less than 5'5" is considerably smaller. It is important to be able to conceptualize the normal curve as a probability distribution because statistical convention sets acceptable probability levels for rejecting the null hypothesis at .05 or .01. As we shall see, when events or outcomes happen very infrequently, that is, only 5 times in 100 or 1 time in 100 (way out in the left or right tail of the curve), we wonder if they belong to that distribution or perhaps to a different distribution. We will come back to this point later in the book.

All normal curves, regardless of whether they are narrow or spread out, can be divided into areas or units in terms of the standard deviation. Approximately 34% of the area under the normal curve is between the mean and one standard deviation above or below the mean (see Fig. 1.7). If we include both the area to the right *and* to the left of the mean, 68% of the area under the normal curve is within one standard deviation from the mean. Another approximately 13.5% of the area under the normal curve is accounted for by adding a second standard deviation to the first standard deviation. In other words, two standard deviations to the right of the mean account for an area of approximately 47.5%, and two standard deviations to the left *and* right of the mean make up an area of approximately 95% of the normal curve. If we were to subtract 95% from 100%, the remaining 5% relates to that ever present probability or *p* value of .05 needed for statistical significance. Values not falling within two standard deviations of the mean are seen as relatively rare events.

The Standard Normal Curve

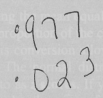

All normal curves can be converted into standard normal curves by setting the mean equal to zero and the standard deviation equal to one. Since all normal curves have the same proportion of the curve within one standard deviation, two standard deviations, and so on, of the mean, this conversion allows comparisons among normal curves with different means and standard deviations. The standard normal distribution has the standard normal distribution units underneath. These units are referred to as *z* scores. If you examine the normal curve table in any statistics book, you can find the areas under the curve for one standard deviation (*z* = 1), two standard deviations (*z* = 2), and so on. As described in Appendix A, it is easy for SPSS to convert raw scores into *standard scores*. This is often done when one wants to aggregate or add together several scores that have quite different means and standard deviations.

Interpretation Questions

1.1 What is the difference between the independent variable and the dependent variable?

1.2 Compare the terms *active independent variable* and *attribute independent variable*. What are the similarities and differences?

1.3 What kind of independent variable is necessary to infer cause? Can one <u>always</u> infer cause from this type of independent variable? If so, why? If not, when can one clearly infer cause, and when might causal inferences be more questionable?

1.4 Compare and contrast associational, difference, and descriptive types of research questions.

1.5   Write three research questions and a corresponding hypothesis regarding variables of interest to you but not in the HSB data set (one associational, one difference, and one descriptive question).

1.6   Using one or more of the following HSB variables, *religion, mosaic score,* and *visualization score:*
   (a) Write an associational question.
   (b) Write a difference question.
   (c) Write a descriptive question.

1.7   If you have categorical, ordered data (such as low income, middle income, high income), what type of measurement would you have? Why?

1.8   (a) What are the differences among nominal, dichotomous, ordinal, and normal variables? (b) In social science research, why is it not important to distinguish between interval and ratio variables?

1.9   What percent of the area under the standard normal curve is between the mean and one standard deviation above the mean?

1.10   (a) How do *z* scores relate to the normal curve? (b) How would you interpret a *z* score of −3.0?

CHAPTER 2

Data Coding and Exploratory Analysis (EDA)

Before computing any inferential statistics, it is necessary to code the data, enter the data into SPSS, and then conduct exploratory data analysis (EDA) as outlined below. This chapter will help you understand your data, help you to see if there are any errors, and help you to know if your data meet basic assumptions for the inferential statistics that you will compute. Throughout this chapter we include syntax for completing the analyses. How to use the point and click method for these analyses is outlined *in SPSS for Introductory Statistics: Use and Interpretation* (Morgan, Leech, Gloeckner, & Barrett, 2011).

Rules for Data Coding

Coding is the process of assigning numbers or symbols to the values or levels of each variable. We want to present some broad suggestions or rules to keep in mind as you proceed. These suggestions are adapted from rules proposed in Newton and Rudestam's (1999) useful book entitled *Your Statistical Consultant*. It is important to note that the recommendations we make are those we find to be most useful in most contexts, but some researchers might propose alternatives, especially for "rules" 1, 2, 4, 5, and 7 below.

1. **All data should be numeric.** Even though it is possible to use letters or words (string variables) as data, it is not desirable to do so. For example, we could code gender as M for male and F for female, but in order to do most statistics with SPSS, you would have to convert the letters or words to numbers. It is easier to do this conversion before entering the data into the computer. We decided to code females as 1 and males as 0. This is called **dummy coding**. In essence, the 0 means "not female." Dummy coding is useful if you will want to use the data in some types of analyses and for obtaining descriptive statistics. For example, the mean of data coded this way will tell you the percentage of participants who fall in the category coded as "1." We could, of course, code males as 1 and females as 0, or we could code one gender as 1 and the other as 2. However, it is crucial that you be consistent in your coding and have a way to remind yourself and others of how you did the coding. In Appendix A, we show how you can provide such a record or **codebook,** which SPSS calls a dictionary or working file.

2. **Each variable for each case or participant must occupy the same column in the SPSS Data Editor.** For most SPSS procedures (**Linear Mixed Models** is an exception), it is important that data from each participant occupy only one line (row), and for all procedures each column must contain data on the same variable for all the participants. The SPSS data editor, into which you will enter data, facilitates this by putting the variable names that you choose at the top of each column. Sometimes a variable is measured more than once for each participant (e.g., pretest and posttest). These data should be entered on the same row in separate columns with somewhat different variable names. An exception to this is for the **Linear Mixed Models** program model (see Chapter 11).

3. **All values (codes) for a variable must be mutually exclus** be recorded for each variable. Some items may allow particip that case, the item should be divided into a separate variable f value of each variable (usually "1") corresponding to yes (chec checked).

Usually, items should be phrased so that persons would logica and all possible options are provided. A final category labeled possible options cannot be listed, but these "other" responses are usually quite diverse and, thus, are usually not very useful for statistical purposes.

4. **Each variable should be coded to obtain maximum information.** Do not collapse categories or values when you set up the codes for them. If needed, let the computer do it later. In general, it is desirable to code and <u>enter data in as detailed a form as available</u>. Thus, enter item raw scores, ages, GPAs, etc. for each participant if you know them. It is good to ask participants to provide information that is quite specific. However, you should be careful not to ask questions that are so specific that the respondent may not know the answer or may not feel comfortable providing it. For example, you will obtain more specific information by asking participants to state their GPA to two decimals than if you asked them to select from a few broad categories (e.g., less than 2.0, 2.0–2.49, 2.50–2.99). However, if students don't know their exact GPA or don't want to reveal it precisely, they may leave the question blank, guess, or write in a difficult to interpret answer.

These issues might lead you to provide a few categories, each with a relatively narrow range of values, for variables such as age, weight, and income. Never collapse such categories before you enter the data into SPSS. For example, if you had age categories for university undergraduates 16–18, 18–20, 21–23, and so on and you realize that there are only a few students in the below 18 group, keep the codes as they are for now. Later you can make a new category of 20 or under by using an SPSS function, **Transform →** **Recode**. <u>If you collapse categories before you enter the data, the additional information </u>will no longer be available.

5. **For each participant, there must be a code or value for each variable**. These codes should be numbers, except when the data are missing. We recommend using blanks when data are missing or unusable, because <u>SPSS is designed to handle blanks as missing values</u>. However, <u>sometimes you may have more than one type of missing data</u>, such as items left blank *and* those that had an answer that was not appropriate or usable. In this case, you may assign numeric codes such as 98 and 99 to them, <u>but you must tell SPSS that these codes are for missing values</u>, or SPSS will treat them as actual data.

6. **Apply coding rules consistently for all participants.** This means that if you decide to treat a certain type of response as, say, missing for one person, you must do the same for all other participants.

7. **Use high numbers (values or codes) for the "agree," "good," or "more" end of a variable that is ordered. If the variable has a negative-sounding label (e.g., aggressiveness) then, higher numbers should refer to more of the trait, which would end up yielding scores in which higher = more negative.** Sometimes you will see questionnaires that use 1 for "strongly agree" and 5 for "strongly disagree." This is not wrong as long as it is clear and consistent. However, you are less likely to get confused when interpreting your results if high values have positive meaning, indicate that something was done (e.g., an algebra 1 course *was taken*), or indicate more of the characteristic.

Make a coding form and/or codebook. You need to make some decisions about how to code the data, especially data that are not already in numerical form. When the responses provided by participants are numbers, the variable is said to be "self-coding." You can just enter the number that was circled or checked on the questionnaire. On the other hand, variables such as *gender* or *ethnicity* have no intrinsic values associated with them, so a number has to be assigned to each level or value.

Fix problems with the completed questionnaires. Examine the questionnaires (or other new data source) for incomplete, unclear, or double answers. The researcher needs to use rules to handle these problems and note the decision on the questionnaires or on a master "coding instructions" sheet or file so that the same rules are used for all cases. For each type of incomplete, blank, unclear, or double answer, you need to make a rule for what to do. As much as possible, you should make these rules before data collection, but there may well be some unanticipated issues. It is important that you apply the rules consistently for all similar problems so as not to bias your results.

Missing data create problems in later data analysis, especially for complex statistics. Thus, we want to use as much of the data provided as is reasonable. The important thing here is that you *must* treat all similar problems the same way. If a participant answered only some of the questions, there will be lots of missing data for that person. We could have a rule such as "if half the items are blank or invalid, we will throw out that whole questionnaire as invalid." In your research report, you should state how many questionnaires were thrown out and for what reason(s). If a participant circled two responses (e.g., 3 and 4 on a 5-point Likert scale), a reasonable decision would be to enter the average or midpoint, 3.50.

Clean up completed questionnaires. Once you have made your rules and decided how to handle each problem, you need to make these rules clear to the person entering the data. A common procedure would be to write your decisions on the questionnaires themselves, perhaps in a different color. You also need to have a master file and hard copy of all the rules that you used.

In the process of understanding your data, different types of analyses and plots will be generated depending on what level of measurement you have. Therefore, it is important to identify whether each of your variables is **nominal, dichotomous, ordinal,** or **normal** (SPSS uses the term **scale**; see Chapter 1). Keep in mind that there are times when whether you call a variable ordinal or scale might change based on your EDA. For example, a variable that you considered to be ordinal may be normally distributed and, thus, better labeled as scale. Remember that making the appropriate choice indicates that you understand your data and should help guide your selection of a statistic.

Exploratory Data Analysis (EDA)

What Is EDA?
After the data are entered into SPSS, the first step to complete (before running any inferential statistics) is EDA, which involves computing various descriptive statistics and graphs. **Exploratory Data Analysis** is used to examine and get to know your data. Chapter 1 and especially this chapter focus on ways to do exploratory data analysis with SPSS. EDA is important to do for several reasons:

1. To see if there are problems in the data such as outliers, nonnormal distributions, problems with coding, missing values, and/or errors inputting the data

2. To examine the extent to which the assumptions of the statistics that you plan to use are met

In addition to these two reasons, which are discussed in this chapter, one could also do EDA for other purposes such as:

3. To get basic information regarding the demographics of subjects to report in the Method section or Results section

4. To examine relationships between variables to determine how to conduct the hypothesis-testing analyses. For example, correlations can be used to see if two or more variables are so highly related that they should be combined (aggregated) for further analyses and/or if only one of them should be included in the central analyses. We created *parents' education* by combining *father's* and *mother's education,* because they are quite highly correlated.

Typically, you would not have research questions for these types of analyses, unless descriptive research questions are part of the study. To show what kinds of descriptive research questions one could answer with EDA, we have included research questions for each of the problems below.

How to Do EDA

There are two general methods used for EDA: generating plots of the data and generating numbers from your data. Both are important and can be very helpful methods of investigating the data. Descriptive statistics (including the minimum, maximum, mean, standard deviation, and skewness), frequency distribution tables, boxplots, histograms, and stem and leaf plots are a few procedures used in EDA.

After collecting data and inputting them into SPSS, many students jump immediately to doing inferential statistics (e.g., *t* tests and ANOVAs). <u>Do not do this!</u> Many times there are errors or problems with the data that need to be located and either fixed, or at least noted, before doing any inferential statistics.

At this point, you are probably asking "Why?" or "I'll do that boring descriptive stuff later while I am writing the methods section." Don't wait! Doing EDA first can prevent many problems down the road.

In the next two sections, we discuss checking for errors and checking assumptions. Some of this discussion reviews basic material, but it is so important that it is worth going over again.

Check for Errors

There are many ways to check for errors; for example:

1. As mentioned above, look over the raw data (questionnaires, interviews, or observation forms) to see if there are inconsistencies, double coding, obvious errors, etc. Do this before entering the data into the computer.

2. Check some, or preferably all, of the raw data (e.g., questionnaires) against the data in your **SPSS Data Editor** file to be sure that errors were not made in the data entry.

3. Compare the minimum and maximum values for each variable in your **Descriptives** output with the allowable range of values in your codebook.

4. Examine the means and standard deviations to see if they look reasonable given what you know about the variables.

5. Examine the *N* column to see if any variables have a lot of missing data, which can be a problem when you do statistics with two or more variables. Missing data could also indicate that there was a problem in data entry.

6. Look for outliers (i.e., extreme scores) in the data.

Check the Assumptions

As noted above, exploratory data analysis can be used to check the assumptions of a statistic. Several assumptions are common to more than one statistic, so in this chapter we will provide an introduction to how to test for them. First, we will define statistical assumptions and briefly discuss several of the most common.

Statistical Assumptions

Every statistical test has assumptions. Statistical assumptions are much like the directions for appropriate use of a product found in an owner's manual. **Assumptions** explain when it is and isn't reasonable to perform a specific statistical test. When the *t* test was developed, for example, the person who developed it needed to make certain assumptions about the distribution of scores, etc., in order to be able to calculate the statistic accurately. If these assumptions are not met, the value that SPSS calculates, which tells the researcher whether the results are statistically significant, will not be completely accurate and may even lead the researcher to draw the wrong conclusion about the results. In each chapter, appropriate statistics and their assumptions are described.

Parametric tests. These include most of the familiar ones (e.g., *t* test, analysis of variance, Pearson correlation, and almost all of the statistics discussed in Chapters 3–11). They usually have more assumptions than nonparametric tests. Parametric tests were designed for data that have certain characteristics, including approximately normal distributions.

Some parametric statistics have been found to be "robust" to violations of one or more of their assumptions. **Robust** means that the assumption can be violated without damaging the validity of the statistic. For example, one assumption of ANOVA is that the dependent variable is normally distributed for each group. Statisticians who have studied these statistics have found that even when data are not completely normally distributed (e.g., they are somewhat skewed), they still can be used under many circumstances.

Nonparametric tests. These tests (e.g., chi-square, Mann-Whitney U, Spearman rho) have fewer assumptions and often can be used when the assumptions of a parametric test are violated. For example, they do not require normal distributions of variables or homogeneity of variances. Unfortunately, there are few nonparametric tests similar to the intermediate statistics discussed in this book so we will have little to say about them here. Appendix B provides a review of most of the basic nonparametric (and parametric) inferential statistics.

Common Assumptions

Independence of observations. The assumption of independence of observations is that there is no relationship between the scores for one person and those of another person. For example, if you know one subject's value on a variable (e.g., *competence*), then this should not help you to guess the value of that variable for any other particular participant. Sometimes, this assumption is violated because one's procedures for sampling participants create systematic bias. For example, "snowball sampling," in which participants recommend other participants for the study, is likely to lead to nonindependence of observations because participants are likely to recommend people who are similar to themselves. Obviously, members of the same family, or the same person measured on more than one occasion, do not comprise independent observations. There are particular methods (matched samples or "repeated measures" methods) designed to deal with the nonindependence of family members or the same person measured several times or participants who are matched on some characteristic.

Homogeneity of variances. Both the *t* test and ANOVA may be affected if the variances (standard deviation squared) of the groups to be compared are substantially different, especially if the number of participants in each group differs markedly. Thus, this is often a critical assumption to meet or correct for. Fortunately, SPSS provides the Levene's test to check this assumption, and it provides ways to adjust the results if the variances are significantly different.

Normality. As mentioned above, many parametric statistics assume that certain variables are distributed approximately normally. That is, the frequency distribution would look like a symmetrical bell-shaped or normal curve, with most subjects having values in the midrange and with a smaller number of subjects with high and low scores. A distribution that is asymmetrical with more high than low scores (or vice versa) is **skewed**. Thus, it is important to check the skewness value. Most statistics books do not provide advice about how to decide whether a variable is at least approximately normal. SPSS recommends that you divide the skewness by its standard error. If the result is less than 2.5 (which is approximately the $p =$ .01 level), then skewness is *not* significantly different from normal. A problem with this method, aside from having to use a calculator, is that the standard error depends on the sample size, so with large samples most variables would be found to be nonnormal. A simpler guideline is that if the skewness is less than plus or minus one ($< +/-1.0$), the variable is at least approximately normal. There are also several other ways to check for normality. In this chapter we will look at two graphical methods: boxplots and frequency polygons. However, remember that *t* tests (if two-tailed) and ANOVA are quite robust to violations of normality.

Linearity. Linearity is the assumption that two variables are related in a linear fashion. If variables are linearly related, then when plotted in a scatterplot the data will fall in a straight line or in a cluster that is relatively straight. Sometimes, if the data are not linearly related (i.e., the plot looks curved) the data can be transformed to make the variables linearly related.

Checking for Errors and Assumptions With Ordinal and Scale Variables

The level of measurement of a variable you are exploring (whether it is nominal, ordinal, dichotomous, or normal/scale) influences the type of exploratory data analysis (EDA) you will want to do. Thus, we have divided this chapter by the measurement levels of the variable because, for some types of variables, certain descriptive statistics will not make sense (e.g., a mean for a nominal variable, or a boxplot for a dichotomous variable). Remember that the researcher has labeled the type of measurement as either nominal, ordinal, or scale when completing the **SPSS Data Editor Variable View.** Remember also that we decided to label dichotomous variables **nominal,** and variables that we assumed were normally distributed were labeled **scale**.

For all of the examples in this chapter, we will be using the *hsbdataB* file, which is on the website. See Appendix A for instructions if you need help with this or getting started with SPSS. Appendix A also shows how to set your computer to print the SPSS syntax on the output.

- Retrieve **hsbdata.sav** from the website. It is desirable to make a working copy of this file. See Appendix A for instructions if you need help with this or getting started. Appendix A also shows how to set your computer to print the syntax.

Problem 2.1: Descriptive Statistics for Ordinal and Scale Variables

For the HSB variables that were labeled as ordinal or scale in the SPSS Variable View, it is important to see if the means make sense (are they close to what you expected?), to examine the minimum and maximum values of the data, and to check the shape of the distribution (i.e., skewness value).

2.1a. Examine the data to get a good understanding of the central tendency, variability, range of scores, and the shape of the distribution for each of the ordinal and scale variables. Which variables are normally distributed?

One way to check these is with the SPSS **Descriptives** command. It is important to examine your data to see if the variables are approximately normally distributed, an assumption of most of the parametric inferential statistics that we will use. To understand if a variable is normally distributed, we compute the skewness index, which helps determine how much a variable's distribution deviates from the distribution of the normal curve. **Skewness** refers to the lack of symmetry in a frequency distribution. Distributions with a long "tail" to the right have a positive skew and those with a long tail on the left have a negative skew. If a frequency distribution of a variable has a large skewness value (larger than 1 or less than -1), that variable is said to deviate from normality. Some of the statistics that we will use later in the book are robust or quite insensitive to violations of normality. Thus, we will assume that it is okay to use them to answer most of our research questions as long as the variables are not extremely skewed. In the case when variables are extremely skewed, you can transform the variables (see Problem 2.9) to hopefully reduce the skewness and use parametric statistics. If transformations cannot reduce the skewness value, then an appropriate nonparametric statistic should be conducted.

The **Descriptives** command will make a compact, space-efficient output. You could instead run the **Frequencies** program because you can get the same statistics with that command. (We will use the Frequencies command later in the chapter.) Now we will compute the mean, standard deviation, skewness, minimum, and maximum for all participants or cases on all the variables that were called ordinal or scale under measure in the **SPSS Data Editor Variable View.** We will <u>not</u> include the nominal variables (*ethnicity* and *religion*) or *gender, algebra1, algebra2, geometry, trigonometry, calculus,* and *math grades,* which are dichotomous variables.

2.1a. First, we will compute **Descriptives** for the **ordinal** variables. These include *father's education, mother's education, grades in h.s.,* and all the "item" variables (*item 01* through *item 14;* be sure to use the reversed items for those that are reversed scored), *math courses taken, mother's education revised, father's education revised,* and *parents' education.* Use these steps:

To get Output 2.1a, select:
- **Analyze → Descriptive Statistics → Descriptives…**
- While holding down the control key (i.e., the key marked "Ctrl"), click on all of the variables in the left box that we called **ordinal** so that they are highlighted. These include *father's education, mother's education, grades in h.s., item 01* to *item 14, math courses taken, mother's education revised, father's education revised,* and *parents' education.*
- Click on the **arrow** button pointing right.
- Be sure that all of the requested variables have moved out of the left window.
- Click on **Options.** The Descriptives: Options window will open.
- Be sure that **Mean** has a check next to it.
- Under **Dispersion,** select **Std. Deviation, Minimum,** and **Maximum** so that each has a check.
- Under **Distribution,** check **Skewness.**
- Click on **Continue** and then click on **OK.**

Compare your output with Output 2.1a.

Output 2.1a: Descriptives for the Ordinal Variables

```
DESCRIPTIVES VARIABLES=faed maed grades item01 item02 item03 item04r item05r item06r
   item07 item08r item09 item10r item11r item12 item13 item14 mathcrs
   maedRevis faedRevis parEduc
   /STATISTICS=MEAN STDDEV MIN MAX SKEWNESS .
```

Descriptive Statistics

	N	Minimum	Maximum	Mean	Std.	Skewness	
	Statistic	Statistic	Statistic	Statistic	Statistic	Statistic	Std. Error
father's education	73	2	10	4.73	2.830	.684	.281
mother's education	75	2	10	4.11	2.240	1.124	.277
grades in h.s.	75	2	8	5.68	1.570	-.332	.277
item01 motivation	74	1	4	2.96	.928	-.763	.279
item02 pleasure	75	1	4	3.52	.906	-1.910	.277
item03 competence	74	1	4	2.82	.897	-.579	.279
item04 reversed	74	1	4	2.84	.922	-.422	.279
item05 reversed	75	1	4	3.39	.971	-1.581	.277
item06 reversed	75	1.00	4.00	2.5733	.97500	.058	.277
item07 motivation	75	1	4	2.76	1.051	-.433	.277
item08 reversed	75	1	4	3.05	.914	-.653	.277
item09 competence	74	1	4	3.32	.760	-1.204	.279
item10 reversed	75	1.00	4.00	3.5867	.73693	-1.869	.277
item11 reversed	75	1	4	3.64	.747	-2.497	.277
item12 motivation	75	1	4	3.00	.822	-.600	.277
item13 motivation	75	1	4	2.67	.794	-.320	.277
item14 pleasure	75	1	4	2.84	.717	-.429	.277
math courses taken	75	0	5	2.11	1.673	.325	.277
mother's educ revised	75	1.00	3.00	1.4667	.68445	1.162	.277
father's educ revised	73	1.00	3.00	1.7397	.85028	.533	.281
parents' education	75	2.00	10.00	4.3933	2.31665	.923	.277
Valid N (listwise)	69						

Next, we will run **Descriptives** for the <u>scale variables</u>: *math achievement, mosaic, visualization, visualization retest, scholastic aptitude test-math, competence, motivation,* and *pleasure scale*. Note that these variables have the symbol ✐ next to them.

2.1b.   What is the distribution of values for variables in our data set that we have conceptualized as scale?

To get Output 2.1b, select:
- **Analyze → Descriptive Statistics → Descriptives…**
- Click on **Reset** to move the ordinal variables back to the left. This also deletes what we chose under **Options**.
- Highlight *math achievement, mosaic, visualization, visualization retest, scholastic aptitude test-math, competence, motivation,* and *pleasure scale* and move them to the **Variables** box.
- Click on **Options** and check the same descriptive statistics as you did in Problem 2.1a.
- Click on **Continue** and then **Ok.**

Compare your output with Output 2.1b.

Output 2.1b: Descriptives for Variables Labeled as Scale

```
DESCRIPTIVES VARIABLES=mathach mosaic visual visual2 satm competence motivation pleasure
  /STATISTICS=MEAN STDDEV IN MAX SKEWNESS .
```

Descriptive Statistics

	N	Minimum	Maximum	Mean	Std.	Skewness	
	Statistic	Statistic	Statistic	Statistic	Statistic	Statistic	Std. Error
math achievement test	75	-1.67	23.67	12.5645	6.67031	.044	.277
mosaic, pattern test	75	-4.0	56.0	27.413	9.5738	.529	.277
visualization test	75	-.25	14.75	5.2433	3.91203	.536	.277
visualization retest	75	.00	9.50	4.5467	3.01816	.235	.277
scholastic aptitude test - math	75	250	730	490.53	94.553	.128	.277
competence scale	73	1.00	4.00	3.2945	.66450	-1.634	.281
motivation scale	73	1.17	4.00	2.8744	.63815	-.570	.281
pleasure scale	75	1.50	4.00	3.1300	.60454	-.682	.277
Valid N (listwise)	71						

Interpretation of Outputs 2.1a and 2.1b

These outputs provide descriptive statistics for all of the variables labeled as **ordinal** (2.1a) and **scale** (2.1b). Notice that the variables are listed down the left column of the outputs and the requested descriptive statistics are listed across the top row. The descriptive statistics included in the output are the number of subjects (**N**), the **Minimum** (lowest) and **Maximum** (highest) scores, the **Mean** (or average) for each variable, the **Std.** (the standard deviation), and the **Skewness** statistic and the **Std. Error** of the skewness. Note, from the bottom line of the outputs, that the **Valid N (listwise)** is 69 for Output 2.1a and 71 for 2.1b rather than 75, which is the number of participants in the data file. This is because the listwise *N* includes only the persons with *no* missing data on <u>any</u> variable requested in the output. Notice that several variables (e.g., *father's education* and *item01* in 2.1a and *motivation* and *competence* in 2.1b) each have one or two participants with missing data.

Using your output to check your data for errors. For both the ordinal and scale variables, check to make sure that all **Means** seem reasonable. That is, you should check your means to see if they are within the ranges you expected (given the information in your codebook and your understanding of the variable). Next, check the output to see that the **Minimum** and **Maximum** are within the appropriate (codebook) range for each variable. If the minimum is smaller or the maximum is bigger than you expected (e.g., 100 for a variable that has only 1–50 for possible values), then you should suspect that there was an error somewhere and you need to check it out. Finally, you should check the *N* column to see if the *N*s are what you were expecting. If it happens that you have more participants missing than you expected, check the original data to see if some were entered incorrectly or inadvertently omitted. If you had calculated the scores you are looking at and you had more missing data than expected, you would also want to check to make sure the calculations were done correctly. Notice that *competence scale* and *motivation scale* each has a few participants missing.

Using the output to check assumptions. The main assumption that we can check from this output is normality. We won't pay much attention to the skewness for *item 01* to *item 14* and *mother's* and *father's education revised*. These ordinal variables have fewer than five levels, and they will not be considered to be scale even though some of them are not very skewed. Usually, if a variable has fewer than five levels, it is best to view it as ordinal; however, it is important to realize that this is our guideline rather than a true requirement. Under some circumstances, such as when four levels represent reasonably equidistant points along an underlying continuous distribution, you might decide to consider a variable normal/scale if it is normally distributed but measured only on a four-point scale. We will not use the four-point-scale "items" as individual variables because we will be combining them to create summated variables (the *motivation* and *competence* and *pleasure* scales) before using inferential statistics.

From Output 2.1a, we can see that, of the variables with five or more levels that we called **ordinal**, four of them (*father's education, grades in h.s., math courses taken,* and *parents' education*) are approximately normally distributed; that is, they have five or more levels and have skewness values between −1 and 1. Thus, we can assume that they are more like scale variables, and we can use inferential statistics that have the assumption of normality. To better understand these variables, it may be helpful to change the **Measure** column in the **Variable View** so that these four variables will be labeled as <u>scale</u>. Note that *mother's education*, with a skewness statistic of 1.12, is more skewed than is desirable but is not grossly skewed. Note that *father's education* is not skewed.

In Output 2.1b, we check the normality assumption for the variables that were labeled as scale to be sure that the variables truly are normally distributed. Look at the skewness value in Output 2.1b to see if it is between −1 and 1. From the output we see that most of these variables have skewness values between −1 and 1, but *competence* at −1.63 is quite skewed.

There are several ways to check this assumption in addition to checking the skewness value. If the mean, median, and mode, which can be obtained with the **Frequencies** command, are approximately equal, then you can assume that the distribution is approximately normally distributed. For example, the mean (490.53), median (490.00), and mode (500) for *scholastic aptitude test-math* are very similar values, and the skewness value is .128 (see Output 2.1b). Thus, we can assume that *SAT-math* is approximately normally distributed.

In addition to numerical methods for understanding your data, there are several graphical methods. SPSS can create histograms with or without the normal curve superimposed and also frequency polygons (line graphs) to roughly assess normality. The trouble is that visual inspection of histograms can be deceiving because some approximately normal distributions may not look very much like a normal curve.

Problem 2.2: Boxplots for Ordinal and Scale Variables

2.2a. What is the distribution of and are there outliers in *math achievement*?

Boxplots of One or Several Variables

Boxplots and **stem-and-leaf plots** can be used to examine some HSB variables. Boxplots are a method of graphically representing ordinal and scale data. They can be made with many different combinations of variables and groups. Using boxplots for one, two, or more variables or groups in the same plot can be useful in helping you understand your data. First, we have produced a boxplot for *math achievement*.

To get Output 2.2a:
- Select **Graphs → Chart Builder.** The **Chart Builder** window should appear. Note: You must have your variables labeled with the appropriate scale of measurement (i.e., nominal, ordinal, or scale) in order to effectively use the Chart Builder.
- Under the **Gallery** tab, click on **Boxplot**. Then, select the boxplot you wish to create. For this example, click on the picture of the single boxplot and drag the picture to the upper box, which is labeled "*Chart preview uses example data*" (the large white box with the blue words).
- Under **Variables:** select *math achievement* and drag it to the blue dotted box labeled "X-Axis."
- Click on **OK.**

Compare your output with Output 2.2a.

Output 2.2a: Boxplot of Math Achievement Test

```
* Chart Builder.
GGRAPH
  /GRAPHDATASET NAME="graphdataset" VARIABLES=mathach MISSING=LISTWISE REPORTMISSING=NO
  /GRAPHSPEC SOURCE=INLINE.
BEGIN GPL
  SOURCE: s=userSource(id("graphdataset"))
  DATA: mathach=col(source(s), name("mathach"))
  DATA: id=col(source(s), name("$CASENUM"), unit.category())
  COORD: rect(dim(1), transpose())
  GUIDE: axis(dim(1), label("math achievement test"))
  ELEMENT: schema(position(bin.quantile.letter(mathach)), label(id))
END GPL.
```

GGraph

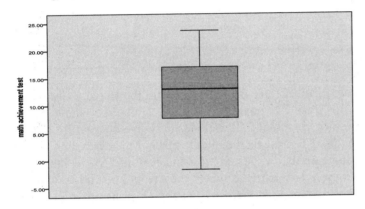

Next, we will create a boxplot with more than one variable in the same plot. To show another way of creating plots, we will use Legacy plots for this example.

2.2b. What are the distributions of and are there outliers in *motivation* and *competence*? How are the distributions of *motivation* and *competence similar* and *different*?

To get Output 2.2a:
- Select **Graphs → Legacy Dialogs → Boxplot** ... The **Boxplot** window should appear.
- Select **Simple** and **Summaries of separate variables**.
- Click on **Define**. The **Define Simple Boxplot: Summaries of Separate Variables** window will appear.
- While holding down the control key (i.e., "Ctrl") highlight both of the variables that you are interested in (in this case they would be *competence* and *motivation*). Click on the arrow to move them into the **Boxes Represent** box.
- Click on **OK**.

Output 2.2b: Boxplots of Competence and Motivation Scales

```
EXAMINE VARIABLES=competence motivation
  /COMPARE VARIABLES
  /PLOT BOXPLOT
  /STATISTICS NONE
  /NOTOTAL
  /MISSING LISTWISE.
```

Explore

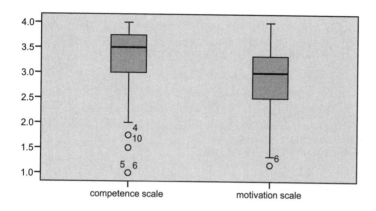

> Notice that there are four outliers for *competence* and one for *motivation* in these boxplots.

Interpretation of Outputs 2.2a and 2.2b

Outputs 2.2a and 2.2b include boxplots generated from **Chart Builder** and from the **Legacy Dialog** command, respectively. We did not include the **Case Processing Summary** tables that show the **Valid *N*, Missing** cases, and **Total** cases. The plot in Output 2.2a includes only one boxplot for our requested variable of *math achievement*. Each "box" represents the middle 50% of the cases, and the "whiskers" at the top and bottom of the box indicate the "expected" top and bottom 25%. If there were **outliers** there would be *O*s and if there were really extreme scores they would be shown with asterisks, above or below the end of the whiskers. Notice that there are not any *O*s or asterisks in the boxplot in Output 2.2a.

For Output 2.2b, notice that there are two separate boxplots, one for competence and one for motivation. As indicated by the *O*s at or below the lower whiskers, the boxplot for *competence* shows there are four outliers, and the boxplot for *motivation* indicates there is one outlier.

Using your output to check your data for errors. If there are *O*s or asterisks, then you need to check the raw data or score sheet to be sure there was not an error. The numbers next to the *O*s indicate which participants these scores belong to. This can be helpful when you want to check to see if these are errors or if they are the actual scores of the subject. If the scores were entered correctly, you can also check to see if the participants with outlier scores differ in any known way from other participants (e.g., also different from the others on a demographic variable or measure of intellectual development). Note that, by default, these numbers refer to the line numbers on the left-hand side, not to any arbitrary participant numbers you might assign to them in your data set.

Using the output to check your data for assumptions. Boxplots can be useful for identifying variables with extreme scores, which can make the distribution skewed (i.e., nonnormal). Also if there are few outliers, if the whiskers are approximately the same length, and if the line in the box is approximately in the middle of the box, then you can assume that the variable is approximately normally distributed. Thus, *math achievement* (Output 2.2a) is near normal, *motivation* (2.2b) is approximately normal, but *competence* (2.2b) is quite skewed and not normal.

Problem 2.3: Boxplots Split by a Dichotomous Variable

Many times researchers are interested in reporting information on one specific variable for multiple subgroups of the participants (e.g., males and females). Creating separate boxplots as well as separate statistics and stem-and-leaf plots can be useful if you want to see if the distributions of scores are very different for the two groups, which would suggest heterogeneity of variances.

2.3. Is there heterogeneity of variances and of the shape of the distribution for males and females for *math achievement*?

To get Output 2.3:
- **Analyze → Descriptive Statistics → Explore.**
- The **Explore** window will appear.
- Click on *math achievement* and move it to the **Dependent List**.
- Next, click on *gender* and move it to the **Factor** (or independent variable) **List.**
- Click on **Both** under **Display.** This will produce both a table of descriptive statistics and two kinds of plots: **Stem-and-Leaf** and **Box-and-Whiskers.**
- Click on **OK**.

Output 2.3: Boxplots Split by Gender With Statistics and Stem-and-Leaf Plots

```
EXAMINE VARIABLES=mathach BY gender
  /PLOT BOXPLOT STEMLEAF
  /COMPARE GROUP
  /STATISTICS DESCRIPTIVES
  /CINTERVAL 95
  /MISSING LISTWISE
  /NOTOTAL.
```

Explore

Gender

Case Processing Summary

		Cases					
		Valid		Missing		Total	
	gender	N	Percent	N	Percent	N	Percent
math achievement test	male	34	100.0%	0	.0%	34	100.0%
	female	41	100.0%	0	.0%	41	100.0%

Descriptives

	gender				Statistic	Std. Error
math achievement test	male	Mean			14.7550	1.03440
		95% Confidence Interval for Mean	Lower Bound		12.6505	
			Upper Bound		16.8595	
		5% Trimmed Mean			14.8454	
		Median			14.3330	
		Variance			36.379	
		Std. Deviation			6.03154	
		Minimum			3.67	
		Maximum			23.7	
		Range			20.0	
		Interquartile Range			10.0005	
		Skewness			-.156	.403
		Kurtosis			-.963	.788
	female	Mean			10.7479	1.04576
		95% Confidence Interval for Mean	Lower Bound		8.6344	
			Upper Bound		12.8615	
		5% Trimmed Mean			10.6454	
		Median			10.3330	
		Variance			44.838	
		Std. Deviation			6.69612	
		Minimum			-1.7	
		Maximum			23.7	
		Range			25.3	
		Interquartile Range			10.5000	
		Skewness			.331	.369
		Kurtosis			-.698	.724

Note that we have circled, for males and for females, three key statistics: mean, variance, and skewness.

gender = male

Stem-and-Leaf Plots

```
math achievement test Stem-and-Leaf Plot for
gender= male
```

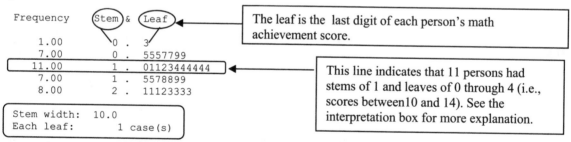

```
 Frequency    Stem &  Leaf

     1.00        0 .  3
     7.00        0 .  5557799
    11.00        1 .  01123444444
     7.00        1 .  5578899
     8.00        2 .  11123333

 Stem width:   10.0
 Each leaf:        1 case(s)
```

The leaf is the last digit of each person's math achievement score.

This line indicates that 11 persons had stems of 1 and leaves of 0 through 4 (i.e., scores between 10 and 14). See the interpretation box for more explanation.

gender = female

Stem-and-Leaf Plots

```
math achievement test Stem-and-Leaf Plot for
gender= female

 Frequency    Stem &  Leaf

     1.00       -0 .  1
     7.00        0 .  1123344
    12.00        0 .  555666778999
    11.00        1 .  00002334444
     5.00        1 .  77779
     5.00        2 .  02233

 Stem width:   10.0
 Each leaf:        1 case(s)
```

1 person had a negative score (stem −0) of −1.

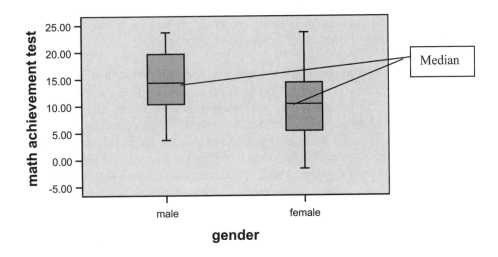

Interpretation of Output 2.3

The first table under **Explore** provides descriptive statistics about the number of males and females with **Valid** and **Missing** data. Note that we have 34 males and 41 females with valid *math achievement test* scores.

The **Descriptives** table contains many different statistics for males and females separately, some of which (e.g., 5% trimmed mean) are not discussed in this book. Note that the average *math achievement test* score is 14.76 for the males and 10.75 for females, but the maximum score for each group is 23.7. We will discuss the variances and skewness below when we discuss assumptions.

The **Stem-and-Leaf Plots,** for each gender separately, are next. These plots are like a histogram or frequency distribution turned on the side. They give a visual impression of the distribution, and they usually show *each* person's score on the dependent variable (*math achievement*). The stem is the first digit of the score and the leaf is the second digit. Note that the legend indicates that **Stem width** equals 10. This means that entries that have 0 for the stem are less than 10, with the leaf indicating the actual number (1–9), those with 1 as the stem range from 10 to 19, etc. Note also that the legend indicates that each **leaf** equals one case. Each number in the **Leaf** column represents the last digit of one person's *math achievement* score. The numbers in the **Frequency** column indicate how many participants had scores in the range represented by that stem. Thus, in the male plot, one student had a **stem** of 0 and a **leaf** of 3, that is, a score of 3. The frequency of male students with leaves between 5 and 9 is 7, and there were three scores of 5, two of 7, and two of 9. Eleven participants had a **stem** of 1 and a **leaf** of 0 to 4; one had a **leaf** of 0 (a score of 10); two had scores of 11, one had a score of 13, and six had a score of 14.

Boxplots are the last part of the output. There are two boxplots (one for males and one for females). By inspecting the plots, we can see that the median score for males is quite a bit higher than that for females, but there is some overlap of the boxes and substantial overlap of the full distributions, with the highest scores being comparable for the two groups but the lowest scores being lower for females. We need to be careful in concluding that males score higher than females, especially based on a small sample of students. In Chapter 8, we will show how an inferential statistic (analysis of covariance) can tell us whether this apparent gender difference is actually due to gender differences in another variable (number of *math courses taken*).

Using the output to check your data for errors. Checking the boxplots and stem-and-leaf plots can help identify outliers that might be data entry errors. In this case, there are none.

Using the output to check your data for assumptions. As noted in the interpretation of Outputs 2.2a and 2.2b, you can tell if a variable is grossly nonnormal by looking at the boxplots. The fact that the median is near the center of the box and the whiskers are reasonably symmetrical suggests a reasonably normal distribution. The stem-and-leaf plots provide similar information. You can also examine the skewness values for each gender separately in the table of **Descriptives** (see the circled skewness values). Note that for both males and females, the skewness values are less than one, which indicates that _math achievement is approximately normal for both genders_. This is an assumption of the *t* test and ANOVA, and multivariate versions of this assumption are required for many of the statistics performed in this book.

The **Descriptives** table also provides the variances for males and females. A key assumption of ANOVA and the *t* test is that the variances are approximately equal (i.e., the assumption of homogeneity of variances). Note that the variance is 36.38 for males and 44.84 for females. These do not seem grossly different, and if we computed a Levene test on the differences in variances between males and females on this variable, we would find that the difference is not statistically significant. (See Appendix B for examples of the Levene test.). Thus, the assumption of homogeneous variances is _not_ violated. The boxplots and stem-and-leaf plots help you see this.

Problem 2.4: Using Tables and Figures for EDA with Dichotomous and Nominal Variables

Descriptives for Dichotomous Variables
We will now use the **Descriptives** command for each of the dichotomous variables. Once again, we could have done **Frequencies**, with or without frequency tables, but we chose Descriptives. This time we selected fewer statistics because the standard deviation, variance, and skewness values are not very meaningful with dichotomous variables.

2.4. What proportion of the sample has a value of "1" for *gender, algebra 1, algebra 2, geometry, trigonometry, calculus,* and *math grades*?

To produce Output 2.4:

- Select **Analyze → Descriptive Statistics → Descriptives**.

After selecting **Descriptives**, you will be ready to compute the *N*, minimum, maximum, and mean for all participants or cases on all selected variables in order to examine the data.

- Before starting this problem, press **Reset** to clear the **Variable** box.
- While holding down the control key (i.e., "Ctrl") *highlight all* of the **dichotomous** variables in the left box. These variables have only two levels: *gender, algebra 1, algebra 2, geometry, trigonometry, calculus,* and *math grades.*
- Click on the **arrow** button pointing right.
- Be sure that all of these variables have moved out of the left window and into the **Variable(s)** window.

- Click on **Options**. The **Descriptives: Options** window will open.
- Select **Mean, Minimum, and Maximum.**
- Unclick **Std. Deviation.**
- Click on **Continue.**
- Click on **OK**.

Compare your output with Output 2.4

Output 2.4: Descriptives for Dichotomous Variables

```
DESCRIPTIVES VARIABLES=gender alg1 alg2 geo trig calc mathgr
/STATISTICS= MEAN MIN MAX .
```

Descriptives

Descriptive Statistics

	N	Minimum	Maximum	Mean	
gender	75	0	1	.55	
algebra 1 in h.s.	75	0	1	.79	79% of students took algebra 1
algebra 2 in h.s.	75	0	1	.47	
geometry in h.s.	75	0	1	.48	
trigonometry in h.s.	75	0	1	.27	
calculus in h.s.	75	0	1	.11	
math grades	75	0	1	.41	
Valid N (listwise)	75				

Interpretation of Output 2.4

Output 2.4 includes only one table of **Descriptive Statistics**. Across the top row are the requested statistics of *N*, **Minimum, Maximum,** and **Mean.** We could have requested other statistics, but they would not be very meaningful for dichotomous variables. Down the left column are the variable labels. The *N* column indicates that all the variables have complete data. The **Valid *N* (listwise)** is 75, which also indicates that all the participants had data for each of our requested variables.

The most helpful column is the **Mean** column. Although the mean is not meaningful for nominal variables with more than two categories, you can use the mean of dichotomous variables to understand what percentage of participants fall into each of the two groups. For example, the mean of *gender* is .55, which indicates that 55% of the participants were coded as 1 (female); thus, 45% were coded 0 (male). Because the mean is greater than .50, there are more females than males. If the mean is close to 1 or 0 (e.g., algebra 1 and calculus), then splitting the data on that dichotomous variable might not be useful because there will be many participants in one group and very few participants in the other.

Using your output to check your data for errors. The **Minimum** column shows that all the dichotomous variables had "0" for a minimum, and the **Maximum** column indicates that all the variables have "1" for a maximum. This is good because it agrees with the codebook.

Problem 2.5: Using Frequency Tables

Displaying frequency tables for variables can help you understand how many participants are in each level of a variable and how much missing data of various types you have. For nominal variables, most descriptive statistics are meaningless. Thus, having a frequency table is usually the best way to understand your nominal variables.

2.5. What are frequencies of values for *ethnicity* (a nominal variable) and for *father's education* (an ordered variable)?

To produce Output 2.5:

- Select **Analyze → Descriptive Statistics → Frequencies**.
- Click on **Reset** if any variables are in the **Variable(s)** box.
- Now *highlight* the **nominal** variable, *ethnicity,* in the left box.
- Click on the **arrow** button pointing right.
- Highlight and move over the **ordinal** variable, *father's education*.
- Be sure the **Display frequency tables box** is checked.
- Do not click on **Statistics** because we do not want to select any this time.
- Click on **OK.**

Compare your output to Output 2.5.

Output 2.5 Frequency Tables for a Nominal Variable and an Ordinal Variable

```
FREQUENCIES VARIABLES=ethnic faed
  /ORDER=  ANALYSIS .
```

Frequencies

Statistics

		ethnicity	father's education
N	Valid	73	73
	Missing	2	2

Frequency Table

ethnicity

		Frequency	Percent	Valid Percent	Cumulative Percent
Valid	Euro-Amer	41	54.7	56.2	56.2
	African-Amer	15	20.0	20.5	76.7
	Latino-Amer	10	13.3	13.7	90.4
	Asian-Amer	7	9.3	9.6	100.0
	Total	73	97.3	100.0	
Missing	multiethnic	1	1.3		
	blank	1	1.3		
	Total	2	2.7		
Total		75	100.0		

father's education

		Frequency	Percent	Valid Percent	Cumulative Percent
Valid	< h.s. grad	22	29.3	30.1	30.1
	h.s. grad	16	21.3	21.9	52.1
	< 2 yrs voc	3	4.0	4.1	56.2
	2 yrs voc	8	10.7	11.0	67.1
	< 2 yrs coll	4	5.3	5.5	72.6
	> 2 yrs coll	1	1.3	1.4	74.0
	coll grad	7	9.3	9.6	83.6
	master's	6	8.0	8.2	91.8
	MD/PhD	6	8.0	8.2	100.0
	Total	73	97.3	100.0	
Missing	System	2	2.7		
Total		75	100.0		

74% of fathers have less than a bachelor's degree.

Interpretation of Output 2.5

There is one **Frequency** table for *ethnicity* and one for *father's education*. The left-hand column shows the **Valid** categories (or levels or values), **Missing** values, and **Total** number of participants. The **Frequency** column gives the number of participants who had each value. The **Percent** column is the percent who had each value, including missing values. For example, in the ethnicity table, 54.7% of all participants were *Euro-American*, 20.0% were *African-American*, 13.3% were *Latino-American*, and 9.3% were *Asian-American*. There also were a total of 2.7% missing: 1.3% were *multiethnic*, and 1.3% were left *blank*. The **valid percent** shows the percentage of those with *nonmissing* data at each value; for example, 56.2% of the 73 students with a single valid ethnic group were *Euro-Americans*. Finally, **Cumulative Percent** is the percentage of subjects in a category *plus* the categories listed above it.

This last column is not very useful with nominal data such as ethnicity but can be quite informative for frequency distributions with several ordered categories. For example, in the distribution of father's education, 74% of the fathers had less than a bachelor's degree (i.e., they had not graduated from college).

Using your output to check your data for errors. Errors can be found by checking to see if the number missing is the number you expected. Also, if you have more than one type of missing data and you assigned different numbers to these (e.g., 98 and 99), you will see the types listed in the first column.

Using the output to check your data for assumptions. Frequency tables are helpful for checking the levels of the variable to see if you have subjects in each one. If one of the levels does not have many subjects in it, it can create problems with difference statistics (see Chapter 4 for an explanation of types of difference statistics).

Problem 2.6: Bar Charts

With **nominal** data, you should not use a graphic that connects adjacent categories because with nominal data there is no necessary ordering of the categories or levels. Thus, it is better to make a bar graph or chart of the frequency distribution of variables like *religion, ethnic group,* or other nominal variables; the points that happen to be adjacent in your frequency distribution are not by necessity adjacent.

2.6. What are the relative numbers of high school students in this sample who report being Protestant, Catholic, and "no religion"?

To produce Output 2.6:

- **Select Analyze → Descriptive Statistics → Frequencies**... The **Frequencies** window should open.
- Click on *religion* and move it into the **Variable(s):** box.
- Click on **Charts...** This will open the **Frequencies: Charts** window.
- Select **Bar charts** and then **Continue**.
- Click on the check mark next to **Display frequency tables**. We do not need the frequency tables in this analysis.
- Click on **OK**.

Compare your output with Output 2.6.

Output 2.6 Frequency Distribution Bar Chart for the Nominal Variable of Religion

```
FREQUENCIES VARIABLES=religion
  /FORMAT=NOTABLE
  /BARCHART  FREQ
  /ORDER=  ANALYSIS .
```

Frequencies

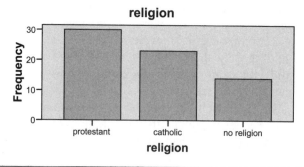

Interpretation of Output 2.6

There are two parts to the output: a statistics table (not shown) and the bar chart. The **Statistics** table indicates the valid *N* and the missing *N*. The **bar chart** presents a bar for each level of the nominal variable. Keep in mind that the order of the bars is arbitrary. The order of the bars can be changed by clicking on the plot and then clicking on the bars. The **Chart Editor Properties** box will appear, and the level can be changed within this window.

Using your output to check your data for errors. Errors can be seen if the levels are not what you were expecting. For example, if you inadvertently entered the wrong number (a number that does not have a category label), you will see a bar for that number, with the number used as a label for the bar. Also, if there are no participants for a level, there will not be a bar for that level.

Using the output to check your data for assumptions. Bar charts are helpful if you are unsure how many categories of a variable actually occur in your data; you can count the number of bars. You can also see the number of participants in each level. It is best if there are approximately the same number of subjects in each level if one wants to use the variable in procedures like ANOVA and MANOVA.

Problem 2.7: Histograms and Frequency Polygons

Histograms (shown in Chapter 1) look much like bar charts except in histograms there is no space between the bars, indicating that there is a continuous variable theoretically underlying the scores (i.e., scores could theoretically be any point on a continuum from the lowest to highest score). Histograms can be used even if the data as measured are not continuous, if the underlying variable is conceptualized as continuous. For example, the *competence scale* items were rated on a four-point scale, but one could, theoretically, have any amount of competence.

2.7a. What is the distribution of *competence*?

There are multiple methods that can be used in SPSS to create a histogram. One method is using **Legacy Dialogs**, as indicated here:

- Select **Graphs → Legacy Dialogs → Histogram…** The **Histogram** window should appear.
- Select *competence* and move it into the **Variable:** box.
- Click on **OK**.

Compare your output with the histogram in Chapter 1.

Frequency Polygons
Output 2.7b is a frequency polygon; it connects the points between the categories, and is best used with **approximately normal** data, but it can be used with ordinal data. SPSS uses the term line graph for frequency polygons.

2.7b. What is the frequency of the scores for *motivation*?

To produce Output 2.7b:

- Select **Graphs → Chart Builder…** The **Chart Builder** window should appear.
- Under the **Gallery** tab, select **Line**. This will produce two choices of line graphs – one with one line (for one variable) and a graph with multiple lines (for multiple variables).
- In this example, we want to select the graph with only one variable. Click on the graph and drag it into the box labeled "*Chart preview uses example data.*"
- Select *motivation scale* and move it into the **X-Axis?** box.
- Click on **OK**.

Compare your output with Output 2.7b.

Output 2.7b. Frequency Polygon Showing Approximately Normal Data

```
* Chart Builder.
GGRAPH
  /GRAPHDATASET NAME="graphdataset" VARIABLES=motivation MISSING=LISTWISE REPORTMISSING=NO
  /GRAPHSPEC SOURCE=INLINE.
BEGIN GPL
  SOURCE: s=userSource(id("graphdataset"))
  DATA: motivation=col(source(s), name("motivation"))
  GUIDE: axis(dim(1), label("motivation scale"))
  GUIDE: axis(dim(2), label("Frequency"))
  ELEMENT: line(position(summary.count(bin.rect(motivation))), missing.wings())
END GPL.
```

GGraph

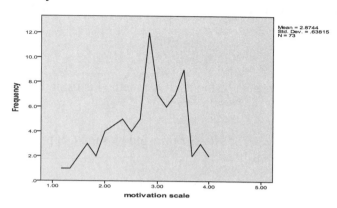

Interpretation of Output 2.7b

The frequency polygon presents frequency **counts** for one variable (listed along the bottom; *motivation scale* in this example). Each level of the variable is listed along the bottom and the counts are listed along the side. We can see from this frequency polygon that the largest number of participants (12) had a motivation level of 2.8, and only about four people had scores of 2.0.

Using your output to check your data for errors. Errors can be seen with the frequency polygon if there are values you were not expecting or if there are larger or smaller counts than you were expecting.

Using the output to check your data for assumptions. We can see that the data are somewhat normally distributed because the highest counts are in the middle, with smaller counts on either end. We would still want to check skewness values as well.

Problem 2.8: Matrix Scatterplots

To check linearity and get a visual idea about whether there is likely to be a problem with multicollinearity (see Chapter 6), we can do matrix scatterplots.

2.8. Are there bivariate linear relationships between the following variables: *math achievement, math courses taken, pleasure scale,* and *mosaic pattern test?*

To develop a scatterplot of *math achievement, math courses taken, pleasure scale,* and *mosaic pattern test,* follow these commands:

- **Graphs → Legacy Dialogs → Scatter/Dot...**
- Click on **Matrix Scatter.**
- Click on **Define**.
- Now, move *math achievement test, math courses taken, pleasure scale,* and *mosaic pattern test* to the **Matrix Variables** box.
- Click on **OK.** You will get Output 2.8, the matrix scatterplot with circles for the data points.
- To change the circles to the Xs (as we have below) double-click on the graph. This will open the **Chart Editor**. Double click again on one of the circles in the Chart Editor. This will open the **Properties** window.
- In the **Properties** window, click on the arrow to the right of **Type**. Select the X.
- Click on **Apply** and then **Close**.
- Close the window for the **Chart Editor** to get back to the **Output** window.

Compare your output with Output 2.8.

Output 2.8: Matrix Scatterplot

```
GRAPH
  /SCATTERPLOT(MATRIX)=mathach mathcrs pleasure mosaic
  /MISSING=LISTWISE .
```

Graph

Note that the points are relatively close to a straight line.

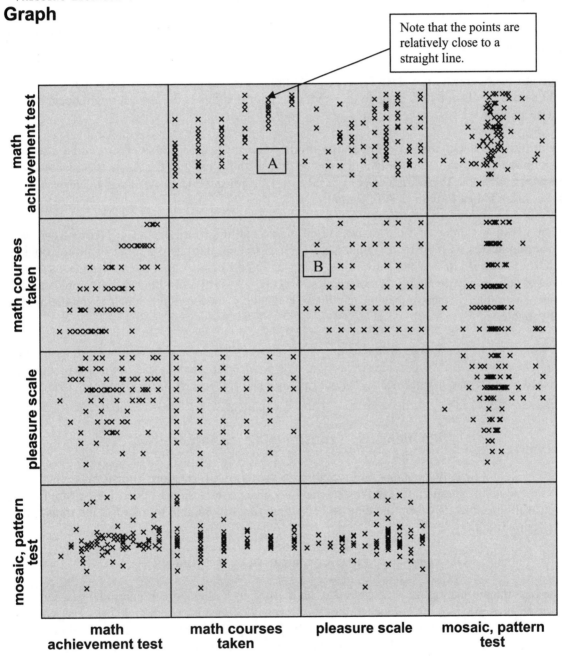

Interpretation of Output 2.8

This matrix scatterplot command in Output 2.8 creates bivariate scatterplots of each entered variable with each of the others. It is most helpful to create a matrix scatterplot when you need to understand the relationships among several variables. In a scatterplot, each X (or O) represents a data point. There are six different bivariate scatterplots in Output 2.8. Keep in mind that there are duplicate relationships shown (i.e., there are two bivariate scatterplots for each pair of variables); you should look either above or below the diagonal empty boxes.

Using your output to check your data for errors. At times, there might be a data point that is extreme; there might be one that is not at all close to the other data points. If this is the case, it might be an outlier, or it might be an error.

Using the output to check your data for assumptions. The clusters or clouds of Xs can be examined for the assumption of linearity. If a straight line can be drawn so that most of the Xs lie relatively close to it, we can assume that the two variables are related in a linear fashion (e.g., see *math achievement* and *math courses taken* indicated with an A in Output 2.8).

If the Xs are not in any order or if they appear to be spread out in a cloud (e.g., see *pleasure* and *math courses taken*, indicated with an B in Output 2.8), we can assume that there is little or no relationship between the variables. If a scatterplot shows little relationship between two predictors, this means there is little chance of collinearity involving these variables. If there is little relationship between a predictor and the dependent variable, it means that the predictor is unlikely to contribute much to predicting the dependent variable.

However, when the clusters appear to be creating a curve rather than a straight line, we can assume the variables might be related in a curvilinear fashion. We would not want to use them in computing a statistic that has the assumption of linearity without fixing this problem first by transforming one or both of the variables, as shown below.

Problem 2.9: Transforming Variables

If the variables do not meet the assumptions, we might consider transformation. Transformations usually increase the difficulty of interpretation of the data and may change the results of the study, so you need to be sure you really need to transform the data and also that you will be able to interpret the transformed variable in your writing.

2.9. Can the normality of the *competence* variable be improved by transforming it?

Finding the best transformation for a variable may be assisted by following certain guidelines, but often trial and error is needed to determine if the transformation was successful. The most common transformations, what the transformation can fix, and the SPSS syntax commands are listed below. If you do not know which transformation is best, start where the arrow is on the figure and go up (for negative skew) or down (for positive skew) one row, or use the arcsine transformation for proportion data. After you transform a variable, you need to rerun the assumptions to see if the newly transformed variable meets the assumptions. If not, go up (for negative skew) or down (for positive skew) one row and use that transformation, and then recheck assumptions. If assumptions are not met, go up or down two rows, etc. If you receive an error message, this may be due to the data not fitting the type of transformation: in this case, pick a different transformation to conduct.

When to use	Transformation	SPSS Syntax
To reduce negative skew	X^3	VAR=(X)**3
	X^2	VAR=(X)**2
Nontransformed variable	X	
To reduce positive skew	log X	VAR=LG10(X)
	$\sqrt{X}$	VAR=SQRT(X)
	1/X	VAR=1/(X)
	$1/X^2$	VAR=1/(X)**2
To stretch both tails of the distribution (proportion data)	Arcsine X	VAR=ARSIN(X)
Note: Nontransformed variable = X		

Start Here →

Fig. 2.1. Transformation ladder.

You can do transformations either through the point-and-click method or with syntax. If you want to compute X^3, X^2, or $1/X^2$, you have to either type in the expression as written or use syntax because these functions are not available as specific choices in the **Compute** command.

To use the point-and-click method, follow these commands:
- **Transform → Compute Variable**. The **Compute Variable** window will open.
- Type a name for the new variable in the **Target Variable** box.
- Click on **Type & Label**. The **Compute Variable: Type and Label** window will open. Label the new variable. We advise including in the label the type of transformation you will be using (e.g., squared).
- Click on **Continue.**
- In the **Compute Variable** window, select **Arithmetic** in the **Function group** box. This will create a sub list of choices in the **Functions and Special Variables** box.
- In the **Functions and Special Variables** box select the type of transformation you wish to use (i.e., Arsin, Log10, Sqrt). If you need help choosing the function you want to try, see Fig. 2.1 for assistance.
- From the list of variables, click on the variable you are interested in transforming.
- Click on the arrow to move it to the **Numeric Expression** box.
- Click on **OK**. If the transformation is not listed under **Functions**, then you can just type it into the **Numeric Expression** box, or you can type it into the syntax listing.

The new variable you computed will appear in the far right column in the **Data View** window. To see if the transformation was successful, retest the assumptions.

To use syntax, follow the guidelines below.

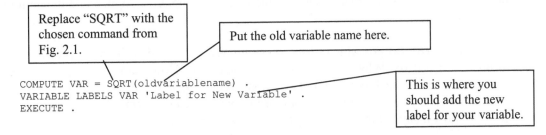

Output 2.9: Transformation of Competence and Descriptive Statistics for the Transformed Variable

```
COMPUTE VAR = (competence)**2 .
VARIABLE LABELS VAR 'SquaredComp' .
EXECUTE .
DESCRIPTIVES
  VARIABLES=VAR
  /STATISTICS=MEAN STDDEV MIN MAX SKEWNESS .
```

Descriptive Statistics

	N	Minimum	Maximum	Mean	Std.	Skewness	
	Statistic	Statistic	Statistic	Statistic	Statistic	Statistic	Std. Error
SquaredComp	73	1.00	16.00	11.2894	3.73342	-.911	.281
Valid N (listwise)	73						

```
COMPUTE VAR = (competence)**3 .
VARIABLE LABELS VAR 'CubedComp' .
EXECUTE .
DESCRIPTIVES
  VARIABLES=VAR
  /STATISTICS=MEAN STDDEV MIN MAX SKEWNESS .
```

Descriptive Statistics

	N	Minimum	Maximum	Mean	Std.	Skewness	
	Statistic	Statistic	Statistic	Statistic	Statistic	Statistic	Std. Error
CubedComp	73	1.00	64.00	39.6027	17.16401	-.445	.281
Valid N (listwise)	73						

Interpretation of Output 2.9

As was shown earlier in Output 2.1b, *competence* is negatively skewed (skewness = −1.634). In order to use this variable with statistics that require a normally distributed variable, we needed to transform it. Since *competence* is negatively skewed, we chose to square it to see if it would be less skewed. Output 2.9 shows the syntax for transforming *competence* by squaring it. After squaring, the skewness = −.911. We might have stopped there; however, −.911 is very close to −1.0 and we wanted it not to be skewed even this much, so we transformed it by cubing (the original values). After the cubic transformation, the skewness value is −.445, which is still slightly skewed but now falls well within the recommended guidelines of $< |1|$ (greater than −1 and less than +1).

Interpretation Questions

2.1   Using Outputs 2.1a and 2.1b: (a) What is the mean *visualization test* score? (b) What is the range for *grades in h.s.?* (c) What is the minimum score for *mosaic pattern test?* How does this compare with the values for that variable as indicated in Chapter 1? Why could the minimum be a negative number?

2.2   Using Outputs 2.1b: (a) For which of the variables that we called scale is the skewness statistic more than +/−1.00? (b) Why is the answer important? (c) How many participants have some missing data? (Hint: Check Chapter 1 if you don't remember the sample size. (d) What percent of students have a valid (nonmissing) *motivation* or *competence* score? (e) Can you tell from Output 2.1b how many are missing both *motivation* and *competence* scores?

2.3   Using Output 2.4: (a) Can you interpret the means? Explain. (b) How many participants are there altogether? (c) How many have complete data (nothing missing)? (d) What percent are *male (if male=0)*? (e) What percent took *algebra 1*?

2.4   Using Output 2.5: (a) 9.6% of what set of participants are *Asian-American?* (b) What percent of students have fathers who had a high school education or less? (c) What percent of fathers (with a known education) have a master's degree or higher?

2.5   In Output 2.8: (a) Why are matrix scatterplots useful? What assumption(s) are tested by them?

Extra SPSS Problems

Using the *college student data.sav* file, do the following problems. Print your outputs, and circle the key parts of the output that you discuss.

2.1   For the variables with five or more ordered levels, compute the skewness. Describe the results. Which variables in the data set are approximately normally distributed/scale? Which ones are ordered but not normal, and can the normality of these variables be improved by transforming them?

2.2   Do a stem-and-leaf plot for *same-sex parent's height* split by *gender*. Discuss the plots.

2.3   Which variables are nominal? Run frequencies for the nominal variables and other variables with fewer than five levels. Comment on the results.

2.4   Do boxplots for *student height* and for *hours of study*. Compare the two plots.

CHAPTER 3
Several Measures of Reliability

This assignment illustrates several of the methods for computing measurement reliability. It is important to assess the reliability of your data prior to conducting inferential statistics. If your reliability tests indicate that your data have low reliability, the results from inferential testing would be suspect. Using existing measures that have already been tested and indicate that the data are reliable can help to increase the chances that your new data will be reliable. Regardless, it is important to assess the level of reliability for your data set, particularly if your sample differs in some way from the standardization sample.

Internal consistency reliability for multiple-item scales. In this assignment, we will compute the most commonly used type of internal consistency reliability, Cronbach's coefficient **alpha**. This measure indicates the consistency of a multiple-item scale. Alpha is typically used when you have several Likert-type items that are summed to make a composite score or **summated scale**. Alpha is based on the mean or average correlation of each item in the scale with every other item. In the social science literature, alpha is widely used, because it provides a measure of reliability that can be obtained during the study from just one testing session or one administration of a questionnaire. In Problems 3.1, 3.2, and 3.3, you will compute alphas for the three math attitude scales (*motivation*, *competence*, and *pleasure*) that items 1 to 14 were designed to assess.

Reliability for one score/measure. In Problem 3.4, you will compute a **correlation coefficient** to check the reliability of *visualization scores*. Several types of reliability can be illustrated by this correlation. If the *visualization retest* was each participant's score from retaking the test a month or so after they initially took it, then the correlation would be a measure of *test–retest reliability*. On the other hand, if the *visualization retest* was a score on an alternative/parallel or equivalent version of the visualization test, then this would be a measure of *equivalent forms reliability*. Imagine that the *visualization test* and the *visualization retest* involved an observer rating of participants' responses to a behavioral test. Then, if two different raters' scores for the this test comprised the *visualization test* and the *retest*, the correlation could be used as an index of *interrater reliability*. This latter type of reliability is needed when behaviors or answers to questions involve some degree of subjective judgment (e.g., when there are open-ended questions or ratings based on observations).

Reliability for nominal variables. In addition to the correlation coefficient, there are several other methods of computing interrater or interobserver reliability. In Problem 3.5, **Cohen's kappa** is used to assess interobserver agreement when the data are nominal.

Assumptions for Measures of Reliability
When two or more measures, items, or assessments are viewed as measuring the same underlying variable(construct), reliability can be assessed. Reliability is used to indicate the extent to which scores are consistent with one another (hopefully, in measuring the intended construct/variable) and the extent to which the data are free from measurement error. It is assumed that each item or score is composed of a true score measuring the underlying construct, plus error; there is almost always some error in the measurement. Therefore, one assumption is that the measures or items are related systematically to one another in a linear manner because they are believed to be measures of the same construct. In addition, because true error should not be correlated systematically with anything else, a second assumption is that the errors (residual) for the different measures or assessments are uncorrelated. If errors are correlated, this means that the residual is not simply error; rather, the different measures not only have the proposed underlying variable in common, but they also have something else systematic in common and reliability estimates may be inflated. An example of a situation in which the assumption of uncorrelated errors might be violated would be when all items are parts

of a cognitive test that is timed. The performance features that are affected by timing the test, in addition to the cognitive skills involved, might systematically affect responses to the items. The best way to determine whether part of the reliability score is due to these extraneous variables is by doing multiple types of reliability assessments (e.g., equivalent forms and test–retest).

Conditions for Measures of Reliability

A condition that is necessary for measures of reliability is that the scores or categories that are being related to one another need to be comparable. If you use split-half reliability, then both halves of the test need to be equivalent. If you use alpha (which we demonstrate in this chapter), then it is assumed that every item is measuring the same underlying construct. It is assumed that respondents should answer similarly on the parts being compared, with any differences being due to measurement error.

- Retrieve your data file: **hsbdataB.**

Problem 3.1: Cronbach's Alpha for the Motivation Scale

The motivation score is composed of six items that were rated on four-point Likert scales, from very atypical (1) to very typical (4). Do the scores for these items go together (interrelate) well enough to add them together for future use as a composite variable labeled *motivation*?

3.1. What is the internal consistency reliability of the math attitude scale that we labeled *motivation*?

Note that you <u>do not actually use the computed motivation scale score</u>. Instead, use the individual items to create the scale temporarily. Let's do reliability analysis for the motivation scale.

- Click on **Analyze → Scale → Reliability Analysis**. You should get a dialog box like Fig. 3.1.
- Now move the variables *item01, item04 reversed, item07, item08 reversed, item12,* and *item13* (the motivation questions) to the **Items** box. Be sure to use *item04 reversed* and *item08 reversed* (<u>not</u> *item04* and *item08*) because a high rating on the original (unreversed) items indicates low motivation. The alpha will be based on the correlation among each pair of items, so they all need to be scored so that higher scores index the same thing (e.g., higher levels of motivation).
- Type **Alpha for Motivation Scale** in the **Scale label** box. Be sure the **Model** is **Alpha** (refer to Fig. 3.1).

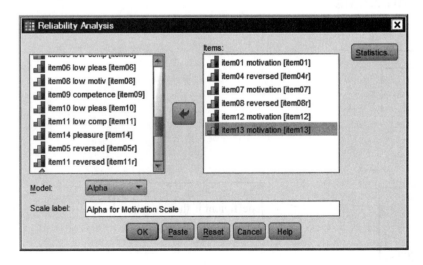

Fig. 3.1. Reliability analysis.

- Click on **Statistics** in the **Reliability Analysis** dialog box and you will see something similar to Fig. 3.2.
- Check the following items: **Item**, **Scale**, and **Scale if item deleted** (all under Descriptives for), **Correlations** (under Inter-Item), **Means**, and **Correlations** (under Summaries).
- Click on **Continue** then **OK**. Compare your syntax and output to Output 3.1.

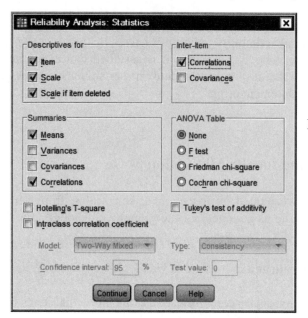

Fig. 3.2. Reliability analysis: Statistics.

Output 3.1: Cronbach's Alpha for the Math Attitude Motivation Scale

```
RELIABILITY
  /VARIABLES=item01 item04r item07 item08r item12 item13
  /SCALE('Alpha for Motivation Scale')  ALL
  /MODEL=ALPHA
  /STATISTICS=DESCRIPTIVE SCALE CORR
  /SUMMARY=TOTAL MEANS CORR .
```

Reliability

Scale: Alpha for Motivation Scale

Case Processing Summary

		N	%
Cases	Valid	73	97.3
	Excluded[a]	2	2.7
	Total	75	100.0

a. Listwise deletion based on all variables in the procedure.

Reliability Statistics

Cronbach's Alpha	Cronbach's Alpha Based on Standardized Items	N of Items
.791	.790	6

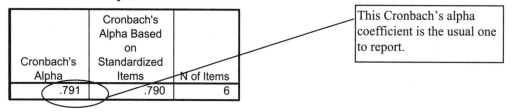

This Cronbach's alpha coefficient is the usual one to report.

Item Statistics

	Mean	Std. Deviation	N
item01 motivation	2.96	.934	73
item04 reversed	2.82	.918	73
item07 motivation	2.75	1.064	73
item08 reversed	3.05	.911	73
item12 motivation	2.99	.825	73
item13 motivation	2.67	.800	73

Descriptive statistics for each item.

Inter-Item Correlation Matrix

	item01 motivation	item04 reversed	item07 motivation	item08 reversed	item12 motivation	item13 motivation
item01 motivation	1.000	.250	.464	.296	.179	.167
item04 reversed	.250	1.000	.551	.576	.382	.316
item07 motivation	.464	.551	1.000	.587	.344	.360
item08 reversed	.296	.576	.587	1.000	.389	.311
item12 motivation	.179	.382	.344	.389	1.000	.603
item13 motivation	.167	.316	.360	.311	.603	1.000

Summary Item Statistics

	Mean	Minimum	Maximum	Range	Maximum / Minimum	Variance	N of Items
Item Means	2.874	2.671	3.055	.384	1.144	.022	6
Inter-Item Correlations	.385	.167	.603	.436	3.604	.020	6

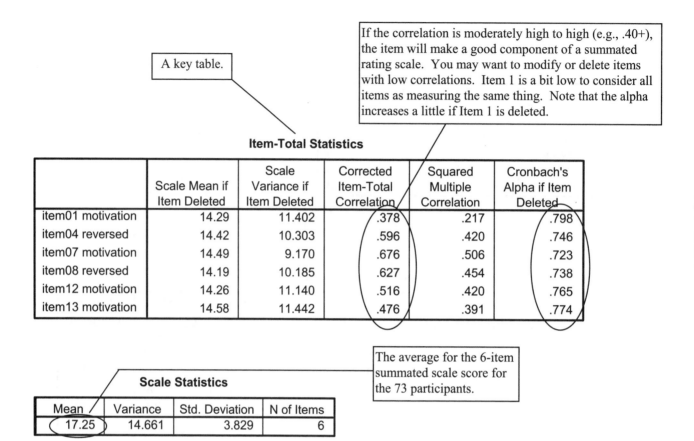

A key table.

If the correlation is moderately high to high (e.g., .40+), the item will make a good component of a summated rating scale. You may want to modify or delete items with low correlations. Item 1 is a bit low to consider all items as measuring the same thing. Note that the alpha increases a little if Item 1 is deleted.

Item-Total Statistics

	Scale Mean if Item Deleted	Scale Variance if Item Deleted	Corrected Item-Total Correlation	Squared Multiple Correlation	Cronbach's Alpha if Item Deleted
item01 motivation	14.29	11.402	.378	.217	.798
item04 reversed	14.42	10.303	.596	.420	.746
item07 motivation	14.49	9.170	.676	.506	.723
item08 reversed	14.19	10.185	.627	.454	.738
item12 motivation	14.26	11.140	.516	.420	.765
item13 motivation	14.58	11.442	.476	.391	.774

The average for the 6-item summated scale score for the 73 participants.

Scale Statistics

Mean	Variance	Std. Deviation	N of Items
17.25	14.661	3.829	6

Interpretation of Output 3.1

The first table shows the number of **Valid** cases, that is, those with no missing data on the selected variables. The second table lists the **Cronbach's Alpha** and an **Alpha Based on Standardized Items**. In general, you will use the unstandardized **alpha** unless the items in the scale have quite different means and standard deviations, as, for example, is the case with *math achievement* ($M = 12.6$, $SD = 6.7$), *grades* ($M = 5.7$, $SD = 1.6$), and *visualization* ($M = 5.2$, $SD = 3.9$); in that case, we would use the standardized alpha. As with other reliability coefficients, alpha should be above .70; however, it is common to see journal articles where one or more scales have somewhat lower alphas (e.g., in the .60–.69 range), especially if there is only a handful of items in the scale. A very high alpha (e.g., greater than .90) probably means that the items are repetitious or that you have more items in the scale than are really necessary for an internally reliable measure of the concept. How to write about this output is found after Problems 3.2 and 3.3.

Third is a table of descriptive statistics for each item, produced by checking **Item** in Fig. 3.2. The fourth table is a matrix showing the **inter-item correlations** of every item in the scale with every other item. The next table provides **Summary Item Statistics** for the **Item Means** and **Correlations**. These tell you, for example, the average, minimum, and maximum of the item means and of the inter-item correlations.

The **Item Total Statistics** table, which we think is the most important, is produced if you check **Scale if item deleted** under **Descriptives for** in the dialog box displayed in Fig. 3.2. This table provides five pieces of information for each item in the scale. The two we find most useful are the **Corrected Item-Total Correlation** and the **Alpha if Item Deleted**. The former is the correlation of each specific item with the sum/total of the <u>other</u> items in the scale. If this correlation is moderately high or high, say, .40 or above, the item is probably at least moderately correlated with most of the other items and will make a good component of this summated rating scale. Items with lower item-total correlations do not fit into this scale as well, psychometrically. If the item-total correlation is negative or too low (less than .30), it is wise to examine the item for wording problems and conceptual fit. You may want to modify or delete such items. You can tell from the last column what the alpha would be if you deleted that item. Compare this with the alpha for the scale with all six items included, which is given in the **Reliability Statistics** table. Deleting a poor item will usually make the alpha go up, but it will usually make only a small difference in the alpha unless the scale has only a few items (e.g., fewer than five) because alpha is based on the number of items as well as their average intercorrelations. Note that we have used items 04 and 08 reversed so that all items would be scored with high motivation as a high number. If we had instead used item 04 or 08, the item-total correlation for them probably would have been negative, indicating a problem.

Problems 3.2 and 3.3: Cronbach's Alpha for the Competence and Pleasure Scales

Again, is it reasonable to add the scores for these items together to form summated measures of the concepts of *competence* and *pleasure*?

3.2. What is the internal consistency reliability of the *competence scale*?

3.3. What is the internal consistency reliability of the *pleasure scale*?

Let's repeat the same steps as before to check the reliability of the following scales and then compare your output to 3.2 and 3.3.

- For the *competence scale,* use *item03, item05 reversed, item09,* and *item11 reversed.*
- Remember to change the **Scale Label** to "Alpha for Competence Scale."
- For the *pleasure scale,* use *item02, item06 reversed, item10 reversed,* and *item14.*
- Change the **Scale Label** to "Alpha for Pleasure Scale."

Output 3.2: Cronbach's Alpha for the Math Attitude Competence Scale

```
RELIABILITY
  /VARIABLES=item03 item05r item09 item11r
  /SCALE('Alpha for Competence Scale')  ALL
  /MODEL=ALPHA
  /STATISTICS=DESCRIPTIVE SCALE CORR
  /SUMMARY=TOTAL MEANS CORR .
```

Reliability

Scale: Alpha for Competence Scale

Case Processing Summary

		N	%
Cases	Valid	73	97.3
	Excluded^a	2	2.7
	Total	75	100.0

a. Listwise deletion based on all variables in the procedure.

Reliability Statistics

Cronbach's Alpha	Cronbach's Alpha Based on Standardized Items	N of Items
.796	.792	4

Item Statistics

	Mean	Std. Deviation	N
item03 competence	2.82	.903	73
item05 reversed	3.41	.940	73
item09 competence	3.32	.762	73
item11 reversed	3.63	.755	73

Inter-Item Correlation Matrix

	item03 competence	item05 reversed	item09 competence	item11 reversed
item03 competence	1.000	.742	.325	.513
item05 reversed	.742	1.000	.340	.609
item09 competence	.325	.340	1.000	.399
item11 reversed	.513	.609	.399	1.000

Summary Item Statistics

	Mean	Minimum	Maximum	Range	Maximum / Minimum	Variance	N of Items
Item Means	3.295	2.822	3.630	.808	1.286	.117	4
Inter-Item Correlations	.488	.325	.742	.417	2.281	.025	4

Item-Total Statistics

	Scale Mean if Item Deleted	Scale Variance if Item Deleted	Corrected Item-Total Correlation	Squared Multiple Correlation	Cronbach's Alpha if Item Deleted
item03 competence	10.36	3.844	.680	.560	.706
item05 reversed	9.77	3.570	.735	.622	.675
item09 competence	9.86	5.092	.405	.181	.832
item11 reversed	9.55	4.473	.633	.417	.736

Scale Statistics

Mean	Variance	Std. Deviation	N of Items
13.18	7.065	2.658	4

Output 3.3: Cronbach's Alpha for the Math Attitude Pleasure Scale

```
RELIABILITY
  /VARIABLES=item02 item06r item10r item14
  /SCALE('Alpha for Pleasure Scale')  ALL
  /MODEL=ALPHA
  /STATISTICS=DESCRIPTIVE SCALE CORR
  /SUMMARY=TOTAL MEANS CORR .
```

Reliability

Scale: Alpha for Pleasure Scale

Case Processing Summary

		N	%
Cases	Valid	75	100.0
	Excluded[a]	0	.0
	Total	75	100.0

a. Listwise deletion based on all
variables in the procedure.

Reliability Statistics

Cronbach's Alpha	Cronbach's Alpha Based on Standardized Items	N of Items
.688	.704	4

Item Statistics

	Mean	Std. Deviation	N
item02 pleasure	3.5200	.90584	75
item06 reversed	2.5733	.97500	75
item10 reversed	3.5867	.73693	75
item14 pleasure	2.8400	.71735	75

Inter-Item Correlation Matrix

	item02 pleasure	item06 reversed	item10 reversed	item14 pleasure
item02 pleasure	1.000	.285	.347	.504
item06 reversed	.285	1.000	.203	.461
item10 reversed	.347	.203	1.000	.436
item14 pleasure	.504	.461	.436	1.000

Summary Item Statistics

	Mean	Minimum	Maximum	Range	Maximum / Minimum	Variance	N of Items
Item Means	3.130	2.573	3.587	1.013	1.394	.252	4
Inter-Item Correlations	.373	.203	.504	.301	2.488	.012	4

Item-Total Statistics

	Scale Mean if Item Deleted	Scale Variance if Item Deleted	Corrected Item-Total Correlation	Squared Multiple Correlation	Cronbach's Alpha if Item Deleted
item02 pleasure	9.0000	3.405	.485	.278	.615
item06 reversed	9.9467	3.457	.397	.217	.685
item10 reversed	8.9333	4.090	.407	.211	.662
item14 pleasure	9.6800	3.572	.649	.422	.528

Scale Statistics

Mean	Variance	Std. Deviation	N of Items
12.5200	5.848	2.41817	4

Example of How to Write About Problems 3.1, 3.2, and 3.3

Method

To assess whether the data from the six variables that were summed to create the motivation score formed a reliable scale, Cronbach's alpha was computed. The alpha for the six items was .79, which indicates that the items form a scale that has reasonable internal consistency reliability. Similarly, the alpha for the competence scale (.80) indicated good internal consistency, but the .69 alpha for the pleasure scale indicated minimally adequate reliability.

Problem 3.4: Test–Retest Reliability Using Correlation

3.4. Is there support for the test–retest reliability of the two *visualization test scores*?

Let's do a Pearson *r* for *visualization test* and *visualization retest* scores.
- Click on **Analyze → Correlate → Bivariate**.
- Move variables *visualization* and *visualization retest* into the variable box.
- Do <u>not</u> select **flag significant correlations** because statistical significance is not important for reliability assessment; rather we should focus on the magnitude of the correlations. Reliability coefficients should be positive and greater than .70; statistical significance is not considered because we are not doing inferential statistics but instead are trying to see if our sample's data are reliable.
- Click on **Options.**
- Click on **Means and Standard deviations**.
- Click on **Continue** and then **OK**. Do your syntax and output look like Output 3.4?

Output 3.4: Pearson *r* for the Visualization Score

```
CORRELATIONS
  /VARIABLES=visual visual2
  /PRINT=TWOTAIL SIG
  /STATISTICS DESCRIPTIVES
  /MISSING=PAIRWISE .
```

Correlations

Descriptive Statistics

	Mean	Std. Deviation	N
visualization test	5.2433	3.91203	75
visualization retest	4.5467	3.01816	75

Correlations

		visualization test	visualization retest
visualization test	Pearson Correlation	1	.885
	Sig. (2-tailed)		.000
	N	75	75
visualization retest	Pearson Correlation	.885	1
	Sig. (2-tailed)	.000	
	N	75	75

> This is the correlation between the first and second visualization test. It should be higher than .70.

> 75 participants have both visualization scores.

Interpretation of Output 3.4

The first table provides the descriptive statistics for the two variables, *visualization test* and *visualization retest*. The second table indicates that the correlation of the two visualization scores is very high ($r = .89$) so there is strong support for the test–retest reliability of the *visualization* score. This correlation is significant, $p < .001$, but we are not as concerned about the significance because we are not doing inferential statistics; instead we are interested in the size of the relationship between the variables in this sample to see if our data are reliable.

Example of How to Write About Problem 3.4

Method

A Pearson's correlation was computed to assess test–retest reliability of the visualization test scores, $r(75) = .89$. This indicates that there is good test–retest reliability for these data.

Problem 3.5: Cohen's Kappa With Nominal Data

When we have two nominal categorical variables with the *same* values (usually two raters' observations or scores using the same codes), we can compute Cohen's kappa to check the reliability or agreement between the measures. Cohen's kappa is preferable over simple percentage agreement because it corrects for the probability that raters will agree due to chance alone. In the *hsbdataB*, the variable *ethnicity* is the ethnicity of the student as reported in the school records. The variable *ethnicity reported by student* is the ethnicity of the student reported by the student. Thus, we can compute Cohen's kappa to check the agreement between these two ratings.

3.5. What is the reliability coefficient for the *ethnicity* codes (based on school records) and *ethnicity reported by the student*?

To compute the kappa:
- Click on **Analyze → Descriptive Statistics → Crosstabs**.
- Move *ethnicity* to the **Rows** box and *ethnicity reported by students* to the **Columns** box.
- Click **Statistics…** This will open the **Crosstabs: Statistics** dialog box.
- Click on **Kappa**.
- Click on **Continue** to go back to the Crosstabs dialog window.
- Then click on **Cells…** and request the **Observed** under **Counts** and **Total** under **Percentages**.
- Click on **Continue** and then **OK**. Compare your syntax and output with Output 3.5.

Output 3.5: Cohen's Kappa With Nominal Data

```
CROSSTABS
  /TABLES=ethnic  BY ethnic2
  /FORMAT= AVALUE TABLES
  /STATISTIC=KAPPA
  /CELLS= COUNT TOTAL
  /COUNT ROUND CELL .
```

Crosstabs

Case Processing Summary

| | Cases | | | | | |
| | Valid | | Missing | | Total | |
	N	Percent	N	Percent	N	Percent
ethnicity * ethnicity reported by student	71	94.7%	4	5.3%	75	100.0%

ethnicity * ethnicity reported by student Crosstabulation

| | | | ethnicity reported by student | | | | |
			Euro-Amer	African-Amer	Latino-Amer	Asian-Amer	Total
ethnicity	Euro-Amer	Count	40	1	0	0	41
		% of Total	56.3%	1.4%	.0%	.0%	57.7%
	African-Amer	Count	2	11	1	0	14
		% of Total	2.8%	15.5%	1.4%	.0%	19.7%
	Latino-Amer	Count	0	1	8	0	9
		% of Total	.0%	1.4%	11.3%	.0%	12.7%
	Asian-Amer	Count	0	1	0	6	7
		% of Total	.0%	1.4%	.0%	8.5%	9.9%
Total		Count	42	14	9	6	71
		% of Total	59.2%	19.7%	12.7%	8.5%	100.0%

This is one of six disagreements. They are in squares off the diagonal. Note that, in contrast to correlation matrices, one should look at elements above and below the diagonal, as they both involve disagreements.

Agreements between school records and students' answers are shown in circles on the diagonal.

As a measure of reliability, kappa should be high (usually $\geq .70$).

Symmetric Measures

		Value	Asymp. Std. Error[a]	Approx. T[b]	Approx. Sig.
Measure of Agreement	Kappa	.858	.054	11.163	.000
N of Valid Cases		71			

a. Not assuming the null hypothesis.

b. Using the asymptotic standard error assuming the null hypothesis.

Interpretation of Output 3.5

The **Case Processing Summary** table shows that 71 students have data on both variables and 4 students have missing data. The **Cross-tabulation** table of *ethnicity* and *ethnicity reported by student* is next. The cases where the school records and the student agree are on the diagonal and circled. There are 65 (40 + 11 + 8 + 6) students with such agreement or consistency. The **Symmetric Measures** table shows that kappa = .86, which is very good. Because **kappa** is a measure of reliability, it usually should be .70 or greater. Because we are not doing inferential statistics (we are not inferring this result is indicative of relationships in a larger population), we are not concerned with the significance value. However, because it corrects for chance, the value of kappa tends to be somewhat lower than some other measures of interobserver reliability, such as percentage agreement.

Example of How to Write About Problem 3.5

Method

Cohen's kappa was computed to check the reliability of reports of student ethnicity by the student in relation to school records. The resulting kappa of .86 indicates that both school records and students' reports provide similar information about students' ethnicity.

Interpretation Questions

3.1. Using Outputs 3.1, 3.2, and 3.3, make a table indicating the number of items, mean inter-item correlation, and the alpha coefficient for each of the scales. Discuss the relationship between mean inter-item correlation and alpha and how this is affected by the number of items.

3.2. For the *competence scale*, what item has the *lowest* corrected item-total correlation? What would be the alpha if that item were deleted from the scale?

3.3   For the pleasure scale (Output 3.3), what item has the highest item-total correlation? Comment on how alpha would change if that item were deleted.

3.4. Using Output 3.4: (a) What is the test–retest reliability of the *visualization* score? (b) Is it acceptable? (c) As indicated above, correlations can be used to indicate test–retest reliability, alternate forms reliability, or interrater reliability, depending on exactly how the scores were obtained. Indicate what information about the measures of *visualization* would be provided, if what we have called the *visualization retest* score was instead an alternate form rather than a retest using the same measure. (d) If this were a measure of interrater reliability, what would be the procedure for measuring *visualization* and *visualization retest* scores?

3.5   Using Output 3.5: What is the interrater reliability of the ethnicity codes? What does this mean?

Extra SPSS Problems

The extra problems at the end of this and each of the following chapters use data sets provided by us or by SPSS and included on the website for this book. The name of the data set is provided in each problem.

3.1   Using the satisf.sav data file, determine the internal consistency reliability (Cronbach's coefficient alpha) of a proposed six-item satisfaction scale. Use the price, variety, organization, service, item quality, and overall satisfaction items, which are five-point Likert-type ratings. In other words, do the six satisfaction items interrelate well enough to be used to create a composite score for satisfaction? Explain.

3.2   A judge from each of seven different countries (e.g., Russia, U.S.) rated 300 participants in an international competition on a 10-point scale. In addition, an "armchair enthusiast" rated the participants. What is the interrater reliability of the armchair enthusiast (judge 8) with <u>each</u> of the other seven judges? Use the judges.sav data file. Comment.

3.3   Two consultants rated 20 sites for a future research project. What is the level of agreement or interrater reliability (using Cohen's kappa) between the raters? Use the site.sav data. Comment.

3.4   A researcher wants to measure how much love married couples have. To measure love, she develops four questions. Using the love.sav data file, determine the internal consistency reliability (Cronbach's coefficient alpha) of a proposed four-item love scale. Comment.

CHAPTER 4

Exploratory Factor Analysis and Principal Components Analysis

Exploratory factor analysis (EFA) and principal components analysis (PCA) both are methods that are used to help investigators represent a large number of relationships among normally distributed or scale variables in a simpler (more parsimonious) way. Both of these approaches determine which, of a fairly large set of items, "hang together" as groups or are answered most similarly by the participants. EFA also can help assess the level of construct (factorial) validity in a dataset regarding a measure purported to measure certain constructs. A related approach, **confirmatory factor analysis,** in which one tests very specific models of how variables are related to underlying constructs (conceptual variables), requires additional software and is beyond the scope of this book so it will not be discussed.

The primary difference, conceptually, between **exploratory factor analysis** and **principal components analysis** is that in EFA one postulates that there is a smaller set of unobserved (latent) variables or constructs underlying the variables actually observed or measured (this is commonly done to assess validity), whereas in PCA one is simply trying to mathematically derive a relatively small number of variables to use to convey as much of the information in the observed/measured variables as possible. In other words, EFA is directed at *understanding* the relations among variables by understanding the constructs that underlie them, whereas PCA is simply directed toward enabling one to derive fewer variables to provide the same information that one would obtain from the larger set of variables.

There are actually a number of different ways of computing factors for factor analysis; in this chapter, we will use only one of these methods, **principal axis factor analysis** (PA). We selected this approach because it is highly similar mathematically to PCA. The primary difference, computationally, between PCA and PA is that in the former the analysis typically is performed on an ordinary correlation matrix, complete with the correlations of each item or variable with itself. In contrast, in PA factor analysis, the correlation matrix is modified such that the correlations of each item with itself are replaced with a "communality"—a measure of that item's relation to all other items (usually a squared multiple correlation). Thus, with PCA the researcher is trying to reproduce all information (variance and covariance) associated with the set of variables, whereas PA factor analysis is directed at understanding only the covariation among variables.

Conditions for Exploratory Factor Analysis and Principal Components Analysis

There are two main conditions necessary for factor analysis and principal components analysis. The first is that there need to be relationships among the variables. Further, the larger the sample size, especially in relation to the number of variables, the more reliable the resulting factors. Sample size is less crucial for factor analysis to the extent that the communalities of items with the other items are high, or at least relatively high and variable. Ordinary principal axis factor analysis should never be done if the number of items/variables is greater than the number of participants.

Assumptions for Exploratory Factor Analysis and Principal Components Analysis

The methods of extracting factors and components that are used in this book do not make strong distributional assumptions; normality is important only to the extent that skewness or outliers affect the observed correlations or if significance tests are performed (which is rare for EFA and PCA). The normality of the distribution can be checked by computing the skewness value. Maximum likelihood estimation, which we will not cover, does require multivariate normality; the variables need to be normally distributed and the joint distribution of all the variables should be normal. Because both principal axis factor analysis and principal components analysis are based on correlations, independent sampling is required and the variables should be related to each other (in pairs) in a linear fashion. The assumption of linearity can be assessed with matrix scatterplots, as shown in Chapter 2. Finally, each of the variables should be correlated at a moderate level with some of the other variables. Factor analysis and principal components analysis seek to explain or reproduce the correlation matrix, which would not be a sensible thing to do if the correlations all hover around zero. Bartlett's test of sphericity addresses this assumption. However, if correlations are too high, this may cause problems with obtaining a mathematical solution to the factor analysis.

- Retrieve your data file: **hsbdataB.sav.**

Problem 4.1: Factor Analysis on Math Attitude Variables

In Problem 4.1, we perform a principal axis factor analysis on the math attitude variables. Factor analysis is more appropriate than PCA when one has the belief that there are latent variables underlying the variables or items measured. In this example, we have beliefs about the constructs underlying the math attitude questions; we believe that there are three constructs: *motivation*, *competence*, and *pleasure*. Now, we want to see if the items that were written to index each of these constructs actually do "hang together"; that is, we wish to determine empirically whether participants' responses to the motivation questions are more similar to each other than to their responses to the competence items, and so on. Conducting factor analysis can assist us in validating the data: if the data do fit into the three constructs that we believe exist, then this gives us support for the construct validity of the math attitude measure in this sample. The analysis is considered exploratory factor analysis even though we have some ideas about the structure of the data because our hypotheses regarding the model are not very specific; we do not have specific predictions about the size of the relation of each observed variable to each latent variable, etc. Moreover, we "allow" the factor analysis to find factors that best fit the data, even if this deviates from our original predictions.

4.1   Are there three constructs (*motivation*, *competence*, and *pleasure*) underlying the math attitude questions?

To answer this question, we will conduct a factor analysis using the principal axis factoring method and specify the number of factors to be three (because our conceptualization is that there are three math attitude scales or factors: *motivation*, *competence*, and *pleasure*).

- **Analyze → Dimension Reduction → Factor...** to get Fig. 4.1.
- Next, select the variables *item01* through *item14*. <u>Do not</u> include *item04r* or any of the other reversed items because we are including the unreversed versions of those same items.

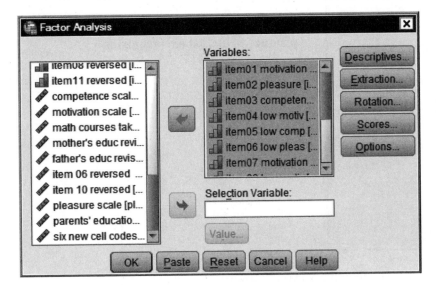

Fig. 4.1. Factor analysis.

- Now click on **Descriptives...** to produce Fig. 4.2.
- Then click on the following: **Initial solution** (under **Statistics**), **Coefficients, Determinant,** and **KMO and Bartlett's test of sphericity** (under **Correlation Matrix**).
- Click on **Continue** to return to Fig. 4.1.

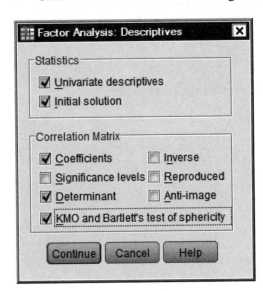

Fig. 4.2. Factor analysis: Descriptives.

- Next, click on **Extraction...** This will give you Fig. 4.3.
- Select **Principal axis factoring** from the **Method** pull-down menu.
- *Unclick* **Unrotated factor solution** (under **Display**). We will examine this only in Problem 4.2. We also usually would check the **Scree plot** box. However, again, we will request and interpret the scree plot only in Problem 4.2.
- Click on **Fixed number of factors** under **Extract,** and type **3** in the box. This setting instructs the computer to extract three math attitude factors.
- Click on **Continue** to return to Fig. 4.1.

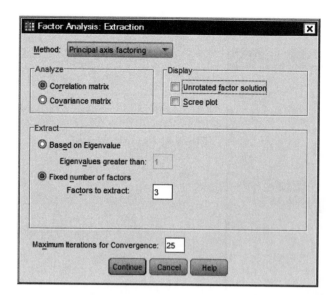

Fig. 4.3. Extraction method to produce principal axis factoring.

- Now click on **Rotation…** in Fig. 4.1, which will give you Fig. 4.4.
- Click on **Varimax**, then make sure **Rotated solution** is also checked. Varimax rotation creates a solution in which the factors are orthogonal (uncorrelated with one another), which can make results easier to interpret and to replicate with future samples.
- Click on **Continue**.

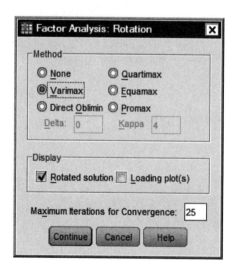

Fig. 4.4. Factor analysis: Rotation.

- Next, click on **Options…**, which will give you Fig. 4.5.
- Click on **Sorted by size**.
- Click on **Suppress absolute values less than** and type **.3** (point 3) in the box (see Fig. 4.5). Suppressing small factor loadings makes the output easier to read.
- Click on **Continue** then **OK**. Compare Output 4.1 with your output and syntax.

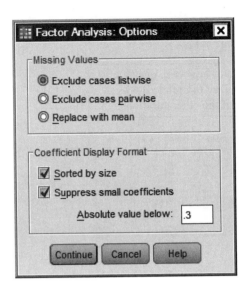

Fig. 4.5. Factor analysis: Options.

Output 4.1: Factor Analysis for Math Attitude Questions

```
FACTOR
  /VARIABLES item01 item02 item03 item04 item05 item06 item07 item08 item09 item10 item11 item12
item13 item14
  /MISSING LISTWISE
  /ANALYSIS item01 item02 item03 item04 item05 item06 item07 item08 item09 item10 item11 item12
item13 item14
  /PRINT UNIVARIATE INITIAL CORRELATION DET KMO EXTRACTION ROTATION
  /FORMAT SORT BLANK(.3)
  /CRITERIA FACTORS(3) ITERATE(25)
  /EXTRACTION PAF
  /CRITERIA ITERATE(25)
  /ROTATION VARIMAX
  /METHOD=CORRELATION.
```

Factor Analysis

Descriptive Statistics

	Mean	Std. Deviation	Analysis N
item01 motivation	2.99	.918	71
item02 pleasure	3.58	.822	71
item03 competence	2.82	.915	71
item04 low motiv	2.21	.909	71
item05 low comp	1.61	.948	71
item06 low pleas	2.44	.996	71
item07 motivation	2.77	1.072	71
item08 low motiv	1.96	.917	71
item09 competence	3.32	.770	71
item10 low pleas	1.41	.748	71
item11 low comp	1.38	.763	71
item12 motivation	2.99	.837	71
item13 motivation	2.68	.807	71
item14 pleasure	2.86	.723	71

Pairs of items with relatively high correlations (e.g., > .40) will probably have high loadings from the same factor.

Indicates how each question is associated (correlated) with each of the other questions.

Correlation Matrix[a]

		item01 motivation	item02 pleasure	item03 competence	item04 low motiv	item05 low comp	item06 low pleas	item07 motivation	item08 low motiv	item09 competence	item10 low pleas	item11 low comp	item12 motivation	item13 motivation	item14 pleasure
Correlation	item01 motivation	1.000	.484	.626	-.305	-.745	-.165	.461	-.340	.209	.071	-.441	.186	.187	.040
	item02 pleasure	.484	1.000	.389	-.166	-.547	-.312	.361	-.176	.219	-.389	-.401	.116	.028	.475
	item03 competence	.626	.389	1.000	-.348	-.743	-.209	.423	-.248	.328	.027	-.513	.165	.170	.068
	item04 low motiv	-.305	-.166	-.348	1.000	.363	.323	-.596	.576	-.120	.102	.396	-.391	-.334	-.063
	item05 low comp	-.745	-.547	-.743	.363	1.000	.260	-.538	.276	-.351	.130	.605	-.187	-.169	-.166
	item06 low pleas	-.165	-.312	-.209	.323	.260	1.000	-.268	.192	-.131	.217	.418	-.044	.001	-.499
	item07 motivation	.461	.361	.423	-.596	-.538	-.268	1.000	-.606	.228	-.169	-.331	.347	.361	.180
	item08 low motiv	-.340	-.176	-.248	.576	.276	.192	-.606	1.000	-.243	.067	.370	-.392	-.308	-.117
	item09 competence	.209	.219	.328	-.120	-.351	-.131	.228	-.243	1.000	-.109	-.407	.406	.286	-.020
	item10 low pleas	.071	-.389	.027	.102	.130	.217	-.169	.067	-.109	1.000	.250	-.059	-.062	-.447
	item11 low comp	-.441	-.401	-.513	.396	.605	.418	-.331	.370	-.407	.250	1.000	-.148	-.006	-.238
	item12 motivation	.186	.116	.165	-.391	-.187	-.044	.347	-.392	.406	-.059	-.148	1.000	.607	.068
	item13 motivation	.187	.028	.170	-.334	-.169	.001	.361	-.308	.286	-.062	-.006	.607	1.000	-.030
	item14 pleasure	.040	.475	.068	-.063	-.166	-.499	.180	-.117	-.020	-.447	-.238	.068	-.030	1.000

a. Determinant = .001

Should be greater than .0001. If very close to zero, collinearity is too high. If zero, no solution is possible.

Low correlations (e.g., < .20) usually will not have high loadings from the same factor.

KMO and Bartlett's Test

Tests of assumptions.

Kaiser-Meyer-Olkin Measure of Sampling Adequacy.		.770
Bartlett's Test of Sphericity	Approx. Chi-Square	433.486
	df	91
	Sig.	.000

Should be greater than .70 indicating sufficient items for each factor.

Should be significant (less than .05), indicating that the correlation matrix is significantly different from an identity matrix, in which correlations between variables are all zero.

Communalities

	Initial
item01 motivation	.660
item02 pleasure	.542
item03 competence	.598
item04 low motiv	.562
item05 low comp	.772
item06 low pleas	.382
item07 motivation	.607
item08 low motiv	.533
item09 competence	.412
item10 low pleas	.372
item11 low comp	.591
item12 motivation	.499
item13 motivation	.452
item14 pleasure	.479

Extraction Method: Principal Axis Factoring.

These initial communalities represent the relation between the variable and all other variables (i.e., the squared multiple correlation between the item and all other items) before rotation. If many or most communalities are low (< .30), a small sample size is more likely to distort results.

Eigenvalues refer to the variance accounted for, in terms of the number of "items' worth" of variance each explains. So, Factor 1 explains almost as much variance as in five items.

Percent of covariation among items accounted for by each factor before and after rotation.

Total Variance Explained

Factor	Initial Eigenvalues			Rotation Sums of Squared Loadings		
	Total	% of Variance	Cumulative %	Total	% of Variance	Cumulative %
1	4.888	34.916	34.916	3.017	21.549	21.549
2	2.000	14.284	49.200	2.327	16.621	38.171
3	1.613	11.519	60.719	1.784	12.746	50.917
4	1.134	8.097	68.816			
5	.904	6.459	75.275			
6	.716	5.113	80.388			
7	.577	4.125	84.513			
8	.461	3.293	87.806			
9	.400	2.857	90.664			
10	.379	2.710	93.374			
11	.298	2.126	95.500			
12	.258	1.846	97.346			
13	.217	1.551	98.897			
14	.154	1.103	100.000			

Extraction Method: Principal Axis Factoring.

Half of the variance is accounted for by the first three factors.

Factor Matrix[a]

a. 3 factors extracted. 12 iterations required.

Rotated Factor Matrix[a]

	Factor		
	1	2	3
item05 low comp	-.897		
item03 competence	.780		
item01 motivation	.777		
item11 low comp	-.572	.355	
item12 motivation		.721	
item13 motivation		.667	
item08 low motiv		-.619	
item04 low motiv		-.601	
item07 motivation	.412	.585	
item09 competence		.332	
item14 pleasure			-.797
item10 low pleas			.580
item02 pleasure	.487		-.535
item06 low pleas			.515

The items cluster into these three groups defined by the highest loading on each item.

Extraction Method: Principal Axis Factoring.
Rotation Method: Varimax with Kaiser Normalization.

a. Rotation converged in 5 iterations.

Factor Transformation Matrix

Factor	1	2	3
1	.747	.552	-.370
2	-.162	.692	.704
3	.645	-.466	.606

We will ignore this; it was used to convert the initial factor matrix into the rotated factor matrix.

Extraction Method: Principal Axis Factoring.
Rotation Method: Varimax with Kaiser Normalization.

Interpretation of Output 4.1

The factor analysis program generates a variety of tables depending on which options you have chosen. The first table includes **Descriptive Statistics** for each variable and the **Analyses N,** which in this case is 71 because several items have one or more participants missing. It is especially important to check the Analysis N when you have a small sample, scattered missing data, or one variable with lots of missing data. In the latter case, it may be wise to run the analysis without that variable. The second table in Output 4.1 is a **correlation matrix** showing how each of the 14 items is associated with each of the other 13. Note that some of the correlations are high (e.g., + or −.60 or greater) and some are low (i.e., near zero). Relatively high correlations indicate that two items are associated and will probably be grouped together by the factor analysis.

Next, several assumptions are tested. The **determinant** (located under the correlation matrix) should be more than .0001. Here, it is .001 so this assumption is met. If the determinant is zero, then a factor analytic solution cannot be obtained, because this would require dividing by zero, which would mean that at least one of the items can be understood as a linear combination of some set of the other items. The **Kaiser-Meyer-Olkin (KMO)** measure should be greater than .70 and is inadequate if less than .50. The KMO test tells us whether or not enough items are predicted by each factor. The **Bartlett** test should be significant (i.e., a significance value of less than .05); this means that the variables are correlated highly enough to provide a reasonable basis for factor analysis.

The **Total Variance Explained** table shows how the variance is divided among the 14 possible factors. Note that four factors have **eigenvalues** (a measure of explained variance) greater than 1.0, which is a common criterion for a factor to be useful. When the eigenvalue is less than 1.0 the factor explains less information than a single item would have explained. Most researchers would not consider the information gained from such a factor to be sufficient to justify keeping that factor. Thus, if you had not specified otherwise, the computer would have looked for the best four-factor solution by "rotating" four factors. Because we specified that we wanted only three factors rotated, only three will be rotated.

For this and all analyses in this chapter, we will use an *orthogonal* rotation (varimax). This means that the final factors will be at right angles with each other. As a result, we can assume that the information explained by one factor is independent of the information in the other factors. Note that if we create scales by summing or averaging items with high loadings from each factor, these *scales* will *not* necessarily be uncorrelated; it is the best-fit *vectors* (factors) that are orthogonal. We rotate the factors so that they are easier to interpret. Rotation makes it so that, as much as possible, different items are explained or predicted by different underlying factors, and each factor explains more than one item. This is a condition called simple structure. Although this is the *goal* of rotation, in reality, this is not always achieved. One thing to look for in the **Rotated Matrix** of factor loadings is the extent to which simple structure is achieved.

The **Rotated Factor Matrix** table, which contains these loadings, is key for understanding the results of the analysis. Note that the analysis has sorted the 14 math attitude questions (*item01* to *item14*) into three somewhat overlapping groups of items, as shown by the circled items. The items are sorted so that the items that have the highest loading (not considering whether the correlation is positive or negative) from factor 1 (four items in this analysis) are listed first, and they are sorted from the one with the highest factor weight or loading (i.e., *item05*, with a loading of −.897) to the one with the lowest loading from that first factor (*item11*). Actually, every item has some loading from every factor, but we requested for loadings less than |.30| (|.30| means the absolute value, or value without considering the sign) to be excluded from the output, so there are blanks where low loadings exist.

Next, the six items that have their highest loading from factor 2 are listed from highest loading (*item12*) to lowest (*item9*). Finally, the four items on which factor 3 loads most highly are listed in order. Loadings resulting from an orthogonal rotation are correlation coefficients between each item and the factor, so they range from −1.0 through 0 to + 1.0. A negative loading just means that the question needs to be interpreted in the opposite direction from the way it is written for that factor (e.g., *item05* "I am a little slow catching on to new topics in math" has a negative loading from the competence factor, which indicates that the people scoring <u>higher</u> on this item are <u>lower</u> in competence). Usually, factor loadings lower than |.30| are considered low, which is why we suppressed loadings less than |.30|. On the other hand, loadings of |.40| or greater are typically considered high. This is just a guideline, however, and one could set the criterion for "high" loadings as low as .30 or as high as .50. Setting the criterion lower than .30 or higher than .50 would be very unusual.

The investigator should examine the content of the items that have high loadings from each factor to see if they fit together conceptually and can be named. Items 5, 3, and 11 were intended to reflect a perception of *competence* at math, so the fact that they all have strong loadings from the same factor provides some support for their being conceptualized as pertaining to the same construct. On the other hand, *item01* was intended to measure *motivation* for doing math, but it is highly related to this same *competence* factor. In retrospect, one can see why this item could also be interpreted as competence. The item reads, "I practice math skills until I can do them well." Unless one felt one could do math problems well, this would not be true. Likewise, *item02*, "I feel happy after solving a hard problem," although intended to measure *pleasure* at doing math (and having its strongest loading there), might also reflect competence at doing math, in that, again, one could not endorse this item unless one had solved hard problems, which one could only do if one were good at math. On the other hand, *item09*, which was originally conceptualized as a competence item, had no really strong loadings. *Item11*, as mentioned earlier, had a high loading for the first factor, as expected. However, it also had a moderate loading for Factor 3, which seems to be a (low) pleasure factor. This item reads, "I have some difficulties doing math as well as other kids my age." Can you think of why this might be related to low *pleasure*?

Every item has a weight or loading from every factor, but in a "clean" factor analysis almost all of the loadings that are not in the circles that we have drawn on the **Rotated Factor Matrix** will be low (blank or less than |.40|). The fact that both Factors 1 and 3 load highly on *item02* and fairly highly on *item11*, and the fact that Factors 1 and 2 both load highly on *item07* is common but undesirable, in that one wants only one factor to predict each item.

Example of How to Write About Problem 4.1

Results

Principal axis factor analysis with varimax rotation was conducted to assess the underlying structure for the 14 items of the Math Motivation Questionnaire. (The assumption of independent sampling was met. The assumptions of normality, linear relationships between pairs of variables, and the variables' being correlated at a moderate level were checked.) Three factors were requested, based on the fact that the items were designed to index three constructs: motivation, competence, and pleasure. After rotation, the first factor accounted for 21.5% of the variance, the second factor accounted for 16.6%, and the third factor accounted for 12.7%. Table 4.1 displays the items and factor loadings for the rotated factors, with loadings less than .40 omitted to improve clarity.

Table 4.1
Factor Loadings for the Rotated Factors

Item	Factor Loading			Communality
	1	2	3	
Slow catching on to new topics	−.90			.77
Solve math problems quickly	.78			.60
Practice math until do well	.78			.66
Have difficulties doing math	−.57			.59
Try to complete math even if takes long		.72		.50
Explore all possible solutions		.67		.45
Do not keep at it long if problem challenging		−.62		.53
Give up easily instead of persisting		−.60		.56
Prefer to figure out problems without help	.41	.59		.61
Really enjoy working math problems			−.80	.48
Smile only a little when solving math problem			.58	.37
Feel happy after solving hard problem	.49		−.54	.54
Do not get much pleasure out of math			.52	.38
Eigenvalues	3.02	2.33	1.78	
% of variance	21.55	16.62	12.75	

Note. Loadings < .40 are omitted.

The first factor, which seems to index competence, had strong loadings on the first four items. Two of the items indexed low competence and had negative loadings. The second factor, which seemed to index motivation, had high loadings on the next five items in Table 4.1. "I prefer to figure out the problem without help" had its highest loading from the second factor but had a cross-loading over .4 on the competence factor. The third factor, which seemed to index low pleasure from math, loaded highly on the last four items in the table. "I feel happy after solving a hard problem" had its highest loading from the pleasure factor but also had a strong loading from the competence factor.

Problem 4.2: Principal Components Analysis on Achievement Variables

Principal components analysis is most useful if one simply wants to reduce a relatively large number of variables to a smaller number of variables that still capture the same information. In this problem we will look at the initial (unrotated) solution because we might want to use the first, unrotated, principal component to summarize all of the variables if it explains most of the variance rather using multiple, rotated components. This would especially be true if the scree plot suggests a large drop-off after the first component in variance explained (eigenvalues), so we will look at the scree plot too.

4.2 Run a principal components analysis to see how the five "achievement" variables cluster. These variables are *grades in h.s., math achievement, mosaic pattern test, visualization test,* and *scholastic aptitude test – math.*

- Click on **Analyze → Dimension Reduction → Factor...**
- First press **Reset**.
- Next select the variables *grades in h.s., math achievement, mosaic pattern test, visualization test,* and *scholastic aptitude test – math,* similar to what we did in Fig. 4.1.

- In the **Descriptives** window (Fig. 4.2), check **Univariate descriptives, Initial solution, Coefficients, Determinant**, and **KMO and Bartlett's test of sphericity**.
- In the **Extraction** window (Fig. 4.3), use the default **Method** of **Principal components**. Be sure that **unrotated factor solution** and **Eigenvalues over 1** checked. Also, request a **Scree plot** (to see if one component would do a good job in summarizing the data or if a different number of components would be preferable to the default based on the criterion of components with eigenvalues over 1).
- In the **Rotation** window (Fig. 4.4), check **Varimax**. Under **Display**, check **Rotated solution** and **Loading plot(s)**.
- Click on **Continue** and then **OK**.

We have requested a principal components analysis for the extraction and some different options for the output to contrast with the earlier one. Compare Output 4.2 with your syntax and output.

Output 4.2: Principal Components Analysis for Achievement Scores

```
FACTOR
  /VARIABLES grades mathach mosaic visual satm
  /MISSING LISTWISE
  /ANALYSIS grades mathach mosaic visual satm
  /PRINT UNIVARIATE INITIAL CORRELATION DET KMO EXTRACTION ROTATION
  /PLOT EIGEN ROTATION
  /CRITERIA MINEIGEN(1) ITERATE(25)
  /EXTRACTION PC
  /CRITERIA ITERATE(25)
  /ROTATION VARIMAX
  /METHOD=CORRELATION .
```

Factor Analysis

Descriptive Statistics

	Mean	Std. Deviation	Analysis N
grades in h.s.	5.68	1.570	75
math achievement test	12.5645	6.67031	75
mosaic, pattern test	27.413	9.5738	75
visualization test	5.2433	3.91203	75
scholastic aptitude test - math	490.53	94.553	75

Correlation Matrix[a]

		grades in h.s.	math achievement test	mosaic, pattern test	visualization test	scholastic aptitude test - math
Correlation	grades in h.s.	1.000	.504	-.012	.127	.371
	math achievement test	.504	1.000	.213	.423	.788
	mosaic, pattern test	-.012	.213	1.000	.030	.110
	visualization test	.127	.423	.030	1.000	.356
	scholastic aptitude test - math	.371	.788	.110	.356	1.000

a. Determinant = .210

KMO and Bartlett's Test

Kaiser-Meyer-Olkin Measure of Sampling Adequacy.		.615
Bartlett's Test of Sphericity	Approx. Chi-Square	111.440
	df	10
	Sig.	.000

This is acceptable because KMO is >.5 but indicated there may not be enough items for one of the components.

Communalities

	Initial	Extraction
grades in h.s.	1.000	.493
math achievement test	1.000	.869
mosaic, pattern test	1.000	.949
visualization test	1.000	.330
scholastic aptitude test - math	1.000	.748

Extraction Method: Principal Component Analysis.

The first component explains less than ½ of the variance, so we probably will want to rotate more than one component.

Total Variance Explained

Component	Initial Eigenvalues			Extraction Sums of Squared Loadings			Rotation Sums of Squared Loadings		
	Total	% of Variance	Cumulative %	Total	% of Variance	Cumulative %	Total	% of Variance	Cumulative %
1	2.379	47.579	47.579	2.379	47.579	47.579	2.340	46.805	46.805
2	1.010	20.198	67.777	1.010	20.198	67.777	1.049	20.972	67.777
3	.872	17.437	85.214						
4	.560	11.197	96.411						
5	.179	3.589	100.000						

Extraction Method: Principal Component Analysis.

Scree Plot

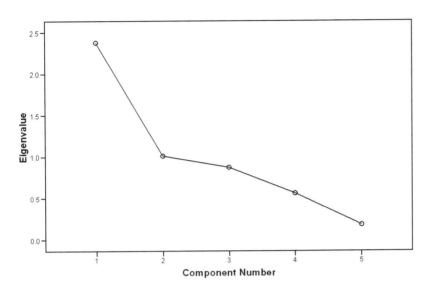

The Scree plot shows that after the first two components, differences between the eigenvalues decline (the curve flattens), and they are less than 1.0. This again supports a two-component solution.

Component Matrix[a]

	Component	
	1	2
grades in h.s.	.624	-.322
math achievement test	.931	.044
mosaic, pattern test	.220	.949
visualization test	.571	-.056
scholastic aptitude test - math	.865	-.020

Extraction Method: Principal Component Analysis.

a. 2 components extracted.

This unrotated matrix should not be interpreted; it provides information about how the loadings change when the solution is rotated. However, the first unrotated component provides the simplest summary of the variables. In this case, it appears that if one used the first component only as the basis for creating summary scores, such scores would not include mosaic, pattern score, which does not have a high loading for the first component.

Rotated Component Matrix[a]

	Component	
	1	2
grades in h.s.	.669	-.213
math achievement test	.911	.200
mosaic, pattern test	.057	.972
visualization test	.573	.041
scholastic aptitude test - math	.856	.126

Extraction Method: Principal Component Analysis.
Rotation Method: Varimax with Kaiser Normalization.

a. Rotation converged in 3 iterations.

Even after rotation, mosaic is predicted by its own component, which does not have strong loadings on any of the other variables.

Component Transformation Matrix

Component	1	2
1	.986	.168
2	-.168	.986

Extraction Method: Principal Component Analysis.
Rotation Method: Varimax with Kaiser Normalization.

Component Plot in Rotated Space

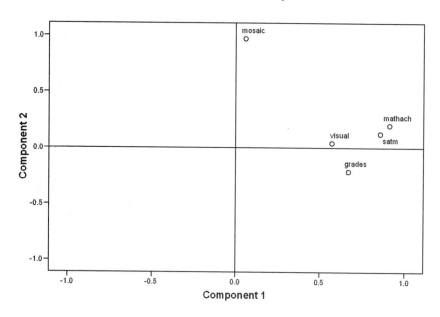

Interpretation of Output 4.2

Compare Output 4.2 with your output and syntax in Output 4.1. Note that in addition to the tables in Output 4.1 you have: (a) a **Scree Plot**; (b) an unrotated **Component Matrix**, which should not be interpreted (however, if you want to compute only one variable that provides the most information about the set of variables, a linear combination of the variables with high loadings from the first unrotated component matrix would be used); (c) a **Rotated Component Matrix**, which contains the loadings (even those < .3) for each component (it is similar to the rotated factor matrix in Output 4.1); and (d) the **Component Plot** of the component loadings.

Both the **Scree Plot** and the eigenvalues support the conclusion that these five variables can be reduced to two components. Note that the scree plot flattens out after the second component. However, the second component is very poorly defined, relating only to one variable. Thus, one may decide to use only one summary variable, based on all variables except *mosaic*, or to redo the PCA after omitting *mosaic*. It usually is best for components to be defined by at least four variables.

Note that the default setting we used does not sort the variables in the **Rotated Component Matrix** by magnitude of loadings and does not suppress low loadings. Thus, you have to organize the table yourself; that is, *math achievement, scholastic aptitude test, grades in h.s.,* and *visualization,* in that order, have high Component 1 loadings, and *mosaic* is the only variable with a high loading for Component 2.

Researchers usually give names to rotated components in a fashion similar to that used in EFA; however, there is no assumption that this indicates a variable that underlies the measured items. Often, a researcher will aggregate (add or average) the items that define (have high loadings for) each component and use this composite variable in further research. Actually, the same thing is often done with EFA factor loadings; however, the implication of the latter is that this composite variable is an index of the underlying construct.

The plot of the component loadings gives one a visual representation of the loadings, plotted in space. This shows how closely related the items are to each other and to the components.

Example of How to Write About Problem 4.2

Results

Principal components analysis with varimax rotation was conducted to assess how five "achievement" variables clustered. These variables were *grades in h.s., math achievement, mosaic pattern test, visualization test,* and *scholastic aptitude test – math.* (The assumption of independent sampling was met. The assumptions of normality, linear relationships between pairs of variables, and the variables being correlated at a moderate level were checked and *mosaic pattern test* did not meet the assumptions, in that it was correlated at a low level with all other variables.) Two components were rotated, based on the eigenvalues over 1 criterion and the scree plot. After rotation, the first component accounted for 46.8% of the variance, and the second component accounted for 21.0% of the variance. Table 4.2 displays the items and component loadings for the rotated components, with loadings less than .25 omitted to improve clarity. Results suggest, in keeping with zero-order correlations, that *mosaic pattern test* scores are not substantially related to the other measures and should not be aggregated with them but that the other measures form a coherent component.

Table 4.2
Component Loadings for the Rotated Components (N = 75)

Item	Component Loading 1	2	Communality
Grades in high school	.67		.49
Math achievement	.91		.87
Visualization test	.57		.33
Scholastic aptitude test – math	.86		.75
Mosaic pattern test		.97	.95
Eigenvalues	2.38	1.01	
% of variance	46.81	20.97	

Note. Loadings < .25 are omitted.

Interpretation Questions

4.1   Using Output 4.1: (a) Are the factors in Output 4.1 close to the conceptual composites (motivation, pleasure, competence) indicated in Chapter 1? (b) How might you name the three factors in Output 4.1? (c) Why did we use factor analysis rather than principal components analysis for this exercise?

4.2   Using Output 4.2: (a) Were any of the assumptions that were tested violated? Explain. (b) Describe the main aspects of the correlation matrix, the rotated component matrix, and the plot in Output 4.2.

4.3   What does the plot in Output 4.2 tell us about the relation of *mosaic* to the other variables and to component 1? How does this plot relate to the rotated component matrix?

Extra SPSS Problems

4.1   Using the *judges.sav* data file, do exploratory factor analysis to see if the seven variables (the judges' countries) can be grouped into two categories: former communistic block countries (Russia, China, and Romania) and non-communist countries (U.S., South Korea, Italy, and France). What, if any, assumptions were violated?

4.2   Using the *satisf.sav* data file, see if the six satisfaction scales can be reduced to a smaller number of variables.

4.3   Using the *love.sav* data file, see if the four love questions can be grouped into one category. What, if any, assumptions were violated?

4.4   Using the *1991 U.S. General Social Survey.sav* data file, do exploratory factor analysis to see if the health variables (hlth1 to hlth9) and the work variables (work1 to work9) fall into two categories: health and work. Were any assumptions violated?

CHAPTER 5

Selecting and Interpreting Inferential Statistics

To understand the information in this chapter, it will be necessary to remember or to review the sections in Chapter 1 about **variables** and levels of **measurement** (nominal, dichotomous, ordinal, and approximately normal/scale). It is also necessary to remember the distinction we made between difference and associational research questions and between **descriptive** and **inferential statistics**. This chapter focuses on inferential statistics, which as the name implies refers to statistics that make inferences about population values based on the sample data that you have collected and analyzed. What we call **difference inferential statistics** lead to inferences about the differences (usually mean differences) between groups in the populations from which the samples were drawn. **Associational inferential statistics** lead to inferences about the association or relationship between variables in the population. Thus, the purpose of inferential statistics is to enable the researcher to make generalizations beyond the specific sample data. Before we describe how to select and interpret inferential statistics, we will introduce design classifications.

General Design Classifications for Difference Questions

Many research questions focus on whether there is a statistically significant difference between two or more groups or conditions. The designs in this section all regard this type of design.

Labeling difference question designs. Brief descriptive labels identify the design for other researchers and also guide us toward appropriate statistics to use. We do not have design classifications for the descriptive or associational research questions, so this section applies only to difference questions. Designs are usually labeled in terms of (a) the <u>overall type of design</u> (between-groups or within-subjects), (b) the <u>number of independent variables</u>, and (c) the <u>number of levels within each independent variable</u>.

When a group comparison or difference question is asked, the independent variable and design can be classified as between-groups or within-subjects. Understanding this distinction is one essential aspect of determining the proper statistical analysis for this type of question.

Between-groups designs. These are designs where <u>each participant</u> in the research is in <u>one and only one condition or group</u>. For example, there may be three groups (or levels or values) of the independent variable, *treatment type*. If the investigator wished to have 20 participants in each group, then 60 participants would be needed to carry out the research.

Within-subjects or repeated-measures designs. These designs are conceptually the opposite of between-groups designs. In within-subjects (sometimes called dependent) designs, each participant in the research <u>receives or experiences all of the conditions or levels</u> of the independent variable. These designs also include examples where the participants are matched by the experimenter or in some natural way (e.g., twins, husband and wife, or mother and child). When each participant is assessed more than once, these designs are also referred to as **repeated-measures designs**. Repeated-measures designs are common in longitudinal research and intervention research. Comparing performance on the same dependent variable assessed before and after intervention (pretest and posttest) is a common example of a repeated-measures design. We might call the independent variable in such a study "time of measurement" or "change over time." Our HSB data did not really have a within-subjects aspect to the design. However, one of the variables is repeated (*visualization* with two levels: *visualization test* and *visualization retest*) and one is within (*education*, each student has both a *mother's education* and *father's education*). To demonstrate a **within-subjects design** and the use of **repeated-measured ANOVA**, we will use another data set, called **Product Data**, which is found on the companion website. This small data set has **within-subjects data**, a rating by each participant for each of four different products (e.g., DVDs, but they could be any four stimuli). The same types of analysis could be done if, instead of each participant rating four different products in the same session, the ratings were done for satisfaction with the same product at four times. In that case, the data would be **repeated-measures data.** In addition, to demonstrate a **doubly multivariate** design, in which there are **repeated** assessments of several measures, we will use the data set called **mixedMANOVAdata**.

Single-factor designs.　If the design has only one <u>independent variable</u> (in either a between-groups design or a within-subjects design), then it should be described as a basic or <u>single-factor or one-way design</u>. **Factor** and **way** are other names for difference independent variables. Note that the number of factors or "ways" refers to the number of *independent variables* not the number of *levels* of an independent variable. For example, a between-groups design with one independent variable that has four levels is a single-factor or one-way between-groups design with four levels. If the design is a within-subjects design with four levels, then it would be described as a single-factor, repeated-measures design with four levels (e.g., the same test being given four times).

Between-groups factorial designs.　When there is <u>more than one group difference independent variable,</u> and each level of each variable (factor) is possible in combination with each level of each of the other variable, the design is called **factorial**. For example, a factorial design could have two independent variables (i.e., factors) *gender* and *ethnicity*, allowing for male and female members of each ethnic group. In these cases, the number of levels of *each* variable (factor) becomes important in the description of the design. If *gender* had two levels (i.e., males and females) and *ethnicity* had three levels (e.g., European-American, Hispanic-American, and African-American), then this design is a 2 × 3 between-groups factorial design. In this 2 × 3 notation, then, the *number* of numbers is the number of factors or ways, and the *numbers themselves* refer to the number of levels of each of those factors. This design could also be called a two-way or two-factor design because there are two independent variables.

Mixed factorial designs.　If the design has a <u>between-groups variable and a within-subjects independent variable, it is called a **mixed design**.</u> For example, if the independent variables are *gender* (a between-groups variable) and *time of measurement* (with pretest and posttest as within-subjects levels); this is a 2 × 2 mixed factorial design with repeated measures on the second factor. The mixed design is common in experimental studies with a pretest and posttest.

Remember, when describing a design, that <u>each independent variable is described using one number, which is the number of levels for that variable</u>. Thus a design description with two numbers (e.g., 3 × 4) has two independent variables or factors, which have three and four levels, respectively. The <u>dependent variable is not part of the design</u> description, so it was not considered in this section.

Selection of Inferential Statistics

It is time to think about how to decide which of the many possible inferential statistics to use. Because many statistical tests are introduced, don't be concerned if you don't know about all of the tests mentioned. You should come back to this chapter later, from time to time, when you have to make a decision about which statistic to use, and by then, the tests will be more familiar.

In Fig 5.1, we present eight steps to guide you in the selection of a proper inferential statistical test for data analysis. Remember that **difference questions** <u>compare groups</u> and utilize the statistics, which we call **difference inferential statistics**. These statistics (e.g., *t* test and analysis of variance) are shown in Tables 5.1 and 5.3.

Associational questions utilize what we call **associational inferential statistics**. The statistics in this group <u>examine the association or relationship between two or more variables</u> and are shown in Tables 5.2 and 5.4. This distinction between difference and associational statistics is somewhat of a simplification; you will see that there is often more than one possible statistic that can be used.

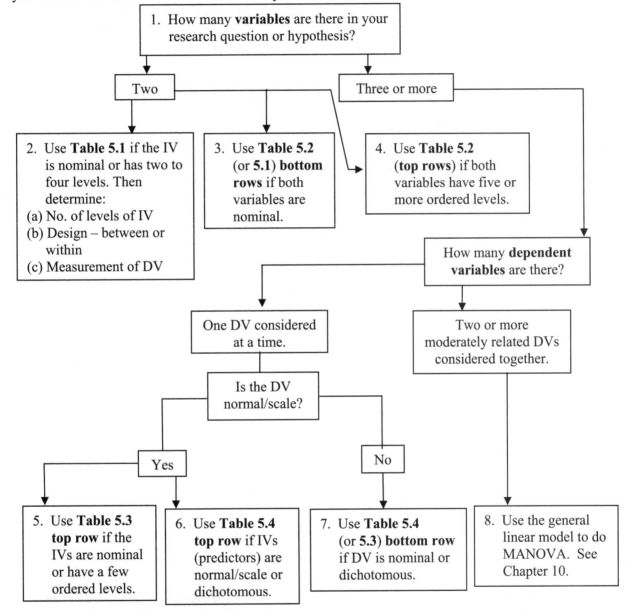

Fig. 5.1. A decision tree to help select an appropriate inferential statistic from Tables 5.1 to 5.4 (IV = independent variable; DV = dependent variable).

Using Tables 5.1 to 5.4 to Select Inferential Statistics

As with research questions and hypotheses discussed in Chapter 1, we divide inferential statistics into basic and complex. For ***basic* (or bivariate) statistics**, there is *one* independent and *one* dependent variable, and you will use Table 5.1 or 5.2. These basic statistics are discussed in more detail in our companion book, Morgan, Leech, Gloeckner, and Barrett (2011). For **complex statistics**, there are three or more variables. We decided to call them **complex** rather than **multivariate**, which is more common in the literature, because there is not unanimity about the definition of multivariate, and several complex statistics (e.g., factorial ANOVA) are not usually classified as multivariate. For complex statistics, you will use Tables 5.3 or 5.4. The complex statistics shown in Tables 5.3 and 5.4 are discussed in the remaining chapters in this book, and assignments and outputs are given demonstrating how to compute them using SPSS19. There are many other statistics, but these four tables include most of the inferential statistics that you will encounter in reading research articles. Note that the boxes in the decision tree are numbered to correspond to the numbers in the text below, which expands some on the decision tree or flowchart.

1. Decide <u>how many variables</u> there are in your research question or hypothesis. If there are only two variables, use Tables 5.1 or 5.2. If there is *more* than one independent and/or more than one dependent variable (i.e., three or more variables) in this research question, use Tables 5.3 and 5.4.

Basic (Two Variable) Statistics

2. If the <u>independent variable is nominal (i.e., has unordered levels)</u> or has a <u>few (2–4) ordered levels</u>, use Table 5.1. Then, your question is a **basic (two variable) difference question** to compare groups.

Table 5.1. *Selection of an Appropriate Inferential Statistic for Basic, Two Variable, Difference Questions or Hypotheses*

Scale of Measurement of **Dependent Variable** ↓	COMPARE ↓	One Factor or Independent Variable with **2 Levels** or **Categories**/Groups/Samples		One Independent Variable **3 or More Levels** or Groups	
		Independent Samples or Groups **(Between)**	Repeated Measures or Related Samples **(Within)**	Independent Samples or Groups **(Between)**	Repeated Measures or Related Samples **(Within)**
Dependent Variable Approximates **Normal /Scale** Data and Assumptions Not Markedly Violated	MEANS	INDEPENDENT SAMPLES *t* TEST **Ch. 5** or ONE-WAY ANOVA **App B**	PAIRED SAMPLES *t* TEST **App B**	ONE-WAY ANOVA **App B**	GLM REPEATED-MEASURES ANOVA **Ch. 9**
Dependent Variables Clearly **Ordinal** or Parametric Assumptions Markedly Violated	MEAN RANKS	MANN-WHITNEY **App B**	WILCOXON **App B**	KRUSKAL-WALLIS **App B**	FRIEDMAN **Ch. 9**
Dependent Variable **Nominal** or **Dichotomous**	COUNTS	CHI-SQUARE **App B**	McNemar	CHI-SQUARE **App B**	Cochran Q Test

Note. After each statistic, we provide in bold (e.g., Ch. 3, App B) the chapter or appendix in which the computation and interpretation of that statistic is discussed. It is acceptable to use statistics that are in the box(es) below the appropriate statistic, but there is usually some loss of power. It is not acceptable to use statistics in boxes above the appropriate statistic or ones in another column.

You must then determine: (a) whether there are <u>two *or* more than two levels</u> (also called categories or groups or samples) of your *independent* variable, (b) whether the design is <u>between-groups or within-subjects</u>, and (c) whether the <u>measurement level</u> of the *dependent* variable is (i) <u>normal/scale</u> and parametric assumptions are not markedly violated, *or* (ii) <u>ordinal</u>, *or* (iii) <u>nominal *or* dichotomous</u>. The answers to these questions lead to a specific box in Table 5.1 and statistics such as **independent** or **paired sample *t* tests**, **one-way ANOVA, chi-square,** and several other nonparametric tests.

3. If <u>both variables are nominal or dichotomous</u>, you could ask either a **difference question** (use the bottom row of Table 5.1, e.g., **chi-square**) or an **associational question** and use the bottom row of Table 5.2 (**phi or Cramer's V**). Note, in the second to bottom row of Table 5.2, we have included **eta**, an associational statistic used with one nominal and one normal or scale variable. We will later see it used as an effect size measure with ANOVAs. There are many *nonparametric associational measures*, some of which are in the bottom three rows of Table 5.2.

Table 5.2. *Selection of an Appropriate Inferential Statistic for Basic, Two Variable, Associational Questions or Hypotheses*

Level (Scale) of Measurement of **Both Variables** ⬇	RELATE ⬇	Two Variables or Scores for the Same or Related Subjects
Variables Are Both **Normal /Scale** and Assumptions Not Markedly Violated	SCORES	PEARSON (*r*) or BIVARIATE REGRESSION **Ch. 5, App B**
Both Variables at Least **Ordinal** Data or Distributional Assumptions Markedly Violated	RANKS	KENDALL TAU or SPEARMAN (RHO) **App B**
One Variable Is **Normal /Scale** and One Is **Nominal**		ETA **Ch. 8**
Both Variables Are **Nominal** or **Dichotomous**	COUNTS	PHI or CRAMER'S V **App B**

4. If both variables have <u>many (we suggest five or more) *ordered*</u> levels, use Table 5.2 (top two rows). Your research question would be a **basic** two variable (bivariate) **associational question**. Which row you use depends on *both* variables. If both are normal/scale, then you would probably select the **Pearson product moment correlation** or **bivariate regression** (top row). Regression should be used if one has a clearly directional hypothesis, with an independent and dependent variable. Correlation is chosen if one is simply interested in how the two variables are related. If one or both variables are ordinal or grossly skewed, the second row (**Kendall's tau** or **Spearman rho**) is a better choice.

Complex (3 or More Variable) Questions and Statistics

It is possible to break down a complex research problem or question into a series of basic (bivariate) questions and analyses. However, <u>there are advantages to combining them into one complex analysis; additional information is provided, and a more accurate overall picture of the relationships is obtained.</u>

5. If you have one normally distributed (scale) dependent variable and two (or perhaps three or four) independent variables, each of which is nominal or has a few (2–4) ordered levels, you will use the top row of Table 5.3 and one of three types of **factorial ANOVA**. These analysis of variance (ANOVA) statistics answer **complex difference questions**.

The last two rows of Table 5.3 involve situations in which there is more than one, categorical independent variable and there is an ordinal or dichotomous dependent variable. Although we do not cover these analyses in this book, we want you to know that it is possible to perform analyses on such data with SPSS, using the programs included in all capital letters. Similarly, note that in Table 5.4 **generalized estimating equations**, which is not covered in this book but is available in SPSS 15.0 and later versions, can be used to analyze data when there is a normal and/or dichotomous independent variable with at least one random and/or nested variable and a dichotomous dependent variable.

6. The statistics in Table 5.4 are used to answer **complex associational questions**. If you have two or more independent or predictor variables and one normal (scale) dependent variable, the statistics in the top row of Table 5.4, including **multiple regression**, are appropriate.

7. For an appropriate complex associational statistic when the dependent variable is dichotomous or nominal, consult the bottom row of Table 5.4. In general, **logistic regression** is used if the dependent variable is dichotomous and some or all the independent variables are dichotomous. **Discriminant analysis** can best be used if the independent variables are all ordered/scale and can be used if the dependent variable is nominal with more than two categories (not discussed in this book).

Table 5.3. *Selection of the Appropriate Complex (Two or More Independent Variables) Statistic to Answer Difference Questions or Hypotheses*

Dependent Variable(s) ↓	Two or More Independent Variables		
	All Between Groups	**All Within Subjects**	**Mixed (Between and Within)**
One **Normal/ Scale** Dependent Variable	GLM, Factorial ANOVA or ANCOVA **Ch. 8**	GLM With Repeated Measures on All Factors **Ch. 9**[a]	GLM With Repeated Measures on Some Factors **Ch. 9**[a]
More Than One **Normal/Scale** Dependent Variable	GLM, Multivariate MANOVA or MANCOVA **Ch. 10**	GLM Doubly multivariate MANOVA With Repeated Measures on All Factors **Ch.10**[b]	GLM Doubly multivariate MANOVA With Repeated Measures on Some Factors **Ch. 10**
Ordinal Dependent Variable	Generalized Linear Models	Generalized Estimating Equations	Generalized Estimating Equations
Dichotomous Dependent Variable	Log Linear; Generalized Linear Models	Generalized Estimating Equations	Generalized Estimating Equations

[a] In Chapter 9, both a multivariate analysis (MANOVA) and a univariate analysis are performed.
[b] In Chapter 10, the doubly multivariate example also has a between-groups factor, so it is actually a mixed design.

8. Use a **MANOVA** (second row of Table 5.3) if you have two or more normal (scale) dependent variables treated simultaneously. **MANOVA** is a better choice than several ANOVAs if the dependent variables are related statistically and conceptually.

Table 5.4. *Selection of the Appropriate Complex Associational Statistic for Predicting a Single Dependent/Outcome Variable From Several Independent Variables*

One Dependent or Outcome Variable ↓	Several Independent or Predictor Variables			
	All Normal / Scale	Some Normal Some or All Dichotomous (2 Categories)	Some or All Nominal (Categorical With More than 2 Categories)	Normal and/or Dichotomous, With at Least One Random and/or Nested Variable
Normal/Scale (Continuous)	MULTIPLE REGRESSION Ch. 6	MULTIPLE REGRESSION Ch. 6 or GLM Ch.8	GLM Ch. 8	LINEAR MIXED MODELS Ch. 11
Dichotomous	DISCRIMINANT ANALYSIS Ch. 7	LOGISTIC REGRESSION Ch. 7	LOGISTIC REGRESSION Ch. 7	Generalized Estimating Equations

Occasionally you will see a research article in which a dichotomous *dependent variable* was used with a *t* test, ANOVA, or Pearson correlation. Because of the special nature of dichotomous variables, this is not necessarily wrong, as would be the use of a nominal (three or more unordered levels) dependent variable with these parametric statistics. However, we think that it is usually a better practice to use the same statistics with dichotomous variables that you would use with nominal variables, except that it is appropriate to use dichotomous independent variables in multiple regression (see Table 5.4).

Other Multivariate (Complex) Statistics

Not shown, in part because they did not fit the format of the tables, are six complex associational statistics for analyzing a number of variables at a time, which you may see in the literature. **Cronbach's alpha,** a technique used to assess the internal consistency reliability of multiple item scales, is discussed, along with some other reliability measures, in Chapter 3. In **exploratory factor analysis**, one postulates that there is a smaller set of latent variables or constructs. Factor analysis and **principal components analysis,** which is used to reduce a relatively large number of variables to a smaller number of groups of variables, are discussed in Chapter 4. **Canonical correlation** involves correlation of linear combinations of one set of variables with linear combinations of another set of variables. Thus, it is useful when you have two sets of variables and want to see the patterns of correlations between the two sets. How to compute it with syntax is shown in Chapter 10.

Because it cannot be computed using SPSS (without the extra program called AMOS), **structural equation models (SEM)** are not discussed in this book. SEM are models that describe relationships among latent (unobserved) variables and manifest (observed) variables.

Multilevel linear models (sometimes called hierarchical linear models, or HLM) enable one to model nested data (data in which certain variables are present only in a subset of one's data) over time. Both SEM and HLM provide tests of the accuracy of proposed models, and both are very useful for drawing better inferences from large sets of data. However, it is important to realize that, despite the language sometimes used in discussing SEM and HLM, even they do not enable one to determine causal relationships (e.g., see the APA Task Force on Statistical Inference report, Wilkinson et al., 1999, p. 600). How to compute multilevel models using SPSS is described in Chapter 11.

The General Linear Model

Whether or not there is a relationship between variables can be answered in two ways. For example, if each of two variables provides approximately normally distributed data with five or more levels, then Fig. 5.1 and Table 5.2 indicate that the statistic to use is either the Pearson correlation or bivariate regression, and that would be our recommendation. However, some researchers choose to divide the independent variable into a few categories such as low, medium, and high and then do a one-way ANOVA. In another example, some researchers who start with an independent variable that has only a few (say, two to four) *ordered* categories may choose to do a correlation instead of a one-way ANOVA. Although these choices are not necessarily wrong, we do not think they are the best practice. In the first example, information is lost by dividing a continuous independent variable into a few categories. In the second example, there would be a restricted range, which tends to decrease the size of the correlation coefficient.

In the above examples, we recommended one of the choices, but the fact that there are two choices raises a bigger and more complex issue. Statisticians point out, and can prove mathematically, that the distinction between difference and associational statistics is an artificial one, in that ANOVA and multiple regression using dummy variables are often mathematically the same. In fact, SPSS calculates ANOVA and MANOVA using this regression approach. The bottom of Fig. 5.2 shows these parallels and that, although we have made a distinction between difference and associational inferential statistics,

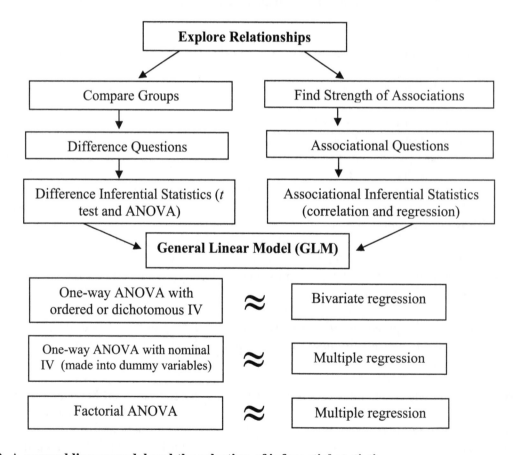

Fig. 5.2. A general linear model and the selection of inferential statistics.

they both serve the purpose of exploring (top box) relationships and both are subsumed by the general linear model (middle box). Statisticians state that all common parametric statistics are relational. Thus, the full range of methods used to analyze one continuous dependent variable and one or more independent variables, either continuous or categorical, are mathematically similar. The model on which this is based is called the **general linear model (GLM)**. The idea is that the relationship between the independent and dependent variables can be expressed by an equation with weights for each of the independent/predictor variables plus an error term.

What this means is that if you have a continuous, normally distributed dependent/outcome variable and several levels of an unordered, nominal independent variable, it would be appropriate to analyze them with either multiple regression or a one-way ANOVA. It is multiple regression rather than bivariate regression because there are multiple independent dummy variables comprising the comparisons among levels of the independent variable. You will get the same answer with regard to the significance level if you use either of these approaches using SPSS. Note in Fig. 5.1 and Table 5.3 that SPSS uses the GLM to perform a variety of statistics including factorial ANOVA and MANOVA. Although we recognize that our distinction between difference and associational parametric statistics is a simplification, we think it is useful conceptually in that it better represents how researchers think about their research questions and hypotheses, which form the basis for the analyses. We hope that this introduction to GLM is helpful.

Interpreting the Results of a Statistical Test

In the following chapters, we present information about how to check assumptions, do analyses, interpret complex statistics, and write results. For each statistic, the program produces a number or **calculated value** based on the specific data in your study. They are labeled t, F, etc., or just **value**.

Statistical Significance

The calculated value is compared to a **critical value** (found in a statistics table or stored in the computer's memory) that takes into account the degrees of freedom, which are usually based on the number of participants. Figure 5.3 shows how to interpret any inferential test once you know the probability level (p or sig.) from the computer or statistics table. In general, if the calculated value of the statistic (e.g., t, F) is relatively large, the probability or p is small (e.g., .05, .01, .001). If the probability is *less than* the preset alpha level (usually .05), we can say that the results are **statistically significant** or that they are statistically significant at the .05 level or that $p < .05$. We can also reject the null hypothesis of no difference or no relationship. Note that, using SPSS computer printouts, it is quite easy to determine statistical significance because the (truncated) actual significance or probability level (p) is printed so you do not have to look up a critical value in a table. SPSS labels this p value **Sig**. so all of the common inferential statistics have a common metric, the significance level or **Sig**. This level is also the probability of a Type I error or the probability of rejecting the null hypothesis when it is actually true. Thus, regardless of what specific statistic you use, if the Sig. or p is small (less than your preset alpha level, which is usually .05) the finding is *statistically* significant, and you can reject the null hypothesis of no difference or no association.

Sig.[a]	Meaning	Null Hypothesis	Interpretation
1.00	$p = 1.00$	Do Not Reject	Not Statistically Significant (could be due to chance)
.50	$p = .50$		
.06	$p = .06$		
.05	$p \leq .05$	Reject [b]	Statistically Significant [c] (not likely due to chance)
.01	$p = .01$		
.000	$p < .001$		

[a] SPSS uses **Sig.** to indicate the significance or probability level (p) of all inferential statistics. This is just a sample of Sig. values, which could be any value from 0 to 1.

[b] $p \leq .05$ is the typical alpha level that researchers use to assess whether the null hypothesis should be rejected. However, sometimes researchers use more liberal levels (e.g., .10 in exploratory studies) or more conservative levels (e.g., .01).

[c] Statistically significant does *not* mean that the results have practical significance or importance.

Fig. 5.3. Interpreting inferential statistics using the SPSS Sig.

Practical Significance Versus Statistical Significance

Students, and sometimes researchers, misinterpret statistically significant results as being practically or clinically important. But statistical significance is not the same as practical significance or importance. With large samples, you can find statistical significance even when the differences or associations are very small/weak. Thus, in addition to statistical significance, we will examine **effect size**. It is quite possible, with a large sample, to have a statistically significant result that is weak (i.e., has a small effect size). Remember that the null hypothesis is that there is *no* difference or *no* association. A statistically significant result with a small effect size means that we can be very confident that there is *some* difference or association, but it is probably small and may not be practically important.

Confidence Intervals

An approach that can be used either as an alternative to null hypothesis significance testing (NHST) or to supplement NHST is **confidence intervals**. These intervals provide more information than NHST alone and *may* provide more practical information. Suppose one knew that an increase in reading scores of five points would lead to a functional increase in reading performance. Two methods of instruction were compared. The result showed that students who used the new method scored statistically significantly higher than those who used the other method. According to NHST, we would reject the null hypothesis of no difference between methods and conclude that our new method is better. If we apply confidence intervals to this same study, we can determine an interval that contains the *population mean difference* 95% of the time. If the lower bound of that interval is greater than five points, we can be confident that using this method of instruction would lead to a practical or functional increase in reading levels. If however, the confidence interval ranged from, say, 1 to 11, the result would be statistically significant, but the mean difference in the population could be as little as 1 point or as big as 11 points. Given these results, we could not be confident that there would be a practical increase in reading using the new method.

Effect Size

A statistically significant outcome does not give information about the strength or size of the outcome. Therefore, it is important to know, in addition to information on statistical significance, the size of the effect. **Effect size** is defined as the strength of the relationship between the independent variable and the dependent variable and/or the magnitude of the difference between levels of the independent variable with respect to the dependent variable. Statisticians have proposed many effect size measures that fall mainly into three types or families: the r family, the d family, and risk potency measures.

The r family of effect size measures. One method of expressing effect sizes is in terms of strength of association. The most well-known variant of this approach is the **Pearson correlation coefficient, r.** Using Pearson r, effect sizes are always less than $|1.0|$,[1] varying between -1.0 and $+1.0$ with 0 representing no effect and $+1$ or -1 the maximum effect. This *family* of effect sizes also includes many other associational statistics, such as rho (r_s), phi (ϕ), eta (η), and the multiple correlation (R).

The d family of effect size measures. The d family focuses on magnitude of difference rather than strength of association. If one compares two groups, the effect size (d) can be computed by subtracting the mean of the second group from the mean of the first group and dividing by the pooled standard deviation of both groups. The general formula is on the left. If the two groups have equal ns, the pooled SD is the average of the SDs for the two groups. When ns are unequal, the formula on the right is the appropriate one.

$$d = \frac{M_A - M_B}{SD_{pooled}} \qquad d = \frac{M_A - M_B}{\sqrt{\dfrac{(n_A - 1)SD_A^2 + (n_B - 1)SD_B^2}{n_A + n_B - 2}}}$$

There are many other formulas for d family effect sizes, but they all express effect size in standard deviation units. Thus, a d of .5 means that the groups differ by one half of a pooled standard deviation. Using d, effect sizes usually vary from 0 to $+$ or -1, but d can be more than 1.

Risk potency effect sizes. These measures are based on data with dichotomous independent and dependent variables. There are many such effect size measures, usually expressed as ratios or percentages, including *odds ratios, relative risk reduction,* and *risk difference (RD)*. The use of these effect size measures is discussed in Chapter 7.

To summarize, the r effect size is most commonly used when the independent and dependent variables are continuous. The d effect size is used when the independent variable is dichotomous and the dependent variable is continuous. Finally, risk potency effect sizes are used when the independent and dependent variables are both dichotomous (binary). However, as implied in Table 5.5, most effect sizes can be converted from one family to another.

Issues about effect size measures. Unfortunately, as just indicated, there are many different effect size measures and little agreement about which to use. Although d is the most commonly discussed effect size measure for differences, it is not available on SPSS outputs. However, d can be calculated by hand with the formulas shown earlier, based on information in the SPSS printout. The correlation coefficient, r, and other measures of the strength of association such as phi (ϕ), eta^2 (η^2), and R^2 are available in SPSS.

There is disagreement among researchers about whether it is best to express effect size as the unsquared or squared r family statistic (e.g., r or r^2). It has been common to use the squared versions because they indicate the percentage of variance in the dependent variable that can be predicted from the independent variable(s). However, some statisticians argue that these usually small percentages give you an

---

[1] The absolute value of 1 is shown as $|1.0|$. Absolute value means the numeric value without considering sign. Thus, $< |1.0|$ means that the value is between -1 and $+1$. See Table 5.5 for examples.

underestimated impression of the strength or importance of the effect. Thus, we (like Cohen, 1988) decided to use the unsquared statistics (r, ϕ, η, and R) as our r family indexes.

Although the fourth edition of the *Publication Manual of the American Psychological Association* recommended that researchers report effect sizes, relatively few researchers did so before 1999 when the APA Task Force on Statistical Inference stated that effect sizes should *always* be reported for your primary results (Wilkinson & The APA Task Force, 1999). The fifth edition (APA, 2001) adopted this recommendation of the Task Force, so we and more and more journal articles discuss the size of the effect as well as whether the result was statistically significant.

Interpreting Effect Sizes

Assuming that you have computed an effect size measure, how should it be interpreted? Table 5.5 provides guidelines for interpreting the size of the "effect" for six common effect size measures based on Cohen (1988) and Vaske, Gliner, and Morgan (2002).

Table 5.5. *Interpretation of the Strength of a Relationship (Effect Sizes)*

General Interpretation of the Strength of a Relationship	The d Family [a] d	The r Family [b] r and ϕ	R	η (eta)	Risk Potency RD (%)
Much larger than typical	$\geq |1.00|^{c, d}$	$\geq |.70|$	$|.70|+$	$|.45|+$	≥ 52
Large or larger than typical	$|.80|$	$|.50|$	$|.51|$	$|.37|$	43
Medium or typical	$|.50|$	$|.30|$	$|.36|$	$|.24|$	28
Small or smaller than typical	$|.20|$	$|.10|$	$|.14|$	$|.10|$	11

[a] d values can vary from 0.0 to + or −infinity, but d greater than one is relatively uncommon.

[b] r family values can vary from 0.0 to + or −1.0, but except for reliability (i.e., same concept measured twice), r is rarely above .70. In fact, some of these statistics (e.g., phi) have a restricted range in certain cases; that is, the maximum phi may be less then 1.0.

[c] We interpret the numbers in this table as a range of values. For example, a d greater than .90 (or less than −.90) would be described as "much larger than typical," a d between say .70 and .90 would be called "larger than typical," and d between say .60 and .70 would be "typical to larger than typical." We interpret the other three columns similarly.

[d] Note that | | indicates absolute value of the coefficient. The absolute magnitude of the coefficient, rather than its sign, is the information that is relevant to effect size. R and eta usually are calculated by taking the square root of a squared value, so that the sign usually is positive.

Note that these guidelines are based on the effect sizes *usually found* in studies in the behavioral sciences. Thus, they do not have absolute meaning and are relative only to typical findings in these areas. For that reason, we suggest using larger than typical instead of large, typical instead of medium, and smaller than typical instead of small. The guidelines will not apply to all subfields in the behavioral sciences, and they definitely will not apply to fields where the usually expected effects are either larger or smaller. It is advisable to examine the research literature to see if there is information about typical effect sizes on the topic.

Cohen (1988) provided research examples of what we labeled small, medium, and large effects to support the suggested d and r family values. Many researchers would not consider a correlation (r) of .5 to be very strong because only 25% of the variance in the dependent variable is predicted. However, Cohen argued that a d of .8 (and an r of .5, which he showed are mathematically similar) are "grossly perceptible and therefore large differences, as (for example is) the mean difference in height between 13- and 18-year-old girls" (p. 27). Cohen stated that a small effect may be difficult to detect, perhaps because it is in a less well-controlled area of research. Cohen's medium size effect is "…visible to the naked eye. That is, in the course of normal experiences, one would become aware of an average difference in IQ between clerical and semi-skilled workers..." (p. 26).

Even effect size is not the same as practical significance. Although effect size measures indicate the strength of the relationship and, thus, are more relevant for practical significance than statistical significance, they are not direct measures of the importance of a finding. As implied above, what constitutes a large or important effect depends on the specific area studied, the context, and the methods used. Furthermore, practical significance always involves a judgment by the researcher and the consumers (e.g., clinicians, clients, teachers, school boards) of research that takes into account such factors as cost and political considerations. A common example is that the effect size of taking daily aspirin and its effect on heart attacks is quite small, but the practical importance is high because preventing heart attacks is a life or death matter, the cost of aspirin is low, and side effects are uncommon. On the other hand, a curriculum change could have a large effect size but be judged to not be practical because of high costs and/or extensive opposition to its implementation.

Confidence intervals of the effect size. Knowing the confidence interval around an effect size can provide information useful to making a decision about practical significance or importance. If the confidence interval is narrow, one would know that the effect size in the population is close to the computed effect size. On the other hand, if the confidence interval is large (as is usually the case with small samples) the population effect size could fall within a wide range, making it difficult to interpret the computed effect size for purposes of estimating practical significance. Similar to the example described earlier, if the lower bound of the confidence interval was more than a minimum effect size agreed to indicate a practically significant effect, one could then be quite confident that the effect was important or practical. Unfortunately, SPSS does not provide confidence intervals for effect size measures, and it is not easy to compute them by hand.

Power

To understand power, first we need to discuss **error.** There are two types of error, **Type I** and **Type II**. Type I error occurs when the researcher rejects the null hypothesis when it is true. Type I error is determined by the significance level (α). For example, if a 5% level of significance is chosen, then the Type I error rate is 5%. Stated another way, α represents the conditional probability of making a Type I error when the null hypothesis is true.

Type II error occurs when the null hypothesis is accepted but the alternative hypothesis is true. The conditional probability of making a Type II error under the alternative hypothesis is denoted by β. Figure 5.4 shows the relationships among the different types of error, the truth, and the researcher's decisions.

Statistical power is the conditional probability of rejecting the null hypothesis (i.e., accepting the alternative hypothesis) when the alternative hypothesis is true. Power can be viewed as how likely it is that the researcher will find a relationship or difference that really exists. It is represented by $1-\beta$. Having low power increases the probability of committing a Type II error. Moreover, having a small sample size, which is the most important controllable source of low power, may also increase the probability of committing a Type I error if the sample is a poor representation of the population.

There are three factors that affect statistical power: (a) the level of significance, (b) effect size, and (c) sample size.

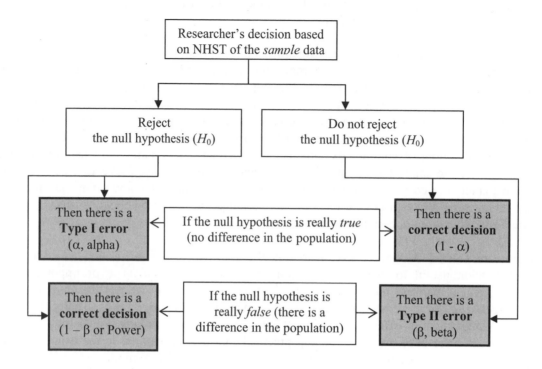

Fig. 5.4. Flowchart showing the four possible outcomes (two correct and two errors) that could result from a decision to reject or not reject a null hypothesis.

Increasing the level of significance will increase power. For example, instead of using an alpha level of .05, a researcher could use an alpha of .10. However, the problem with this approach is that this will also increase the probability of rejecting the null hypothesis when it is actually true. Changing the alpha level is not common practice since most research journals expect the use of .05 as an a priori value for alpha, and most researchers do not want to allow a probability of .10 for Type I error. Ocassionallty, in small sample exploratory studies, researchers will use alpha < .10 to increase power. The reverse is also sometimes the case; in large sample studies, the researcher may set alpha at < .01 to decrease power.

The larger the effect size, the easier it will be to attain significance with less power. With high power (usually due to very large sample sizes), even small effect sizes will attain statistical significance. This is one of the problems with too much power; researchers might find a statistically significant result and consider it to be important, when in fact it represents a small difference (i.e., a small effect size) which is not very meaningful. Although the null hypothesis is not more likely to be *true* (alpha ensures this), the effect is so close to being zero that for practical purposes the null hypothesis should be considered true. That is, when one achieves statistical significance with a small effect size (but large N), the probability that one has falsely rejected the null hypothesis is still .05, but the amount of difference from zero is not large enough to justify the manipulation, intervention, or inference about meaningful group differences.

The factor that can be most readily manipulated by the researcher to increase power is the sample size. The larger the sample size, the greater the likelihood of rejecting the null hypothesis. The concern here is that if the sample size is very large, one should not overinterpret significance alone. One, rather, should pay close attention to effect sizes, confidence intervals, and other information that will help one draw conclusions about the practical importance of an effect of the magnitude that was observed, because even small effect sizes that might not be important will be found statistically significant.

Power of .80 or greater is recommended by Cohen (1965) to detect a medium effect with an alpha level of .05. This recommendation was based on considering the ratio of the probability of committing a Type I error (i.e., 5%) to the probability of committing a Type II error (i.e., $1-.80 = .20$). The most common type of power analysis is **a priori power analysis**. A priori power analysis is done prior to collecting data in order to determine the sample size needed to have adequate (usually $\geq .80$) power. This type of power analysis is helpful, as it allows the researcher to select a sample size that is large enough to lead to a rejection of the null hypothesis for a given effect size. In order to determine the needed sample size we would need to estimate three factors: alpha level, power, and effect size. For example, a researcher might assume the following: an alpha level = .05, power = .80, and a medium effect size ($d = .50$). Then, using either Cohen's (1988) tables or a computer program, we can determine the needed sample size.

Although a priori power analysis is based on <u>estimated</u> values, **post hoc power** analysis, which SPSS labels as **Observed power**, can be used to determine the <u>exact</u> amount of power found in a study. As with a priori power, post hoc power should be $\geq .80$. If post hoc power is low and the result is non-statistically significant with a medium to large effect size, then it is possible that a difference does exist within the data, but there was not enough power to detect it. On the other hand, if post hoc power is high and the result is statistically significant with a small effect size, then it is possible that the statistically significant difference is not meaningful; it might be a small difference that is trivially different from the null hypothesis.

Steps in Interpreting Inferential Statistics

In order to properly interpret inferential statistics, we recommend the following steps:

1. <u>Decide whether to reject the null hypothesis</u>. However, that is not enough for a full interpretation. If you find that the outcome is statistically significant, you need to answer at least two *more* questions. Figure 5.5 summarizes the steps for how to more fully interpret the results of an inferential statistic.

2. <u>What is the direction of the effect</u>? Difference inferential statistics compare groups so it is necessary to state which group performed better. We discuss how to do this in Chapters 8, 9, and 10. For associational inferential statistics (e.g., correlation), the sign is very important, so you must indicate whether the association or relationship is positive or negative. We discuss how to interpret correlations in Chapters 3, 4, and 6, as part of the chapters on reliability, factor analysis, and multiple regression, respectively.

3. <u>What is the size of the effect</u>? You should include effect size, confidence intervals, or both in the description of your results. Unfortunately, SPSS does not always provide effect sizes and confidence intervals, so for some statistics we have to compute or estimate the effect size by hand or use an effect size calculator, several of which are available online.

4. Although not shown in Fig. 5.5, the researcher or the consumer of the research should make a <u>judgment about whether the result has practical or clinical significance or importance</u>. To do so, they need to take into account the effect size, the costs of implementing change and the probability and severity of any side effect or unintended consequences. Previously, we discussed the fact that with high power and a small effect size a statistically significant finding (even one with $p < .001$) *may* be trivial and of little practical significance.

| <u>Nontechnical Question</u> | <u>Statistical Answer</u> |

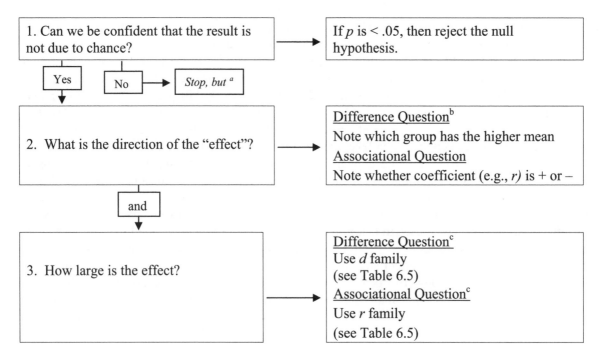

^a If you have a small sample *(N)*, it is possible to have a nonsignificant result (it may be due to chance) and yet a large effect size. If so, an attempt to replicate the study with a larger sample may be justified.

^b If there are three or more means or a significant interaction, a post hoc test (e.g., Tukey) will be necessary for complete interpretation.

^c Interpretation of effect size is based on Cohen (1988) and Table 6.5. A "large" effect is one that Cohen stated is "grossly perceptible." It is larger than typically found but does not necessarily explain a large amount of variance. You might use confidence intervals in addition to or instead of effect sizes.

Fig. 5.5. Steps in the interpretation of an inferential statistic.

A Review of How to Select and Interpret Basic Inferential Statistics

As a review, we now provide an extended example based on the HSB data. We will walk you through the process of identifying the variables, research questions, and approach and then show how we selected appropriate statistics and interpreted the results for two basic research questions.

Problem 5.1
Suppose your research problem was **to investigate whether** *males and females differ in math achievement*.

Identification of the variables and their measurement. The research problem specifies two variables: *gender* and *math achievement,* so the problem and question will be considered "basic." The latter appears to be the outcome or dependent variable. *Gender* is the independent or predictor variable because it is *presumed* to be an influence on *math achievement* scores. What is the level of measurement for these variables? *Gender* is clearly dichotomous (male or female). The *math achievement* test has many levels, with more scores somewhere in the middle than high or low. It is necessary to confirm that *math achievement* is at least approximately normally distributed by requesting that SPSS compute the skewness as we did in Chapter 2.

Research question. There are several possible ways the research question could be stated and more than one statistic that could be used with these variables. However, we will focus on one research question and inferential statistic because they answer this research problem and fit our earlier recommendations for good choices. Because the independent variable has only a few levels (in this case two) or categories, we recommend that you phrase this as a difference question such as:

5.1. Is there a difference between individuals of male and female *gender* in average *math achievement* scores?

Type of research question. Note that there are only two variables and the focus is a group difference (the difference between the male group and the female group). Thus, using Fig. 5.1, you should refer to Table 5.1 to find a statistic to help answer this *basic difference question*.

Selection of an appropriate statistic. After computing the skewness value for *math achievement*, when you examine Table 5.1 you will see that this first question would be appropriately answered with an *independent samples t test* because (a) the independent variable has only two values (male and female), (b) the design is between-groups (males and females form two independent groups), and (c) the dependent variable (*math achievement*) is normal or scale data.

Syntax and results output for research question 1. In Output 5.1, we provide the syntax and output, using the *hsbdataB.sav* data set, for an independent samples *t* test to see if there was a difference between male and female students on math achievement. Appendix B, Review of Basic Statistics, shows the steps used in the point-and-click method, the syntax, key parts of the output, and a brief interpretation for the basic statistics covered in our *IBM SPSS for Introductory Statistics* book (Morgan et al., 2010). Detailed interpretations of the outputs and an example of how to write about the outputs in a research report are presented in our 2010 Introductory SPSS book.

Output 5.1: Independent Samples *t* Test Comparing Males and Females

```
T-TEST GROUPS = gender(0 1)
  /MISSING = ANALYSIS
  /VARIABLES = mathach
  /CRITERIA = CI(.95) .
```

T-Test

Group Statistics

	gender	N	Mean	Std. Deviation	Std. Error Mean
math achievement test	male	34	14.7550	6.03154	1.03440
	female	41	10.7479	6.69612	1.04576

Independent Samples Test

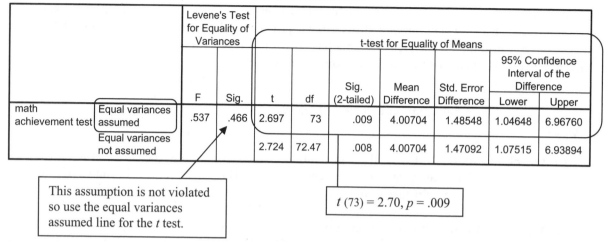

		Levene's Test for Equality of Variances		t-test for Equality of Means							
										95% Confidence Interval of the Difference	
		F	Sig.	t	df	Sig. (2-tailed)	Mean Difference	Std. Error Difference		Lower	Upper
math achievement test	Equal variances assumed	.537	.466	2.697	73	.009	4.00704	1.48548		1.04648	6.96760
	Equal variances not assumed			2.724	72.47	.008	4.00704	1.47092		1.07515	6.93894

This assumption is not violated so use the equal variances assumed line for the *t* test.

$t(73) = 2.70, p = .009$

Interpretation of Output 5.1

You can see from the **Group Statistics** table that the 34 males had an average *math achievement test* score of 14.76, while the 41 females had an average score of 10.75. The **Independent Samples Test** table has two main parts: **Levene's test**, for the assumption of equal variances, and the *t* **test for Equality of Means**.

A critical assumption of the *t* test is that the variances (standard deviation squared) of the two groups (males and females) are approximately equal. In this case, those variances are 6.03^2 and 6.70^2. Levene's test provides an *F* and a Sig. (*p*), which in this example is not statistically significant because it is .47, much greater than .05. Thus, the variances are not statistically significantly different. This is not the *t* test; it assesses an assumption! Because Levene's test is not statistically significant, the assumption is not violated, and, in this case, we use the top (Equal Variances Assumed) line to interpret and report the *t* test. Note that SPSS could make this output more clear if it had been broken into three tables with a separate table for Levene's test and with the labels about about equal variances (assumed or not) next to the appropriate *t*, *df*, etc.

The appropriate *t* to use is 2.70 with 73 degrees of freedom (34 + 41−2 = 73) and *p* = .009. Thus, there is a statistically significant difference between the male and female students; we can reject the null hypothesis of no difference in the population of male and female students. (Note these data were collected 20+ years ago so they may well not apply to current scores on math achievement; moreover, we will learn in another assignment that these gender differences seem to be mediated by the number of math courses males and females took.) The **Mean Difference** in *math achievement* between males and females in this sample was 4.01. The 95% **Confidence Interval of the Difference**, shown in the two right-hand columns, tells us that if we repeated the study 100 times, 95 of the times the true (population) difference would fall within the confidence interval, which for *math achievement* is between 1.05 points and 6.97 points. Note that if the **Upper** and **Lower** bounds have the same sign (either + and + in this case, or − and −), we know that the difference is statistically significant because the null finding of zero difference lies *outside* of the confidence interval. On the other hand, if zero lies between the upper and lower limits, there could be no difference. The lower limit of the confidence interval on *math achievement* tells us that the difference between males and females could be as small as 1.05 points out of 25, which is the maximum possible score.

Effect size measures for *t* tests are not provided in the printout but can be estimated relatively easily using the formula and interpretation of *d* provided in this chapter. For *math achievement*, the difference between the means (4.01) would be divided by about 6.4, an estimate of the pooled (weighted average) standard deviation. Thus, *d* would be approximately .60, which is, according to Cohen (1988), a medium- to large-sized "effect." The *d* of .60 is a somewhat larger than typical effect size. This means that the difference is greater than typical of the statistically significant findings in the behavioral sciences. A *d* of .60 may or may not be a large enough difference to use for recommending programmatic changes (i.e., be practically significant).

We found a statistically significant *t* with the hsbdata and a sample of 75 participants. However, if we had only 20 participants, it is very likely that the *t* would not have been statistically significant because the *t* value is influenced strongly by sample size.

Whether the statistic is statistically significant only means the result is unlikely to be due to chance. In addition you have to state the direction of the result and the effect size and/or the confidence interval. Because males had the higher mean, we can be quite confident that males in the population are at least a little better at math achievement, on average, than females. If the difference was not statistically significant, it is best *not* to make any comment about which mean was higher because the difference could be due to chance. Likewise, if the difference was not statistically significant, we recommend that you do not discuss or *interpret* the effect size. However, you should provide the *d* in a table or provide means and standard deviations so that effect sizes could be computed if a researcher wanted to use this study in a meta-analysis.

Confidence intervals might help you decide if the difference in *math achievement* scores was large enough to have practical significance. For example, we found (from the lower bound of the confidence interval) that you only could be confident that there was a 1.05 point difference between males and females. Then you could decide whether that is a big enough difference to justify, for example, a programmatic change.

Problem 5.2

A second research problem might be **to investigate the relationship between *math courses taken* and *math achievement*.** Again, the dependent or outcome variable is *math achievement*. We can think of *math courses taken* as the predictor or independent variable because it occurred before the math test and is presumed to have an effect on math achievement scores. Both *math courses taken* and *math achievement* have more than five ordered levels and are not highly skewed so can be considered approximately normally distributed or scale variables.

Because there are only two variables in this problem and because the independent or predictor variable (*math courses taken*) has five or more ordered levels, we would suggest that the research question be written as a basic associational question as follows.

5.2. *Is the number of math courses taken predictive of later math achievement?*

Type of research question. This second question is a **basic associational question** because there are only two variables and both have many ordered levels. Thus, use Table 5.2 for this question.

Selection of an appropriate statistic. As you can see from Table 5.2, research question 2 would be answered with **bivariate regression** because both *math courses taken* and *math achievement* are normally distributed data, and we are viewing one variable, *math courses taken,* as the predictor of the other variable.

Syntax and output for research question 2. Again, Appendix B provides the general point-and-click instructions for computing **bivariate**, or **simple**, **regression**, as in this example. The syntax and output showing the regression of *math achievement test* score on the number of *math courses taken* is shown in Output 5.2

Output 5.2: Regression of Math Achievement on Math Courses Taken

```
REGRESSION
  /MISSING LISTWISE
  /STATISTICS COEFF OUTS CI R ANOVA
  /CRITERIA=PIN(.05) POUT(.10)
  /NOORIGIN
  /DEPENDENT mathach
  /METHOD=ENTER mathcrs   .
```

Regression

Variables Entered/Removed[b]

Model	Variables Entered	Variables Removed	Method
1	math courses taken[a]	.	Enter

a. All requested variables entered.

b. Dependent Variable: math achievement test

Model Summary

Model	R	R Square	Adjusted R Square	Std. Error of the Estimate
1	.794[a]	.631	.626	4.08162

a. Predictors: (Constant), math courses taken

ANOVA[b]

Model		Sum of Squares	df	Mean Square	F	Sig.
1	Regression	2076.327	1	2076.327	124.632	.000[a]
	Residual	1216.154	73	16.660		
	Total	3292.481	74			

a. Predictors: (Constant), math courses taken

b. Dependent Variable: math achievement test

Coefficients[a]

Model		Unstandardized Coefficients		Standardized Coefficients	t	Sig.	95% Confidence Interval for B	
		B	Std. Error	Beta			Lower Bound	Upper Bound
1	(Constant)	5.895	.761		7.747	.000	4.378	7.411
	math courses taken	3.166	.284	.794	11.164	.000	2.601	3.731

a. Dependent Variable: math achievement test

Interpretation of Output 5.2

The unstandardized regression coefficient (B) for predicting *math achievement* from *math courses taken* is 3.17; the standardized coefficient (β) is .79; the significance level (**Sig.**) or *p* is printed as .000 (but see below how to report it) and the degrees of freedom for the *F* test are 1 for the numerator (Regression) and 73 for the denominator (Residual). The regression coefficient is the slope of the best fit line predicting *achievement* from *math courses taken.* In a report, this would usually be written as B = 3.17, $F(1,73)$ = 124.63, $p < .001$; $r = .79$. Note that the standardized coefficient or β in a bivariate regression such as this is equal to the *r* or **Pearson correlation** relating these two variables. The model summary labels this correlation as *R*, because if this were a multiple regression the value in the table would be the multiple *R*, which is represented with a capital letter. However, in the bivariate case, this is simply the Pearson correlation. The significance, or *p*-value, follows and is stated as < .001; SPSS truncates Sig. values less than .001 to .000, but the probability cannot be zero. So, we report $p < .001$.

The regression predicting *math achievement* from *math courses taken* is statistically significant because the "Sig" is less than .05. Thus, we can reject the null hypothesis of no association and state that *math courses taken* is a statistically significant predictor of *math achievement*. Using the R^2 from the Model Summary table, we can say that $r^2 = .63$, indicating that 63% of the variance in *math achievement* is predicted by *math courses taken* In nontechnical language, students who have taken a lot of math courses generally have higher *math achievement* scores. Because the relation is positive, this means that taking many *math courses* is generally associated with high achievement, a medium number of courses taken with medium achievement, and low with low. If the regression were statistically significant and negative (e.g., −3.17), a high number of *math courses taken* would be predictive of low achievement. If the regression were not statistically significant, there would be <u>no</u> statistically significant systematic association between *math courses taken* and *math achievement*. In that case, you could not predict anything about *math achievement* from knowing how many math courses someone had taken. In addition to statistical significance and the sign of the regression coefficient, you should note and comment on the effect size for a full interpretation of the correlation. In this case, the correlation is .79, so the effect size is much larger than typical (see Table 6.5). This is a very strong correlation.

Note that if *N* were 6 a larger value of the regression coefficient would be required to obtain statistical significance. On the other hand, if *N* were 500 only a very small regression coefficient would be necessary to achieve statistical significance. In the latter case, you could be quite sure the association was not zero, but the effect size would be small or less than typical.

Complex Research Questions and Statistics

This review of the *t* test and regression assumes that your research problem considered only two variables at a time. Many research problems involve three or more variables and, thus, require what we call complex research questions and statistics, which are the subject of this book. There are advantages to considering the above three independent variables (*gender, math courses taken,* and *math achievement*) together rather than separately, as we did in research questions 1 and 2.

There are at least three statistics that you will compute in this book that can be used to consider *gender, math courses taken,* and *math achievement* together. The first is **multiple regression**, which is discussed in Chapter 6. If you examine Table 5.4, you will see that with two (or more) independent variables that are scale and/or dichotomous and one dependent variable that is approximately normal (scale) data, an appropriate associational statistic would be multiple regression. A research question, which subsumes both questions 1 and 2 above, could be:

Is there a combination of *gender* and *math courses* that predicts *math achievement*?

Selection of an appropriate statistic. As just stated, multiple regression could be used to answer this question. As you can see in Table 5.4, multiple regression is appropriate because we are trying to predict a normally distributed variable (*math achievement*) from two independent variables. The independent or predictor variables are *math courses taken* (normal or scale) and *gender* (a dichotomous or dummy variable).

Based on our discussion of the general linear model (GLM) and Fig. 5.2, a **two-way factorial ANOVA** is another statistic that could be used to consider both *gender* and *math courses* simultaneously. However, to use ANOVA, the several levels of *math courses taken* would have to be recoded into two or three levels (perhaps high, medium, and low). Because information is lost when you do such a recode, we would not recommend factorial ANOVA for this example.

Another possible statistic to use for this example is **analysis of covariance (ANCOVA)** using gender as the independent variable and math courses taken as the covariate. We will demonstrate in Chapter 8 how we can control for differences in the number of math courses taken by using math courses as a covariate, and we will see that these results importantly change the conclusions we would have drawn from the *t* test examining gender differences in math achievement that was described in this chapter.

We will discuss the interpretation of multiple regression results in Chapter 6 and factorial ANOVA and ANCOVA in Chapter 8. You will see that we will obtain more information about the relationships among these three variables by doing these complex statistics than by doing only the *t* test and regression.

Review of Writing About Your Outputs

One of the goals of this book is to help you write a research report or thesis/dissertation using the SPSS outputs. In each of the following chapters, we will provide an **Interpretation** of each output as well as an example of how you might write about and make a table from the results provided by the output. As a review of how to write about a *t* test and regression, we have provided this section, which could be from a thesis based on the expanded HSB data used in the assignments in this book.

Before demonstrating how you might write about the results of research questions 1 and 2 above, we want to make several important points. Several books that will help you write a research paper and make appropriate tables are listed in *For Further Reading* at the back of this book. Note especially the APA manual (2010), Nicol and Pexman (2010), and Morgan, Reichart, and Harrison (2002). The examples below and in the following chapters are only one way to write about SPSS outputs. There are other good ways.

Based on your SPSS outputs, you should include, in your **Method** section, descriptive statistics about the demographics (e.g., gender, age, ethnicity) of the participants. You should also put evidence related to the reliability and validity of your data in the **Method** section as well as reporting whether statistical assumptions of the inferential statistics were met or how adjustments were made if assumptions were not met.

The **Results** chapter or section includes a description (but not a discussion) of the findings in words and tables. Your Results section should include the following numbers about each statistically significant finding (in a table or the text):

1. The value of the statistic (e.g., $t = 2.05$ or $r = .30$)
2. The degrees of freedom (often in parentheses) and for chi-square the N (e.g., $df = 2$, $N = 49$)
3. The exact p (Sig. Value in SPSS: e.g., $p = .048$)
4. The direction of the finding (e.g., by stating which mean is larger or the sign of the correlation, if the statistic is statistically significant)
5. An index of effect size

When not shown in a table, the above information should be provided in the text as shown below. In addition to the numerical information, describe your statistically significant results in words, including the variables related, the direction of the finding, and an interpretive statement about the size/strength of the effect, perhaps based on Cohen (1988) or Table 5.5. Realize that these terms are only rough estimates of the magnitude of the "effect" based on what is typical in the behavioral sciences but not necessarily your topic. If there is literature about the effect size in your area, use that to decide what is typical.

If your paper includes a table, it is usually not necessary or advisable to include all the details about the value of the statistic, degrees of freedom, and p in the text, because they are in the table. If you have a table, you must refer to it by number (e.g., Table 1) in the text and describe the main points, but do not repeat all of it or the table is not necessary.You should not describe, in the text, the direction of the finding or the effect size of statistically non-significant findings, because the results could well be due to chance. The **Discussion** chapter or section puts the findings in context in regard to the research literature, theory, and the purposes of the study. You may also attempt to explain why the results turned out the way they did.

Example of How to Write About Outputs 5.1 and 5.2

Results

To investigate whether males and females differ in math achievement, a t test was computed. (The following assumptions were tested and met: (a) groups are approximately the same size, (b) the variances of the two populations are equal, (c) observations were independent, and (d) the dependent variable was approximately normally distributed.) There was a statistically significant difference between male and female students on math achievement: $t (73) = 2.70$, $p = .009$, $d = .60$. Males ($M = 14.75$, $SD = 6.03$) scored higher than females ($M = 10.75$, $SD = 6.69$), and the effect size was larger than typical for this topic. The confidence interval for the difference between the means was 1.05 to 6.97, indicating that the difference could be as small as one point, which is probably not a practically important difference, but it could also be as large as seven points.

Simple linear regression was computed to investigate whether the number of math courses taken predicted later math achievement. (Assumptions of linearity and normal distributions were checked and met.) Math courses taken ($M = 2.11$, $SD = 1.67$) significantly predicted math achievement ($M = 12.56$, $SD = 6.67$), $F(1, 73) = 124.63$, $p < .001$, adjusted $R^2 = .63$. According to Cohen (1988) this is a large effect size. The unstandardized regression weights, presented in Table 5.6, indicate that when the number of math courses increases by one unit math achievement increases by 3.17 units.

Table 5.6
Simple Linear Regression Analysis Summary for Math Courses Taken
Predicting Math Achievement (N = 74)

Variable	B	SEB	β
Math courses taken	3.17	.28	.79***
Constant	5.90	.76	

Note. $R^2 = .63$; $F(1,73) = 124.63$, $p < .001$.
***$p < .001$.

We will present examples of how to write about the results of the complex statistics discussed in this book in the appropriate chapters. Note that measures of reliability (e.g., Cronbach alpha, discussed in Chapter 3) and principal components analysis (Chapter 4) are usually discussed in the **Method** section, unless they are the focus of the research questions for the study. Chapters 6–10 present complex statistics that might be used to answer your complex research questions.

In conclusion, after the above review, you should be ready to study each of the complex statistics in Tables 5.3 and 5.4 and learn more about their computation and interpretation. Hopefully this review has brought you up to speed. It would be wise for you to review this chapter, especially the tables and figures from time to time. If you do, you will have a good grasp of how the various statistics fit together, when to use them, and how to interpret the results. You will need this information to understand the chapters that follow.

Interpretation Questions

5.1   Is there only one appropriate statistic to use for each research design? Explain your answer.

5.2   When $p < .05$, what does this signify?

5.3   Interpret the following related to effect size:
       a) $d = .25$ c) $R = .53$ e) $d = 1.15$
       b) $r = .35$ d) $r = .13$ f) $\eta = .38$

5.4   The confidence interval of the difference between means was $-.30$ to 4.0. Explain what this indicates.

5.5   What statistic would you use if you had two independent variables, income group (< \$10,000, \$10,000–\$30,000, > \$30,000) and ethnic group (Hispanic, Caucasian, African-American), and one normally distributed dependent variable (self-efficacy at work)? Explain.

5.6   What statistic would you use if you had one independent variable, geographic location (North, South, East, West), and one dependent variable (satisfaction with living environment, Yes or No)? Explain.

5.7   What statistic would you use if you had three normally distributed (scale) independent variables and one dichotomous independent variable (weight of participants, age of participants, height of participants and gender) and one dependent variable (positive self-image), which is normally distributed? Explain.

5.8 What statistic would you use if you had one between-groups independent variable, one repeated-measures independent variable, each with two levels, and one normally distributed dependent variable?

5.9 What statistic would you use if you had one, repeated-measures, independent variable with two levels and one ordinal dependent variable?

5.10 What statistic would you use if you had one, between-groups, independent variable with four levels and three normally distributed dependent variables?

5.11 What statistic would you use if you had three normally distributed independent variables, one dichotomous independent variable, and one dichotomous dependent variable?

CHAPTER 6

Multiple Regression

Multiple regression is one type of complex associational statistical method. Already, we have done assignments using another complex associational method, Cronbach's alpha, which, like multiple regression, is based on a correlation matrix of all the variables to be considered in a problem. In addition to multiple regression, two other complex associational analyses, **logistic regression** and **discriminant analysis** will be computed in the next chapter. Like multiple regression, logistic regression and discriminant analysis have the general purpose of predicting a dependent or criterion variable from *several* independent or predictor variables. As you can tell from examining Table 5.4, these three techniques for predicting one outcome measure from several independent variables vary in the level of measurement and type of independent variables and/or type of outcome variable.

There are several different ways of computing multiple regression that are used under somewhat different circumstances. We will have you use several of these approaches, so that you will be able to see that the method one uses to compute multiple regression influences the information one obtains from the analysis. If the researcher has no prior ideas about which variables will create the best prediction equation and has a reasonably small set of predictors, then **simultaneous regression** is the best method to use. It is preferable to use the **hierarchical method** when one has an idea about the *order* in which one wants to enter predictors and wants to know how prediction by certain variables *improves on* prediction by others. Hierarchical regression appropriately corrects for capitalization on chance, whereas, **stepwise**, another method available in SPSS in which variables are entered sequentially, does not. Both simultaneous regression and hierarchical regression require that you specify exactly which variables serve as predictors, and they provide significance levels based on this number of predictors. Sometimes you have a relatively large set of variables that you think may be good predictors of the dependent variable, but you cannot enter such a large set of variables without sacrificing the power to find significant results. In such a case, stepwise regression might be used. However, as indicated earlier, stepwise regression capitalizes on chance more than many researchers find acceptable. In essence, stepwise regression "tries out" all possible predictors but uses only the number of predictors actually selected for the final model when correcting degrees of freedom for the number of predictors. Many researchers would suggest that a better approach would be to aggregate correlated predictors, thereby reducing the number of predictors.

Conditions of Multiple Linear Regression

There are a few important conditions for **multiple regression**. For multiple regression, the *dependent* or outcome variable should be an interval or scale level variable, which is normally distributed in the population from which it is drawn. The *independent* variables should be mostly interval- or scale-level variables, but multiple regression can also have dichotomous independent variables, which are called dummy variables. **Dummy variables** are often nominal categories that have been given numerical codes, usually 1 and 0. The 0 stands for whatever the 1 is not and is thus said to be "dumb" or silent. Thus, when we use *gender*, for instance, as a dummy variable in multiple regression, we're really coding it as 1 = female and 0 = not female (i.e., male). This gets complex when there are more than two nominal categories. In that case, we need to convert the multiple category variable to a *set* of dichotomous variables indicating presence versus absence of the categories. For example, if we were to use the ethnic group variable, we would have to code it into several dichotomous dummy variables such as *Euro-American* and *not Euro-American*, *African-American* and *not African-American*, and *Latino-American* and *not Latino-American*.

A condition that can be extremely problematic as well is **multicollinearity**, which can lead to misleading and/or inaccurate results. Multicollinearity (or collinearity) occurs when there are high intercorrelations among some set of the predictor variables. In other words, multicollinearity happens when two or more predictors contain much of the same information.

Although a correlation matrix indicating the intercorrelations among all pairs of predictors is helpful in determining whether multicollinearity is likely to be a problem, it will not always indicate that the condition exists. Multicollinearity may occur because several predictors, taken *together*, are related to some other predictors or set of predictors. For this reason, it is important to test for multicollinearity when doing multiple regression.

Assumptions of Multiple Linear Regression

There are many assumptions to consider, but we will focus on the major ones that are easily tested with SPSS. The assumptions for multiple regression include the following: that the relationship between each of the predictor variables and the dependent variable is linear and that the error, or residual, is normally distributed and uncorrelated with the predictors.

- Retrieve your data file: **hsbdataB.sav**.

Problem 6.1: Using the Simultaneous Method to Compute Multiple Regression

To reiterate, the purpose of multiple regression is to predict an interval (or scale) dependent variable from a combination of several interval/scale and/or dichotomous independent/predictor variables. In the following assignment, we will see if *math achievement* can be predicted better from a combination of several of our other variables, such as the *motivation scale, grades in high school*, and *mother's* and *father's education*. In Problems 6.1 and 6.3, we will run the multiple regression using alternate methods provided by SPSS. In Problem 6.1, we will assume that all seven of the predictor variables are important and that we want to see what is the highest possible multiple correlation of these variables with the dependent variable. For this purpose, we will use the method that SPSS calls **Enter** (often called **simultaneous regression**), which tells the computer to consider all the variables at the same time. In Problem 6.3, we will use the hierarchical method.

6.1. How well does the combination of *motivation, competence, pleasure, grades in high school, father's education, mother's education,* and *gender* predict *math achievement*?

In this problem, the computer will enter/consider all the variables into the model at the same time. Also, we will ask which of these seven predictors contribute significantly to the multiple correlation/regression.

It is a good idea to check the correlations among the predictor variables prior to running the multiple regression to determine if the predictors are correlated such that multicollinearity is highly likely to be a problem. This is especially important to do when one is using a relatively large set of predictors and/or if, for empirical or conceptual reasons, one believes that some or all of the predictors might be highly correlated. If variables are highly correlated (e.g., correlated at .50 or .60 and above), then one might decide to combine (aggregate) them into a composite variable or eliminate one or more of the highly correlated variables if the variables do not make a meaningful composite variable. For this example, we will check correlations between the variables to see if there might be multicollinearity problems. We typically also would create a scatterplot matrix to check the assumption of linear relationships of each predictor with the dependent variable and a scatterplot between the predictive equation and the residual to check for the assumption that these are uncorrelated. In this problem, we will not do so because we will show you how to do these assumption checks in Problem 6.2.

- Click on **Analyze → Correlate → Bivariate...** The **Bivariate Correlations** window will appear.

- Select the variables *motivation scale, competence scale, pleasure scale, grades in h.s., father's education, mother's education,* and *gender* and click them over to the **Variables** box.
- Click on **Options**. Under **Missing Values** click on **Exclude cases listwise.**
- Click on **Continue** and then click on **OK**. A correlation matrix like the one in Output 6.1a should appear.

Output 6.1a: Correlation Matrix

```
CORRELATIONS
  /VARIABLES=motivation competence pleasure grades faed maed gender
  /PRINT=TWOTAIL NOSIG
  /MISSING=LISTWISE.
```

Correlations

> High correlations among predictors indicate it is likely that there will be a problem with multicollinearity.

Correlations[a]

		motivation scale	competence scale	pleasure scale	grades in h.s.	father's education	mother's education	gender
motivation scale	Pearson Correlation	1	.517**	.277*	.020	.049	.115	-.178
	Sig. (2-tailed)		.000	.021	.872	.692	.347	.143
competence scale	Pearson Correlation	.517**	1	.413**	.216	.031	.234	-.037
	Sig. (2-tailed)	.000		.000	.075	.799	.053	.760
pleasure scale	Pearson Correlation	.277*	.413**	1	-.081	.020	.108	.084
	Sig. (2-tailed)	.021	.000		.509	.869	.378	.492
grades in h.s.	Pearson Correlation	.020	.216	-.081	1	.315**	.246*	.162
	Sig. (2-tailed)	.872	.075	.509		.008	.042	.182
father's education	Pearson Correlation	.049	.031	.020	.315**	1	.649**	-.266*
	Sig. (2-tailed)	.692	.799	.869	.008		.000	.027
mother's education	Pearson Correlation	.115	.234	.108	.246*	.649**	1	-.223
	Sig. (2-tailed)	.347	.053	.378	.042	.000		.065
gender	Pearson Correlation	-.178	-.037	.084	.162	-.266*	-.223	1
	Sig. (2-tailed)	.143	.760	.492	.182	.027	.065	

**. Correlation is significant at the 0.01 level (2-tailed).

*. Correlation is significant at the 0.05 level (2-tailed).

a. Listwise N=69

The correlation matrix indicates large correlations between *motivation* and *competence* and between *mother's education* and *father's education*. If predictor variables are highly correlated and conceptually related to one another, we would usually aggregate them, not only to reduce the likelihood of multicollinearity but also to reduce the number of predictors (which typically increases power). If predictor variables are highly correlated but conceptually are distinctly different (so aggregation does not seem appropriate), we might decide to eliminate the less important predictor before running the regression. However, if we have reasons for wanting to include both variables as separate predictors, we should run collinearity diagnostics to see if collinearity actually is a problem. For this problem, we also want to show how the collinearity problems created by these highly correlated predictors affect the Tolerance values and the significance of the beta coefficients, so we will run the regression without altering the variables. To run the regression, follow the steps below:

- Click on the following: **Analyze → Regression → Linear...** The **Linear Regression** window (Fig. 6.1) should appear.

- Select *math achievement* and click it over to the **Dependent** box (dependent variable).
- Next select the variables *motivation scale, competence scale, pleasure scale, grades in h.s., father's education, mother's education,* and *gender* and click them over to the **Independent(s)** box (independent variables).
- Under **Method**, be sure that **Enter** is selected.

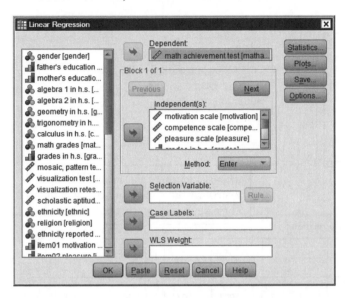

Fig. 6.1. Linear regression.

- Click on **Statistics,** click on **Estimates** (under **Regression Coefficients**), and click on **Model fit, Descriptives, Part and partial correlations**, and **Collinearity diagnostics** (see Fig. 6.2).

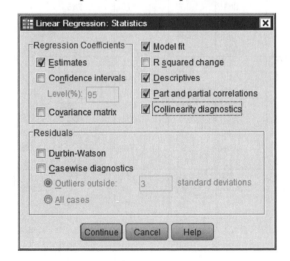

Fig. 6.2. Linear regression: Statistics.

- Click on **Continue**.
- Click on **OK**.

Compare your output and syntax to Output 6.1b.

Output 6.1b: Multiple Linear Regression, Method = Enter

```
REGRESSION
  /DESCRIPTIVES MEAN STDDEV CORR SIG N
  /MISSING LISTWISE
  /STATISTICS COEFF OUTS R ANOVA COLLIN TOL ZPP
  /CRITERIA=PIN(.05) POUT(.10)
  /NOORIGIN
```

```
/DEPENDENT mathach
/METHOD=ENTER motivatn competnc pleasure grades faed maed gend.
```

Regression

Descriptive Statistics

	Mean	Std. Deviation	N
math achievement test	12.7536	6.66293	69
motivation scale	2.8913	.62676	69
competence scale	3.3188	.62262	69
pleasure scale	3.1486	.60984	69
grades in h.s.	5.71	1.573	69
father's education	4.65	2.764	69
mother's education	4.07	2.185	69
gender	.54	.502	69

N is 69 because six participants have some missing data.

Correlations with *math achievement*.

This is a repeat of the correlation matrix we did earlier, indicating high correlations among some predictors.

Correlations

		math achievement test	motivation scale	competence scale	pleasure scale	grades in h.s.	father's education	mother's education	gender
Pearson Correlation	math achievement test	1.000	.256	.260	.085	.470	.416	.387	-.272
	motivation scale	.256	1.000	.517	.277	.020	.049	.115	-.178
	competence scale	.260	.517	1.000	.413	.216	.031	.234	-.037
	pleasure scale	.085	.277	.413	1.000	-.081	.020	.108	.084
	grades in h.s.	.470	.020	.216	-.081	1.000	.315	.246	.162
	father's education	.416	.049	.031	.020	.315	1.000	.649	-.266
	mother's education	.387	.115	.234	.108	.246	.649	1.000	-.223
	gender	-.272	-.178	-.037	.084	.162	-.266	-.223	1.000
Sig. (1-tailed)	math achievement test	.	.017	.015	.243	.000	.000	.001	.012
	motivation scale	.017	.	.000	.011	.436	.346	.173	.072
	competence scale	.015	.000	.	.000	.037	.400	.026	.380
	pleasure scale	.243	.011	.000	.	.254	.435	.189	.246
	grades in h.s.	.000	.436	.037	.254	.	.004	.021	.091
	father's education	.000	.346	.400	.435	.004	.	.000	.014
	mother's education	.001	.173	.026	.189	.021	.000	.	.032
	gender	.012	.072	.380	.246	.091	.014	.032	.
N	math achievement test	69	69	69	69	69	69	69	69
	motivation scale	69	69	69	69	69	69	69	69
	competence scale	69	69	69	69	69	69	69	69
	pleasure scale	69	69	69	69	69	69	69	69
	grades in h.s.	69	69	69	69	69	69	69	69
	father's education	69	69	69	69	69	69	69	69
	mother's education	69	69	69	69	69	69	69	69
	gender	69	69	69	69	69	69	69	69

Significance level of correlations with *math achievement*.

Variables Entered/Removed[b]

Model	Variables Entered	Variables Removed	Method
1	gender, competence scale, father's education, pleasure scale, grades in h.s., motivation scale, mother's education [a]	.	Enter

a. All requested variables entered.

b. Dependent Variable: math achievement test

Multiple correlation coefficient.

Indicates that 36% of the variance in the dependent variable can be predicted from the independent variables.

Model Summary

Model	R	R Square	Adjusted R Square	Std. Error of the Estimate
1	.653[a]	.426	.360	5.33030

a. Predictors: (Constant), gender, competence scale, father's education, pleasure scale, grades in h.s., motivation scale, mother's education

ANOVA[b]

Model		Sum of Squares	df	Mean Square	F	Sig.
1	Regression	1285.701	7	183.672	6.465	.000[a]
	Residual	1733.137	61	28.412		
	Total	3018.838	68			

a. Predictors: (Constant), gender, competence scale, father's education, pleasure scale, grades in h.s., motivation scale, mother's education

b. Dependent Variable: math achievement test

Indicates that the combination of these variables significantly ($p < .001$) predicts the dependent variable.

Coefficients[a]

Model		Unstandardized Coefficients		Standardized Coefficients	t	Sig.	Correlations			Collinearity Statistics	
		B	Std. Error	Beta			Zero-order	Partial	Part	Tolerance	VIF
1	(Constant)	-6.875	4.850		-1.418	.161					
	motivation scale	1.614	1.237	.152	1.305	.197	.256	.165	.127	.695	1.439
	competence scale	.122	1.388	.011	.088	.930	.260	.011	.008	.559	1.788
	pleasure scale	.912	1.215	.083	.750	.456	.085	.096	.073	.761	1.314
	grades in h.s.	1.901	.478	.449	3.975	.000	.470	.454	.386	.738	1.354
	father's education	.301	.332	.125	.907	.368	.416	.115	.088	.495	2.019
	mother's education	.327	.407	.107	.803	.425	.387	.102	.078	.528	1.893
	gender	-3.543	1.441	-.267	-2.459	.017	-.272	-.300	-.239	.797	1.254

a. Dependent Variable: math achievement test

Only *grades* and *gender* are significantly contributing to the equation. However, all of the variables need to be included to obtain this result, since the overall *F* value was computed with all the variables in the equation.

Grades and *gender* are also explain the most unique variance in math achievement. We can see this through the squaring the semi-partial correlations [i.e., *grades* = 21% ($.454^2$) and *gender* = 9% ($-.300^2$)].

Tolerance and VIF give the same information (Tolerance = 1/VIF). They tell us if there is multicollinearity. If the Tolerance value is low ($< 1-R^2$), then there is probably a problem with multicollinearity. In this case, since adjusted R^2 is .36, and $1-R^2$ is about .64, then tolerances are low for *competence* and *mother's* and *father's education*.

This gives you more information about collinearity in the model. Eigenvalues should be close to 1, variance proportions should be high for just one variable on each dimension, and Condition Indexes should be under 15 (15 – 30 is usually considered to indicate weak or possible collinearity; over 30 to indicate problematic collinearity). Low eigenvalues and high condition indexes can indicate collinearity difficulties, particularly when more than one variable has a large variance proportion for that dimension. In this example, none of the condition indexes is extremely high, but dimensions 4 – 8 have rather low eigenvalues, dimensions 6 – 8 have somewhat high condition indexes, and both father's education and mother's education primarily are explained by the same dimension. All of these suggest possible collinearity issues.

Collinearity Diagnostics[a]

Model	Dimension	Eigenvalue	Condition Index	Variance Proportions							
				(Constant)	motivation scale	competence scale	pleasure scale	grades in h.s.	father's education	mother's education	gender
1	1	7.043	1.000	.00	.00	.00	.00	.00	.00	.00	.00
	2	.550	3.578	.00	.00	.00	.00	.00	.04	.02	.48
	3	.211	5.773	.00	.02	.01	.01	.00	.18	.09	.32
	4	.086	9.038	.00	.00	.00	.00	.05	.47	.79	.01
	5	.055	11.303	.00	.02	.00	.07	.65	.21	.03	.07
	6	.027	16.146	.02	.62	.00	.40	.02	.01	.00	.10
	7	.015	21.602	.42	.08	.72	.00	.00	.07	.06	.01
	8	.013	23.538	.55	.26	.26	.52	.28	.02	.01	.00

a. Dependent Variable: math achievement test

Interpretation of Output 6.1

First, the output provides the usual descriptive statistics for all eight variables. Note that N is 69 because six participants are missing a score on one or more variables. Multiple regression uses only the participants who have complete data for all the variables. The next table is a correlation matrix similar to the one in Output 6.1a. Note that the first column shows the correlations of the other variables with *math achievement* and that *motivation, competence, grades in high school, father's education, mother's education*, and *gender* are all significantly correlated with *math achievement*. As we observed before, several of the predictor/independent variables are highly correlated with each other, that is, *competence* and *motivation* (.517) and *mother's education* and *father's education* (.649).

The **Model Summary** table shows that the multiple correlation coefficient (R), using all the predictors simultaneously, is .65 ($R^2 = .43$), and the **adjusted R^2** is .36, meaning that 36% of the variance in *math achievement* can be predicted from *gender, competence*, etc. combined. Note that the adjusted R^2 is lower than the unadjusted R^2. This is, in part, related to the number of variables in the equation. The adjustment is also affected by the magnitude of the effect and the sample size. Because so many independent variables were used, especially given difficulties with collinearity, a reduction in the number of variables might help us find an equation that explains more of the variance in the dependent variable. It is helpful to use the concept of parsimony with multiple regression and use the smallest number of predictors needed.

The **ANOVA** table shows that $F = 6.47$ and is significant. This indicates that the combination of the predictors significantly predict *math achievement*.

One of the most important tables is the **Coefficients** table. It indicates the **standardized beta coefficients**, which are interpreted similarly to correlation coefficients or factor weights (see Chapter 3). The t value and the **Sig** opposite each independent variable indicates whether that variable is significantly contributing to the equation for predicting *math achievement* from the whole set of predictors. Thus, *h.s. grades* and *gender*, in this example, are the only variables that are significantly adding anything to the prediction when the other five variables are already considered. It is important to note that all the variables are being considered together when these values are computed. Therefore, if you delete one of the predictors that is not significant, it can affect the size of the betas and levels of significance for other predictors. This is particularly true if high collinearity exists.

Another important aspect of the **Coefficients** table are the Correlations and, in this example of using Enter, the Partial correlations. These values, when they are squared, give us an indication of the amount of unique variance, or variance that is not explained by any of the other variables, each independent variable is explaining in the outcome variable (in this example, *math achievement*). In the output, we can see that *competence* explains the least amount of unique variance ($.011^2 < 1\%$) and *grades in high school* explains the most ($.454^2 = 21\%$).

Moreover, as the **Tolerances** in the **Coefficients** table suggest, and as we will see in Problem 6.2, these results are somewhat misleading. Although the two parent education measures were significantly correlated with *math achievement*, they did not contribute to the multiple regression predicting *math achievement*. What has happened here is that these two measures were also highly correlated with each other, and multiple regression eliminates all overlap between predictors. Thus, neither *father's education* nor *mother's education* had much to contribute when the other was also used as a predictor. Note that tolerance for each of these variables is $< .64$ ($1 - .36$), indicating that too much multicollinearity (overlap between predictors) exists. The same is true for *competence*, once *motivation* and *pleasure* are entered. One way to handle multicollinearity is to combine variables that are highly related if that makes conceptual sense. For example, you could make a new variable called *parents' education*, as we will for Problem 6.2.

Problem 6.2: Simultaneous Regression Correcting Multicollinearity

In Problem 6.2, we will use the combined/average of the two variables, *mother's education* and *father's education*, and then recompute the multiple regression after omitting *competence* and *pleasure*.

We combined *father's education* and *mother's education* because it makes conceptual sense and because these two variables are quite highly related ($r = .65$). We know that entering them as two separate variables created problems with multicollinearity because tolerance levels were low for these two variables, and, despite the fact that both variables were significantly and substantially correlated with *math achievement*, neither contributed significantly to predicting *math achievement* when taken together.

When it does not make sense to combine the highly correlated variables, one can eliminate one or more of them. Because the conceptual distinction between *motivation*, *competence*, and *pleasure* was important for us and because *motivation* was more important to us than *competence* or *pleasure*, we decided to delete the latter two scales from the analysis. We wanted to see if *motivation* would contribute to the prediction of *math achievement* if its contribution was not canceled out by *competence* and/or *pleasure*. *Motivation* and *competence* are so highly correlated that they create problems with multicollinearity. We eliminate *pleasure* as well, even though its tolerance is acceptable, because it is virtually uncorrelated with *math achievement*, the dependent variable, yet it is correlated with *motivation* and *competence* and because the **Collinearity Diagnostics** table indicates that it is contributing to the collinearity difficulties. Given its low correlation with *math achievement*, it is unlikely to contribute meaningfully to the prediction of *math achievement*, and its inclusion would serve only to reduce power and potentially reduce the predictive power of *motivation*. It would be particularly important to eliminate a variable such as *pleasure* if it were more strongly correlated with another predictor that remains in the equation, as this can lead to particularly misleading results.

6.2. Rerun Problem 6.1 using the *parents' education* variable (*pareduc*) instead of *faed* and *maed* and omitting the *competence* and *pleasure scales*.

First, we created a matrix scatterplot (as in Chapter 2) to see if the variables are related to each other in a linear fashion. You can use the syntax in Output 6.2 or use the **Analyze → Scatter** windows as shown below.

- Click on **Graphs → Legacy Dialogs → Scatter/Dot…**
- Select **Matrix Scatter** and click on **Define.**
- Move *math achievement, motivation, grades, parents' education*, and *gender* into the **Matrix Variables:** box.
- Click on **Options**. Check to be sure that **Exclude cases listwise** is selected.
- Click on **Continue** and then **OK**.

Then run the regression using the following steps:

- Click on the following: **Analyze → Regression → Linear...** The **Linear Regression** window (Fig. 6.1) should appear. This window may still have the variables moved over to the **Dependent** and **Independent(s)** boxes. If so, click on **Reset**.
- Move *math achievement* into the **Dependent** box.
- Next select the variables *motivation, grades in h.s., parents' education,* and *gender* and move them into the **Independent(s)** box (independent variables).
- Under **Method**, be sure that **Enter** is selected.

- Click on **Statistics,** click on **Estimates** (under **Regression Coefficients**), and click on **Model fit, Descriptives**, and **Collinearity diagnostics** (see Fig. 6.2).
- Click on **Continue**.

Then, we added a plot to the multiple regression to see the relationship of the predictors and the residual. To make this plot follow these steps:

- Click on **Plots…** (in Fig. 6.1 to get Fig. 6.3).

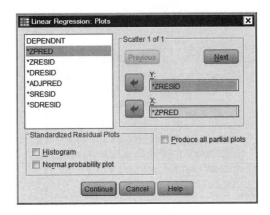

Fig. 6.3. **Linear regression: Plots.**

- Move **ZRESID** to the **Y:** box.
- Move **ZPRED** to the **X:** box. This enables us to check the assumption that the predictors and residual are uncorrelated.
- Click on **Continue**.
- Click on **OK**.

To make the residual plot easier to read, we added a reference line at 0. To do this, follow the steps below:

- Double click on the residual plot. The **Chart Editor** window will open.
- Click on **Options → Y Axis Reference Line**. The **Properties** window will appear.
- Highlight the number in the box next to **Position:** and type a **0**. We are telling SPSS that we want a reference line positioned at 0 on the Y axis.
- Click on **Apply** and then **Close**.
- Close the Chart Editor window.

Refer to Output 6.2 for comparison.

Output 6.2: Multiple Linear Regression with Parents' Education, Method = Enter

```
GRAPH
  /SCATTERPLOT(MATRIX)=mathach motivation grades parEduc gender
  /MISSING=LISTWISE .

REGRESSION
  /DESCRIPTIVES MEAN STDDEV CORR SIG N
  /MISSING LISTWISE
  /STATISTICS COEFF OUTS R ANOVA COLLIN TOL ZPP
  /CRITERIA=PIN(.05) POUT(.10)
  /NOORIGIN
  /DEPENDENT mathach
  /METHOD=ENTER motivation grades parEduc gender
  /SCATTERPLOT=(*ZRESID , *ZPRED) .
```

Graph

> The top row shows four scatterplots (relationships) of the dependent variables with each of the predictors. To meet the assumption of linearity, a straight line, as opposed to a curved line, should fit the points relatively well.

> Dichotomous variables have two columns (or rows) of data points. If the data points bunch up near the top of the left column and the bottom of the right, the correlation will be negative (and vice versa). Linearity would be violated if the data points bunch at the center of one column and at the ends of the other column.

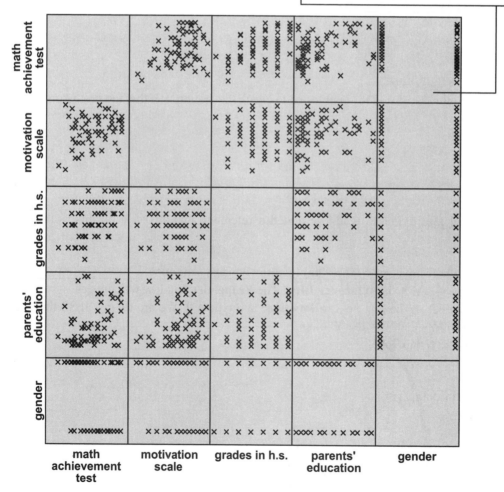

Regression

Descriptive Statistics

	Mean	Std. Deviation	N
math achievement test	12.6028	6.75676	73
motivation scale	2.8744	.63815	73
grades in h.s.	5.68	1.589	73
parents' education	4.3836	2.30266	73
gender	.55	.501	73

Note that $N = 73$, indicating that eliminating competence and pleasure reduced the amount of missing data.

Note that all the predictors are significantly related to *math achievement*. Multiply Sig by 2 to get the two-tailed significance level.

None of the relationships among predictors is greater than .25.

Correlations

		math achievement test	motivation scale	grades in h.s.	parents' education	gender
Pearson Correlation	math achievement test	1.000	.316	.504	.394	-.303
	motivation scale	.316	1.000	.084	.090	-.209
	grades in h.s.	.504	.084	1.000	.250	.115
	parents' education	.394	.090	.250	1.000	-.227
	gender	-.303	-.209	.115	-.227	1.000
Sig. (1-tailed)	math achievement test	.	.003	.000	.000	.005
	motivation scale	.003	.	.241	.225	.038
	grades in h.s.	.000	.241	.	.016	.166
	parents' education	.000	.225	.016	.	.027
	gender	.005	.038	.166	.027	.
N	math achievement test	73	73	73	73	73
	motivation scale	73	73	73	73	73
	grades in h.s.	73	73	73	73	73
	parents' education	73	73	73	73	73
	gender	73	73	73	73	73

Variables Entered/Removed[b]

Model	Variables Entered	Variables Removed	Method
1	gender, grades in h.s., motivation scale, parents' education[a]	.	Enter

This indicates we used simultaneous regression in this problem.

a. All requested variables entered.

b. Dependent Variable: math achievement test

Model Summary[b]

Model	R	R Square	Adjusted R Square	Std. Error of the Estimate
1	.678[a]	.459	.427	5.11249

The adjusted R square indicates that we have a fairly good model, explaining about 43% of the variance in *math achievement*.

a. Predictors: (Constant), gender, grades in h.s., motivation scale, parents' education

b. Dependent Variable: math achievement test

ANOVA[b]

Model		Sum of Squares	df	Mean Square	F	Sig.
1	Regression	1509.723	4	377.431	14.440	.000[a]
	Residual	1777.353	68	26.138		
	Total	3287.076	72			

Our model significantly predicts *math achievement*.

a. Predictors: (Constant), gender, grades in h.s., motivation scale, parents' education

b. Dependent Variable: math achievement test

Coefficients[a]

Model		Unstandardized Coefficients		Standardized Coefficients	t	Sig.	Collinearity Statistics	
		B	Std. Error	Beta			Tolerance	VIF
1	(Constant)	-5.444	3.605		-1.510	.136		
	motivation scale	2.148	.972	.203	2.211	.030	.944	1.059
	grades in h.s.	1.991	.400	.468	4.972	.000	.897	1.115
	parents' education	.580	.280	.198	2.070	.042	.871	1.148
	gender	-3.631	1.284	-.269	-2.828	.006	.877	1.141

a. Dependent Variable: math achievement test

Here are the values to check for multicollinearity. Note that all tolerances are well over .57 $(1-R^2)$.

Collinearity Diagnostics[a]

Model	Dimension	Eigenvalue	Condition Index	Variance Proportions				
				(Constant)	motivation scale	grades in h.s.	parents' education	gender
1	1	4.337	1.000	.00	.00	.00	.01	.01
	2	.457	3.082	.00	.00	.00	.07	.68
	3	.135	5.665	.02	.07	.02	.85	.17
	4	.052	9.120	.01	.20	.87	.06	.06
	5	.019	15.251	.97	.73	.11	.01	.08

a. Dependent Variable: math achievement test

Casewise Diagnostics[a]

Case Number	Std. Residual	math achievement test
63	-3.174	1.00

a. Dependent Variable: math achievement test

Residuals Statistics[a]

	Minimum	Maximum	Mean	Std. Deviation	N
Predicted Value	1.5029	22.2180	12.6028	4.57912	73
Residual	-16.2254	10.3169	.0000	4.96845	73
Std. Predicted Value	-2.424	2.100	.000	1.000	73
Std. Residual	-3.174	2.018	.000	.972	73

a. Dependent Variable: math achievement test

Charts

Because the dots are scattered, it indicates the data meet the assumptions of the errors being normally distributed and the variances of the residuals being constant.

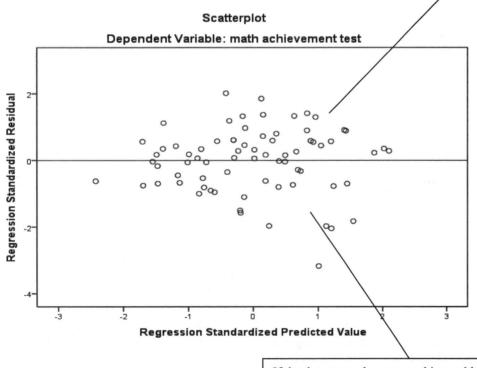

Scatterplot

Dependent Variable: math achievement test

If the dots created a pattern, this would indicate the residuals are not normally distributed, the residual is correlated with the independent variables, and/or the variances of the residuals are not constant.

Interpretation of Output 6.2
This output begins with the **scatterplot matrix**, which shows that the independent variables are generally linearly related to the dependent variable of *math achievement*, meeting this assumption. One should check the matrix scatterplots to see if there are curvilinear relationships between any of the variables; in this example, there are none. If the variables had not met this assumption, we could have transformed them, aggregated some, and/or eliminated some independent variables. (See Chapter 2 for how to do transformations.) There are also only low to moderate relationships among the predictor variables in the **Correlations** table. This is good. The other assumptions are checked in the **residual scatterplot** at the end of the output, which indicates that the errors are normally distributed, the variances of the residuals are constant, and the residual is relatively uncorrelated with the linear combination of predictors.

The next important part of the output to check is the **Tolerance** and VIF values in the **Coefficients** table for the existence of multicollinearity. In this example, we do not need to worry about multicollinearity because the Tolerance values are close to 1.

The **Model Summary** table gives the *R* (.68) and **Adjusted *R* square** (.43). Thus, this model is predicting 43% of the variance in *math achievement*. If we want to compare this model to that in Problem 6.1, we use the Adjusted *R* square to see which model is explaining more of the variance in the dependent variable. Interestingly, this model is predicting more of the variance in *math achievement* than the model in Problem 6.1, despite using fewer predictors.

As can be seen from the **ANOVA** table, the model of *motivation, grades in h.s., parents' education*, and *gender* significantly predicts *math achievement*, $F(4, 68) = 14.44$, $p < .001$.

We can see from the **Coefficients** table that now <u>all</u> of the predictors are significantly contributing to the equation (see the **Sig.** column) and each of the variables has increased the amount of unique variance that it is explaining.

Example of How to Write About Output 6.2
Results
    Multiple regression was conducted to determine the best linear combination of gender, grades in h.s., parents' education, and motivation for predicting math achievement test scores. (Assumptions of linearity, normally distributed errors, and uncorrelated errors were checked and met.) The means, standard deviations, and intercorrelations can be found in Table 6.1. This combination of variables significantly predicted math achievement, $F(4,68) = 14.44$, $p < .001$, with all four variables significantly contributing to the prediction. The adjusted R squared value was .43. This indicates that 43% of the variance in math achievement was explained by the model. According to Cohen (1988), this is a large effect. The beta weights, presented in Table 6.2, suggest that good grades in high school contributes most to predicting math achievement and that being male, having high math motivation, and having parents who are more highly educated also contribute to this prediction.

Table 6.1

Means, Standard Deviations, and Intercorrelations for Math Achievement and Predictor Variables (N = 73)

Variable	M	SD	1	2	3	4
Math Achievement	12.60	6.76	.32**	.50**	.39**	−.30**
Predictor variable						
1. Motivation scale	2.87	.64	-	.08	.09	−.21*
2. Grades in h.s.	5.68	1.59		-	.25*	.12
3. Parents' education	4.38	2.30			-	−.23*
4. Gender	.55	.50				-

*p < .05; **p < .01.

Table 6.2

Simultaneous Multiple Regression Analysis Summary for Motivation, Grades in High School, Parents' Education, and Gender Predicting Math Achievement (N = 73)

Variable	B	SEB	β
Motivation scale	2.15	.97	.20*
Grades in h.s.	1.99	.40	.47**
Parents' education	.58	.28	.20*
Gender	−3.63	1.2□	−.27**
Constant	−5.4□	3.61	

Note. $R^2 = .46$; $F(4,68) = 14.44$, $p < .001$
*p < .05; **p < .01.*

Problem 6.3: Hierarchical Multiple Linear Regression

In Problem 6.3, we will use the **hierarchical** approach, which is used when you want to enter the variables in a series of blocks or groups. This enables the researcher to see if each new group of variables adds anything to the prediction produced by the previous blocks of variables. This approach is an appropriate method to use when the researcher has a priori ideas about how the predictors go together to predict the dependent variable. In our example, we will enter *gender* first and then see if *motivation*, *grades in h.s.*, *parents' education*, and *math courses taken* make an additional contribution. This method is intended to control for or eliminate the effects of *gender* on the prediction.

6.3 If we control for *gender* differences in *math achievement*, do any of the other variables significantly add anything to the prediction over and above what *gender* contributes?

We will include all of the variables from the previous problem; however, this time we include *math courses taken*, and we will enter the variables in two separate blocks to see how *motivation, grades in high school, parents' education,* and *math courses taken* improve on prediction from *gender* alone.

- Click on the following: **Analyze → Regression → Linear...**
- Click on **Reset**.
- Select *math achievement* and click it over to the **Dependent** box (dependent variable).
- Next, select *gender* and move it over to the **Independent(s)** box (independent variables).
- Select **Enter** as your **Method** (see Fig. 6.4).

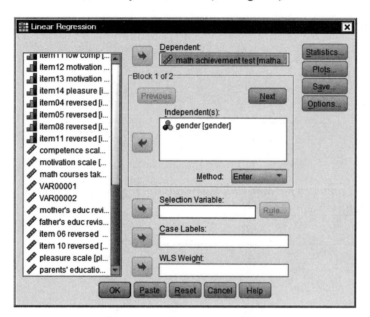

Fig. 6.4. Linear regression.

- Click on **Next** beside **Block 1 of 1.** You will notice it changes to **Block 2 of 2**.
- Then move *motivation scale, grades in h.s., parents' education,* and *math courses taken* to the **Independent(s)** box (independent variables).
- Under **Method**, select **Enter**. The window should look like Fig. 6.5.

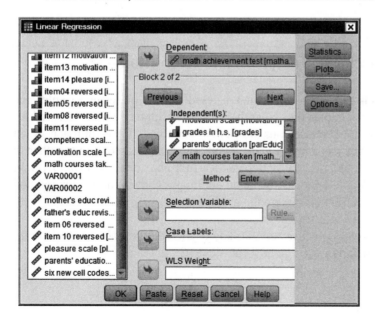

Fig. 6.5. Hierarchical regression.

- Click on **Statistics,** click on **Estimates** (under **Regression Coefficients**), and click on **Model fit** and *R* **squared change** (See Fig. 6.2.).
- Click on **Continue**.
- Click on **OK**.

Compare your output and syntax to Output 6.3.

Output 6.3: Hierarchical Multiple Linear Regression

```
REGRESSION
  /MISSING LISTWISE
  /STATISTICS COEFF OUTS R ANOVA CHANGE
  /CRITERIA=PIN(.05) POUT(.10)
  /NOORIGIN
  /DEPENDENT mathach
  /METHOD=ENTER gender
  /METHOD=ENTER motivation grades parEduc mathcrs.
```

Regression

Variables Entered/Removed[b]

Model	Variables Entered	Variables Removed	Method
1	gender[a]	.	Enter
2	grades in h.s., motivation scale, parents' education, math courses taken	.	Enter

In the first column of this table there are two models (1 and 2). This indicates that first we tested a model with *gender* as a predictor, and then we added the other predictors and tested that model (Model 2).

a. All requested variables entered.

b. Dependent Variable: math achievement test

Footnotes provide you with relevant information.

Model Summary

Model	R	R Square	Adjusted R Square	Std. Error of the Estimate	Change Statistics R Square Change	F Change	df1	df2	Sig. F Change
1	.303[a]	.092	.079	6.48514	.092	7.158	1	71	.009
2	.809[b]	.654	.628	4.12003	.562	27.228	4	67	.000

a. Predictors: (Constant), gender

b. Predictors: (Constant), gender, grades in h.s., motivation scale, parents' education, math courses taken

The Model Summary output shows there were two models run: Model 1 (in the first row) and Model 2 (in the second row). It also shows that the addition of *grades, motivation, parents' education,* and *math courses taken* significantly improved on the prediction by *gender* alone, explaining about 55% additional variance.

ANOVA^c

Model		Sum of Squares	df	Mean Square	F	Sig.
1	Regression	301.026	1	301.026	7.158	.009^a
	Residual	2986.050	71	42.057		
	Total	3287.076	72			
2	Regression	2149.773	5	429.955	25.329	.000^b
	Residual	1137.303	67	16.975		
	Total	3287.076	72			

a. Predictors: (Constant), gender

b. Predictors: (Constant), gender, grades in h.s., motivation scale, parents' education, math courses taken

c. Dependent Variable: math achievement test

> Note that now gender is no longer a significant predictor of math achievement; the only significant predictor is *math courses taken.*

Coefficients^a

Model		Unstandardized Coefficients		Standardized Coefficients	t	Sig.
		B	Std. Error	Beta		
1	(Constant)	14.838	1.129		13.144	.000
	gender	-4.080	1.525	-.303	-2.675	.009
2	(Constant)	2.042	3.151		.648	.519
	gender	-1.042	1.117	-.077	-.933	.354
	motivation scale	.914	.808	.086	1.131	.262
	grades in h.s.	.418	.412	.098	1.014	.314
	parents' education	.066	.241	.023	.276	.784
	math courses taken	2.749	.448	.681	6.141	.000

a. Dependent Variable: math achievement test

Excluded Variables^b

Model		Beta In	t	Sig.	Partial Correlation	Collinearity Statistics Tolerance
1	motivation scale	.264^a	2.358	.021	.271	.956
	grades in h.s.	.546^a	5.784	.000	.569	.987
	parents' education	.343^a	3.132	.003	.351	.949
	math courses taken	.782^a	10.392	.000	.779	.902

a. Predictors in the Model: (Constant), gender

b. Dependent Variable: math achievement test

Interpretation of Output 6.3

We rechecked the assumptions for this problem, since we added the variable *math courses taken*. All the assumptions were met.

The **Descriptives** and **Correlations** tables would have been the same (except for the addition of the variable *math courses taken*) as those in Problem 6.2 if we had checked the Descriptive box in the Statistics window.

The other tables in this output are somewhat different than the previous two outputs. This difference is because we entered the variables in two steps. Therefore, this output has two models listed, Model 1 and Model 2. The information in Model 1 is for *gender* predicting *math achievement*. The information in Model 2 is *gender* plus *motivation, grades in h.s., parents' education,* and *math courses taken* predicting *math achievement*.

In the **Model Summary** table, we have three new and important pieces of information: R^2 **change**, *F* **change**, and **Sig. F change**. The R^2 **change** tells you how much the R^2 *increases* when you add the new predictors entered in the second step (Model 2). The **F change**, and **Sig. F change** tell you whether this change is statistically significant, i.e., that the additional variables significantly improved on the first model that had only gender as a predictor. In this case, the change is significant, $F(4,67) = 27.23$, $p < .001$. This test is based on the unadjusted R^2, which does not adjust for the fact that there are more predictors, so it is also useful to compare the adjusted R^2 for each model, to see if it increases even after the correction for more predictors. The adjusted R^2 also suggests that Model 2 is better than Model 1 given the large increase in the adjusted R^2 value from $R^2 = .08$ to $R^2 = .63$. Furthermore, as we will see in the next table, Model 2 is highly significant. However, this in itself does not show you that the new model significantly *improved* on the prior model. It is quite possible for the second model to be significant without its improving to a significant degree on the prior model.

We can see from the **ANOVA** table that when *gender* is entered by itself it is a significant predictor of *math achievement*, $F(1,71) = 7.16$, $p = .009$; however, when the other predictors are entered, gender is no longer a significant predictor of *math achievement*. This means that boy's apparent superiority over girls in math achievement could be completely explained by the other predictors. In the final model, only *math courses taken* significantly predicts *math achievement* $p < .001$, and the overall model with the addition of the other predictor variables is significant as well $F(5,67) = 25.33$, $p < .001$. If one wants to make comparisons among predictors to see how much each is contributing to the prediction of the dependent variable, it is best to look at the **Standardized Coefficients** (beta weights), especially when variables are on very different scales, as in this example in which gender, a dichotomous variable, is included. On the other hand, the **Unstandardized Coefficients** give you a better understanding of how the variables, as measured, are weighted to best predict the outcome.

Included in the **Excluded Variables** table are the **Partial Correlations**. As noted in the previous example, these values, when they are squared, give us an indication of the amount of unique variance, or variance that is not explained by any of the other variables, each independent variable is explaining in the outcome variable (in this example, *math achievement*). In the output, we can see that *motivation* explains the least amount of unique variance ($.271^2 = 7\%$) and *math courses taken* explains the most ($.779^2 = 61\%$).

Example of How to Write About Output 6.3
Results

To investigate how well grades in high school, motivation, parents' education, and math courses taken predict math achievement test scores, after controlling for gender, a hierarchical linear regression was computed. (The assumptions of linearity, normally distributed errors, and uncorrelated errors were checked and met.) Means and standard deviations are presented in Table 6.1. When gender was entered alone, it significantly predicted math achievement, $F(1,71) = 7.16$, $p = .009$, adjusted $R^2 = .08$. However, as indicated by the R^2, only 8% of the variance in math achievement could be predicted by knowing the student's gender. When the other variables were added, they significantly improved the prediction, R^2 change = .56, $F(4,67) = 27.23$, $p < .001$, and gender no longer was a significant predictor. The entire group of variables significantly predicted math achievement, $F(5,67) = 25.33$, $p < .001$, adjusted $R^2 = .63$. This is a large effect according to Cohen (1988). The beta weights and significance values, presented in Table 6.3, indicates which variable(s) contributes most to predicting math achievement, when gender, motivation, parents' education, and grades in high school are entered together as predictors. With this combination of predictors, math course taken has the highest beta (.68), and is the only variable that contributes significantly to predicting math achievement.

Table 6.3

Hierarchical Multiple Regression Analysis Summary Predicting Math Achievement from Motivation, Demographic Variables, and Math Courses Taken, When Controlling for Gender (N = 73).

Variable	B	SEB	β	R^2	ΔR^2
Step 1				.09	.09
Gender	−4.08	1.53	−.30*		
Constant	14.84	1.13			
Step 2				.65	.56
Gender	−1.04	1.12	-.08		
Grades in h.s.	.42	.41	.10		
Parents' ☐ ☐ ☐ education	.07	.24	.02		
Motivation scale	.914	.81	.09		
Math courses taken	2.75	.45	.68**		
Constant	2.04	3.15			

*$p < .05$; **$p < .01$.

Interpretation Questions

6.1   In Output 6.1: (a) What information suggests that we might have a problem of collinearity? (b) How does multicollinearity affect results? (c) What is the adjusted R^2 and what does it mean?

6.2   Using Output 6.2: (a) How does combining (aggregating) *mother's education* and *father's education* and eliminating *competence* and *pleasure scales* change the results from those in Output 6.1? (b) Why did we aggregate *mother's education* and *father's education*? (c) Why did we eliminate the *competence* and *pleasure scales*?

6.3   In Output 6.3: (a) Compare the adjusted R^2 for Model 1 and Model 2. What does this tell you? (b) Why would one enter *gender* first? (c) How did entering the additional variables change our interpretation of the significant effect of gender when it alone was entered? (d) Compare the results of Output 6.2 and Output 6.3. How did findings change for *grades in high school*, *parents' education*, and *motivation* change when you also enter *math courses taken*?

Extra SPSS Problems

6.1   Open the **World95.sav** data file. You will use this data set for Extra SPSS Problems 6.1–6.3. Using People living in cities (*urban*), People who read (*literacy*), Infant mortality (*babymort*), Gross domestic product (*gdp_cap),* AIDS cases *(aids),* and daily calorie intake (*calories)* as independent variables and Average male life expectancy (*lifeexpm*) as the dependent variable, conduct a linear regression.
   a. Is the regression significant?
   b. What is the Adjusted R Square?
   c. Is multicollinearity an issue for this analysis, according to the criteria we have been using? Are tolerances high? What does this imply?
   d. Which variables are weighted most highly in the regression equation? Which betas are significant?

6.2   Rerun the analysis from Extra SPSS Problem 6.1, but this time omit *babymort* as a predictor.
   a. Is the regression significant?
   b. What is the Adjusted R Square?
   c. Is multicollinearity an issue for this analysis, according to the criteria we have been using? Are tolerances high? How have tolerances and multicollinearity been affected by leaving out *babymort*?
   d. Which variables are weighted most highly in the regression equation? Which betas are significant?

6.3.   Run a hierarchical regression, using Average female life expectancy (*lifeexpf*) as the dependent variable, entering Average male life expectancy (*lifeexpm*) as the first block and then the same predictors from Extra SPSS Problem 6.2 for the second block. Be sure to check R square change under statistics.
   a. Is the regression significant?
   b. What is the Adjusted R Square?
   c. Is multicollinearity an issue for this analysis, according to the criteria we have been using? Are tolerances high? How have tolerances and multicollinearity been affected by including *lifeexpm* as a predictor?

d. Which variables are weighted most highly in the regression equation? Which betas are significant? Do any variables predict *lifeexpf* after *lifeexpm* is taken into account? Which variables might you want to eliminate from the equation? Why?

6.4. Open the 1991 U.S. General Social Survey.sav data file. Run a hierarchical regression, using Highest year of school completed (*educ*) as the dependent variable, entering Highest year school completed, father (*paeduc*) and Highest year school completed, mother (*maeduc*) as the first block, and then Number of brothers and sisters (*sibs*), Number of children (*childs*), and Age of respondent (*age*) for the second block. Be sure to check *R* square change under statistics.

   a. Is the regression significant?
   b. What is the Adjusted *R* Square?
   c. Is multicollinearity an issue for this analysis, according to the criteria we have been using? Are tolerances high? How have tolerances and multicollinearity been affected by including *sibs, child,* and *age* as a predictors?
   d. Which variables are weighted most highly in the regression equation? Which betas are significant? Do any variables predict *educ* after *paeduc* and *maeduc* are taken into account? Are there any variables that you might want to eliminate from the equation? Why?

CHAPTER 7
Logistic Regression and Discriminant Analysis

Logistic regression and discriminant analysis, like multiple regression, are useful when you want to predict an outcome or dependent variable from a set of predictor variables. They are similar to a linear regression in many ways. However, logistic regression and discriminant analysis are more appropriate when the dependent variable is categorical. Logistic regression is useful because it does not rely on some of the assumptions on which multiple regression and discriminant analysis are based. As with other forms of regression, multicollinearity (high correlations among the predictors) can lead to problems for both logistic and discriminant analysis.

Logistic regression is helpful when you want to predict a categorical variable from a set of predictor variables. **Binary logistic regression** is similar to linear regression except that it is used when the dependent variable is dichotomous. **Multinomial logistic regression** is used when the dependent/outcome variable has more than two categories, but that is complex and less common so we will not discuss it here. Logistic regression also is useful when some or all of the independent variables are dichotomous; others can be continuous.

Discriminant analysis, on the other hand, is most useful when you have several continuous independent variables and, as in logistic regression, an outcome or dependent variable that is categorical. The dependent variable can have more than two categories. If so, then more than one discriminant function will be generated (number of functions = number of levels of the dependent variable minus 1). For the sake of simplicity, we will limit our discussion to the case of a dichotomous dependent variable here. Discriminant analysis is useful when you want to build a predictive model of group membership based on several observed characteristics of each participant. Discriminant analysis creates a linear combination of the predictor variables that provides the best discrimination between the groups.

Assumptions of Logistic Regression
Logistic regression, unlike multiple regression and discriminant analysis, has very few assumptions, which is one reason this technique has become popular, especially in health-related fields. There are no distributional assumptions; however, observations must be independent and independent variables must be linearly related to the logit (natural log of the odds ratio) of the dependent variable.

Conditions of Logistic Regression
Conditions for binary logistic regression include that the dependent or outcome variable needs to be dichotomous and, like most other statistics, that the outcomes are mutually exclusive; that is, a single case can be represented only once and must be in one group or the other. Finally, logistic regression requires large samples to be accurate: Some say there should be a minimum of 20 cases per predictor, with a minimum of 60 total cases. These requirements need to be satisfied prior to doing statistical analysis with SPSS. As with multiple regression, multicollinearity is a potential source of confusing or misleading results and needs to be assessed.

Assumptions and Conditions of Discriminant Analysis
The assumptions of discriminant analysis include that the relationships between all pairs of predictors must be linear, multivariate normality must exist within groups, and the population covariance matrices for predictor variables must be equal across groups. A linear relationship between all pairs of predictors and homogeneity of variance-covariance matrices can be diagnosed through a matrix scatterplot. Discriminant analysis is, however, fairly robust to these assumptions, although violations of multivariate normality may affect accuracy of estimates of the probability of correct classification. If multivariate nonnormality is suspected, then logistic regression should be used.

Multicollinearity is again an issue with which you need to be concerned. It is also important that the sample size of the smallest group (35 in Problem 7.3) exceed the number of predictor variables in the model (there are four in Problem 7.3, so this assumption is met). The linearity assumption as well as the assumption of homogeneity of variance-covariance matrices can be tested, as we did for multiple regression in Chapter 6, by examining a matrix scatterplot. If the spreads of the scatterplots are roughly equal, then the assumption of homogeneity of variance-covariance matrices can be assumed. This assumption can also be tested with Box's M.

In Problems 7.1 and 7.2, we will use logistic regression to predict a dichotomous outcome (whether students will take *algebra 2*) from continuous and dichotomous predictors. In Problem 7.1, we will enter all four predictors simultaneously into the equation. This is similar to the first multiple regression problem in Chapter 6. In Problem 7.2, we use a hierarchical approach, in which blocks of variables are entered sequentially. In Problem 7.3, we will use discriminant analysis to do the same problem that we did with logistic regression in Problem 7.1 in order to compare the two techniques.

- Get your **hsbdataB** data file.

Problem 7.1: Logistic Regression

7.1. Is there a combination of *gender*, *parents' education*, *mosaic*, and *visualization test* that predicts whether students will take *algebra 2*?

Let's try a logistic regression to predict a dichotomous (two category) dependent variable when the independent variables (called covariates in SPSS) are either dichotomous or normal/scale.

First, we should check for multicollinearity. Because tolerance and VIF scores are not available through the logistic regression command, one way to compute these values is through the linear regression command, using *algebra 2* as the dependent variable and *gender, mosaic, visualization test*, and *parents' education* as independent variables. If you did this, you would find that the tolerance statistics are all above .87, with an adjusted R^2 of .253, so there is little multicollinearity. (See Chapter 6 for how to do this.)

Use these commands to compute the logistic regression:
- **Analyze → Regression → Binary Logistic** to get to Fig. 7.1.
- Move *algebra 2 in h.s.* into the **Dependent** variable box.
- Move *gender, mosaic, visualization test,* and *parents' education* into the **Covariates** box.
- Make sure **Enter** is the selected **Method**. (This enters all the variables in the covariates box into the logistic regression equation simultaneously.)
- Click on **Options** to produce Fig. 7.2.

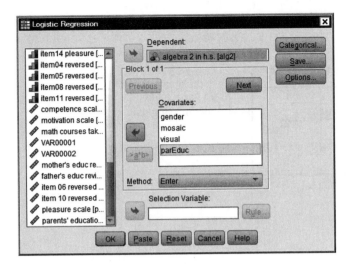

Fig. 7.1. Logistic regression.

- Check **CI for exp(B),** and be sure **95** is in the box (which will provide confidence intervals for the odds ratio of each predictor's contribution to the equation).
- Click on **Continue**.

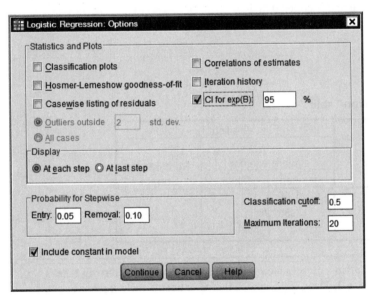

Fig. 7.2. Logistic regression: Options.

- Click on **OK**. Does your output look like Output 7.1?

Output 7.1: Logistic Regression, Method = Enter

```
LOGISTIC REGRESSION VARIABLES alg2
  /METHOD=ENTER gender mosaic visual parEduc
  /PRINT=CI(95)
  /CRITERIA=PIN(0.05) POUT(0.10) ITERATE(20) CUT(0.5).
```

Case Processing Summary

Unweighted Cases[a]		N	Percent
Selected Cases	Included in Analysis	75	100.0
	Missing Cases	0	.0
	Total	75	100.0
Unselected Cases		0	.0
Total		75	100.0

No participants have missing data.

a. If weight is in effect, see classification table for the total number of cases.

Dependent Variable Encoding

Original Value	Internal Value
not taken	0
taken	1

Algebra 2 is the dependent outcome variable and is coded 0 or 1.

Block 0: Beginning Block

Classification Table[a,b]

			Predicted		
			algebra 2 in h.s.		Percentage
Observed			not taken	taken	Correct
Step 0	algebra 2 in h.s.	not taken	40	0	100.0
		taken	35	0	.0
	Overall Percentage				53.3

a. Constant is included in the model.

b. The cut value is .500

40 students didn't take *algebra 2* and 35 did. 53% did not take algebra 2. Thus, if one stated that no students took *algebra 2*, one would correct 53.3% of the time.

Variables in the Equation

		B	S.E.	Wald	df	Sig.	Exp(B)
Step 0	Constant	-.134	.231	.333	1	.564	.875

Only the constant is in the equation.

Gender, *visual*, and *parents' education* are each separately significantly related to *algebra 2*.

Variables not in the Equation

			Score	df	Sig.
Step 0	Variables	GENDER	5.696	1	.017
		MOSAIC	.480	1	.488
		VISUAL	10.339	1	.001
		PAREDUC	12.559	1	.000
	Overall Statistics		22.031	4	.000

Block 1: Method=Enter

Omnibus Tests of Model Coefficients

		Chi-square	df	Sig.
Step 1	Step	24.231	4	.000
	Block	24.231	4	.000
	Model	24.231	4	.000

The overall model is significant when all four independent variables are entered.

Model Summary

Step	-2 Log likelihood	Cox & Snell R Square	Nagelkerke R Square
1	79.407	.276	.369

These are similar to R^2 and give a rough estimate of the variance that can be predicted from the combination of the four variables.

Note that 33/40 (83%) of those who didn't take *algebra 2* were predicted correctly with this model, but 71% of those who did were predicted correctly.

Classification Table[a]

			Predicted		
			algebra 2 in h.s.		Percentage Correct
	Observed		not taken	taken	
Step 1	algebra 2 in h.s.	not taken	33	7	82.5
		taken	10	25	71.4
	Overall Percentage				77.3

a. The cut value is .500

> *Parents' education* and *visualization*, but not *gender*, are significant predictors when all four variables are considered together, even though gender was a significant predictor when used alone. This suggests that even though tolerances were acceptable, there was sufficient correlation between some set of predictors and *gender* to keep *gender* from making a significant contribution once the other predictors were included. *Mosaic* fails to predict *algebra2* whether used alone or with the other predictors. Furthermore, because the CI's are very close to 1, this indicates that these may not be significant.

Variables in the Equation

		B	S.E.	Wald	df	Sig.	Exp(B)	95.0% C.I.for EXP(B) Lower	Upper
Step 1ᵃ	GENDER	-.497	.577	.742	1	.389	.609	.197	1.884
	MOSAIC	-.030	.031	.892	1	.345	.971	.913	1.032
	VISUAL	.190	.075	6.428	1	.011	1.209	1.044	1.400
	PAREDUC	.380	.131	8.418	1	.004	1.462	1.131	1.889
	Constant	-1.736	1.159	2.243	1	.134	.176		

a. Variable(s) entered on step 1: GENDER, MOSAIC, VISUAL, PAREDUC.

Interpretation of Output 7.1

There are three main parts to this output. First, two tables provide descriptive information (see callout boxes). Next, there are three tables in **Block 0** that provide information about the baseline situation, when only the constant is in the equation or model. That is, how well can we predict *algebra 2* without using *gender, parents' education, mosaic,* or *visualization test,* if we predicted that all the students would *not take algebra 2*? The last section of four tables is below **Block 1.** They show the results when the four predictors are entered simultaneously.

The first table under **Block 0**, the initial **Classification Table**, shows the percentage of correct predictions (53%) if all of the students were predicted to be in the larger (*algebra 2 not taken*) group. The first **Variables in the Equation** table shows that if you predicted that all students would not take *algebra 2*, the odds of successful prediction would *not* be significantly different from 50–50 (i.e., no better than chance).

The **Variables not in the Equation** table shows that three of the four variables (*gender, parents' education,* and *visualization test*) are, individually, significant predictors of whether a student would take *algebra 2* or not. *Mosaic* is not a significant predictor.

Logistic regression in SPSS provides several ways to interpret the results of using these four variables (*gender, parents' education, mosaic,* and *visualization test*) as predictors of whether students took *algebra 2*. The last four tables in Output 7.1 show these several ways. The **Omnibus Tests of Model Coefficients** table indicates that, when we consider all four predictors together, the **Model** or equation is significant ($\chi^2 = 24.23$, $df = 4$, $N = 75$, $p < .001$).

The **Model Summary** table includes two different ways of estimating R^2 (percent of variance accounted for) as was done in multiple regression. These "pseudo" R^2 estimates (.28 and .37) indicate that approximately 28% or 37% of the variance in whether students took *algebra 2* can be predicted from the linear combination of the four independent variables. The Cox & Snell R^2 (28%) is usually an underestimate.

The final **Classification Table** indicates how well the combination of variables predicts *algebra 2*. In this problem we have tried to predict, from four other variables, whether or not students would take *algebra 2*. Note from the classification table that, overall, 77% of the participants were predicted correctly. The independent/covariate variables were better at helping us predict who would *not* take *algebra 2* (83% correct) than at who would take it (71% correct).

Note that in the **Variables in the Equation** table, only *parents' education* and *visualization test* are significant. *Gender* is not significant, which is probably due to several factors: 1) the fact that SE (standard error) is quite high relative to B, which makes the Wald statistic lower, 2) the fact that *gender* is dichotomous, and 3) the fact that in this sample, *gender* is modestly (.25 and .28) but significantly related to *visualization test* and *parents' education,* so when they are already included, *gender* does not add enough to be significant ($p = .389$). Note that **Exp(B)** gives the odds ratios for each variable. The odds ratio ([EXP (B)] with confidence interval) for *parents' education* was 1.46 (95% CI = 1.13−1.89) and for *visualization test* was 1.21 (CI = 1.04−1.4). These indicate that the odds of taking *algebra 2* improve by 1.46 for each unit increase in *parents' education* and by about 1.21 for every unit increase in *visualization test* score. With SPSS, the odds are for the outcome that is coded as "1," so in this case, it would be for those students who had taken *algebra 2*. For odds ratios that are less than 1, there is a decrease in the likelihood of taking *algebra 2* for every increase in the predictor variable.

Odds ratios and risk ratios are common examples of a third group or family of effect size measures, called **risk potency** measures. Although odds ratios and risk ratios are common effect size measures when both variables are dichotomous (also called binary), especially in the health-related literature, they are somewhat difficult to interpret clearly. Furthermore, there are no agreed-upon standards for what represents a large ratio because the ratio may approach infinity if the outcome is very rare or very common, even when the association is near random.

Example of How to Write About Problem 7.1
Results
     Logistic regression was conducted to assess whether the four predictor variables*, gender*, *parents' education*, *mosaic pattern test*, and *visualization test*, significantly predicted whether or not a student took *algebra 2*. (The assumptions of observations being independent and independent variables being linearly related to the logit were checked and met.) When all four predictor variables are considered together, they significantly predict whether or not a student took *algebra 2*, $\chi^2 = 24.23$, $df = 4$, $N = 75$, $p < .001$. Table 7.1 presents the odds ratios, which suggest that the odds of taking *algebra 2* are increasingly greater as parents' education and student visualization scores increase.

Table 7.1
Logistic Regression Predicting Who Will Take Algebra 2

Variable	B	SE	Odds ratio	p
Gender	−.50	.58	.61	.389
Parents' education	.38	.13	1.46	.004
Mosaic	−.03	.03	.97	.345
Visualization test	.19	.08	1.21	.011
Constant	−1.74	1.16	.18	.134

Problem 7.2: Hierarchical Logistic Regression

We will rerun Problem 7.1, but this time we will enter the background variables *gender* and *parents' education* first and then, on the second step or block, enter *mosaic* and *visualization test*.

7.2. If we control for *gender* and *parents' education*, will *mosaic* and/or *visualization test* add to the prediction of whether students will take *algebra 2*?

Now use the same dependent variable and covariates except enter *gender* and *parents' education* in **Block 1** and then enter *mosaic* and *visualization test* in **Block 2**. Use these commands:

- Select **Analyze** → **Regression** → **Binary Logistic...**
- Click on **Reset.**
- Move *algebra 2 in h.s.* into the **Dependent:** variable box.
- Move *gender* and *parents' education* into the **Covariates** box (in this problem we actually are treating them as covariates in that we remove variance associated with them first; however, in SPSS all predictors are called **Covariates**).
- Make sure **Enter** is the selected **Method.**
- Click on **Next** to get Block **2 of 2** (see Fig. 7.1 if you need help).
- Move *mosaic* and *visualization test* into the **Covariates** box.
- Click on **Options.**
- Check **CI for exp(B),** and be sure **95** is in the box (which will provide confidence intervals for the odds ratio of each predictor's contribution to the equation).
- Click on **Continue.**
- Click on **OK.** Does your output look like Output 7.2?

Output 7.2: Logistic Regression

```
LOGISTIC REGRESSION   VARIABLES alg2
  /METHOD = ENTER gender parEduc
  /METHOD = ENTER mosaic visual
  /PRINT = CI(95)
  /CRITERIA = PIN(.05) POUT(.10) ITERATE(20) CUT(.5) .
```

Case Processing Summary

Unweighted Cases[a]		N	Percent
Selected Cases	Included in Analysis	75	100.0
	Missing Cases	0	.0
	Total	75	100.0
Unselected Cases		0	.0
Total		75	100.0

a. If weight is in effect, see classification table for the total number of cases.

Dependent Variable Encoding

Original Value	Internal Value
not taken	0
taken	1

Again, *algebra 2* is the dependent variable and is coded 0 for not taken and 1 for taken.

Block 0: Beginning Block

Classification Table[a,b]

			Predicted		
			algebra 2 in h.s.		Percentage
Observed			not taken	taken	Correct
Step 0	algebra 2 in h.s.	not taken	40	0	100.0
		taken	35	0	.0
	Overall Percentage				53.3

a. Constant is included in the model.

b. The cut value is .500

> If we predicted that no one would take *algebra 2*, we would be correct 53% of the time, which is not significant, $p = .56$.

Variables in the Equation

		B	S.E.	Wald	df	Sig.	Exp(B)
Step 0	Constant	-.134	.231	.333	1	.564	.875

> Both *gender* and *parents' education* are significant predictors when entered separately.

Variables not in the Equation

			Score	df	Sig.
Step 0	Variables	GENDER	5.696	1	.017
		PAREDUC	12.559	1	.000
	Overall Statistics		14.944	2	.001

Block 1: Method=Enter

> *Gender* and *parents' education* are entered in Block 1, the first step.

Omnibus Tests of Model Coefficients

		Chi-square	df	Sig.
Step 1	Step	16.109	2	.000
	Block	16.109	2	.000
	Model	16.109	2	.000

> The combination of *gender* and *parents' education* significantly predicts who will take *algebra 2*.

Model Summary

Step	-2 Log likelihood	Cox & Snell R Square	Nagelkerke R Square
1	87.530	.193	.258

> These are estimates of how much knowing a student's *gender* and *parents' education* helps you predict whether or not the student will take *algebra 2*.

Classification Table[a]

			Predicted		
			algebra 2 in h.s.		Percentage Correct
Observed			not taken	taken	
Step 1	algebra 2 in h.s.	not taken	32	8	80.0
		taken	14	21	60.0
	Overall Percentage				70.7

a. The cut value is .500

> We can predict who will not take *algebra 2* (80%) better than we can predict who will (60%).

Variables in the Equation

		B	S.E.	Wald	df	Sig.	Exp(B)	95.0% C.I.for EXP(B)	
								Lower	Upper
Step 1[a]	gender	-.858	.522	2.707	1	.100	.424	.152	1.178
	parEduc	.374	.127	8.638	1	.003	1.454	1.133	1.866
	Constant	-1.297	.681	3.625	1	.057	.273		

a. Variable(s) entered on step 1: gender, parEduc.

> When both *gender* and *parents' education* are entered, *gender* is no longer significant.

Block 2: Method=Enter

Omnibus Tests of Model Coefficients

		Chi-square	df	Sig.
Step 1	Step	8.123	2	.017
	Block	8.123	2	.017
	Model	24.231	4	.000

> Note that adding *mosaic* and *visual* to the equation increases the prediction significantly.

Model Summary

Step	-2 Log likelihood	Cox & Snell R Square	Nagelkerke R Square
1	79.407	.276	.369

> Note that these pseudo R^2s and percentage correct are higher than they were when only *gender* and *parents' education* were entered and that they are the same as we found when all variables were entered simultaneously.

Classification Table[a]

			Predicted		
			algebra 2 in h.s.		Percentage Correct
Observed			not taken	taken	
Step 1	algebra 2 in h.s.	not taken	33	7	82.5
		taken	10	25	71.4
	Overall Percentage				77.3

a. The cut value is .500

Note that neither *gender* nor *mosaic* is significant when all of these variables are entered together.

Variables in the Equation

		B	S.E.	Wald	df	Sig.	Exp(B)	95.0% C.I.for EXP(B) Lower	Upper
Step 1ᵃ	gender	-.497	.577	.742	1	.389	.609	.197	1.884
	parEduc	.380	.131	8.418	1	.004	1.462	1.131	1.889
	mosaic	-.030	.031	.892	1	.345	.971	.913	1.032
	visual	.190	.075	6.428	1	.011	1.209	1.044	1.400
	Constant	-1.736	1.159	2.243	1	.134	.176		

a. Variable(s) entered on step 1: mosaic, visual.

Interpretation of Output 7.2

The first four tables are the same as in Output 7.1. In this case, we have an additional step or block (Block 2). **Block 1** shows the **Omnibus Chi-Square, Model Summary, Classification Table,** and **Variables in the Equation** when *gender* and *parents' education* were entered as covariates. Note that the Omnibus Test is statistically significant ($\chi^2 = 16.11$, $p < .001$). With only *gender* and *parents' education* entered, overall we can predict correctly 71% of the cases. Note from the last table in Block 1, that *gender* is not significant ($p = .100$) when it and *parents' education* are both in the equation.

In **Block 2,** we entered *mosaic* and *visualization test* to see if they would add to the predictive power of *gender* and *parents' education*. They do, as indicated by the **Step** in the **Omnibus Tests** table ($\chi^2 = 8.12$, $p = .017$). Note in the same table that the overall **Model** ($\chi^2 = 24.23$, $p < .001$) with all four predictors entered is significant. In this example, there is only one step in each block so the four tables in **Block 2** all say **Step 1**. The last three tables, as would be expected, are the same as those from Problem 7.1.

Problem 7.3: Discriminant Analysis

Discriminant analysis is appropriate when you want to predict which group participants will be in (in this example, who took *algebra 2*). The procedure produces a discriminant function (or for more than two groups, a set of discriminant functions) based on linear combinations of the predictor variables that provide the best overall discrimination among the groups. The grouping or dependent variable can have more than two values, but this will increase the complexity of the output and interpretation. The codes for the grouping variable must be integers. You need to specify their minimum and maximum values, as we will in Fig. 7.3. Cases with values outside these bounds are excluded from the analysis.

Discriminant analysis (DA) is similar to multivariate analysis of variance (MANOVA, discussed in Chapter 10), except that the independent and dependent variables are switched; thus, the conceptual basis for the study is typically different. In DA, one is trying to devise one or more predictive equations to maximally discriminate people in one group from those in another group; in MANOVA, one is trying to determine whether group members differ significantly on a set of several measures. The assumptions for DA are similar to those for MANOVA.

7.3 What combination of *gender*, *parents' education*, *mosaic*, and *visualization test* best distinguishes students who take *Algebra 2* from those who do not?

This is a similar question to the one that we asked in Problem 7.1, but this time we will use discriminant analysis, so the way of thinking about the problem is a little different.

You can use discriminant analysis instead of logistic regression when you have a categorical outcome or grouping variable if you have all continuous independent variables. It is best not to use dichotomous predictors for discriminant analysis, except when the dependent variable has a nearly 50-50 split as is true in this case.

To check the condition of multicollinearity, follow these commands:

- Select **Analyze → Regression → Linear**.
- Highlight *algebra 2 in h.s.* and move it into the **Dependent:** box.
- Hold down the shift key and highlight *gender*, *parents' education*, *mosaic*, and *visualization test* and move them into the **Independent(s):** box.
- Click on **Statistics…** and **The Linear Regression: Statistics** window will open.
- Check the box next to **Collinearity diagnostics**.
- Click on **Continue** and **OK**.

To check the assumption of homogeneity of variance-covariance matrices across groups we created scatterplots (below) after splitting the data by the grouping variable (in this case *algebra 2 in h.s.*). To split the file into groups, follow these steps to use **Split File**.

- Select **Data → Split File.**
- Select **Compare groups.**
- Move *algebra 2 in h.s.* into the **Groups Based on:** box.
- Click on **OK**.

Then do a scatterplot, selecting "matrix scatter," as shown in Chapter 2, with *gender*, *parents' education*, *mosaic*, and *visualization test* as the variables.

Don't forget to turn off the split file command before you run other analyses:

- Select **Data → Split File.**
- Select **Analyze all cases, do not create groups.**
- Click on **OK**.

Next, follow these steps to do the Discriminant Analysis:
- Select **Analyze → Classify → Discriminant**…
- Move *algebra 2 in h.s.* into the **Grouping Variable** box (see Fig. 7.3).

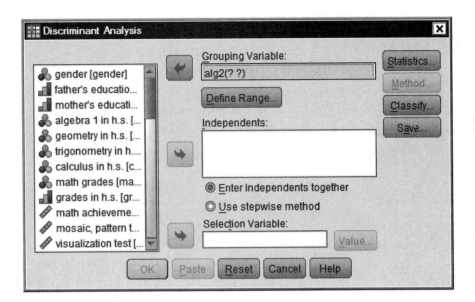

Fig. 7.3. Discriminant
analysis.

- Click on **Define Range** and enter **0** for **Minimum** and **1** for **Maximum** (see Fig. 7.4).
- Click on **Continue** to return to Fig. 7.3.

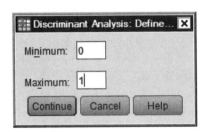

Fig. 7.4. Discriminant analysis:
Define range.

- Now move *gender, parents' education, mosaic,* and *visualization test* into the **Independents** box.
- Make sure **Enter independents together** is selected.
- Click on **Statistics**.
- Select **Means, Univariate ANOVAs,** and **Box's M** (see Fig. 7.5). Click on **Continue**.

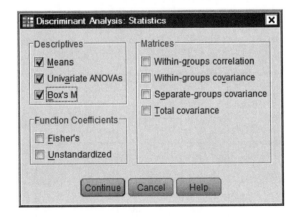

Fig. 7.5. Discriminant analysis: Statistics.

- Click on **Classify** to get Fig. 7.6.
- Check **Summary Table** under **Display**.
- Click on **Continue**.

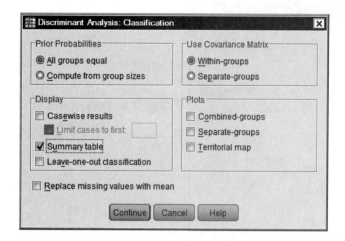

Fig. 7.6. Discriminant analysis: Classification.

- Finally, click on **OK** and compare your output to Output 7.3.

Output 7.3: Discriminant Analysis, Enter Independents Together

```
REGRESSION
  /MISSING LISTWISE
  /STATISTICS COEFF OUTS R ANOVA COLLIN TOL
  /CRITERIA=PIN(.05) POUT(.10)
  /NOORIGIN
  /DEPENDENT alg2
  /METHOD=ENTER gender parEduc mosaic visual.

SORT CASES BY alg2 .
SPLIT FILE
  LAYERED BY alg2 .
GRAPH
  /SCATTERPLOT(MATRIX)=gender parEduc mosaic visual
  /MISSING=LISTWISE .
SPLIT FILE
  OFF.

DISCRIMINANT
  /GROUPS=alg2(0 1)
  /VARIABLES=gender parEduc mosaic visual
  /ANALYSIS ALL
  /PRIORS  EQUAL
  /STATISTICS=MEAN STDDEV UNIVF BOXM TABLE
  /CLASSIFY=NONMISSING POOLED .
```

> The Tolerance and VIF assess multicollinearity. Since the Tolerance values are close to 1 and the VIF values are low, collinearity does not seem to be a problem.

Regression

Coefficients[a]

Model		Unstandardized Coefficients B	Unstandardized Coefficients Std. Error	Standardized Coefficients Beta	t	Sig.	Collinearity Statistics Tolerance	Collinearity Statistics VIF
1	(Constant)	.125	.209		.597	.553		
	gender	-.101	.108	-.101	-.938	.351	.873	1.145
	parents' education	.076	.023	.352	3.390	.001	.933	1.072
	mosaic, pattern test	-.005	.005	-.101	-.999	.321	.997	1.003
	visualization test	.039	.013	.306	2.924	.005	.920	1.087

a. Dependent Variable: *algebra 2* in h.s.

Graph

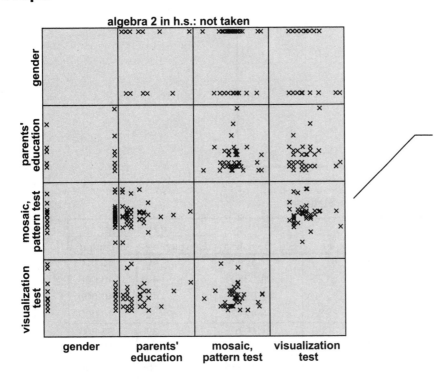

algebra 2 in h.s.: not taken

Compare the corresponding scatterplots for the two groups. The scatterplots for the same variables appear to be similar in variability for the two groups, suggesting that the assumption of homogeneity of variance-covariance matrices is met.

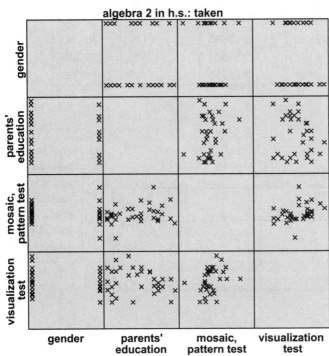

algebra 2 in h.s.: taken

Analysis Case Processing Summary

Unweighted Cases		N	Percent
Valid		75	100.0
Excluded	Missing or out-of-range group codes	0	.0
	At least one missing discriminating variable	0	.0
	Both missing or out-of-range group codes and at least one missing discriminating variable	0	.0
	Total	0	.0
Total		75	100.0

Group Statistics

algebra 2 in h.s.		Mean	Std. Deviation	Valid N (listwise) Unweighted	Weighted
not taken	gender	.6750	.47434	40	40.000
	parents' education	3.5125	1.68891	40	40.000
	mosaic, pattern test	28.1250	12.03188	40	40.000
	visualization test	3.8938	3.42122	40	40.000
taken	gender	.4000	.49705	35	35.000
	parents' education	5.4000	2.54026	35	35.000
	mosaic, pattern test	26.6000	5.67088	35	35.000
	visualization test	6.7857	3.91037	35	35.000
Total	gender	.5467	.50117	75	75.000
	parents' education	4.3933	2.31665	75	75.000
	mosaic, pattern test	27.4133	9.57381	75	75.000
	visualization test	5.2433	3.91203	75	75.000

Tests of Equality of Group Means

	Wilks' Lambda	F	df1	df2	Sig.
gender	.924	6.000	1	73	.017
parents' education	.833	14.683	1	73	.000
mosaic, pattern test	.994	.470	1	73	.495
visualization test	.862	11.672	1	73	.001

Gender, parents' education, and *visualization* are each significant predictors by themselves. *Mosaic* is not.

Box's Test of Equality of Covariance Matrices

Analysis 1

Log Determinants

algebra 2 in h.s.	Rank	Log Determinant
not taken	4	6.904
taken	4	6.258
Pooled within-groups	4	7.101

The ranks and natural logarithms of determinants printed are those of the group covariance matrices.

Test Results

Box's M		36.324
F	Approx.	3.416
	df1	10
	df2	24432.818
	Sig.	.000

Tests null hypothesis of equal population covariance matrices.

> This indicates that the assumption of homogeneity of the covariance matrices has not been met, according to this test. However, this test is strongly influenced by nonnormality and may not be accurate. We checked this assumption with matrix scatterplots for each group, and these suggested the assumption was not badly violated. We could use logistic regression instead of discriminant analysis if we are concerned about the degree to which we met this assumption.

Summary of Canonical Discriminant Functions

> We can square the Canonical correlation to compute the effect size for the discriminant function.

Eigenvalues

Function	Eigenvalue	% of Variance	Cumulative %	Canonical Correlation
1	.416[a]	100.0	100.0	.542

a. First 1 canonical discriminant functions were used in the analysis.

> Wilks' lambda can be used to compute an overall effect size for the analysis (partial $\eta^2 = 1-\Lambda^{1/3} = 1 - (.706)^{1/3} = 1 - .89 = .11$).

Wilks' Lambda

Test of Function(s)	Wilks' Lambda	Chi-square	df	Sig.
1	.706	24.692	4	.000

> This indicates that the predictors significantly discriminate the groups.

Standardized Canonical Discriminant Function Coefficients

	Function
	1
gender	-.213
parents' education	.706
mosaic, pattern test	-.220
visualization test	.624

This table indicates how heavily each variable is weighted in order to maximize discrimination of groups. In this example, *parents' education* and *visual* are weighted more than *gender* and *mosaic*.

Structure Matrix

	Function
	1
parents' education	.695
visualization test	.620
gender	-.445
mosaic, pattern test	-.124

Pooled within-groups correlations between discriminating variables and standardized canonical discriminant functions
Variables ordered by absolute size of correlation within function.

These are the correlations of each independent variable with the standardized discriminant function. They show that *parent's education*, *visualization*, and *gender* all have notable correlations with the function, but *mosaic* does not. Gender is negatively related, indicating male status is related to the function.

Functions at Group Centroids

	Function
algebra 2 in h.s.	1
not taken	-.595
taken	.680

Unstandardized canonical discriminant functions evaluated at group means

Classification Statistics

Classification Processing Summary

Processed		75
Excluded	Missing or out-of-range group codes	0
	At least one missing discriminating variable	0
Used in Output		75

Prior Probabilities for Groups

		Cases Used in Analysis	
algebra 2 in h.s.	Prior	Unweighted	Weighted
not taken	.500	40	40.000
taken	.500	35	35.000
Total	1.000	75	75.000

Classification Results[a]

		algebra 2 in h.s.	Predicted Group Membership		Total
			not taken	taken	
Original	Count	not taken	32	8	40
		taken	10	25	35
	%	not taken	80.0	20.0	100.0
		taken	28.6	71.4	100.0

a 76.0% of original grouped cases correctly classified.

> This shows how well the model predicts who will take *algebra 2*. For example, 80% of those who did not take algebra 2 were correctly predicted.

Interpretation of Output 7.3

The **Group Statistics** table provides basic descriptive statistics for each of the independent/predictor variables for each outcome group (did not take *algebra 2* and did take it) separately and for the whole sample. The **Tests of Equality of Group Means** table shows which independent variables are significant predictors by themselves; it shows the variables with which there is a statistically significant difference between those who took *algebra 2* and those who did not. As was the case when we used logistic regression, *gender*, *parents' education*, and *visualization test* are statistically significant.

Similar to factorial ANOVA, discriminant analysis has two types of effect size: one effect size describes the variance for the entire analysis (i.e., partial η^2), and the other effect size describes the variances associated with each discriminant function. To compute partial η^2 we can use the following formula, partial $\eta^2 = 1 - \Lambda^{1/3}$. Wilks' lambda is represented with the "Λ" symbol, and the value of Λ is found in the **Wilks' Lambda** table. Thus, for this output, partial $\eta^2 = 1 - \Lambda^{1/3} = 1 - .706^{1/3} = 1 - .89 = .11$. This is considered a larger than typical effect size. To compute an effect size that describes the variance associated with each discriminant function, we square the Canonical correlation value found in the **Eigenvalues** table, $(.542)^2 = .294$.

Note, from the **Standardized Canonical Discriminant Function Coefficients** table, that only *parents' education* and *visualization test* are weighted heavily to maximize the discrimination between groups. Because *gender* correlates with *parents' education,* it has a low function coefficient. But in the **Structure Matrix** table, *gender* has a higher ($-.45$) correlation because it is correlated with the discriminant function that best predicts who took *algebra 2* and who did not.

The last table is similar to the classification table for logistic regression. It shows how well the combination of four independent variables classifies or predicts who will take *algebra 2*. Note that overall, 76% of the sample was classified correctly. As with logistic regression, discriminant analysis did better at predicting who did not take *algebra 2* (80% correct) than it did at predicting who would take it (71% correct).

Example of How to Write About Problem 7.3

Results

Discriminant analysis was conducted to assess whether the four predictors, gender, parents' education, mosaic, and visualization test, could distinguish those who took *algebra 2* from those who did not. (The assumptions of that the relationships between all pairs of predictors must be linear, multivariate normality must exist within groups, and the population covariance matrices for predictor variables must be equal across groups were checked and all were met except the assumption of homogeneity of variances.) Wilks' lambda was significant, $\lambda = .71$, $\chi^2 = 24.69$, $p < .001$, partial $\eta^2 = .11$, which indicates that the model including these four variables was able to significantly discriminate the two groups. Table 7.2 presents the standardized function coefficients, which suggest that parents' education and the visualization test contribute most to distinguishing those who took *algebra 2* from those who did not, using these predictors. The classification results show that the model correctly predicts 80% of those who did not take *algebra 2* and 71% of those who did take *algebra 2*. The correlation coefficients in the table indicate the extent to which each variable correlates with the resulting discriminant function. Note that even though gender didn't contribute strongly to the discriminant function, it is moderately highly (negatively) correlated with the overall discriminant function.

Table 7.2

Standardized Function Coefficients and Correlation Coefficients

	Standardized function coefficients	Correlations between variables and discriminant function
Parents'education	.71	.70
Visualization test	.62	.62
Gender	−.21	-.45
Mosaic, pattern test	−.22	−.12

Interpretation Questions

7.1.   Using Output 7.1: (a) When all four predictors are included, which variables make significant contributions to predicting who took *algebra 2*? (b) How accurate is the overall prediction? (c) How well do the variables predict who actually <u>took</u> *algebra 2*? (d) How about the prediction of who *did not* take it?

7.2.   Compare Outputs 7.1 and 7.2. How are they different and why?

7.3.   In Output 7.3: (a) What do the discriminant function coefficients and the structure coefficients tell us about how the predictor variables combine to predict who took *algebra 2*? (b) How accurate is the prediction/classification overall and for who would not take *algebra 2*? (c) How do the results in Output 7.3 compare to those in Output 7.1, in terms of success at classifying and contribution of different variables to the equation?

7.4.   Comparing Outputs 7.3 and 7.1, what kind of information does the discriminant analysis provide that is not provided by the logistic regression?

7.5.   In Output 7.2: Why might one want to do a hierarchical logistic regression?

7.6.   (a) In Output 7.1: How can one tell which variables are contributing more to the classification of participants using logistic regression? (b) In Output 7.3: How can one tell which variables are contributing to the classification of participants using discriminant analysis? What is the difference between the function coefficients and the coefficients in the structure matrix?

Extra SPSS Problems

Access the Wuensch_logistic data set. These data are from a published study by Wuensch and Poteat (1998) in the *Journal of Social Behavior and Personality*. Context: College students ($N = 315$) were asked to pretend that they were serving on a university research committee hearing a complaint against animal research being conducted by a member of the university faculty. The DV was whether or not to withdraw the researcher's authorization to conduct the research (Decision, 0=stop, 1=continue).

7.1.   Run a logistic regression analysis predicting decision from gender alone.
   a.   Is the logistic regression significant?
   b.   What overall percentage of students was correctly classified as to whether they continue or discontinue the research? How accurately was each decision predicted?

7.2.   Run a second analysis with gender, idealism, and relativism as predictors (Keep in mind that persons who score high on relativism reject the notion of universal moral principles, preferring personal and situational analysis of behavior. Persons who score high on idealism believe that ethical behavior will always lead only to good consequences, never to bad consequences, and never to a mixture of good and bad consequences).
   a.   How does the results for Block 0 compare with the results in the first analysis? Why?
   b.   Examine the "Classification Table" in Block 1. Does a model with gender, idealism, and realism predict better than a model with only gender? Why do you say this?
   c.   Interpret the odds ratios provided for each predictor in "Variables in the Equation."
   d.   Examine the B coefficients. Are subjects who are more idealistic likely to decide to stop (0) or continue (1) the research? How about subjects are more realistic (relativism)?

7.3.   Do a discriminant function analysis using these same variables.
   a.   Is the discriminative function significant?
   b.   Which predictor(s) contribute significantly to predicting whether individuals would continue the research or stop the research?
   c.   What overall percentage of students were correctly classified as to whether they would continue the research or not? How accurately were students who would continue the research predicted? How accurately were students who would not continue the research predicted? How do these results differ from those for the logistic regression?
   d.   Given the results of both of these analyses, what would you conclude about your understanding of these students' tendency to continue or stop the research? Describe your conclusions in nontechnical terms, making sure to describe the statistical results of the discriminant function analysis.

CHAPTER 8

Factorial ANOVA and ANCOVA

In this chapter, we will introduce two complex difference statistics: factorial analysis of variance (ANOVA) and analysis of covariance (ANCOVA). Both factorial ANOVA and ANCOVA tell you whether considering more than one independent variable at a time gives you additional information over and above what you would get if you did the appropriate *basic* inferential statistics for each independent variable separately. Both of these inferential statistics have two or more independent variables and one scale (normally distributed) dependent variable. **Factorial ANOVA** is used when there is a small number of independent variables (usually two or three), and each of these variables has a small number of levels or categories (usually two to four).

ANCOVA typically is used to adjust or control for differences between the groups based on another, typically interval-level variable, called the covariate. For example, imagine that we found that boys and girls differ on math achievement. However, this could be due to the fact that boys take more math courses in high school. ANCOVA allows us to adjust the math achievement scores based on the relationship between number of math courses taken and math achievement. We can then determine if boys and girls still have different math achievement scores after making the adjustment. ANCOVA can also be used if one wants to use one or more discrete or nominal variables and one or two continuous variables to predict differences in one dependent variable.

Assumptions of Factorial ANOVA and ANCOVA

The assumptions for factorial ANOVA and ANCOVA include that the observations are independent, the variances of the groups are equal (homogeneity of variances), and the dependent variable is normally distributed for each group. Assessing whether the observations are independent (i.e., each participant's score is not related systematically to any other participant's score) is a design issue that should be evaluated prior to entering the data into SPSS. Using random sampling is the best way of ensuring that the observations are independent; however, this is not possible in behavioral research that requires voluntary participation. The most important thing to avoid is having known relationships among participants in the study (e.g., several family members or several participants obtained through "snowball" sampling included as "separate" participants). Second, to test the assumption of homogeneity of variances, SPSS computes Levene's statistic, which can be requested using the General Linear Model command. It is important to have homogeneity of variances, particularly if sample sizes differ across levels of the independent variable(s). The third assumption is that the dependent variable needs to be normally distributed. Factorial ANOVA is robust against violations of the assumption of the normal distributions of the dependent variable. To test this assumption you can compare boxplots or compute skewness values through the Explore command for the dependent variable for each group (cell) defined by each combination of the levels of the independent variables.

Additional Assumptions for ANCOVA

For ANCOVA there is a fourth assumption that there is a linear relationship between the covariates and the dependent variable. This can be checked with a scatterplot (or matrix scatterplot if there is more than one covariate). The regression slopes for the covariates (in relation to the dependent variable) need to be the same for each group (this is called homogeneity of regression slopes). This assumption is one of the most important assumptions, and it can be checked with an *F* test on the interaction of the independent variables with the covariate. If the *F* test is significant, then this assumption has been violated.

- Retrieve **hsbdataB** from your data file.

Problem 8.1: Factorial (Two-Way) ANOVA

We would use a *t* test or one-way ANOVA to examine differences between two or more groups (comprising the levels of *one* independent variable or factor) on a continuous dependent variable. These designs, in which there is only one independent variable and it is a discrete or categorical variable, are called single-factor designs. In this problem, we will compare groups formed by combining *two* independent variables. The appropriate statistic for this type of problem is called a **two-factor**, **two-way**, or **factorial ANOVA**. One can also have factorial ANOVAs in which there are more than two independent variables. If there are three independent variables, one would have a three-factor or three-way ANOVA. It is unusual, but possible, to have more than three factors as well. Factorial ANOVA is used when there are two or more independent variables (each with a few categories or values) and a between-groups design.

8.1 Are there differences in *math achievement* for people varying on *math grades* and/or *father's education revised,* and is there a significant interaction between *math grades* and *father's education* on *math achievement*? (Another way to ask this latter question: Do the "effects" of *math grades* on *math achievement* vary depending on level of *father's education revised*?)

Follow these commands:
- **Analyze → General Linear Model → Univariate**.
- Move *math achievement* to the **Dependent Variable** box.
- Move the first independent variable, *math grades,* to the **Fixed Factor(s)** box and then move the second independent variable, *father's educ revised* (<u>not *father's education*</u>), to the **Fixed Factor(s)** box (see Fig. 8.1).

Now that we know the variables we will be dealing with, let's determine our options.

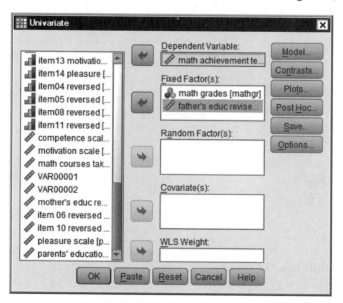

Fig. 8.1. GLM: Univariate.

- Click on **Plots** and move *faedRevis* to the **Horizontal Axis** and *mathgr* to the **Separate Lines** box in Fig. 8.2. This "profile plot" will help you picture the interaction (or absence of interaction) between your two independent variables. Note, the plots will be easier to interpret if you put *father's educ revised* with its three values on the horizontal axis and create separate lines for the variable (math grades) that has two levels.
- Then press **Add**. You will see that *mathgr* and *faedRevis* have moved to the **Plots** window as shown at the bottom of Fig. 8.2.

- Click on **Continue** to get back Fig.8.1.

Fig. 8.2. Univariate: Profile plots.

- Select **Options** and check **Descriptive statistics, Estimates of effect size, Observed power,** and **Homogeneity tests** in Fig. 8.3.

Fig. 8.3. Univariate: Options.

- Click on **Continue**. This will take you back to Fig. 8.1.
- Click on **OK**. Compare your output with Output 8.1.

Output 8.1: GLM General Factorial (Two-Way) ANOVA

```
UNIANOVA mathach  BY mathgr faedRevis
  /METHOD = SSTYPE(3)
  /INTERCEPT = INCLUDE
  /PLOT = PROFILE(faedRevis*mathgr)
  /PRINT = OPOWER ETASQ HOMOGENEITY DESCRIPTIVE
  /CRITERIA = ALPHA(.05)
  /DESIGN = mathgr faedRevis mathgr*faedRevis .
```

Univariate Analysis of Variance

Between-Subjects Factors

		Value Label	N
math grades	0	less A-B	43
	1	most A-B	30
father's educ revised	1.00	HS grad or less	38
	2.00	Some College	16
	3.00	BS or More	19

The six-boxed cell means will be shown in the plot.

Descriptive Statistics

Dependent Variable: math achievement test

math grades	father's educ revised	Mean	Std. Deviation	N
less A-B	HS grad or less	9.8261	5.03708	23
	Some College	12.8149	5.05553	9
	BS or More	12.3636	7.18407	11
	Total	11.1008	5.69068	43
most A-B	HS grad or less	10.4889	6.56574	15
	Some College	16.4284	3.43059	7
	BS or More	21.8335	2.84518	8
	Total	14.9000	7.00644	30
Total	HS grad or less	10.0877	5.61297	38
	Some College	14.3958	4.66544	16
	BS or More	16.3509	7.40918	19
	Total	12.6621	6.49659	73

Levene's Test of Equality of Error Variances[a]

Dependent Variable: math achievement test

F	df1	df2	Sig.
2.548	5	67	.036

Tests the null hypothesis that the error variance of the dependent variable is equal across groups.

a. Design: Intercept+mathgr+faedRevis+mathgr * faedRevis

This indicates that the assumption of homogeneity of variances has been violated. Because Levene's test is significant, we know that the variances are significantly different. Luckily, SPSS uses the regression approach to calculate ANOVA, so this problem is less important. Nevertheless, this violation should be considered when deciding which post hoc test to use.

This eta squared indicates that 24% of the variance in *math achievement* can be predicted from *father's education*.

Tests of Between-Subjects Effects

Dependent Variable: math achievement test

Source	Type III Sum of Squares	df	Mean Square	F	Sig.	Partial Eta Squared	Noncent. Parameter	Observed Power[a]
Corrected Model	1029.236[b]	5	205.847	6.863	.000	.339	34.315	.997
Intercept	12094.308	1	12094.308	403.230	.000	.858	403.230	1.000
mathgr	325.776	1	325.776	10.862	.002	.139	10.862	.901
faedRevis	646.015	2	323.007	10.769	.000	.243	21.538	.987
mathgr * faedRevis	237.891	2	118.946	3.966	.024	.106	7.931	.693
Error	2009.569	67	29.994					
Total	14742.823	73						
Corrected Total	3038.804	72						

a. Computed using alpha = .05

b. R Squared = .339 (Adjusted R Squared = .289)

The *R* Squared value is the percent of variance in *math achievement* predictable from both independent variables and the interaction.

Focus on these three *F*s and Sig values, especially the *Mathgr × FaedRevis* interaction.

Profile Plots

Plot for students with high *math grades*.

Estimated Marginal Means of math achievement test

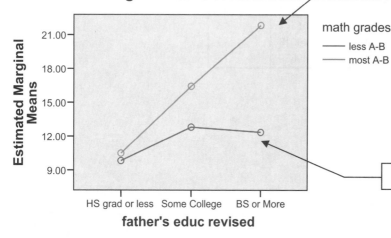

Note that for students whose fathers have a BS or more, there is a big difference in *math achievement* between those with high and low *math grades*. However, there is little difference for students whose fathers are high school grads or less.

Plot for students with low *math grades*.

Interpretation of Output 8.1

The **GLM Univariate** program allows you to print the means and counts, measures of effect size (eta²), and the plot of the interaction, which is helpful in interpreting it. The first table in Output 8.1 shows the two levels of *math grades* (0 and 1), with 43 participants indicating "less A–B" (low math grades) and 30 reporting "most A–B" (high grades). *Father's education revised* had three levels (low, medium, and high education) with 38 participants reporting HS grad or less, 16 indicating some college, and 19 with a BS or more. The second table, **Descriptive Statistics,** shows the cell and marginal (total) means; both are very important for interpreting the ANOVA table and explaining the results of the test for the interaction.

The second table is **Levene's Test of Equality of Error Variances**, which tests the homogeneity of variances. It is important to check whether Levene's test is significant; if it is significant ($p < .05$) the variances are different, and thus this assumption is violated. If it is not significant ($p > .05$), then the assumption is met. Whether this assumption has been met is important to remember when we do post hoc tests.

The ANOVA table, called **Tests of Between-Subjects Effects**, is the key table. Note that the word "effect" in the title of the table can be misleading because this study was not a randomized experiment. Thus, you should not report that the differences in the dependent variable were *caused* by the independent variable. Usually you will ignore the information about the corrected model and intercept and skip down to the interaction *F (mathgr*faedRevis)*. It is important to look at the interaction first because it may change the interpretation of the separate "main effects" of each independent variable.

In this case, the interaction is statistically significant, $F (2,67) = 3.97$, $p = .024$. This means that the "effect" of *math grades* on *math achievement* depends on which *father's education* level is being considered. If you find a significant interaction, you should examine the **profile plots** of cell means to visualize the differential effects. If there is a significant interaction, the lines on the profile plot will not be parallel. In this case, the plot indicates that *math achievement* is relatively low for both groups of students whose fathers had relatively low education (*high school grad or less*). However, for students whose fathers have a high education level (*BS or more*), differences in *math grades* seem to have a large "effect" on *math achievement*. This interpretation, based on a visual inspection of the plots, needs to be checked with inferential statistics. When the interaction is statistically significant, you should analyze the "**simple effects**" (differences between means for one variable at each particular level of the other variable). We will illustrate two methods for statistically analyzing the simple effects in Problem 8.2.

Now examine the main effects of *math grades* and of *father's education revised*. Note that both are statistically significant, but because the interaction is significant this is somewhat misleading. The plots show that the effect of *math grades* does not seem to hold true for those whose fathers had the least education. Note also the callout boxes about the adjusted R squared and eta squared. **Eta**, the correlation ratio, is used when the independent variable is *nominal* and the dependent variable (*math achievement* in this problem) is *scale*. Eta is an indicator of the proportion of variance that is due to between-groups differences. **Adjusted R^2** refers to the multiple correlation coefficient, squared and adjusted for number of independent variables, N, and effect size. Like r^2, eta squared and R^2 indicate how much variance or variability in the dependent variable can be predicted; however, the multiple R^2 is used when there are several independent variables, and the r^2 is used when there is only one independent variable. In this problem, the eta^2 values for the three key Fs vary from .106 to .243 (you can take the square root of this to get eta, which in this case varies from .325 to .493). Because eta and R, like r, are indexes of association, they can be used to interpret the effect size. However, the guidelines according to Cohen (1988) for eta and R are somewhat different (for eta: small = .10, medium = .24, and large = .37; for R: small = .10, medium =.36, and large = .51).

In this example, **eta** for *math grades* is about .37 ($\sqrt{.139} = .37$) and, thus, according to Cohen (1988) a large effect. Eta for *father's education* (revised) is about .49, a large effect. The interaction eta is about .33, close to a large effect. The overall **adjusted R** is about .54, a large effect, but not really bigger than for father's education alone, when you consider the different criteria for "large" for eta vs. R. Notice that the adjusted R^2 is lower than the unadjusted (.29 vs. .34). The reason for this is that the adjusted R^2 takes into account (and adjusts for) several things including the fact that not just one but three factors (*mathgr, faedRevis,* and the interaction), some of which have more than two levels, were used to predict *math achievement*.

An important point to remember is that statistical significance depends heavily on the sample size so that with 1,000 subjects, a much lower F or r will be significant than if the sample is 10 or even 100. Statistical significance just tells you that you can be quite sure that there is at least a tiny relationship between the independent and dependent variables. Effect size measures, which are more independent of sample size, tell how strong the relationship is and, thus, give you some indication of its importance.

The **Observed Power** for *math grades* was .90, and for *father's education revised* it was .99. These indicate extremely high power, which means we might find statistically significant results even with small effect sizes. For these two factors this was not a problem because the effect sizes were large (eta = .373 and .493). Observed power for the interaction of *math grades* and *father's education revised* was .69. Because it is less than .80, there was relatively low power. But, because the effect size for the interaction was close to large (eta = .326), we had enough power to detect this difference.

How to write the results for Problem 8.1 is included after the interpretation box for Problem 8.2.

Problem 8.2: Post Hoc Analyses of a Significant Interaction

We have described, in the interpretation of Output 8.1, how to visually inspect and interpret the Profile Plots when there is a statistically significant interaction. In Problems 8.2b and 8.2c we will illustrate two ways to test the simple effects statistically.

In the interpretation of Output 8.1, we indicated that you should examine the interaction *F* first. If it is statistically significant, it provides important information and means that the results of the main effects may be misleading. Figure 8.4 is a decision tree that illustrates this point and guides the analysis in this section. It shows two ways to examine the simple effects when you have a significant interaction. You would <u>use either contrasts or post hoc tests, not both</u>.

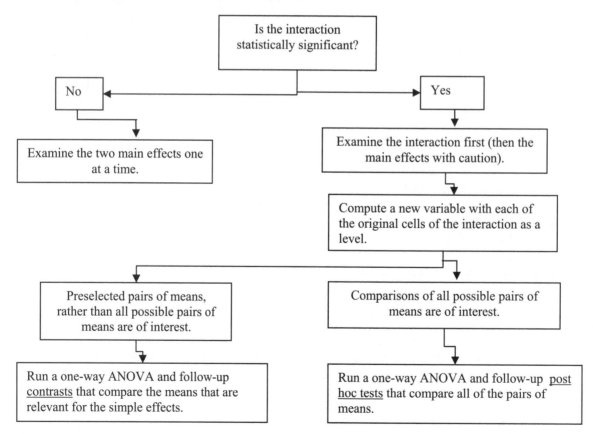

Fig. 8.4. Steps in analyzing a two-way factorial ANOVA.

8.2. Which simple effects of *math grades* (at each level of *father's education revised*) are statistically significant?

8.2a. Computation of the New Cellcode Variable

To analyze the simple effects, we first need to compute a new variable with each of the original cells as a level. To do this, do the following commands.

- Select **Transform → Compute Variable...** You will see the **Compute Variable** window, Fig. 8.5.

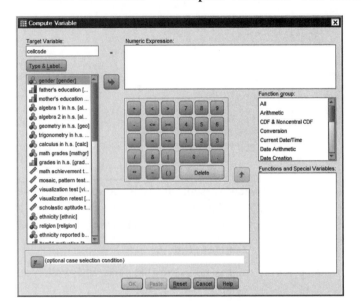

Fig. 8.5. Compute variable window.

- Under **Target Variable**, type *cellcode*. This is the name of the new variable you will compute.
- Click on **Type and Label.** You will see the **Compute Variable: Type and Label** window (Fig. 8.6).
- Type *six new cell codes* in the label box.

Fig. 8.6. Compute variable: Type and label.

- Click on **Continue**. You will see the **Compute Variable** window (Fig. 8.5) again.
- In the **Numeric Expression** box, type the number 1. This will be the first value or level for the new variable.
- Next, click on the **If...** button in Fig. 8.5 to produce Fig. 8.7.
- **Select Include if case satisfies condition**.
- Type *mathgr = 0 & faedRevis = 1* in the window. You are telling SPSS to compute level 1 of the new variable, *cellcode,* so that it combines the first level of *math grades* (0) and the first level of *father's education revised* (1) (see Fig. 8.7).

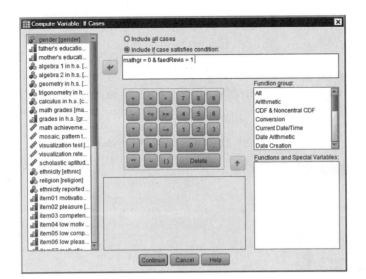

Fig. 8.7. Compute variable: If cases.

- Click on **Continue to** return to Fig. 8.5.
- Click on **OK**. If you look at your Data View or Variable View screen, you will see a new variable called *cellcode*. In the **Data View** screen, you should also notice that several of the cases now show a value of 1. Those are the cases where the original variables of *math grades* and *father's education revised* met the requirements you just computed.

You will need to repeat this process for the other five levels of this new variable. We will walk you through the process once more.

- Select **Transform**→ **Compute Variable** to see the **Compute Variable** window (see Fig. 8.5).
- Ensure that *cellcode* is still in the target variable box.
- Delete the *1* on the **Numeric Expression** box.
- Type *2* in the **Numeric Expression** box.
- Click on the **If…** button.
- Ensure that **Include if case satisfies condition** is selected.
- Type *mathgr=1 & faedRevis=1* in the box. You are now telling SPSS to use the other (higher) level of *math grades* with the first level of *father's education revised*.
- Click on **Continue**.
- Click on **OK**.
- SPSS will ask you if you want to change the existing variable. Click on **OK**. This means that you want to add this second level to the *cellcode* variable. If you look at the **Data View** screen, you will notice that some of the cases now indicate a value of 2.
- Complete the above steps for the remaining four levels: Level 3 of cellcode: *mathgr = 0 & faedRevis = 2*; Level 4: *mathgr = 1 & faedRevis = 2*; Level 5: *mathgr = 0 & faedRevis = 3;* and Level 6: *mathgr = 1 & faedRevis = 3.*

To simplify the output and help you remember what levels you have created, you should add value labels to the *cellcode* variable as we have done in Output 8.2b. See Appendix A if you don't know how to do this, and see Output 8.2b for the labels we used.

Output 8.2a

```
IF (mathgr = 0 & faedRevis = 1 ) cellcode = 1 .
EXECUTE .
IF (mathgr = 1 & faedRevis = 1 ) cellcode = 2 .
EXECUTE .
IF (mathgr = 0 & faedRevis = 2 ) cellcode = 3 .
EXECUTE .
IF (mathgr = 1 & faedRevis = 2 ) cellcode = 4 .
EXECUTE .
IF (mathgr = 0 & faedRevis = 3) cellcode = 5 .
EXECUTE .
IF (mathgr = 1 & faedRevis = 3) cellcode = 6 .
EXECUTE .
```

Next, you will use this new variable, *cellcode,* to examine the statistical significance of differences among certain of the six cells. This will help us to interpret the simple effects that we discussed above. We will demonstrate two types of follow-up tests (**Post Hoc tests** and **Contrasts**), but you should choose the most appropriate, not both. Remember, **Post Hoc tests** are appropriate when the researcher does not have a clear idea of which levels of the independent variable she/he wishes to compare or wants to compare all pairs of levels. Therefore, with **Post Hoc tests** all possible combinations will be compared. **Contrasts** compare a limited number of preselected pairs of means rather than all possible pairs of means. We will use the GLM univariate program to do post hocs in Problem 8.2b, but we could have used the **Oneway** program as we did in 8.2c.

8.2b. Computation of Post Hoc Tests

- Select **Analyze** → **General Linear Model** → **Univariate**. (This will produce Fig. 8.1.)
- Click on **Reset.**
- Move *math achievement* to the **Dependent** (variable) box.
- Move *six new cell codes* to the **Fixed Factor(s)** box.
- Click on **Post Hoc...** The **Univariate: Post Hoc Multiple Comparisons for Observed Means** window (not shown) will appear.
- Highlight *cellcode* in the **Factors** box. Click on the arrow to move it into the **Post Hoc Tests for**: box.
- Click on the **Games-Howell** post hoc test under **Equal Variances Not Assumed** because the Levene's test for homogeneity was significant in Output 8.1. (If Levene's test for homogeneity had not been significant, we could use the Tukey post hoc test here.)
- Click on **Continue** to get Fig. 8.1. Select Options to get Fig. 8.3.
- Check **Descriptive statistics**, **Estimates of effect size,** and **Observed power**. (Don't check homogeneity tests; we already know that it is significant.)
- Click on **Continue** and **OK.**

Output 8.2b.

```
UNIANOVA mathach  BY cellcode
  /METHOD = SSTYPE(3)
  /INTERCEPT = INCLUDE
  /POSTHOC = cellcode (GH)
  /PRINT = DESCRIPTIVE ETASQ OPOWER
  /CRITERIA = ALPHA(.05)
  /DESIGN = cellcode.
```

Univariate Analysis of Variance

Between-Subjects Factors

		Value Label	N
six new cell codes	1.00	low math and low faed	23
	2.00	high math and low faed	15
	3.00	low math and med faed	9
	4.00	high math and med faed	7
	5.00	low math and high faed	11
	6.00	high math and high faed	8

Descriptive Statistics

Dependent Variable: math achievement test

six new cell codes	Mean	Std. Deviation	N
low math and low faed	9.8261	5.03708	23
high math and low faed	10.4889	6.56574	15
low math and med faed	12.8149	5.05553	9
high math and med faed	16.4284	3.43059	7
low math and high faed	12.3636	7.18407	11
high math and high faed	21.8335	2.84518	8
Total	12.6621	6.49659	73

All combinations of pairs of these six cell code means will be compared (twice) in the Games-Howell Multiple Comparisons table.

The overall *cellcode* ANOVA is, $F(5, 67) = 6.86$, $p < .001$, eta = .58 so there are differences among the cells and a large effect size.

Tests of Between-Subjects Effects

Dependent Variable: math achievement test

Source	Type III Sum of Squares	df	Mean Square	F	Sig.	Partial Eta Squared	Noncent. Parameter	Observed Power[a]
Corrected Model	1029.236[b]	5	205.847	6.863	.000	.339	34.315	.997
Intercept	12094.308	1	12094.308	403.230	.000	.858	403.230	1.000
cellcode	1029.236	5	205.847	6.863	.000	.339	34.315	.997
Error	2009.569	67	29.994					
Total	14742.823	73						
Corrected Total	3038.804	72						

a. Computed using alpha = .05

b. R Squared = .339 (Adjusted R Squared = .289)

Post Hoc Tests

six new cell codes

Each pair of cell means is compared twice in this table. We have crossed out the duplicates. It may be helpful for you to do the same on your output. The simple effects (circled) are discussed in the 8.2b Interpretation and Fig. 8.10.

Multiple Comparisons

Dependent Variable: math achievement test

Games-Howell

(I) six new cell codes	(J) six new cell codes	Mean Difference (I-J)	Std. Error	Sig.	95% Confidence Interval	
					Lower Bound	Upper Bound
low math and low faed	high math and low faed	-.6628	1.99426	.999	-6.8183	5.4928
	low math and med faed	-2.9888	1.98569	.667	-9.4625	3.4849
	high math and med faed	-6.6023*	1.66866	.013	-12.0371	-1.1676
	low math and high faed	-2.5375	2.40729	.892	-10.3670	5.2919
	high math and high faed	-12.0074*	1.45431	.000	-16.5343	-7.4805
high math and low faed	low math and low faed	.6628	1.99426	.999	-5.4928	6.8183
	low math and med faed	-2.3260	2.39035	.921	-9.8239	5.1718
	high math and med faed	-5.9396	2.13429	.103	-12.6633	.7842
	low math and high faed	-1.8748	2.75060	.982	-10.4995	6.7500
	high math and high faed	-11.3446*	1.97125	.000	-17.5256	-5.1637
low math and med faed	low math and low faed	2.9888	1.98569	.667	-3.4849	9.4625
	high math and low faed	2.3260	2.39035	.921	-5.1718	9.8239
	high math and med faed	-3.6135	2.12629	.554	-10.6007	3.3736
	low math and high faed	.4513	2.74440	1.000	-8.2882	9.1907
	high math and high faed	-9.0186*	1.96258	.005	-15.5383	-2.4989
high math and med faed	low math and low faed	6.6023*	1.66866	.013	1.1676	12.0371
	high math and low faed	5.9396	2.13429	.103	-.7842	12.6633
	low math and med faed	3.6135	2.12629	.554	-3.3736	10.6007
	low math and high faed	4.0648	2.52451	.605	-4.1231	12.2527
	high math and high faed	-5.4051	1.64108	.057	-10.9371	.1270
low math and high faed	low math and low faed	2.5375	2.40729	.892	-5.2919	10.3670
	high math and low faed	1.8748	2.75060	.982	-6.7500	10.4995
	low math and med faed	.4513	2.74440	1.000	-9.1907	8.2882
	high math and med faed	4.0648	2.52451	.605	-12.2527	4.1231
	high math and high faed	-9.4699*	2.38826	.014	-17.3147	-1.6250
high math and high faed	low math and low faed	12.0074*	1.45431	.000	7.4805	16.5343
	high math and low faed	11.3446*	1.97125	.000	5.1637	17.5256
	low math and med faed	9.0186*	1.96258	.005	2.4989	15.5383
	high math and med faed	5.4051	1.64108	.057	-.1270	10.9371
	low math and high faed	9.4699*	2.38826	.014	1.6250	17.3147

Based on observed means.

*. The mean difference is significant at the .05 level.

Interpretation of Output 8.2b

The second table is **Descriptive Statistics** showing the six new cell code means computed in Output 8.2a. The **Tests of Between-Subjects Effects** table provides an overall or omnibus ANOVA (circled) that indicates there are significant differences among the six *cellcode* means. However, we are almost always more interested in the comparisons of <u>pairs or other subsets of the means</u>. Post hoc multiple comparisons allow you to test all combinations of pairs of means or at least more combinations of interest than are allowed using contrasts.

The **Multiple Comparisons** table is very complex. It includes comparisons of all possible combinations of pairs of cellcode means, twice. We have crossed out duplicates to simplify the table some. Even then there are 15 paired comparisons, and some are more meaningful than others. One useful set of comparisons is to test the difference between high and low math grades at each level of *father's education*. We have done this in Output 8.2c and Fig. 8.11 with contrasts. Similar comparisons are made in this table. Can you find them?

Another set of meaningful comparisons is identified by the circles in the **Multiple Comparisons** table and by Fig. 8.10. These post hoc comparisons show that there are no significant differences between any of the three pairs of means for the low math grades line in Fig. 8.10. The p values for comparisons 1, 2, and 3 are .667, .892, and 1.00, respectively. Can you see them in the figure and table?

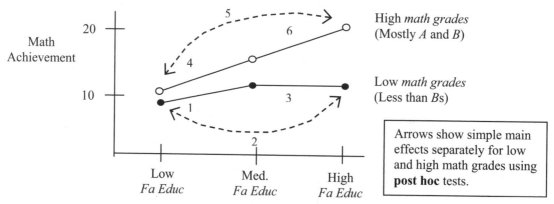

Fig. 8.10. Interaction plot showing simple effects for father's education.

In regard to students who had high math grades (the top line), there was not a significant difference between the low and medium father's education groups (comparison 4, $p = .103$) or between the medium and high father's education groups (6, $p = .057$). However, there was a difference for the high math grades students between those with father's who were HS grads or less (low) and those with a B.S. or more (high); this is comparison 5 and $p < .001$.

Example of How to Write About Problems 8.1 and 8.2 With Post Hoc Tests
Results

Table 8.1 shows that there was a significant interaction between the effects of math grades and father's education on math achievement, $F(2,67) = 3.97$, $p = .024$, partial eta^2 = .11. (The assumptions of independent observations, homogeneity of variances, and normal distributions of the dependent variable for each group were checked. The assumption of homogeneity of variances was violated; thus, results should be viewed with caution. The assumption of normal distributions of the dependent variable for each group was not violated.) Table 8.2 shows the number of subjects, the mean, and standard deviation of math achievement for each cell. Games-Howell post hoc tests revealed that, of students with low math grades, level of father's education did not seem to be associated with differences in math achievement. In contrast, for those who had mostly A and Bs in math, high father education was associated with statistically significantly higher math achievement than low father education ($p < .001$, $d = 2.02$). This effect size is considered large according to the literature.

Table 8.1
Two-Way Analysis of Variance for Math Achievement as a Function of Math Grades and Father's Education

Variable and source	df	MS	F	p	η^2
Math grades	1	325.78	10.86	.002	.14
Father's education	2	323.01	10.77	<.001	.24
Grades*father's educ	2	118.95	3.97	.024	.11
Error	67	29.99			

Table 8.2
Means, Standard Deviations, and n for Math Achievement as a Function of Math Grades and Father's Education

Father's education	Low math grades			High math grades			Total	
	n	M	SD	n	M	SD	M	SD
HS grad or less	23	9.83	5.04	15	10.49	6.57	10.09	5.61
Some college	9	12.81	5.06	7	16.43	3.43	14.40	4.67
BS or more	11	12.36	7.18	8	21.83	2.85	16.35	7.41
Total	43	11.10	5.69	30	14.90	7.01	12.66	6.50

8.2c. Computation of Contrasts

If you have preselected a limited number of comparisons between means, the appropriate follow-up test is **Contrasts**. Note that the maximum number of contrasts that you can do is limited in an SPSS run to the number of levels of the independent variable minus one, so that the number of contrasts will not exceed the number of degrees of freedom. To do **Contrasts** follow the steps below.

- Select **Analyze→ Compare Means→ One Way ANOVA....** You will see the **One Way ANOVA** window. (See Fig. 8.8.)
- Move *math achievement* into the **Dependent List:** box by clicking on the top **arrow** button.
- Move *six new cell codes* into the **Factor:** box by clicking on the bottom **arrow** button.

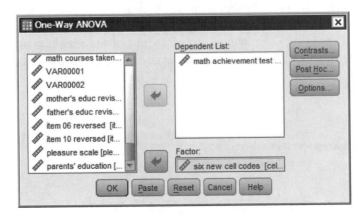

Fig. 8.8. One-Way ANOVA.

Now, we will compute Contrasts. In this case, we want to compare the math achievement of high versus low math grade students at each of the three levels of father's education. This is done by telling SPSS specific cell means to contrast. For example, if we want to compare only the first and second means while ignoring the other four means, we would write a contrast statement as follows 1 −1 0 0 0 0. This can be done with the SPSS syntax or using the point and click method as shown below.

- Click on the **Contrasts...** button to see Fig. 8.9.
- Enter 1 in the **Coefficients:** window.
- Then click on **Add,** which will move the 1 to the larger window.
- Next enter −1 and press **Add**; enter 0, press **Add**; enter another 0, press **Add.**
- Enter a third 0, press **Add**; enter a fourth 0. Fig 8.9 is how the window should look just before you press **Add** the final time. This compares the math achievement scores of students with low versus high *math grades* if their fathers have the lowest level of education.
- Now press **Next** so that the Fig. 8.9 says **Contrast 2 of 2.**
- Now enter the following coefficients as you did for the first contrast: 0 0 1 −1 0 0. Be sure to press **Add** after you enter each number. This compares the math achievement scores of students with low versus high grades if their fathers have the middle level of education.
- Press **Next** and enter the following **Coefficients** for **Contrast 3 of 3**: 0 0 0 0 1 −1. This compares the math achievement scores of students with low versus high grades if their fathers have the highest level of education.

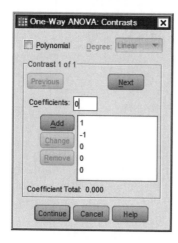

Fig. 8.9. One-Way ANOVA: Contrasts.

Thus, what we have done with the above instructions is simple effects, first comparing students with high and low *math grades* who have fathers with *less than a high school education*. Second, we have compared students with high and low *math grades* who have fathers with *some college*. Finally, we have compared students with high and low *math grades* who have fathers with a *B.S. or more*. Look back at how we computed the cellcode variable (or the syntax and Descriptives in Output 8.2c) to see why this is true. Note that in cases like this it might be easier to type the syntax, which is part of the reason many experienced SPSS users prefer to use syntax. However, you must type the syntax exactly correctly or the program will not run.

- Click on **Continue**.
- Click on **Options.**
- Click on **Descriptive** and **Homogeneity of variance test.**
- Click on **Continue.**
- Click on **OK**.

Output 8.2c: Contrasts for Comparing New Cell Means

```
ONEWAY mathach BY cellcode
 /CONTRAST= 1 -1 0 0 0 0
 /CONTRAST= 0 0 1 -1 0 0
 /CONTRAST= 0 0 0 0 1 -1
 /STATISTICS DESCRIPTIVES HOMOGENEITY
 /MISSING ANALYSIS.
```

Oneway

Pairs of means to be compared.

Descriptives

math achievement test

	N	Mean	Std. Deviation	Std. Error	95% Confidence Interval for Mean		Minimum	Maximum
					Lower Bound	Upper Bound		
1.00	23	9.8261	5.03708	1.05030	7.6479	12.0043	2.33	21.0
2.00	15	10.4889	6.56574	1.69527	6.8529	14.1249	1.00	22.7
3.00	9	12.8149	5.05553	1.68518	8.9289	16.7009	5.00	18.7
4.00	7	16.4284	3.43059	1.29664	13.2557	19.6012	14.3	23.7
5.00	11	12.3636	7.18407	2.16608	7.5373	17.1900	1.00	23.7
6.00	8	21.8335	2.84518	1.00592	19.4549	24.2121	15.7	23.7
Total	73	12.6621	6.49659	.76037	11.1463	14.1779	1.00	23.7

Test of Homogeneity of Variances

math achievement test

Levene Statistic	df1	df2	Sig.
2.548	5	67	.036

As in Output 8.1, the assumption of equal variances is violated, so we will select contrast tests that do not assume equal variances.

ANOVA

math achievement test

	Sum of Squares	df	Mean Square	F	Sig.
Between Groups	1029.236	5	205.847	6.863	.000
Within Groups	2009.569	67	29.994		
Total	3038.804	72			

The overall F is significant at $p < .001$. Note that this is the same as the *cellcode* F in Output 8.2b.

Contrast 1 looks at the difference between codes 1 and 2 (having lower and higher math grades if fathers have low education).

Contrast Coefficients

Contrast	Six new cell codes					
	1.00	2.00	3.00	4.00	5.00	6.00
1	1	-1	0	0	0	0
2	0	0	1	-1	0	0
3	0	0	0	0	1	-1

Because Levene's test was significant we will use this.

Note, only the third contrast is significant.

Contrast Tests

		Contrast	Value of Contrast	Std. Error	t	df	Sig. (2-tailed)
math achievement test	Assume equal variances	1	-.6628	1.81759	-.365	67	.717
		2	-3.6135	2.75997	-1.309	67	.195
		3	-9.4699	2.54478	-3.721	67	.000
	Does not assume equal variances	1	-.6628	1.99426	-.332	24.512	.742
		2	-3.6135	2.12629	-1.699	13.819	.112
		3	-9.4699	2.38826	-3.965	13.858	.001

Difference between contrasted means.

The Contrast Tests table shows the significance level of the three simple main effects shown in Fig. 8.11.

Interpretation of Output 8.2c

This output is the result of doing the bottom left-hand step, shown in Fig. 8.4, for interpreting a statistically significant interaction. Using Output 8.2c, we can examine three main simple effects statistically. The first table, **Descriptives**, provides the means of the *six new cell code* groups that will be compared, two at a time, as shown in the **Contrast Coefficients** table. The second table is **Levene's** test for the assumption that the variances are equal or homogeneous. In this case, the Levene's test is significant, so the assumption is violated and the variances cannot be assumed to be equal. The third table is the **ANOVA** table. Again, the overall F (6.86) is significant ($p < .001$), which indicates that there are significant differences somewhere. The **Contrast Tests** table helps us identify which simple effects were statistically significant. We will focus on one set of simple effects in our interpretation, the ones based on *t* tests that do not assume equal variances. Note that we have circled three **Sigs.** (the significance level or *p*). These correspond to the three simple effects shown with **arrows** in our drawing of the interaction plot (Fig. 8.11). For example, the left-hand arrow (and the first contrast) compares *math achievement* scores for both high and low *math grades* of students whose fathers have a relatively low education level.

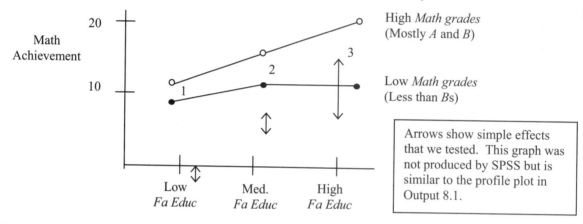

Fig. 8.11. Interaction plot showing three simple effects.

The contrasts confirm statistically what we thought from visual inspection of the profile plot in Output 8.1. As you can see in Fig. 8.11 and the circled parts of the **Contrast Tests** table, there is not a significant difference ($p = .742$) in *math achievement* between students with high and low *math grades* when their *father's education* is low. Likewise, the difference between students with high and low *math grades* when their *father's education* is medium (some college), although bigger (3.61 points), is not statistically significant ($p = .112$). However, when *father's education* is high, students with high (mostly *A*s and *B*s) *math grades* do much better (9.47 points) on the achievement test than those with low grades ($p = .001$). Thus, *math achievement* depends both on students' *math grades* and their *father's education*. It would also be possible to examine the simple effects for high and low math grades separately (the two lines) as we did in the interpretation for 8.2b, but it is usually not necessary to do both types of simple effects to understand the interaction.

Example of How to Write About Problems 8.1 and 8.2 With Contrasts
Results

Table 8.3 shows that there was a significant interaction between the effects of math grades and father's education on math achievement, F (2,67) = 3.97, p = .024, partial eta^2 = .11. (The assumptions of independent observations, homogeneity of variances, and normal distributions of the dependent variable for each group were checked. The assumption of homogeneity of variances was violated; thus, results should be viewed with caution. The assumption of normal distributions of the dependent variable for each group was not violated.) Table 8.4 shows the number of subjects, the mean, and standard deviation of math achievement for each cell. Simple effects contrast analyses revealed that, of students with highly educated fathers, those who had mostly A and B grades had higher math achievement than did students who had lower grades, t (13.86) = −3.97, p = .001). Simple effects at the other levels of father education were not significant, indicating that for students whose fathers were less educated, students with higher and lower math grades had similar math achievement scores

Table 8.3
Two-Way Analysis of Variance for Math Achievement as a Function of Math Grades and Father's Education

Variable and source	df	MS	F	p	η^2
Math grades	1	325.78	10.86	.002	.14
Father's education	2	323.00	10.77	<.001	.24
Grades*father's educ	2	118.95	3.97	.024	.11
Error	67	29.99			

Table 8.4
Means, Standard Deviations, and n for Math Achievement as a Function of Math Grades and Father's Education

Father's education	Low math grades			High math grades			Total	
	n	M	SD	n	M	SD	M	SD
HS grad or less	23	9.83	5.04	15	10.49	6.57	10.09	5.61
Some college	9	12.81	5.06	7	16.43	3.43	14.40	4.67
BS or more	11	12.36	7.18	8	21.83	2.85	16.35	7.41
Total	43	11.10	5.69	30	14.90	7.01	12.66	6.50

Problem 8.3: Analysis of Covariance

ANCOVA is an extension of ANOVA that typically provides a way of statistically controlling for the effects of continuous or scale variables that you are concerned about but that are not the focal point or independent variable(s) in the study. These continuous variables are called **covariates** (or sometimes, control variables). Covariates usually are variables that may cause you to draw incorrect inferences about the prediction of the dependent variable from the independent variable, if not controlled (then are possible confounds). It is also possible to use ANCOVA when you are interested in examining a combination of a categorical (nominal) variable and a continuous (scale) variable as predictors of the dependent variable. In this latter case, you would not consider the covariate to be an extraneous variable but rather a variable that is of interest in the study. SPSS will allow you to determine the significance of the contribution of the covariate as well as whether the nominal variables (factors) significantly predict the dependent variable, over and above the "effect" of the covariate.

In the HSB data, boys have significantly higher *math achievement* scores than girls. To see if the males' higher math achievement scores are due to differences in the number of math courses taken by the male and female students, we will use *math courses taken* as a covariate and do ANCOVA.

8.3 Do boys have higher *math achievement* than girls if we control for differences in the number of *math courses taken*?

To answer this question, first, we need to assess the assumption of homogeneity of regression slopes:
- **Analyze → General Linear Model → Univariate.**
- Next, move *math achievement* to the **Dependent** box, *gender* to the **Fixed Factor** box, and *math courses taken* to the **Covariates** box (see Fig. 8.12).

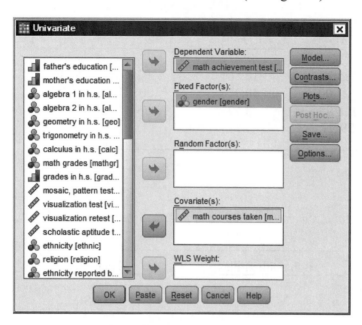

Fig. 8.12. GLM: Univariate.

- Click on **Model** and then click on the button next to **Custom** under **Specify Model** (see Fig. 8.13).

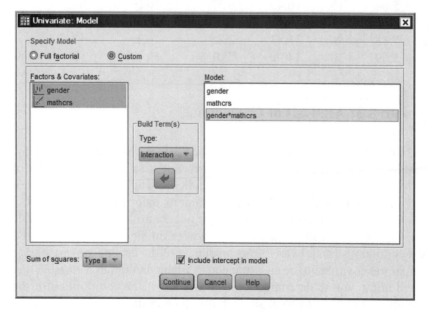

Fig. 8.13. Univariate: Model.

- Move *gender* from the **Factor & Covariates** box to the **Model** box. Do the same for *mathcrs*.
- Next highlight *gender* again, but hold down the "Shift" key and highlight *mathcrs*. This will allow you to have both *gender* and *mathcrs* highlighted at the same time. Click on the arrow to move both variables together to the **Model** box. This will make *gender*mathcrs*.

- Click on **Continue** and then **OK**. Your syntax and output should look like the beginning of Output 8.3.

Next, do the following:
- **Analyze → General Linear Model → Univariate.**
- Click on **Reset.**
- Next, move *math achievement* to the **Dependent** box, *gender* to the **Fixed Factor** box, and *math courses taken* to the **Covariates** box (see Fig. 8.12).
- Click on **Options** to get Fig. 8.14.

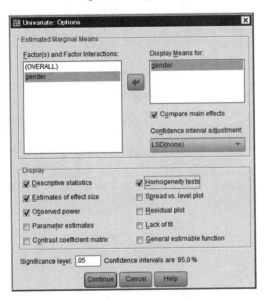

Fig. 8.14. GLM: Univariate options.

- Select **Descriptive statistics, Estimates of effect size, Observed power,** and **Homogeneity tests.**
- Move *gender* into the box labeled **Display Means for** (see Fig. 8.14).
- Click on **Compare main effects** to include output that will show which levels are statistically significantly different from one another.
- Be sure **LSD(none)** is in the **Confidence interval adjustment** pull-down menu.
- Click on **Continue** and then **OK**. Your syntax and output should look like the rest of Output 8.3.

Output 8.3: Analysis of Covariance (ANCOVA)

```
UNIANOVA mathach BY gender WITH mathcrs
  /METHOD = SSTYPE(3)
  /INTERCEPT = INCLUDE
  /CRITERIA = ALPHA(.05)
  /DESIGN = gender mathcrs gender*mathcrs.
```

Univariate Analysis of Variance

Between-Subjects Factors

		Value Label	N
gender	0	male	34
	1	female	41

Tests of Between-Subjects Effects

Dependent Variable: math achievement test

Source	Type III Sum of Squares	df	Mean Square	F	Sig.
Corrected Model	2085.698[a]	3	695.233	40.903	.000
Intercept	833.723	1	833.723	49.051	.000
gender	8.94E-005	1	8.94E-005	.000	.998
mathcrs	1775.937	1	1775.937	104.486	.000
gender * mathcrs	3.369	1	3.369	.198	.658
Error	1206.783	71	16.997		
Total	15132.393	75			
Corrected Total	3292.481	74			

a. R Squared = .633 (Adjusted R Squared = .618)

> Recall that this analysis was done to check the assumption of homogeneity of regression slopes, not to test a hypothesis. The factor and covariate do not interact, so the assumption of homogeneity of regression slopes has been met.

```
UNIANOVA
  mathach  BY gender  WITH mathcrs
  /METHOD = SSTYPE(3)
  /INTERCEPT = INCLUDE
  /EMMEANS = TABLES(gender) WITH(mathcrs=MEAN)
  /PRINT = DESCRIPTIVE ETASQ OPOWER HOMOGENEITY
  /CRITERIA = ALPHA(.05)
  /DESIGN = mathcrs gender .
```

Univariate Analysis of Variance

Between-Subjects Factors

		Value Label	N
gender	0	male	34
	1	female	41

Descriptive Statistics

Dependent Variable: math achievement test

gender	Mean	Std. Deviation	N
male	14.7550	6.03154	34
female	10.7479	6.69612	41
Total	12.5645	6.67031	75

> Note that the mean score of males was four points higher than females on math before the ANCOVA.

Levene's Test of Equality of Error Variances [a]

Dependent Variable: math achievement test

F	df1	df2	Sig.
5.572	1	73	.021

Tests the null hypothesis that the error variance of the dependent variable is equal across groups.

a. Design: Intercept+mathcrs+gender

> This is significant ($p < .05$); therefore, it indicates that the assumption of homogeneity of variances has been violated. However, because cell sizes are similar (34 and 41), this is not a big problem, especially given the way SPSS calculates the ANCOVA.

Tests of Between-Subjects Effects

Dependent Variable: math achievement test

Source	Type III Sum of Squares	df	Mean Square	F	Sig.	Partial Eta Squared	Noncent. Parameter	Observed Power[a]
Corrected Model	2082.329[b]	2	1041.164	61.946	.000	.632	123.892	1.000
Intercept	946.381	1	946.381	56.306	.000	.439	56.306	1.000
mathcrs	1783.894	1	1783.894	106.136	.000	.596	106.136	1.000
gender	6.001	1	6.001	.357	.552	.005	.357	.091
Error	1210.152	72	16.808					
Total	15132.393	75						
Corrected Total	3292.481	74						

a. Computed using alpha = .05

b. R Squared = .632 (Adjusted R Squared = .622)

The covariate (*mathcrs*) is significant, but the gender difference is not significant.

Notice that the power for the covariate (*mathcrs*) is extremely high (1.0), and for *gender* it is very low (.09).

Estimated Marginal Means

gender

Dependent Variable: math achievement test

gender	Mean	Std. Error	95% Confidence Interval	
			Lower Bound	Upper Bound
male	12.893[a]	.726	11.446	14.340
female	12.292[a]	.658	10.981	13.603

a. Covariates appearing in the model are evaluated at the following values: math courses taken = 2.11.

Note that the means are similar after differences in *math courses taken* were controlled.

Pairwise Comparisons

Dependent Variable:math achievement test

(I) gender	(J) gender	Mean Difference (I-J)	Std. Error	Sig.[a]	95% Confidence Interval for Difference[a]	
					Lower Bound	Upper Bound
male	female	.602	1.007	.552	-1.405	2.609
female	male	-.602	1.007	.552	-2.609	1.405

Based on estimated marginal means

Univariate Tests

Dependent Variable:math achievement test

	Sum of Squares	df	Mean Square	F	Sig.	Partial Eta Squared	Noncent. Parameter	Observed Power[a]
Contrast	6.001	1	6.001	.357	.552	.005	.357	.091
Error	1210.152	72	16.808					

The F tests the effect of gender. This test is based on the linearly independent pairwise comparisons among the estimated marginal means.

a. Computed using alpha = .05

Interpretation of Output 8.3

The ANCOVA (**Tests of Between-Subject Effects**) table is interpreted in much the same way as ANOVA tables in earlier outputs. The covariate (*mathcrs*) has a highly significant "effect" on math achievement, as should be the case. However, the "effect" of gender is no longer significant, $F(1,72) = .36$, $p = .55$. You can see from the **Estimated Marginal Means** table that the statistically adjusted math achievement means for boys and girls are quite similar once differences in the number of *math courses taken* were accounted for.

The **Observed Power** for *math courses taken* was 1.0, which indicates extremely high power. For gender the observed power was .091. This is very low power. The effect size for gender is also very small (eta = .071), so it may be that we have overlooked an important gender difference because of this low power. It is possible that once the strong relation between the number of math courses taken and math achievement was taken into account, there was no longer an important "effect" of gender on math achievement.

We include the **Pairwise Comparisons** table to show how to produce a post hoc test for the multiple levels of the independent variable. In our example, this table is not helpful since our overall test was not significant. If we had found a significant difference among an independent variable that had three or more levels, the Pairwise Comparison table would show which levels were significantly different from one another. We would also need to calculate an effect size (i.e., Cohen's *d*) for each pair that was statistically significantly different. To do so, we need to calculate the standard deviation for the estimated marginal means by using the formula: $SD = SE(\sqrt{n})$. We would use this standard deviation and the new estimated marginal means to calculate Cohen's *d*.

The **Univariate Test** table can be ignored since it gives us the same information as the **Tests of Between-Subject Effects** table.

Example of How to Write About Problems 8.3

Results

An analysis of covariance was used to assess whether boys have higher math achievement than girls after controlling for differences between boys and girls in the number of math courses taken (Table 8.6). (The following assumptions were checked, (a) independence of observations, (b) normal distribution of the dependent variable, (c) homogeneity of variances, (d) linear relationships between the covariates and the dependent variable, and (e) homogeneity of regression slopes. The assumption of homogeneity of variances was violated; however, because cell sizes were similar (34 and 41), this violation did not present an issue. All other assumptions were met.) Results indicate that after controlling for the number of math courses taken, there is not a significant difference between boys and girls in math achievement, $F(1, 72) = .36$, $p = .552$, partial eta$^2 = .60$. Table 8.5 presents the means and standard deviations for boys and girls on math achievement before and after controlling for number of math courses taken. As is evident from this table, virtually no difference between boys and girls remains after differences in number of math courses taken are controlled.

Table 8.5

Adjusted and Unadjusted Gender Means and Variability for Math Achievement Using Math Grades as a Covariate

		Unadjusted		Adjusted	
	N	M	SD	M	SE
Males	34	14.76	6.03	12.89	.73
Females	41	10.75	6.70	12.29	.66

Table 8.6

Analysis of Covariance for Math Achievement as a Function of Gender, Using Number of Math Courses Taken as a Covariate

Source	df	MS	F	p	eta^2
Math courses	1	1783.89	106.14	<.001	.60
Gender	1	6.00	.36	.552	.01
Error	72	16.81			

Interpretation Questions

8.1 In Output 8.1: (a) Is the interaction significant? (b) Examine the profile plot of the cell means that illustrates the interaction. Describe it in words. (c) Is the main effect of *father's education* significant? Interpret the eta squared. (d) Is the "effect" of *math grades* significant? (e) Why did we put the word effect in quotes? (f) How might focusing on the main effects be misleading?

8.2 (a) Interpret, in words, the post hoc multiple comparisons shown in Output 8.2b. (b) Interpret the contrasts shown in Output 8.2c. (c) When would you use post hoc tests instead of contrasts?

8.3   In Output 8.3: (a) Is the adjusted main effect of *gender* significant? (b) What are the adjusted *math achievement* means (marginal means) for males and females? (c) Is the effect of the covariate (*mathcrs*) significant? (d) What do (a) and (c) tell us about *gender* differences in *math achievement* scores?

Extra SPSS Problems

8.1.   Using the college student data.sav file, do *gender* and *marital status* seem to have an effect on *student's height* and do *gender* and *marital status* interact? Run the appropriate SPSS analysis and interpret the results.

8.2.   A county is interested in assessing the costs of its road construction (*cost*): whether it is more expensive in the South Florida District or in other districts in the county (*district*) in relation to whether the contractors were found through competitive contracts or fixed contracts (*status*). Using the Road construction bids.sav data set, conduct factorial ANOVA.
           (a) Are these factors independently significant in the level of *cost*?
           (b) Is there a significant interaction effect between the *district* and the *status* on the *cost*?
           (c) How much total variance in *cost* can be attributed to these variables?
           (d) If a post hoc test is necessary, conduct an appropriate test and discuss the results.

8.3.   Answer the following question using the Mall rentals.sav data file. Do people with higher levels of education (*edu*) have a shorter time for getting a mall rental (*interval*) than people with lower levels of education if we control for differences in the number of *status*?

8.4.   Open the Employee data.sav file. Do male or female (*gender*) employees have higher salaries (*salbegin*) if we control for the number of months they have been employed (*jobtime*)?

CHAPTER 9
Repeated-Measures and Mixed ANOVAs

In this chapter, you will analyze a new data set that includes repeated measure data. These data allow you to compare four products (or these could be four instructional programs), each of which was evaluated by 12 consumers/judges (6 male and 6 female). The analysis requires statistical techniques for **within-subjects** and **mixed designs.**

In Problem 9.1, to do the analysis, you will do a **repeated-measures ANOVA,** using the **General Linear Model** program (called **GLM**) in SPSS. In Problem 9.3, you will use the same GLM program to do a **mixed ANOVA,** one that has a repeated-measures independent variable *and* a between-groups independent variable. In Problem 9.2, you will use a nonparametric statistic, the **Friedman** test, which is similar to the repeated-measures ANOVA. SPSS does not have a nonparametric equivalent to the mixed ANOVA.

Chapter 5 provides several tables to help you decide what statistic to use with various types of difference statistics problems. Tables 5.1 and 5.3 include the statistics used in this chapter. Please refer back to Chapter 5 to see how these statistics fit into the big picture.

Assumptions of Repeated-Measures ANOVA
The assumptions of repeated-measures ANOVA are similar to those for between-groups ANOVA, and include independence of observations (except when the dependent data comprise the "within-subjects" or "repeated-measures" factor), normality, and homogeneity of variances. However, in addition to variances, which involve deviations from the mean of each person's score on one measure, the repeated-measures design includes more than one measure for each person. Thus, covariances, which compare deviations from the mean, need to meet certain assumptions as well. The homogeneity assumption for repeated-measures designs, known as sphericity, requires equal variances and covariances for each level of the within-subjects variable. Another way of thinking about sphericity is that, if one created new variables for each pair of within-subjects variable levels by subtracting each person's score for one level of the repeated-measures variable from that same person's score for the other level of the within subject variable, the variances for all of these new difference scores would be equal. For example, if you have three groups (Group A, Group B, and Group C) sphericity is assessing the following: variance$_{A-B} \cong$ variance$_{A-C} \cong$ variance$_{B-C}$. Unfortunately, it is rare for behavioral science data to meet the sphericity assumption, and violations of this assumption can seriously affect results. However, fortunately, there are good ways of dealing with this problem—either by adjusting the degrees of freedom or by using a multivariate approach to repeated measures. Both of these are discussed later in this chapter. One can test for the sphericity assumption using the Mauchly's test, the Box test, the Greenhouse-Geisser test, and/or the Huynh-Feldt tests (see below). Even though the repeated-measures ANOVA is fairly robust to violations of normality, the dependent variable should be approximately normally distributed for each level of the independent variable.

Assumptions of the Friedman Test
There are two main assumptions of the Friedman test. First, all of the data must come from populations having the same continuous distribution. This is not as stringent as the assumption of normality, which is the common assumption for ANOVA tests. The assumption of a continuous distribution can be checked by creating histograms. The second assumption is independence of observations, which is a design issue.

Assumptions of Mixed ANOVA

The assumptions for mixed ANOVA are similar to those for repeated-measures ANOVA, except that the assumption of sphericity must hold for levels of the within-subjects variable at each level of between-subjects variables. This can be tested using SPSS with Box's M through the Multivariate General Linear Model.

The Product Data Set

- Open the SPSS for Windows program. Open the **Product** data set. Do <u>not</u> retrieve the **hsbdata** for this assignment.

In this study, each of the 12 participants (or subjects) has evaluated four products that vary in cost (e.g., four brands of DVD players) on 1–7 Likert scales. Product A is the most expensive (i.e., $400), Product B is less expensive (i.e., $300), Product C costs only $200, and Product D is $100. You will find the data presented in the SPSS data editor once you have opened the product data set.

- Click on the **Data View** tab at the bottom of the screen to get Fig 9.1.

	A_$400	B_$300	C_$200	D_$100	gender
1	7	7	6	6	1
2	7	6	6	5	1
3	6	5	5	4	1
4	6	4	4	3	1
5	5	3	3	2	1
6	4	2	2	1	1
7	6	5	5	4	2
8	5	4	5	4	2
9	4	3	4	3	2
10	3	2	3	2	2
11	2	1	2	1	2
12	1	1	1	1	2

Note that this is what the data view for your product data looks like. In most studies the N would be larger.

Fig. 9.1. Data view for the product data.

Figure 9.1 shows the **Data View** for 12 participants who were asked to rate four *products* (*A_$400, B_$300, C_$200, D_$100*) from 1 (very low quality) to 7 (very high quality). The participants were also asked their *gender* (1 = male, 2 = female). Thus, subjects 1–6 are males, and 7–12 are females.

- Click on the **Variable View** tab to see the names and labels of the variables as shown in Fig. 9.2.

	Name	Type	Width	Decimals	Label	Values	Missing	Columns	Align	Measure	Role
1	p1	Numeric	1	0	Product 1	{1, Very Lo...	None	8	Right	Ordinal	Input
2	p2	Numeric	1	0	Product 2	{1, Very Lo...	None	8	Right	Ordinal	Input
3	p3	Numeric	1	0	Product 3	{1, Very Lo...	None	8	Right	Ordinal	Input
4	p4	Numeric	1	0	Product 4	{1, Very Lo...	None	8	Right	Ordinal	Input
5	gender	Numeric	1	0	Gender	{1, Male}...	None	8	Right	Nominal	Input

Fig. 9.2. Variable view.

We have labeled the measurement of the four *products* **scale** because the frequency distribution of each is approximately normal. We label *gender* and other dichotomous variables as nominal; however, despite this traditional designation for dichotomous variables, dichotomous variables, unlike other types of nominal variables, provide meaningful averages (indicating percentage of participants falling in each category) and can be used in multiple and logistic regression as if they were ordered. Furthermore, many dichotomous variables (but not *gender*) even have an implied order (e.g., 0 = do not have the characteristic and 1 = have the characteristic; thus, a score of 1 indicates more of the characteristic than does a score of 0).

In repeated-measures (also called within-subjects) analyses, SPSS creates the **Within-Subjects Factor** or independent variable from two or more existing variables (in this case *A_$400, B_$300, C_$200, D_$100*). These then become levels of the new independent variable. In this example, we will call the new variable *product*, and it has four levels (*A_$400*, etc.), indicating which product was being rated. In order for a set of variables to be converted into a meaningful within-subject factor, the scores on each of the existing variables (which will become levels of the new within-subjects variable) have to be comparable (e.g., ratings on the same seven-point Likert scale) and each participant has to have a score on each of the variables. The within-subject factor could be based on related or matched subjects (e.g., the ratings of a product by mother, father, and child from each family) instead of a single participant having repeated scores. The within-subjects design should be used whenever there are known dependencies in the data, such as when the same questions are systematically asked of multiple family members (e.g,, there is a mother, father, and child rating for each family) that would otherwise violate the between-subjects assumption of independent observations. The **dependent variable** for the data in Fig. 9.1 could be called *product ratings* and would be the scores/ratings for each of the four products. Thus, the independent variable, *product*, indicates which product is being rated, and the dependent variable is the rating itself. Note that *gender* is a between-subjects independent variable that will be used in Problem 9.3.

Problem 9.1: Repeated-Measures ANOVA

The GLM repeated-measures procedure provides a variety of analysis of variance procedures to use when the same measurement is made several times on each subject or the same measurement is made on several related subjects. The single-factor repeated-measures ANOVA, which we will use for Problem 9.1, is appropriate when you have one independent variable with two or more levels that represent the occasions on which repeated measures were made, the family member who was responding to the questions, or other similar categories involving non-independent assessments of the same measure and one outcome variable. If there are only two levels of the independent variable, the sphericity assumption is not a problem because there is only one pair of levels. If between-subjects factors are specified, they divide the sample into groups. There are no between-subjects (also called between-groups) factors in this problem. Finally, you can use a multivariate or univariate approach to testing repeated-measures effects.

9.1. Are there differences among the average ratings for the four *product*s?

Let's test whether there are differences among the average ratings of the four *product*s. We are assuming the *product* ratings are scale/normal data. Follow these commands:

- **Analyze → General Linear Model → Repeated Measures** (see Fig. 9.3).
- <u>Delete</u> the **factor 1** from the **Within-Subject Factor Name** box and <u>replace</u> it with the name **product**, our name for the repeated-measures independent variable that SPSS will generate from the four products.
- Type **4** in the **Number of Levels** box since there are four products established in the data file.
- Click on **Add** so the screen looks like Fig. 9.3, then click on **Define** to get Fig. 9.4.

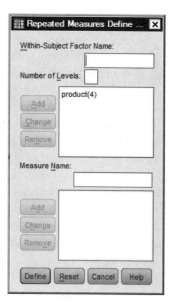

Fig. 9.3. Repeated measures GLM define factor(s).

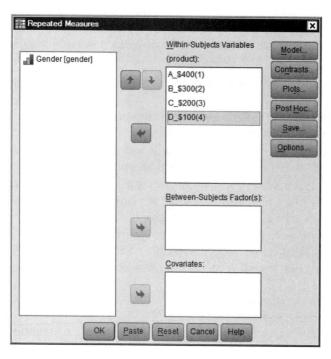

Fig. 9.4. GLM repeated measures.

- Now move *A_$400, B_$300, C_$200, D_$100* over to the **Within-Subjects Variables** box.
- Click on **Contrasts.** Be sure **Polynomial** is in the parenthesis after *product* (see Fig. 9.5). SPSS does not provide post hoc tests for the within-subjects (repeated-measures) effects, so we will use contrasts. If the products are ordered, let's say, by price, we can use the polynomial contrasts that are interpreted below. If we wanted to use a different type of contrast, we could change the type by clicking on the arrow under **Change Contrast**.
- Click on **Continue** to get Fig. 9.4 again.

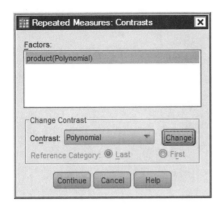

Fig 9.5. Repeated measures: Contrasts.

- Click on **Options** to get Fig. 9.6.
- Click on **Descriptive statistics**, **Estimates of effect size,** and **Observed power.**

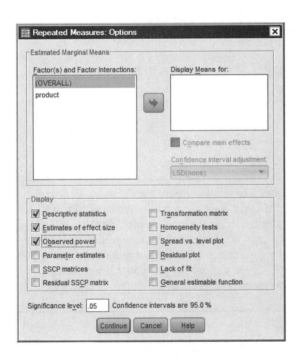

Fig 9.6. Repeated measures: Options.

- Click on **Continue**, then on **OK**.

Compare your syntax and output with Output 9.1.

Output 9.1: Repeated-Measures ANOVA Using the General Linear Model Program

```
GLM A_$400 B_$300 C_$200 D_$100
  /WSFACTOR=Product D Polynomial
  /METHOD=SSTYPE(3)
  /PRINT=DESCRIPTIVE ETASQ OPOWER
  /CRITERIA=ALPHA(.05)
  /WSDESIGN=product.
```

General Linear Model

Within-Subjects Factors

Measure:MEASURE_1

product	Dependent Variable
1	A_$400
2	B_$300
3	C_$200
4	D_$100

Descriptive Statistics

	Mean	Std. Deviation	N
Product A, $400	4.67	1.923	12
Product B, $300	3.58	1.929	12
Product C, $200	3.83	1.642	12
Product D, $100	3.00	1.651	12

> This shows four similar multivariate tests of the within-subjects effect. These are actually a form of MANOVA, which is discussed in the next chapter. In this case, all four tests have the same Fs, and are significant. If the sphericity assumption is violated, a multivariate test could be used or one could use the procedure shown below, which corrects the degrees of freedom.

Multivariate Tests[c]

Effect		Value	F	Hypothesis df	Error df	Sig.	Partial Eta Squared	Noncent. Parameter	Observed Power[a]
product	Pillai's Trace	.864	19.065[b]	3.000	9.000	.000	.864	57.194	1.000
	Wilks' Lambda	.136	19.065[b]	3.000	9.000	.000	.864	57.194	1.000
	Hotelling's Trace	6.355	19.065[b]	3.000	9.000	.000	.864	57.194	1.000
	Roy's Largest Root	6.355	19.065[b]	3.000	9.000	.000	.864	57.194	1.000

a. Computed using alpha = .05

b. Exact statistic

c.
  Design: Intercept
  Within Subjects Design: product

The epsilons, which are estimates of the degree of sphericity in the population, are less than 1.0, indicating that the sphericity assumption is violated. The "lower-bound" indicates the lowest value that epsilon could be. The highest epsilon possible is always 1.0. When sphericity is violated, you can either use the multivariate results or use epsilons to adjust the numerator and denominator *dfs*. Typically, when epsilons are less than .75, use the Greenhouse-Geisser epsilon, but use Huynh-Feldt if epsilon > .75.

Mauchly's Test of Sphericity[b]

Measure: MEASURE_1

Within Subjects Effect	Mauchly's W	Approx. Chi-Square	df	Sig.	Epsilon[a]		
					Greenhouse-Geisser	Huynh-Feldt	Lower-bound
product	.101	22.253	5	.001	.544	.626	.333

Tests the null hypothesis that the error covariance matrix of the orthonormalized transformed dependent variables is proportional to an identity matrix.

a. May be used to adjust the degrees of freedom for the averaged tests of significance. Corrected tests are displayed in the Tests of Within-Subjects Effects table.

b.
  Design: Intercept
  Within Subjects Design: product

Note that 3 and 33 would be the *dfs* to use if sphericity were not violated. Because it is, we will use the Greenhouse-Geisser correction, which multiplies 3 and 33 by epsilon, which in this case is .544, yielding *dfs* of 1.63 and 17.95.

Tests of Within-Subjects Effects

Measure: MEASURE_1

Source		Type III Sum of Squares	df	Mean Square	F	Sig.	Partial Eta Squared	Noncent. Parameter	Observed Power[a]
product	Sphericity Assumed	17.229	3	5.743	23.629	.000	.682	70.886	1.000
	Greenhouse-Geisser	17.229	1.632	10.556	23.629	.000	.682	38.565	1.000
	Huynh-Feldt	17.229	1.877	9.178	23.629	.000	.682	44.356	1.000
	Lower-bound	17.229	1.000	17.229	23.629	.001	.682	23.629	.993
Error(product)	Sphericity Assumed	8.021	33	.243					
	Greenhouse-Geisser	8.021	17.953	.447					
	Huynh-Feldt	8.021	20.649	.388					
	Lower-bound	8.021	11.000	.729					

a. Computed using alpha = .05

Significance of linear, quadratic, and cubic trends.

Tests of Within-Subjects Contrasts

Measure: MEASURE_1

Source	product	Type III Sum of Squares	df	Mean Square	F	Sig.	Partial Eta Squared	Noncent. Parameter	Observed Power[a]
product	Linear	13.538	1	13.538	26.532	.000	.707	26.532	.997
	Quadratic	.187	1	.187	3.667	.082	.250	3.667	.416
	Cubic	3.504	1	3.504	20.883	.001	.655	20.883	.985
Error(product)	Linear	5.613	11	.510					
	Quadratic	.563	11	.051					
	Cubic	1.846	11	.168					

a. Computed using alpha = .05

Tests of Between-Subjects Effects

Ignore this. There were no between-groups/subjects variables in this problem.

Measure: MEASURE_1

Transformed Variable: Average

Source	Type III Sum of Squares	df	Mean Square	F	Sig.	Partial Eta Squared	Noncent. Parameter	Observed Power[a]
Intercept	682.521	1	682.521	56.352	.000	.837	56.352	1.000
Error	133.229	11	12.112					

a. Computed using alpha = .05

Interpretation of Output 9.1

The first table identifies the four levels of the within-subjects, repeated-measures independent variable, *product*. The second table gives the *M* and *SD* for each product on the 1–7 rating, which is the dependent variable.

The third table presents four similar **Multivariate Tests** of the within-subjects effect (i.e., whether the four *products* are all rated equally). **Wilks' lambda** is a commonly used multivariate test. Notice that in this case, the *F*s, *df*, and significance are the same for each of the multivariate tests: $F(3, 9) = 19.07$, $p < .001$. The significant *F* means that there is a difference somewhere in how the products are rated. The multivariate tests can be used even if sphericity is violated. However, if epsilons are high, indicating that one is close to achieving sphericity, the multivariate tests may be less powerful (less likely to indicate statistical significance) than the corrected univariate repeated-measures ANOVA. Also note that the observed power is extremely high (1.0); thus it would be possible to have a statistically significant result with a small effect size, which might not be practically meaningful. However, eta is very large ($\sqrt{.864} = .93$) so this is not an issue.

The fourth table indicates that these data violate the sphericity assumption of the univariate approach to repeated-measures analysis of variance. Thus, we should use either the multivariate approach, the appropriate nonparametric test (Friedman), or correct the univariate approach with the **Greenhouse-Geisser** or other similar correction.

You can see in the **Tests of Within-Subjects Effects** that these corrections reduce the degrees of freedom by multiplying them by **Epsilon**. Using the Greenhouse-Geisser epsilon (because it is less than .75), the *df*s become $3 \times .544 = 1.63$ and $33 \times .544 = 17.95$. Even with this adjustment, the **Within-Subjects Effects** (of *product*) is significant, $F(1.63, 17.95) = 23.63$, $p < .001$, as were the multivariate tests. This means that the ratings of the four products are significantly different. However, this overall (*product*) *F* does not tell you which pairs of products have significantly different means.

SPSS has several tests of within-subjects contrasts. We have chosen to use the polynomial contrast on the assumption that the products are ordered, say, from the most expensive as *A_$400* to the least as *D_$100*. The **Tests of Within-Subjects Contrasts** table shows whether the four product means are significantly like a straight line (linear effect), a line with one change in direction (quadratic), and a two bend line (cubic). You can see that there is a highly significant linear trend and a significant cubic trend. Below, we plotted the means using a line graph (**Graphs → Interactive → Line**) to show the trends. Overall, there is a linear decline in ratings from *Product A* (4.67) to *Product D* (3.00). However, *Product B* has a somewhat lower mean (3.58) than *Product C* (3.83) producing the cubic trend.

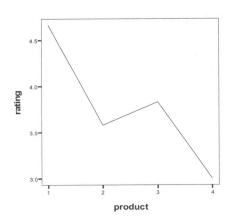

Dot/Lines show Means

In Output 9.1, we ignore the **Tests of Between-Subjects Effects** table because we do not have a between-subjects/groups variable in this analysis.

There is controversy over whether or not it is appropriate to report the univariate F even after a significant multivariate F has been found. Traditionally, univariate F's have been analyzed to understand where the differences are when there is a significant multivariate F. A simulation study found that utilizing univariate ANOVAs kept experimentwise error rate lower than other techniques. The argument against reporting the univariate F is that the univariate F misses the multivariate relationships and has been found in some studies to be incorrect. We recommend reporting the univariate F's for significant multivariate F's.

Example of How to Write About Output 9.1

Results

A repeated-measures ANOVA, with Greenhouse-Geisser correction, was conducted to assess whether there were differences between the average ratings of the four products. (The following assumptions were tested: (a) independence of observations, (b) normality, and (c) sphericity. Independence of observations and normality were met. The assumption of sphericity was violated. Thus, the Greenhouse-Geisser correction was used.) Results indicated that participants did rate the four products differently and that these differences were statistically significant, $F (1.63, 17.95) = 23.63$, $p < .001$, eta^2 = .68. The means and standard deviations for the products listed in order from most expensive to least expensive are presented in Table 9.1. Examination of these means suggests that participants rated more expensive products more highly than less expensive products. Polynomial contrasts indicated, in support of this, that there was a statistically significant linear trend, $F (1, 11) = 26.53$, $p < .001$, eta^2 = .71. However, this finding was qualified by the statistically significant cubic trend, $F (1, 11) = 20.88$, $p = .001$, eta^2 = .66, reflecting the higher rating for Product C than Product B.

Table 9.1

Means and Standard Deviations of the Four Product Ratings

Variable	M	SD
Product A ($400)	4.67	1.92
Product B ($300)	3.58	1.93
Product C ($200)	3.83	1.64
Product D ($100)	3.00	1.65

Problem 9.2: The Friedman Nonparametric Test for Several Related Samples

What could you do if the *product* ratings are <u>ordinal</u> data or the repeated-measures ANOVA assumptions are markedly violated? One answer is to use a nonparametric statistic. As you can tell from Table 5.1, an appropriate nonparametric test for when you have more than two levels of one repeated-measures or related samples (i.e., within-subjects) independent variables is the Friedman test.

9.2. Are there differences among the mean <u>ranks</u> of the *product* ratings?

Let's use *A_$400* to *D_$100* again with the following commands:
*   **Analyze → Nonparametric tests →Legacy Dialogs→ K Related Samples...** and move *product A [A_$400] to product D [D_$100]* to the **Test Variables** box (see Fig. 9.7).
*   Make sure the **Friedman** test type is checked.
*   Then click on **Statistics** to get Fig. 9.8.

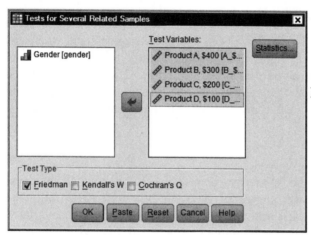

Fig. 9.7. Tests for several related samples.

*   Now click on **Descriptive**.
*   Click on **Continue**, then **OK**. Look at your output and compare it to Output 9.2a.

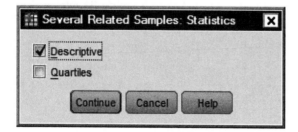

Fig. 9.8. Descriptive statistics for nonparametric tests for several related samples.

Output 9.2a: Nonparametric Tests With Four Related Samples

```
NPAR TESTS
  /FRIEDMAN=A_$400 B_$300 C_$200 D_$100
  /STATISTICS DESCRIPTIVES
  /MISSING LISTWISE.
```

Descriptive Statistics

	N	Mean	Std. Deviation	Minimum	Maximum
Product A, $400	12	4.67	1.923	1	7
Product B, $300	12	3.58	1.929	1	7
Product C, $200	12	3.83	1.642	1	6
Product D, $100	12	3.00	1.651	1	6

Friedman Test

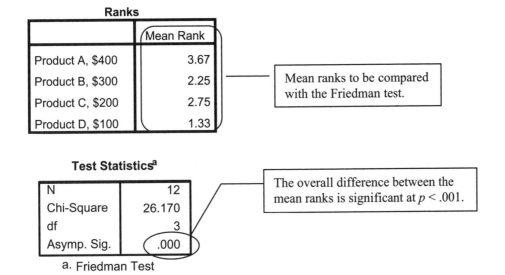

Ranks

	Mean Rank
Product A, $400	3.67
Product B, $300	2.25
Product C, $200	2.75
Product D, $100	1.33

Mean ranks to be compared with the Friedman test.

Test Statistics[a]

N	12
Chi-Square	26.170
df	3
Asymp. Sig.	.000

a. Friedman Test

The overall difference between the mean ranks is significant at $p < .001$.

Interpretation of Output 9.2a

The **Descriptive Statistics** table provides familiar statistics that were useful for interpreting the polynomial contrasts in Output 9.1 but are not themselves used in the Friedman test. Rather, ratings are *ranked*, and the means of these ranks are used in the Friedman test. The **Ranks** table shows the mean rank for each of the four *product*s.

There is not an easy method for calculating effect sizes for the Friedman test. Therefore, we recommend focusing on calculating effect sizes for any follow-up tests that you might do. Below, we will show you how to calculate an effect size for the follow-up Wilcoxon test.

The Friedman **Test Statistics** table shows the results of the null hypothesis that the four related variables come from the same population. For each rater/case, the four variables are ranked from 1 to 4, with 4 being the highest rank. The test statistic is based on these ranks. The **Asymp. Sig.** (asymptotic significance means this is not an exact significance level) of $p < .001$ indicates that there is a statistically significant overall difference among the four mean ranks.

In order to determine which pairs of differences between mean ranks are significant, and thus the likely source of the significant Friedman test, we will perform a nonparametric related-sample test, the Wilcoxon. See Table 5.1 for a more complete view of the different statistical tests used to compare samples.

- **Analyze → Nonparametric tests → Legacy Dialogs → 2 Related Samples** and make sure that **Wilcoxon** is checked.
- Then highlight both *Product A, $400* <u>and</u> *Product B, $300* and click the arrow to move them over together.
- Next, repeat for *Product B, $300* <u>and</u> *Product C, $200* and for *Product C, $200* <u>and</u> *Product D, $100*.
- Click **OK**.

Check to make sure that your syntax and output are like those in Output 9.2b.

Output 9.2b: Follow-Up Paired Comparisons for Significant Friedman

```
NPAR TESTS
  /WILCOXON=A_$400 B_$300 C_$200 WITH B_$300 C_$200 D_$100 (PAIRED)
  /MISSING ANALYSIS.
```

Wilcoxon Signed Ranks Test

Ranks

		N	Mean Rank	Sum of Ranks
Product B, $300 - Product A, $400	Negative Ranks	10[a]	5.50	55.00
	Positive Ranks	0[b]	.00	.00
	Ties	2[c]		
	Total	12		
Product C, $200 - Product B, $300	Negative Ranks	1[d]	3.00	3.00
	Positive Ranks	4[e]	3.00	12.00
	Ties	7[f]		
	Total	12		
Product D, $100 - Product C, $200	Negative Ranks	10[g]	5.50	55.00
	Positive Ranks	0[h]	.00	.00
	Ties	2[i]		
	Total	12		

a. Product B, $300 < Product A, $400

b. Product B, $300 > Product A, $400

c. Product B, $300 = Product A, $400

d. Product C, $200 < Product B, $300

e. Product C, $200 > Product B, $300

f. Product C, $200 = Product B, $300

g. Product D, $100 < Product C, $200

h. Product D, $100 > Product C, $200

i. Product D, $100 = Product C, $200

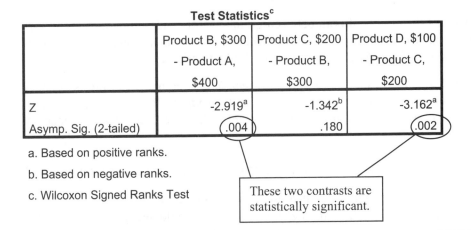

Test Statistics^c

	Product B, $300 - Product A, $400	Product C, $200 - Product B, $300	Product D, $100 - Product C, $200
Z	-2.919^a	-1.342^b	-3.162^a
Asymp. Sig. (2-tailed)	.004	.180	.002

a. Based on positive ranks.

b. Based on negative ranks.

c. Wilcoxon Signed Ranks Test

These two contrasts are statistically significant.

Interpretation of Output 9.2b

Given that there was a significant overall difference between the mean ranks, we followed up the Friedman with Wilcoxon tests. Since the products are ordered and there are four levels, it makes sense to do three orthogonal contrasts, contrasting adjacent pairs. A larger number of comparisons would prevent the comparisons from being independent of one another. Given that three post hoc comparisons were made, it would be desirable to make a Bonferroni correction on alpha, such that p would need to be .05/3 (.017) to be significant. Notice that the contrasts between *products 2* and *1* and between *4* and *3* are significant at this level and that they both indicate that the higher numbered product was given a lower rating than the lower numbered product. On the other hand, the difference between ratings for *products 3* and *2* was not significant. This is not surprising when you look at the mean ranks in Output 9.2a and suggests that the slight increase in ratings for *Product C* compared to *Product B* may not be important. Remember, however, that the Wilcoxon is not performed on the rating scores themselves but rather on the ranks of the ratings.

To calculate an effect size for this analysis, we can compute an r from the z scores and Ns (Total) that are shown in Output 9.2b using the formula $r = \dfrac{z}{\sqrt{N}}$. For Output 9.2b, $r = -.84$ (i.e., $-2.919/3.46$) for the comparison of Product A with Product B. For the comparison of Product C with Product D, $r = -.91$ (i.e., $-3.162/3.46$). Both of these are very large effect sizes.

Example of How to Write About Outputs 9.2a and 9.2b

Results

    A Friedman test was conducted to assess if there were differences among the mean ranks of the product ratings. (Assumptions of independence of observations and continuous distributions were checked and met.) A statistically significant difference was found, χ^2 (3, $N = 12$) = 26.17, $p = .001$. This indicates that there were differences among the four mean ranks. Three orthogonal contrasts were performed using Wilcoxon tests with the Bonferroni correction (*comparison-wise alpha* = .017). The contrasts between Products 1 and 2 ($Z = -2.92$, $p = .004$, $r = -.84$), and between Products 3 and 4 ($Z = -3.16$, $p = .002$, $r = -.91$) were found to be statistically significant; however that between Products 2 and 3 was not statistically significant. In both cases, the statistically significant contrasts indicated that the more expensive product was rated more highly, and the differences were very large according to Cohen (1988).

Problem 9.3: Mixed ANOVA

You can test null hypotheses about the effects of both between-groups factors and within-subjects factors with a **Mixed ANOVA** using the General Linear Model procedure. You can investigate interactions between factors as well as the effects of individual factors on a dependent variable.

Repeat Problem 9.1 except add *gender* to see if there are any *gender* differences as well as *product* differences and if there is an interaction between *gender* and *product*. Is *gender* a between-groups/subjects or within-subjects variable? The answer is important in how you compute and interpret the analysis.

9.3. Are there *gender* as well as *product* differences? Is there an interaction between *gender* and *product*?

- Click on **Analyze → General Linear Model → Repeated Measures** to get Fig. 9.3 again.
- In the **Repeated Measures Define Factor(s)** window (Fig. 9.3), you should see, *product* (4) in the top big box. If so, click on **Define** (if not repeat the steps for Problem 9.1).
- Then move *gender* to the **Between-Subjects Factor(s)** box (Fig. 9.4).
- Click on **Contrasts** to get Fig. 9.5.
- Click on *product(polynomial)* under **Factors.**
- Be sure that **Repeated** is listed under **Contrast**, then click **Change**. This will make it say *product (Repeated)*.
- Click **Continue.**
- Click on **Options** and be sure that **Descriptive Statistics, Estimates of effect size,** and **Observed power** are checked.
- Click **Continue.**
- Click on **Plots.**
- Move *gender* to the **Separate Lines** box and *product* to the **Horizontal Axis** box.
- Click **Continue.**
- Click on **OK.**

Compare your syntax and output with Output 9.3.

Output 9.3: Mixed ANOVA: Product by Gender

```
GLM A_$400 B_$300 C_$200 D_$100 BY gender
  /WSFACTOR=Product D Repeated
  /METHOD=SSTYPE(3)
  /PRINT=DESCRIPTIVE ETASQ OPOWER
  /CRITERIA=ALPHA(.05)
  /WSDESIGN=product
  /DESIGN=gender.
```

General Linear Model

Within-Subjects Factors

Measure:MEASURE_1

product	Dependent Variable
1	A_$400
2	B_$300
3	C_$200
4	D_$100

Between-Subjects Factors

		Value Label	N
Gender	1	Male	6
	2	Female	6

Descriptive Statistics

	Gender	Mean	Std. Deviation	N
Product A, $400	Male	5.83	1.169	6
	Female	3.50	1.871	6
	Total	4.67	1.923	12
Product B, $300	Male	4.50	1.871	6
	Female	2.67	1.633	6
	Total	3.58	1.929	12
Product C, $200	Male	4.33	1.633	6
	Female	3.33	1.633	6
	Total	3.83	1.642	12
Product D, $100	Male	3.50	1.871	6
	Female	2.50	1.378	6
	Total	3.00	1.651	12

> The multivariate test for product and the interaction are significant.

Multivariate Tests[c]

Effect		Value	F	Hypothesis df	Error df	Sig.	Partial Eta Squared	Noncent. Parameter	Observed Power[a]
product	Pillai's Trace	.897	23.152[b]	3.000	8.000	.000	.897	69.455	1.000
	Wilks' Lambda	.103	23.152[b]	3.000	8.000	.000	.897	69.455	1.000
	Hotelling's Trace	8.682	23.152[b]	3.000	8.000	.000	.897	69.455	1.000
	Roy's Largest Root	8.682	23.152[b]	3.000	8.000	.000	.897	69.455	1.000
product * gender	Pillai's Trace	.763	8.606[b]	3.000	8.000	.007	.763	25.818	.925
	Wilks' Lambda	.237	8.606[b]	3.000	8.000	.007	.763	25.818	.925
	Hotelling's Trace	3.227	8.606[b]	3.000	8.000	.007	.763	25.818	.925
	Roy's Largest Root	3.227	8.606[b]	3.000	8.000	.007	.763	25.818	.925

a. Computed using alpha = .05

b. Exact statistic

c.
　　Design: Intercept+gender
　　Within Subjects Design: product

Mauchly's Test of Sphericity[b]

Measure: MEASURE_1

Within Subjects Effect	Mauchly's W	Approx. Chi-Square	df	Sig.	Epsilon[a]		
					Greenhouse -Geisser	Huynh-Feldt	Lower-bound
product	.176	15.138	5	.010	.547	.705	.333

Tests the null hypothesis that the error covariance matrix of the orthonormalized transformed dependent variables is proportional to an identity matrix.

a. May be used to adjust the degrees of freedom for the averaged tests of significance. Corrected tests are displayed in the Tests of Within-Subjects Effects table.

b.

Design: Intercept+gender
Within Subjects Design: product

The *df*s for the univariate test are adjusted using the Greenhouse-Geisser epsilon because of lack of sphericity.

Tests of Within-Subjects Effects

Measure: MEASURE_1

Source		Type III Sum of Squares	df	Mean Square	F	Sig.	Partial Eta Squared	Noncent. Parameter	Observed Power[a]
product	Sphericity Assumed	17.229	3	5.743	41.768	.000	.807	125.303	1.000
	Greenhouse-Geisser	17.229	1.640	10.507	41.768	.000	.807	68.490	1.000
	Huynh-Feldt	17.229	2.114	8.148	41.768	.000	.807	88.317	1.000
	Lower-bound	17.229	1.000	17.229	41.768	.000	.807	41.768	1.000
product * gender	Sphericity Assumed	3.896	3	1.299	9.444	.000	.486	28.333	.993
	Greenhouse-Geisser	3.896	1.640	2.376	9.444	.003	.486	15.487	.924
	Huynh-Feldt	3.896	2.114	1.842	9.444	.001	.486	19.970	.966
	Lower-bound	3.896	1.000	3.896	9.444	.012	.486	9.444	.791
Error(product)	Sphericity Assumed	4.125	30	.138					
	Greenhouse-Geisser	4.125	16.398	.252					
	Huynh-Feldt	4.125	21.145	.195					
	Lower-bound	4.125	10.000	.413					

a. Computed using alpha = .05

Univariate within subjects and interaction trends.

Tests of Within-Subjects Contrasts

Measure: MEASURE_1

Source	product	Type III Sum of Squares	df	Mean Square	F	Sig.	Partial Eta Squared	Noncent. Parameter	Observed Power[a]
product	Linear	13.538	1	13.538	64.209	.000	.865	64.209	1.000
	Quadratic	.187	1	.187	5.000	.049	.333	5.000	.524
	Cubic	3.504	1	3.504	21.345	.001	.681	21.345	.985
product * gender	Linear	3.504	1	3.504	16.621	.002	.624	16.621	.956
	Quadratic	.188	1	.188	5.000	.049	.333	5.000	.524
	Cubic	.204	1	.204	1.244	.291	.111	1.244	.173
Error(product)	Linear	2.108	10	.211					
	Quadratic	.375	10	.038					
	Cubic	1.642	10	.164					

a. Computed using alpha = .05

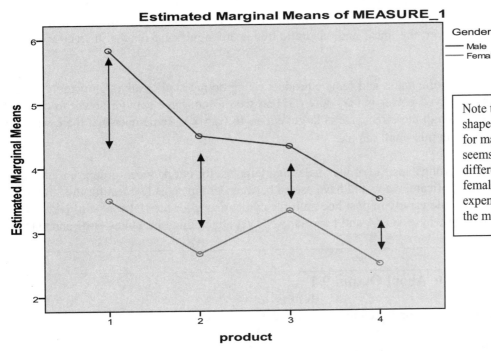

Estimated Marginal Means of MEASURE_1

Note that although the general shape of the curves are similar for males and females, there seems to be a greater difference between males' and females' ratings of the less expensive products relative to the more expensive ones.

Tests of Between-Subjects Effects

The test of whether males and females rate the products differently is not significant.

Measure: MEASURE_1

Transformed Variable: Average

Source	Type III Sum of Squares	df	Mean Square	F	Sig.	Partial Eta Squared	Noncent. Parameter	Observed Power[a]
Intercept	682.521	1	682.521	65.183	.000	.867	65.183	1.000
gender	28.521	1	28.521	2.724	.130	.214	2.724	.321
Error	104.708	10	10.471					

a. Computed using alpha = .05

Interpretation of Output 9.3

Most of these tables are similar in format and interpretation to those in Output 9.1. However, the addition of *gender* as a between-subjects independent variable makes the last table meaningful and adds an interaction (*product * gender*) to both the **Multivariate Tests** table and the univariate (**Tests of Within-Subjects Effects**) tables. Both multivariate and univariate tables indicate that (as in Output 9.1) there are differences among the four *product*s, with a very large effect size (eta). Again, one should interpret the Greenhouse–Geisser univariate test with corrected degrees of freedom given the lack of sphericity. In addition, the interaction of *product* and *gender* is significant according to both univariate and multivariate tests. This means that the downward overall trend for all subjects is somewhat different for males and females. The figure shows that males seem to rate the two inexpensive products more highly than do females, whereas the difference between ratings of males and females isn't as great for the two most expensive products. Recall that the **Tests of Within-Subjects Contrasts** table shows whether the four product means are significantly like a straight line (linear effect), a line with one change in direction (quadratic), and a two-bend line (cubic). Again, there are significant linear and cubic trends, but now the quadratic trend is also significant. For males, there is a linear decline in ratings from *Product A* (5.83) to *Product D* (3.50). For females, *Product B* has a lower mean (2.67) than *Product A* (3.50) and *Product C* (3.33) producing the cubic trend. And then the mean for *Product D* (2.50) is again lower, which produces the quadratic trend. Moreover, the linear and quadratic trends are significant for the interaction between *product* and *gender*.

The last table indicates that the males and female product rating do not statistically significantly differ ($p = .13$). However, the observed power is very low (.32) so we did not have enough power to detect the gender difference even though the effect size is large, eta $= .46$ ($\sqrt{.214}$). Remember that there were only six males and six females in this small sample.

Note that if we had three groups, instead of just males and females, for our between-groups variable and if the ANOVA had been significant, we would have used a between-groups post hoc test for this effect. SPSS provides the same wide variety of post hoc multiple comparisons for the **Between-Subjects Effects** that were available for one-way ANOVA and factorial ANOVAs, including the Tukey HSD and Games Howell.

Example of How to Write About Output 9.3
Results

A mixed ANOVA was conducted to assess whether there were gender and product differences in product ratings. (The following assumptions were tested: (a) independence of observations, (b) normality, and (c) sphericity. Independence of observations and normality were met. The assumption of sphericity was violated. Thus, the Greenhouse-Geisser epsilon was used to correct degrees of freedom.) Results indicated a statistically significant main effect of product, $F (1.64, 16.4) = 41.77$, $p < . 001$, partial eta$^2 = .807$, but not of gender, $F (1, 10) = 2.72$, $p = .13$, partial eta$^2 = .214$. However, the product main effect was qualified by a statistically significant interaction between product and gender, $F (1.64, 16.40) = 9.44$, $p = .003$, partial eta$^2 = .486$. Table 9.1 provides the means and standard deviations for product ratings by gender, and Figure 9.9 graphically represents the interaction between product and gender. Inspection of the figure suggests that males seem to rate the two inexpensive products more highly than do females; whereas the difference between ratings of males and females is less pronounced for the two most expensive products.

Table 9.1.

Means and Standard Deviations of the Quality Ratings for the Four Products Separately by Gender

Product	Males		Females	
	M	*SD*	*M*	*SD*
A, $400	5.83	1.17	3.50	1.87
B, $300	4.50	1.87	2.67	1.63
C, $200	4.33	1.63	3.33	1.63
D, $100	3.50	1.87	2.50	1.65

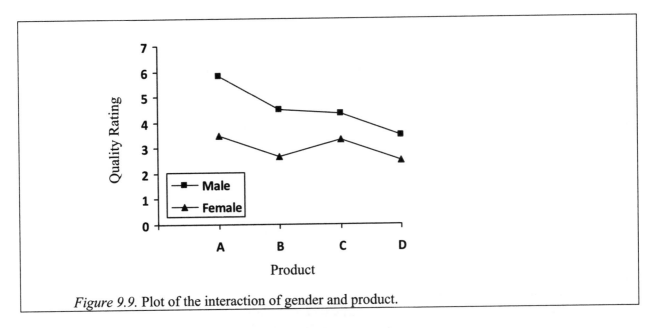

Figure 9.9. Plot of the interaction of gender and product.

Interpretation Questions

9.1.   In Output 9.2a: Explain the results in nontechnical terms.

9.2.   In Output 9.2b: (a) Why did we do three Wilcoxon tests after the Friedman test? Why Wilcoxons rather than paired *t* tests or Mann-Whitney U tests? (b) Explain the results of the Wilcoxon tests in nontechnical terms.

9.3.   In Output 9.3: (a) Is the assumption of sphericity violated? If it is violated, what can you do? (b) How would you interpret the *F* for *product* (within subjects)? (c) Is the interaction between *product* and *gender* significant? How would you describe it in nontechnical terms? (d) Is there a significant difference between the *gender*s? Is a post hoc multiple comparison test needed? Explain.

9.4.   Compare the *F* and significance for *product* in Output 9.3 to the same *F* in Output 9.1. Compare the *F*s for the linear, quadratic, and cubic trends for *product* in Outputs 9.1 and 9.3. Why are some things different?

Extra SPSS Problems

9.1.   Using the Anxiety 2.sav data file find out if there are differences between the average score for the *trails*.

9.2.   Using the Anxiety 2.sav data file: Are there *anxiety* as well as *trial* differences? Is there an interaction between *anxiety* and *trial*? Are post hoc tests needed?

9.3.   Using the New drug.sav data file answer the following research question: Are there significant differences between the average *pulse* rates?

9.4.   Using the New drug.sav data file: Are there drug type as well as pulse rate differences? Is there an interaction between *drug* and *pulse*?

CHAPTER 10

Multivariate Analysis of Variance (MANOVA) and Canonical Correlation

In this chapter, we introduce multivariate analysis of variance (**MANOVA**), which is a complex statistic similar to ANOVA but with multiple dependent variables analyzed together. The dependent variables should be related conceptually, and they should be correlated with one another at a low to moderate level. If they are too highly correlated, there is a risk of multicollinearity. If they are uncorrelated, there is usually no reason to analyze them together. The **General Linear Model** program in SPSS provides you with a multivariate F based on the linear combination of dependent variables that maximally distinguishes your groups. This multivariate result is the MANOVA. SPSS also automatically prints out univariate Fs for the separate univariate ANOVAs for each dependent variable. Similar to repeated measures analysis, these ANOVA results are not usually examined unless the multivariate results (the MANOVA) are statistically significant, and some statisticians believe that they should not be interpreted or reported. It is important to realize that one or more ANOVAs can be significant even if the MANOVA is not, or vice versa, so ANOVAs do not necessarily indicate why a significant MANOVA was significant. However, many people want to know whether there is a significant difference among groups in each variable, considered by itself, and the ANOVAs provide this information. The decision not to look at separate ANOVAs unless the overall MANOVA is significant does reduce Type I error relative to just doing the ANOVAs without this requirement. To determine whether it is typical in your field to report the ANOVA results, check published research studies in your discipline.

In this chapter, you will first do a one-way or single-factor MANOVA. This problem has one independent variable (*father's education revised*) and three dependent variables (*grades, math achievement,* and *visualization test*). One could do three separate one-way ANOVAs; however, doing these analysis would not answer our research question, and we would need to adjust our alpha level so we do not find a significant result by chance. By using MANOVA, you will see how the <u>combination</u> of the three variables distinguishes the groups in one analysis. The second problem is a two-way or **two-factor MANOVA**. It is two-way because there are two independent variables (*math grades* and *gender*) and MANOVA because two test scores are examined simultaneously as dependent variables. Problem 10.3 is a doubly multivariate or **mixed MANOVA**. It is mixed because there is a between-groups independent variable (intervention group) and a repeated-measures independent variable (time: pretest and posttest). It is MANOVA because these are two (or more) dependent variables. Mixed MANOVAs are one way to analyze intervention (experimental) studies that have more than one dependent variable.

Finally, Problem 10.4 uses **canonical correlation** for a problem with two sets of two or more variables each. Canonical correlation relates variables in set 1 to those in set 2.

Assumptions of and Conditions for Independent Samples MANOVA

The assumptions of MANOVA include: independent observations (each person's scores are independent of every other person's scores), multivariate normality, and homogeneity of variance/covariance matrices across groups (variances for each dependent variable are approximately equal in all groups plus covariances between pairs of dependent variables are approximately equal for all groups). Independence of observations is a design issue. Multivariate normality is difficult to check with SPSS. There are three aspects of multivariate normality to be assessed: (a) normality of each variable, (b) the linear combination of the variables should be normally distributed, and (c) all subsets of the variables have multivariate normality. Normality of each variable can be checked through Explore. Bivariate scatterplots will help to assess the linearity between variables, although it will not be assessing the multivariate relationships. MANOVA is robust to violations of multivariate normality and to violations of homogeneity of variance/covariance matrices if groups are of nearly equal size (N of the largest group is no more than about 1.5 times the N of the smallest group). Homogeneity of variance/covariance matrices can be checked with Box's M test or Levene's statistic.

In addition to these assumptions, for all types of MANOVA, another condition that should be examined is the potential for multicollinearity among the dependent variables. Multicollinearity can affect both results and the validity of interpretation of results.

Assumptions of Repeated and Mixed MANOVA

The assumptions of repeated or doubly multivariate (multiple measures obtained on multiple occasions) MANOVA include linearity of relations among the dependent variables and multivariate normality; for mixed MANOVA, an additional assumption is homogeneity of variance-covariance matrices between groups. If the sample sizes in each group are approximately equal, repeated MANOVA is robust to these assumptions. Linearity can be assessed through matrix scatterplots. If sample sizes are not equal, than Box's M test can be conducted to check the homogeneity assumption, and univariate normality can be assessed using plots to help assess the normality assumption. One should also make sure that sample sizes are sufficiently large. If the number of variables times the number of levels of the within-subjects variable approaches the sample size, then the doubly multivariate analysis should not be conducted. Rather, one should either use multiple MANOVAs with only one or two dependent variable each (if there are only two, three, or four dependent variables), or one should aggregate or drop some dependent variables (if there are more dependent variables).

Assumptions of Canonical Correlation

The assumptions of canonical correlation include: linearity (between each variable as well as between the variables and the linear composites), multivariate normality, and homoscedasticity. Because multivariate normality is difficult to assess, univariate normality can be evaluated. Multicollinearity should be assessed as well. All of the assumptions can be evaluated through a matrix scatterplot of the canonical variate scores (the scores are generated by the canonical correlation syntax). It is recommended to have at least 10 subjects per variable in order to have adequate power.

- Retrieve **hsbdataB.sav**. Note: You are to get the **hsbdataB.sav** file, *not the* **product.sav** file from the last lab assignment.

Problem 10.1: GLM Single-Factor Multivariate Analysis of Variance

Sometimes you have more than one dependent variable that you want to analyze simultaneously. The GLM multivariate procedure allows you to analyze differences between levels of one or more (usually nominal level) independent variables, with respect to a linear combination of several dependent variables. One can also include normally distributed variables (covariates) as predictors of the linear combination of dependent variables. When you include both nominal variables and normally distributed variables as predictors, the analysis usually is referred to as **MANCOVA** (multivariate analysis of covariance).

10.1. Are there differences among the three *father's education* groups on a linear combination of *grades*, *math achievement*, and *visualization test*? Also, are there differences between groups on any of these variables separately? Which ones?

Before we answer these questions, we will correlate the dependent variables to see if they are moderately correlated. To do this:

- Select **Analyze→ Correlate→Bivariate**.

- Move *grades in h.s., math achievement test,* and *visualization test* into the **Variables:** box.
- Click on **Options** and select **Exclude cases listwise** (so that only participants with all three variables will be included in the correlations, just as they will be in the MANOVA).
- Click on **Continue**.
- Click on **OK**.

Compare your output with 10.1a.

Output 10.1a: Intercorrelations of the Independent Variables

```
CORRELATIONS
  /VARIABLES=grades mathach visual
  /PRINT=TWOTAIL NOSIG
  /MISSING=LISTWISE .
```

Correlations

> The three circled correlations should be low to moderate.

Correlations^a

		grades in h.s.	math achievement test	visualization test
grades in h.s.	Pearson Correlation	1	.504**	.127
	Sig. (2-tailed)	.	.000	.279
math achievement test	Pearson Correlation	.504**	1	.423**
	Sig. (2-tailed)	.000	.	.000
visualization test	Pearson Correlation	.127	.423**	1
	Sig. (2-tailed)	.279	.000	.

**. Correlation is significant at the 0.01 level (2-tailed).

a. Listwise N=75

Interpretation of Output 10.1a
Look at the correlation table to see if correlations are too high or too low. One correlation is a bit high: the correlation between *grades in h.s.* and *math achievement test* ($r = .504$). Thus, we will keep an eye on it in the MANOVA that follows. If the correlations were .60 or above, we would consider either making a composite variable (in which the highly correlated variables were summed or averaged) or eliminating one of the variables.

Now, to do the actual MANOVA, follow these steps:

- Select **Analyze → General Linear Model → Multivariate**.
- Move *grades in h.s., math achievement,* and *visualization test* into the **Dependent Variables** box.
- Move *father's education revised* into the **Fixed Factor(s)** box (see Fig. 10.1).

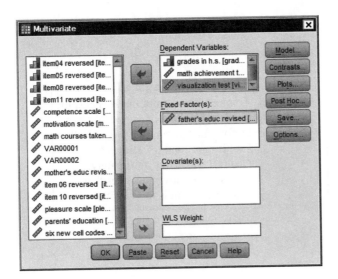

Fig. 10.1. Multivariate.

- Click on **Options**.
- Check **Descriptive statistics, Estimates of effect size, Observed power, Parameter estimates,** and **Homogeneity tests** (see Fig. 10.2). These will enable us to check other assumptions of the test and see which dependent variables contribute most to distinguishing between groups.
- Click on **Continue.**

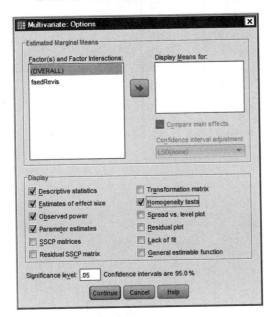

Fig. 10.2 Multivariate options.

- Click on **OK**.

Compare your output with Output 10.1b.

Output 10.1b: One-Way Multivariate Analysis of Variance

```
GLMgrades mathach visual  BY faedRevis
  /METHOD = SSTYPE(3)
  /INTERCEPT = INCLUDE
  /PRINT = DESCRIPTIVE ETASQ OPOWER PARAMETER HOMOGENEITY
  /CRITERIA = ALPHA(.05)
  /DESIGN = faedRevis.
```

General Linear Model

Between-Subjects Factors

		Value Label	N
father's education revised	1	HS grad or less	38
	2	Some College	16
	3	BS or More	19

To meet the assumptions it is best to have approximately equal cell sizes. Unfortunately, here the largest cell (38) is more than 1 ½ times the smallest However, fortunately, Box's test (below) indicates that this assumption is not violated.

Descriptive Statistics

	father's education revised	Mean	Std. Deviation	N
grades in h.s.	HS grad or less	5.34	1.475	38
	Some College	5.56	1.788	16
	BS or More	6.53	1.219	19
	Total	5.70	1.552	73
math achievement test	HS grad or less	10.0877	5.61297	38
	Some College	14.3958	4.66544	16
	BS or More	16.3509	7.40918	19
	Total	12.6621	6.49659	73
visualization test	HS grad or less	4.6711	3.96058	38
	Some College	6.0156	4.56022	16
	BS or More	5.4605	2.79044	19
	Total	5.1712	3.82787	73

Box's Test of Equality of Covariance Matrices

Box's M	18.443
F	1.423
df1	12
df2	10219.040
Sig.	.147

Tests the null hypothesis that the observed covariance matrices of the dependent variables are equal across groups.

a. Design: Intercept+faedRevis

This checks the assumption of homogeneity of covariances across groups.

This indicates that there are no significant differences between the covariance matrices. Therefore, the assumption is not violated and Wilks' lambda is an appropriate test to use (see the **Multivariate Tests** table).

Multivariate Tests[d]

Effect		Value	F	Hypothesis df	Error df	Sig.	Partial Eta Squared	Noncent. Parameter	Observed Power[a]
Intercept	Pillai's Trace	.938	341.884[b]	3.000	68.000	.000	.938	1025.652	1.000
	Wilks' Lambda	.062	341.884[b]	3.000	68.000	.000	.938	1025.652	1.000
	Hotelling's Trace	15.083	341.884[b]	3.000	68.000	.000	.938	1025.652	1.000
	Roy's Largest Root	15.083	341.884[b]	3.000	68.000	.000	.938	1025.652	1.000
faedRevis	Pillai's Trace	.229	2.970	6.000	138.000	.009	.114	17.823	.892
	Wilks' Lambda	.777	3.040[b]	6.000	136.000	.008	.118	18.238	.900
	Hotelling's Trace	.278	3.106	6.000	134.000	.007	.122	18.637	.907
	Roy's Largest Root	.245	5.645[c]	3.000	69.000	.002	.197	16.936	.934

a. Computed using alpha = .05

b. Exact statistic

c. The statistic is an upper bound on F that yields a lower bound on the significance level.

d. Design: Intercept+faedRevis

This is the MANOVA using the Wilks' lambda test.

The degrees of freedom are calculated through complex formulas that include the number of dependent variables, the number of levels of the independent variables, and the number of scores in each cell for the dependent variables.

Because this is significant, we know that the assumption of homogeneity of variances is violated for *math achievement*. We could choose to transform this variable to enable it to meet the assumption. Given that the Box test is not significant and this is the only Levene test that is (barely) significant, we are opting to conduct the analysis anyway but to use corrected follow-up tests.

Levene's Test of Equality of Error Variances[a]

	F	df1	df2	Sig.
grades in h.s.	1.546	2	70	.220
math achievement test	3.157	2	70	.049
visualization test	1.926	2	70	.153

Tests the null hypothesis that the error variance of the dependent variable is equal across groups.

a. Design: Intercept+faedRevis

These are the three univariate analyses of variance.

Tests of Between-Subjects Effects

Source	Dependent Variable	Type III Sum of Squares	df	Mean Square	F	Sig.	Partial Eta Squared	Noncent. Parameter	Observed Power[a]	Eta
Corrected Model	grades in h.s.	18.143[b]	2	9.071	4.091	.021	.105	8.182	.708	
	math achievement test	558.481[c]	2	279.240	7.881	.001	.184	15.762	.945	
	visualization test	22.505[d]	2	11.252	.763	.470	.021	1.526	.175	
Intercept	grades in h.s.	2148.057	1	2148.057	968.672	.000	.933	968.672	1.000	
	math achievement test	11788.512	1	11788.512	332.697	.000	.826	332.697	1.000	
	visualization test	1843.316	1	1843.316	124.973	.000	.641	124.973	1.000	
faedRevis	grades in h.s.	18.143	2	9.071	4.091	.021	.105	8.182	.708	.32
	math achievement test	558.481	2	279.240	7.881	.001	.184	15.762	.945	.43
	visualization test	22.505	2	11.252	.763	.470	.021	1.526	.175	.14
Error	grades in h.s.	155.227	70	2.218						
	math achievement test	2480.324	70	35.433						
	visualization test	1032.480	70	14.750						
Total	grades in h.s.	2544.000	73							
	math achievement test	14742.823	73							
	visualization test	3007.125	73							
Corrected Total	grades in h.s.	173.370	72							
	math achievement test	3038.804	72							
	visualization test	1054.985	72							

a. Computed using alpha = .05

b. R Squared = .105 (Adjusted R Squared = .079)

c. R Squared = .184 (Adjusted R Squared = .160)

d. R Squared = .021 (Adjusted R Squared = -.007)

We have calculated the etas (by taking the square root of the partial eta squared values) to help you interpret these effect sizes.

Parameter Estimates

Dependent Variable	Parameter	B	Std. Error	t	Sig.	95% Confidence Interval Lower Bound	Upper Bound	Partial Eta Squared	Noncent. Parameter	Observed Power[a]
grades in h.s.	Intercept	6.526	.342	19.103	.000	5.845	7.208	.839	19.103	1.000
	[faedRevis=1.00]	-1.184	.418	-2.830	.006	-2.019	-.350	.103	2.830	.797
	[faedRevis=2.00]	-.964	.505	-1.907	.061	-1.972	.044	.049	1.907	.469
	[faedRevis=3.00]	0[b]	.	.	.	.	.	.	.	.
math achievement test	Intercept	16.351	1.366	11.973	.000	13.627	19.075	.672	11.973	1.000
	[faedRevis=1.00]	-6.263	1.673	-3.745	.000	-9.599	-2.927	.167	3.745	.958
	[faedRevis=2.00]	-1.955	2.020	-.968	.336	-5.983	2.073	.013	.968	.159
	[faedRevis=3.00]	0[b]	.	.	.	.	.	.	.	.
visualization test	Intercept	5.461	.881	6.198	.000	3.703	7.218	.354	6.198	1.000
	[faedRevis=1.00]	-.789	1.079	-.732	.467	-2.942	1.363	.008	.732	.111
	[faedRevis=2.00]	.555	1.303	.426	.671	-2.044	3.154	.003	.426	.070
	[faedRevis=3.00]	0[b]	.	.	.	.	.	.	.	.

a. Computed using alpha = .05

b. This parameter is set to zero because it is redundant.

Each of the variables in brackets under **Parameter** comprises a dummy variable devised to distinguish one group from the others. For example, the circled weights (*B*) were devised to maximize differences between the first group (students whose fathers had high school education or less) and *all* other groups (those whose fathers had more education). Note that there are actually just two dummy variables, as a third would provide redundant information.

Interpretation of Output 10.1

The **GLM Multivariate** procedure provides an analysis for "effects" on a linear combination of several dependent variables of one or more fixed factor/independent variables and/or covariates. Note that many of the results (e.g., **Descriptive Statistics, Test of Between Subjects Effects**) refer to the univariate tests.

The first test we encounter is **Box's test of equality of covariance matrices**. This tests whether the covariances among the three dependent variables are the same for the three *father's education* groups. The **Box test** is strongly affected by violations of normality and may not be accurate. If *N*s for the various groups are approximately equal, then the Box test should be ignored. Our largest group ($N = 38$) is 2.3 times larger than our smallest group ($N = 16$), so we should look at the Box test, which is not statistically significant ($p = .147$). Thus, the assumption of homogeneity of covariances is *not* violated. If the Box test had been statistically significant, we would have looked at the correlations among variables separately for the three groups and noted the magnitude of the discrepancies. **Pillai's trace** is the best **Multivariate** statistic to use if there is violation of the homogeneity of covariance matrices assumption and group sizes are similar (not the case here). None of the multivariate tests would be robust if Box's test had been statistically significant and group sizes were very different.

MANOVA provides four multivariate tests (in the **Multivariate Tests** table). These tests examine whether the three *father's education* groups differ on a linear combination of the dependent variables: *grades in h.s.*, *math achievement*, and *visualization test*. Under most conditions when assumptions are met, **Wilks' lambda** provides a good and commonly used multivariate F (in this case $F = 3.04$, $df = 6$, 136, $p = .008$). The "intercept" effect is just needed to fit the line to the data so skip over it. The main part of this multivariate test table to look at is the *faedrevis* effect. This statistically significant F indicates that there are statistically significant differences among the *faedrevis* groups on a linear combination of the three dependent variables.

Next, we see the **Levene's test** table. This tests the assumption of MANOVA and ANOVA that the variances of each variable are equal across groups. If the Levene's test is statistically significant, as it is in this output for *math achievement*, this means the assumption has been violated. Results for *math achievement* should be viewed with caution (or the data could be transformed so as to equalize the variances; see Chapter 2 for how to transform variables).

Because the MANOVA was statistically significant, we will now examine the univariate ANOVA results (in the **Tests of Between-Subjects Effects** table). Note that these tests are identical to the three separate univariate one-way ANOVAs we would have performed if we opted not to do the MANOVA. Because the *grades in h.s.* and *math achievement* dependent variables are statistically significant and there are three levels or values of *father's education*, we would usually do post hoc multiple comparisons or contrasts to see which pairs of means are different.

Both multivariate and univariate (between subjects) tests provide measures of effect size (**eta squared**). For the multivariate test eta is .34 (the square root of .118), which is about a medium effect size. The univariate etas are .32, .43, and .14 for *grades in h.s.*, *math achievement* and *visualization test*, respectively. The first one is a medium effect, and the second is a large effect. The eta for *visualization* indicates a small effect that is not statistically significant ($p = .470$) (See Table 5.5 on page 92 for interpretation of the effect size for eta.) Note that the **Observed Power** for *math achievement* is very high (.945) and relatively high for *grades in h.s.* (.708). The high power indicates we might find statistically significant results with small effect sizes. For these two factors this was not the case because the effect sizes were large (eta = .43, and .32). *Visualization test* had very low observed power (.175), which might explain why this variable did not statistically significantly contribute to the model.

In MANOVA, a linear combination of the dependent variables is created, and groups are compared on that variable. To create this linear combination for each participant, the computer multiplies the participant's score on each variable by a weight (B), with the values of the weights being devised to maximize differences between groups. We see these Bs in the next table **(Parameter Estimates)**, so we can see how the dependent variables are weighted in the equation that maximally distinguishes the groups. Note that in the column under **Parameter** in this table, three variables are listed that seem new. These are the dummy variables that were used to test for differences between groups. The first one [*faedrevis* = 1.00] indicates differences between students whose fathers have a high school education or less and the other students whose fathers have more education. The second one [*faedrevis* = 2.00] indicates differences between students whose fathers have some college education and students in the other two groups. A third dummy variable would provide redundant information and, thus, is not considered; there are k−1 independent dummy variables, where k = number of groups. The next column, headed by **B**, indicates the weights for the dependent variables for that dummy variable. For example, in order to distinguish students whose fathers have a high school education or less from other students, *math achievement* is weighted highest in absolute value (−6.263), followed by *grades in h.s.* (−1.184), and then *visualization test* (−.789). In all cases, students whose fathers have less education score lower than other students, as indicated by the minus signs. This table can also tell us which variables statistically significantly contributed toward distinguishing which groups, if you look at the **sig** column for each dummy variable. For example, both *grades in high school* and *math achievement* contributed statistically significantly toward discriminating group 1 (high school grad or less) from the other two groups, but no variables statistically significantly contributed to distinguishing group 2 (some college) from the other two groups (although grades in high school discriminates group 2 from the others at almost statistically significant levels). *Visualization* does not statistically significantly contribute to distinguishing any of the groups.

We can look at the ANOVA (**Between-Subjects**) and **Parameter Estimates** table results to determine whether the groups differ on each of these variables, examined alone. This will help us in determining whether multicollinearity affected results because if two or more of the ANOVAs are statistically significant, but the corresponding variables are not weighted much (examine the **B** scores) in the MANOVA, this probably is because of multicollinearity. The ANOVAs also help us understand which variables, separately, differ across groups. Note that some statisticians think that it is not appropriate to examine the univariate ANOVAs. Traditionally, univariate Fs have been analyzed to understand where the differences are when there is a statistically significant multivariate F. One argument against reporting the univariate Fs is that it can be confusing to compare the univariate and multivariate results for two reasons. First, the univariate Fs do not take into account the relations among the dependent variables; thus, the variables that are statistically significant in the univariate tests are not always the ones that are weighted most highly in the multivariate test. Second, univariate Fs can be confusing because they will sometimes be statistically significant when the multivariate F is not because the multivariate is adjusted for the number of variables included. Furthermore, if one is using the MANOVA to reduce Type I error by analyzing all dependent variables together, then analyzing the univariate Fs "undoes" this to a large extent, increasing Type I error. One method to compensate for this is to use the Bonferroni correction to adjust the alpha used to determine statistical significance of the univariate Fs. Despite these issues, most researchers elect to examine the univariate results following a statistically significant MANOVA to clarify which variables, taken alone, differ between groups.

Example of How to Write About Output 10.1
Results
A multivariate analysis of variance was conducted to assess if there were differences between the three father's education groups on a linear combination of grades in h.s., math achievement, and

visualization test. (The assumptions of independence of observations and homogeneity of variance/covariance were checked and met. Bivariate scatterplots were checked for multivariate normality.) A statistically significant difference was found, Wilks' $\Lambda = .777$, $F (6, 136) = 3.04$, $p = .008$, multivariate $\eta^2 = .12$. Examination of the coefficients for the linear combinations distinguishing fathers' education groups indicated that grades in high school and math achievement contributed most to distinguishing the groups. In particular, both grades in high school ($\beta = -1.18$, $p = .006$, multivariate $\eta^2 = .10$) and math achievement ($\beta = -6.26$, $p < .001$, multivariate $\eta^2 = .17$) contributed statistically significantly toward discriminating group 1 (high school grad or less) from the other two groups, but no variables statistically significantly contributed to distinguishing group 2 (some college) from the other two groups. Visualization did not contribute statistically significantly to distinguishing any of the groups.

Follow-up univariate ANOVAs indicated that both math achievement and grades in high school, when examined alone, were statistically significantly different for children of fathers with different degrees of education, $F (2,70) = 7.88$, $p = .001$ and $F (2,70) = 4.09$, $p = .021$, respectively.

Problem 10.2: GLM Two-Factor Multivariate Analysis of Variance

MANOVA is also useful when there is more than one independent variable and several related dependent variables. Let's answer the following questions:

10.2. Do students who differ in *math grades* and *gender* differ on a linear combination of two dependent variables (*math achievement*, and *visualization test*)? Do males and females differ in terms of whether those with higher and lower *math grades* differ on these two variables (is there an interaction between *math grades* and *gender*)? What linear combination of the two dependent variables distinguishes these groups?

We already know the correlation between the two dependent variables is moderate ($r = .42$), so we will omit the correlation matrix. Follow these steps:

- Select **Analyze → General Linear Model → Multivariate**.
- Click on **Reset**.
- Move *math achievement* and *visualization test* into the **Dependent Variables** box (see Fig. 10.1 if you need help).
- Move both *math grades* and *gender* into the **Fixed Factor(s)** box.
- Click on **Options**.
- Check **Descriptive statistics, Estimates of effect size, Observed power Parameter estimates,** and **Homogeneity tests** (see Fig. 10.2).
- Click on **Continue**.
- Click on **OK**.

Compare your output with Output 10.2.

Output 10.2: Two-Way Multivariate Analysis of Variance

```
GLMmathach visual  BY mathgr gender
  /METHOD = SSTYPE(3)
  /INTERCEPT = INCLUDE
```

```
/PRINT = DESCRIPTIVE ETASQ OPOWER PARAMETER HOMOGENEITY
/CRITERIA = ALPHA(.05)
/DESIGN = mathgr gender mathgr*gender .
```

General Linear Model

Between-Subjects Factors

		Value Label	N
math grades	0	less A-B	44
	1	most A-B	31
gender	0	male	34
	1	female	41

Descriptive Statistics

	math grades	gender	Mean	Std. Deviation	N
math achievement test	less A-B	male	12.8751	5.73136	24
		female	8.3333	5.32563	20
		Total	10.8106	5.94438	44
	most A-B	male	19.2667	4.17182	10
		female	13.0476	7.16577	21
		Total	15.0538	6.94168	31
	Total	male	14.7550	6.03154	34
		female	10.7479	6.69612	41
		Total	12.5645	6.67031	75
visualization test	less A-B	male	5.7188	4.52848	24
		female	3.2750	2.74209	20
		Total	4.6080	3.97572	44
	most A-B	male	8.1250	4.04188	10
		female	5.2024	3.20119	21
		Total	6.1452	3.69615	31
	Total	male	6.4265	4.47067	34
		female	4.2622	3.10592	41
		Total	5.2433	3.91203	75

Box's Test of Equality of Covariance Matrices

Box's M	12.437
F	1.300
df1	9
df2	12723.877
Sig.	.231

Because $p = .231$ and is _not_ less than .05, we know that, this assumption of homogeneity of covariances across groups is _not_ violated.

Tests the null hypothesis that the observed covariance matrices of the dependent variables are equal across groups.

a. Design: Intercept+mathgr+gender+mathgr * gender

Multivariate Tests[c]

Effect		Value	F	Hypothesis df	Error df	Sig.	Partial Eta Squared	Noncent. Parameter	Observed Power[a]
Intercept	Pillai's Trace	.848	195.012[b]	2.000	70.000	.000	.848	390.025	1.000
	Wilks' Lambda	.152	195.012[b]	2.000	70.000	.000	.848	390.025	1.000
	Hotelling's Trace	5.572	195.012[b]	2.000	70.000	.000	.848	390.025	1.000
	Roy's Largest Root	5.572	195.012[b]	2.000	70.000	.000	.848	390.025	1.000
mathgr	Pillai's Trace	.189	8.155[b]	2.000	70.000	.001	.189	16.310	.952
	Wilks' Lambda	.811	8.155[b]	2.000	70.000	.001	.189	16.310	.952
	Hotelling's Trace	.233	8.155[b]	2.000	70.000	.001	.189	16.310	.952
	Roy's Largest Root	.233	8.155[b]	2.000	70.000	.001	.189	16.310	.952
gender	Pillai's Trace	.200	8.743[b]	2.000	70.000	.000	.200	17.485	.964
	Wilks' Lambda	.800	8.743[b]	2.000	70.000	.000	.200	17.485	.964
	Hotelling's Trace	.250	8.743[b]	2.000	70.000	.000	.200	17.485	.964
	Roy's Largest Root	.250	8.743[b]	2.000	70.000	.000	.200	17.485	.964
mathgr * gender	Pillai's Trace	.005	.171[b]	2.000	70.000	.843	.005	.342	.075
	Wilks' Lambda	.995	.171[b]	2.000	70.000	.843	.005	.342	.075
	Hotelling's Trace	.005	.171[b]	2.000	70.000	.843	.005	.342	.075
	Roy's Largest Root	.005	.171[b]	2.000	70.000	.843	.005	.342	.075

a. Computed using alpha = .05

b. Exact statistic

c. Design: Intercept+mathgr+gender+mathgr * gender

> The effects of *math grades* and *gender* on the combination dependent variable are significant, but the interaction is not.

Levene's Test of Equality of Error Variances[a]

	F	df1	df2	Sig.
math achievement test	1.691	3	71	.177
visualization test	2.887	3	71	.042

Tests the null hypothesis that the error variance of the dependent variable is equal across groups.

a. Design: Intercept+mathgr+gender+mathgr * gender

> Because this is significant, we know that the assumption of homogeneity of variances is violated for visualization. However, since groups are nearly equal in size, the test should not be strongly affected by this violation.

> These etas were computed so you would not have to compute them.

Tests of Between-Subjects Effects

Source	Dependent Variable	Type III Sum of Squares	df	Mean Square	F	Sig.	Partial Eta Squared	Noncent. Parameter	Observed Power[a]	Eta
Corrected Model	math achievement test	814.481[b]	3	271.494	7.779	.000	.247	23.337	.985	
	visualization test	165.986[c]	3	55.329	4.064	.010	.147	12.193	.824	
Intercept	math achievement test	11971.773	1	11971.773	343.017	.000	.829	343.017	1.000	
	visualization test	2082.167	1	2082.167	152.956	.000	.683	152.956	1.000	
mathgr	math achievement test	515.463	1	515.463	14.769	.000	.172	14.769	.966	.41
	visualization test	78.485	1	78.485	5.766	.019	.075	5.766	.659	.27
gender	math achievement test	483.929	1	483.929	13.866	.000	.163	13.866	.957	.40
	visualization test	120.350	1	120.350	8.841	.004	.111	8.841	.835	.33
mathgr * gender	math achievement test	11.756	1	11.756	.337	.563	.005	.337	.088	.07
	visualization test	.958	1	.958	.070	.792	.001	.070	.058	.03
Error	math achievement test	2478.000	71	34.901						
	visualization test	966.510	71	13.613						
Total	math achievement test	15132.393	75							
	visualization test	3194.438	75							
Corrected Total	math achievement test	3292.481	74							
	visualization test	1132.497	74							

a. Computed using alpha = .05

b. R Squared = .247 (Adjusted R Squared = .216)

c. R Squared = .147 (Adjusted R Squared = .111)

Parameter Estimates

Dependent Variable	Parameter	B	Std. Error	t	Sig.	95% Confidence Interval Lower Bound	95% Confidence Interval Upper Bound	Partial Eta Squared	Noncent. Parameter	Observed Power[a]
math achievement test	Intercept	13.048	1.289	10.121	.000	10.477	15.618	.591	10.121	1.000
	[mathgr=0]	-4.714	1.846	-2.554	.013	-8.395	-1.034	.084	2.554	.712
	[mathgr=1]	0[b]	.	.	.	.	.	.	.	.
	[gender=0]	6.219	2.270	2.740	.008	1.693	10.745	.096	2.740	.771
	[gender=1]	0[b]	.	.	.	.	.	.	.	.
	[mathgr=0] * [gender=0]	-1.677	2.890	-.580	.563	-7.440	4.085	.005	.580	.088
	[mathgr=0] * [gender=1]	0[b]	.	.	.	.	.	.	.	.
	[mathgr=1] * [gender=0]	0[b]	.	.	.	.	.	.	.	.
	[mathgr=1] * [gender=1]	0[b]	.	.	.	.	.	.	.	.
visualization test	Intercept	5.202	.865	6.012	.000	3.597	6.808	.370	6.462	1.000
	[mathgr=0]	-1.927	1.153	-1.672	.099	-4.226	.371	.038	1.672	.378
	[mathgr=1]	0[b]	.	.	.	.	.	.	.	.
	[gender=0]	2.923	1.418	2.062	.043	.096	5.749	.056	2.062	.529
	[gender=1]	0[b]	.	.	.	.	.	.	.	.
	[mathgr=0] * [gender=0]	-.479	1.805	-.265	.792	-4.078	3.120	.001	.265	.058
	[mathgr=0] * [gender=1]	0[b]	.	.	.	.	.	.	.	.
	[mathgr=1] * [gender=0]	0[b]	.	.	.	.	.	.	.	.
	[mathgr=1] * [gender=1]	0[b]	.	.	.	.	.	.	.	.

Note that the weights for *math achievement* are larger than those for *visualization test*.

a. Computed using alpha = .05

b. This parameter is set to zero because it is redundant.

Interpretation of Output 10.2

Many of the tables are similar to those in Output 10.1. For the **Descriptive Statistics**, we now see means and standard deviations of the dependent variables for the groups made up of every combination of the two levels of *math grades* and the two levels of *gender*. **Box's test** again is not statistically significant, indicating that the assumption of homogeneity of covariance matrices is met.

The main difference in 10.2, compared with 10.1, for both the **Multivariate Tests** table and the univariate **Tests of Between-Subjects Effects** table, is the inclusion of two main effects (one for each independent variable) and one interaction (of *math grades* and *gender*; shown in the output as *math grades * gender*). The interpretation of this interaction, if it were statistically significant, would be similar to that in Output 10.1. However, note that although both the multivariate main effects of *math grades* and *gender* are statistically significant, the multivariate interaction is not statistically significant. Because the interaction was not statistically significant, we can look at the univariate tests of main effects, but we should not examine the univariate interaction effects.

Levene's test indicates that there is heterogeneity of variances for *visualization test*. Again, we could have transformed that variable to equalize the variances. However, if we consider only the main effects of *gender* and of *math grades* (since the interaction is not statistically significant), then *N*s are approximately equal for the groups (34 and 41 for *gender* and 31 and 44 for *math grades*), so this is less of a concern.

The **Tests of Between-Subjects Effects** table indicates that there are statistically significant main effects of both independent variables on both dependent variables, with medium to large effect sizes. For example, the "effect" of *math grades* on *math achievement* is large (eta = .41) and the effect of *math grades* on *visualization* test is medium (eta = .27). Refer again to Table 5.5. Note that both of these had relatively high power (.97 and .70, respectively).

The **Parameter Estimates** table now has three dummy variables: for the difference between students with less A-B and more A-B (MATHGR = 0), for male versus not male (GEND = 0), as well as for the interaction term (MATHGR = 0 GEND = 0). Thus, we can see that *math achievement* contributes more than *visualization test* to distinguishing students with better and worse math grades as well as contributing more to distinguishing boys from girls.

Example of How to Write About Output 10.2
Results

To assess whether boys and girls with higher and lower math grades have different math achievement and visualization test scores and whether there was an interaction between gender and math grades, a multivariate analysis of variance was conducted. (The assumptions of independence of observations and homogeneity of variance/covariance were checked and met. Bivariate scatterplots were checked for multivariate normality.) The interaction was not statistically significant, Wilks' Λ = .995, F (2, 70) = .17, p =.843, multivariate η^2 = .005. The main effect for gender was statistically significant, Wilks' Λ = .800, F (2, 70) = 8.74, p < .001, multivariate η^2 = .20. This indicates that the linear composite of math achievement and visualization test differs for males and females. The main effect for math grades is also statistically significant, Wilks' Λ = .811, F (2, 70) = 8.15, p = .001, multivariate η^2 = .19. This indicates that the linear composite differs for different levels of math grades. Follow-up ANOVAs (Table 10.2) indicate that effects of both math grades and gender were statistically significant for both math achievement and visualization. Males scored higher on both outcomes and students with higher math grades were higher on both outcomes (see Table 10.1).

Table 10.1

Means and Standard Deviations for Math Achievement and Visualization Test as a Function of Math Grades and Gender

Group	n	Math achievement		Visualization	
		M	SD	M	SD
Low math grades					
Males	24	12.88	5.73	5.72	4.53
Females	20	8.33	5.33	3.28	2.74
High math grades					
Males	10	19.27	4.17	8.13	4.04
Females	21	13.05	7.17	5.20	3.20

Table 10.2

Univariate Effects of Math Grades and Gender on Math Achievement and Visualization Test Scores

Source	Dependent variable	df	F	p	η
Math grades	Math achievement	1	14.77	.001	.41
	☐isualization test	1	5.77	.019	.27
Gender	Math achie☐ement	1	13.87	.001	.40
	Visualization test	1	8.84	.004	.33
Math grades × gender	Math achievement	1	.34	.563	.07
	Visualization test	1	☐.07	.792	.03
Error	Math achievement	71			
	Visualization test	71			

Problem 10.3: Mixed MANOVA

There might be times when you want to find out if there are differences between groups as well as within subjects; this can be answered with Mixed MANOVA.

We have created a new dataset to use for this problem (MixedMANOVAdata).

- Retrieve **MixedMANOVAdata.sav**.

Let's answer the following question:

10.3. Is there a difference between participants in the intervention group (group 1) and participants in the control group (group 2) in the amount of change that occurs over time in scores on two different *outcome* measures?

We will not check the assumptions of linearity, multivariate normality, or homogeneity of variance-covariance matrices because MANOVA is robust against these assumptions when the sample sizes are equal. If our sample sizes had not been approximately equal, we would need to check these assumptions.
- **Analyze → General Linear Model → Repeated Measures** (see Fig. 10.3).
- <u>Delete</u> the **factor 1** from the **Within-Subject Factor Name** box and <u>replace</u> it with the name **time,** our name for the repeated-measures independent variable that SPSS will generate.
- Type *2* in the **Number of Levels** box.
- Click on **Add.**
- In the **Measure Name** box, type *dv1*.
- Click on **Add.**
- In the **Measure Name box,** type *dv2*.
- Click on **Add.** The window should look like Fig. 10.3.

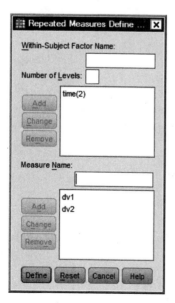

Fig. 10.3. Repeated measures define factor(s).

- Click on **Define,** which changes the screen to a new menu box (see Fig. 9.4 in Chapter 9 if you need help).

- Now while holding down the "shift" key, click on *outcome 1 pretest, outcome 1 posttest, outcome 2 pretest,* and *outcome 2 posttest*. Click on the arrow to move these over to the **Within-Subjects Variables** box.
- Highlight *group* and then click on the arrow to move it over to the **Between-Subjects Factor(s)** box.
- Click on **Plots**. The **Repeated Measures: Profile Plots** window will open.
- Highlight *time* and then click on the arrow to move it to the **Horizontal Axis** box.
- Highlight *group* and then click on the arrow to move it to the **Separate Lines** box.
- Click on **Add**. This is will move the variables down to the **Plots** box.

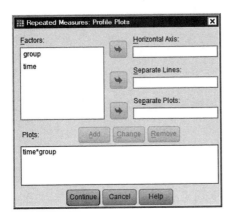

Fig. 10.4. Repeated measures: Profile plots.

- Click on **Continue**.
- Click on **Options**. (see Fig. 9.6 in Chapter 9 if you need help).
- Click on **Descriptive Statistics, Estimates of effect size, Observed power,** and **Homogeneity tests.**
- Click on **Continue**, then on **OK**.

Compare your syntax and output with Output 10.3.

Output 10.3: Repeated Measures MANOVA Using the General Linear Model

```
GLMDV11 DV12 DV21 DV22 BY group
  /WSFACTOR = time 2 Polynomial
  /MEASURE = dv1 dv2
  /METHOD = SSTYPE(3)
  /PLOT = PROFILE(time*group)
  /PRINT = DESCRIPTIVE ETASQ OPOWER HOMOGENEITY
  /CRITERIA = ALPHA(.05)
  /WSDESIGN = time
  /DESIGN = group.
```

General Linear Model

Within-Subjects Factors

Measure	time	Dependent Variable
dv1	1	DV11
	2	DV12
dv2	1	DV21
	2	DV22

Between-Subjects Factors

		Value Label	N
group	1	intervention	10
	2	comparison	10

Descriptive Statistics

	group	Mean	Std. Deviation	N
outcome 1 pretest	intervention	5.00	1.826	10
	comparison	5.10	1.370	10
	Total	5.05	1.572	20
outcome 1 posttest	intervention	10.00	1.414	10
	comparison	5.50	1.780	10
	Total	7.75	2.789	20
outcome 2 pretest	intervention	20.00	7.454	10
	comparison	20.50	6.852	10
	Total	20.25	6.973	20
outcome 2 posttest	intervention	20.50	6.852	10
	comparison	19.00	8.097	10
	Total	19.75	7.340	20

Box's Test of Equality of Covariance Matrices [a]

Box's M	4.936
F	.372
df1	10
df2	1549.004
Sig.	.959

Tests the null hypothesis that the observed covariance matrices of the dependent variables are equal across groups.

a.

Design: Intercept+group
Within Subjects Design: time

This table tells you what effects are statistically significant. In this case, there are statistically significant multivariate main effects of *group* and *time*, but these are qualified by a *group* by *time* interaction. This indicates that the difference between the intervention and control group on the linear combination of the two dependent variables is different at pretest than at posttest. Examination of the means suggests that this is because groups do not differ on either dependent variable at the time of the pretest, but they do differ, particularly on the first dependent variable, at the time of the posttest.

Multivariate Tests[c]

Effect			Value	F	Hypothesis df	Error df	Sig.	Partial Eta Squared	Noncent. Parameter	Observed Power[a]
Between Subjects	Intercept	Pillai's Trace	.955	182.194[b]	2.000	17.000	.000	.955	364.388	1.000
		Wilks' Lambda	.045	182.194[b]	2.000	17.000	.000	.955	364.388	1.000
		Hotelling's Trace	21.435	182.194[b]	2.000	17.000	.000	.955	364.388	1.000
		Roy's Largest Root	21.435	182.194[b]	2.000	17.000	.000	.955	364.388	1.000
	group	Pillai's Trace	.553	10.499[b]	2.000	17.000	.001	.553	20.998	.970
		Wilks' Lambda	.447	10.499[b]	2.000	17.000	.001	.553	20.998	.970
		Hotelling's Trace	1.235	10.499[b]	2.000	17.000	.001	.553	20.998	.970
		Roy's Largest Root	1.235	10.499[b]	2.000	17.000	.001	.553	20.998	.970
Within Subjects	time	Pillai's Trace	.822	39.321[b]	2.000	17.000	.000	.822	78.642	1.000
		Wilks' Lambda	.178	39.321[b]	2.000	17.000	.000	.822	78.642	1.000
		Hotelling's Trace	4.626	39.321[b]	2.000	17.000	.000	.822	78.642	1.000
		Roy's Largest Root	4.626	39.321[b]	2.000	17.000	.000	.822	78.642	1.000
	time * group	Pillai's Trace	.786	31.235[b]	2.000	17.000	.000	.786	62.470	1.000
		Wilks' Lambda	.214	31.235[b]	2.000	17.000	.000	.786	62.470	1.000
		Hotelling's Trace	3.675	31.235[b]	2.000	17.000	.000	.786	62.470	1.000
		Roy's Largest Root	3.675	31.235[b]	2.000	17.000	.000	.786	62.470	1.000

a. Computed using alpha = .05

b. Exact statistic

c.

Design: Intercept+group
Within Subjects Design: time

Note that Mauchly's test of sphericity would be needed only in relation to the assumptions of the follow-up univariate repeated-measures tests (second table below, labeled "univariate tests"); sphericity is not required for the multivariate tests. In this case, it is not needed even for univariate tests because there are only two levels of the within-subjects variable, so sphericity is not an issue and all epsilons are 1.0. The follow-up repeated-measures ANOVAs (see univariate effects table) and contrasts test whether these apparent findings are statistically reliable.

Mauchly's Test of Sphericity[b]

Within Subjects Effect	Measure	Mauchly's W	Approx. Chi-Square	df	Sig.	Epsilon[a] Greenhouse-Geisser	Epsilon[a] Huynh-Feldt	Epsilon[a] Lower-bound
time	dv1	1.000	.000	0	.	1.000	1.000	1.000
	dv2	1.000	.000	0	.	1.000	1.000	1.000

Tests the null hypothesis that the error covariance matrix of the orthonormalized transformed dependent variables is proportional to an identity matrix.

a. May be used to adjust the degrees of freedom for the averaged tests of significance. Corrected tests are displayed in the Tests of Within-Subjects Effects table.

b.

Design: Intercept+group
Within Subjects Design: time

Tests of Within-Subjects Effects

Multivariate[c,d]

Within Subjects Effect		Value	F	Hypothesis df	Error df	Sig.	Partial Eta Squared	Noncent. Parameter	Observed Power[a]
time	Pillai's Trace	.822	39.321[b]	2.000	17.000	.000	.822	78.642	1.000
	Wilks' Lambda	.178	39.321[b]	2.000	17.000	.000	.822	78.642	1.000
	Hotelling's Trace	4.626	39.321[b]	2.000	17.000	.000	.822	78.642	1.000
	Roy's Largest Root	4.626	39.321[b]	2.000	17.000	.000	.822	78.642	1.000
time * group	Pillai's Trace	.786	31.235[b]	2.000	17.000	.000	.786	62.470	1.000
	Wilks' Lambda	.214	31.235[b]	2.000	17.000	.000	.786	62.470	1.000
	Hotelling's Trace	3.675	31.235[b]	2.000	17.000	.000	.786	62.470	1.000
	Roy's Largest Root	3.675	31.235[b]	2.000	17.000	.000	.786	62.470	1.000

a. Computed using alpha = .05

b. Exact statistic

c.
  Design: Intercept+group
  Within Subjects Design: time

d. Tests are based on averaged variables.

> Note that this table provides information that is redundant with the previous multivariate table. You can ignore it.

Univariate Tests

Source	Measure		Type III Sum of Squares	df	Mean Square	F	Sig.	Partial Eta Squared	Noncent. Parameter	Observed Power[a]
time	dv1	Sphericity Assumed	72.900	1	72.900	81.000	.000	.818	81.000	1.000
		Greenhouse-Geisser	72.900	1.000	72.900	81.000	.000	.818	81.000	1.000
		Huynh-Feldt	72.900	1.000	72.900	81.000	.000	.818	81.000	1.000
		Lower-bound	72.900	1.000	72.900	81.000	.000	.818	81.000	1.000
	dv2	Sphericity Assumed	2.500	1	2.500	.240	.630	.013	.240	.075
		Greenhouse-Geisser	2.500	1.000	2.500	.240	.630	.013	.240	.075
		Huynh-Feldt	2.500	1.000	2.500	.240	.630	.013	.240	.075
		Lower-bound	2.500	1.000	2.500	.240	.630	.013	.240	.075
time * group	dv1	Sphericity Assumed	52.900	1	52.900	58.778	.000	.766	58.778	1.000
		Greenhouse-Geisser	52.900	1.000	52.900	58.778	.000	.766	58.778	1.000
		Huynh-Feldt	52.900	1.000	52.900	58.778	.000	.766	58.778	1.000
		Lower-bound	52.900	1.000	52.900	58.778	.000	.766	58.778	1.000
	dv2	Sphericity Assumed	10.000	1	10.000	.960	.340	.051	.960	.153
		Greenhouse-Geisser	10.000	1.000	10.000	.960	.340	.051	.960	.153
		Huynh-Feldt	10.000	1.000	10.000	.960	.340	.051	.960	.153
		Lower-bound	10.000	1.000	10.000	.960	.340	.051	.960	.153
Error(time)	dv1	Sphericity Assumed	16.200	18	.900					
		Greenhouse-Geisser	16.200	18.000	.900					
		Huynh-Feldt	16.200	18.000	.900					
		Lower-bound	16.200	18.000	.900					
	dv2	Sphericity Assumed	187.500	18	10.417					
		Greenhouse-Geisser	187.500	18.000	10.417					
		Huynh-Feldt	187.500	18.000	10.417					
		Lower-bound	187.500	18.000	10.417					

a. Computed using alpha = .05

> This table displays follow-up repeated-measures ANOVAs for each dependent variable, which show that the main effect of time (change from pretest to posttest) is statistically significant only for dependent variable 1 and that the interaction between group and time is statistically significant only for dependent variable 1. This indicates that the change over time is associated with the intervention, but only for dependent variable 1.

This table indicates that there is a statistically significant linear trend only for dependent variable 1 and that this time effect interacted with group. Examination of the means suggests that this interaction indicates that the time effect held only for the intervention group. The linear trend is the only polynomial contrast used because there are only two groups and only two time points, so quadratic or cubic trends are not possible. This table also provides effect sizes (partial eta squared), which indicate that the effects for dv1 were large.

Tests of Within-Subjects Contrasts

Source	Measure	time	Type III Sum of Squares	df	Mean Square	F	Sig.	Partial Eta Squared	Noncent. Parameter	Observed Power[a]
time	dv1	Linear	72.900	1	72.900	81.000	.000	.818	81.000	1.000
	dv2	Linear	2.500	1	2.500	.240	.630	.013	.240	.075
time * group	dv1	Linear	52.900	1	52.900	58.778	.000	.766	58.778	1.000
	dv2	Linear	10.000	1	10.000	.960	.340	.051	.960	.153
Error(time)	dv1	Linear	16.200	18	.900					
	dv2	Linear	187.500	18	10.417					

a. Computed using alpha = .05

Levene's Test of Equality of Error Variances[a]

	F	df1	df2	Sig.
outcome 1 pretest	1.031	1	18	.323
outcome 1 posttest	.288	1	18	.598
outcome 2 pretest	.058	1	18	.813
outcome 2 posttest	.844	1	18	.370

The Levene's test for all of our outcome variables are not significant; thus the assumption is met.

Tests the null hypothesis that the error variance of the dependent variable is equal across groups.

a.

Design: Intercept+group
Within Subjects Design: time

Tests of Between-Subjects Effects

Transformed Variable: Average

Source	Measure	Type III Sum of Squares	df	Mean Square	F	Sig.	Partial Eta Squared	Noncent. Parameter	Observed Power[a]
Intercept	dv1	1638.400	1	1638.400	382.010	.000	.955	382.010	1.000
	dv2	16000.000	1	16000.000	164.807	.000	.902	164.807	1.000
group	dv1	48.400	1	48.400	11.285	.003	.385	11.285	.888
	dv2	2.500	1	2.500	.026	.874	.001	.026	.053
Error	dv1	77.200	18	4.289					
	dv2	1747.500	18	97.083					

a. Computed using alpha = .05

This table indicates that if one averages across the within-subjects variable (time), then the groups differ only on dependent variable 1. This table is misleading because we know that there is no difference at the time of the pretest. In this case, it really does not provide much useful information.

Profile Plots

dv1

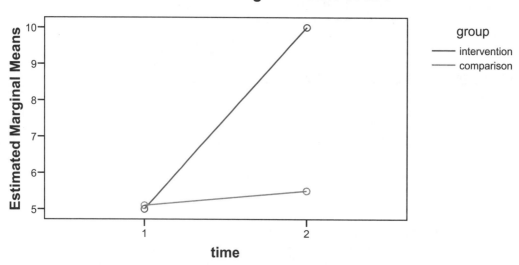

dv2

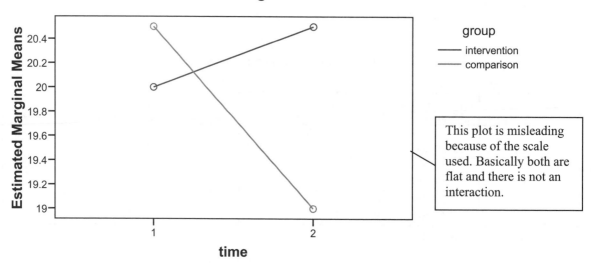

Interpretation of Output 10.3

This example illustrates the utility of the doubly multivariate analysis for testing a pretest-posttest design with intervention and control groups. We see from these results not only that the intervention seemed successful when both *outcome* measures were taken together but also that the effect was statistically significant only for one of the dependent variables, when each was considered separately. Sphericity was not an issue in this case because there were only two levels of the within-subjects variable. If one creates difference scores by subtracting each person's score on the dependent variable at one level of the within-subjects variable from the same dependent variable at each other level of the within-subjects variable, then sphericity exists if the variances of the resulting difference scores are all equal. Because there are only two levels of the within-subjects variable, there is only one set of difference scores, so sphericity has to exist, which is desirable. If we had had more than two levels of the within-subjects variable, then we would have needed to be concerned about the sphericity assumption when examining the univariate results. If epsilons did not approach 1.0, then we would have used the Huynh-Feldt or Greenhouse-Geisser test results, which use an estimate of epsilon to correct the degrees of freedom. Levene's Test for homogeneity of variances was not significant, therefore this assumption was met.

Example of How to Write About Problem 10.3

Results

A doubly multivariate analysis was conducted to assess if there was a difference between participants in the intervention group and participants in the control group in the amount of change in their scores on the two outcome measures. (The sample sizes were equal across the groups; therefore, the assumptions were considered to be met.) Statistically significant multivariate effects were found for the main effects of group, $F(2,17) = 10.5$, $p = .001$ and time $F(2,17) = 39.3$, $p < .001$, as well as for the interaction between group and time, $F(2,17) = 31.2$, $p < .001$. This interaction effect indicates that the difference between the intervention and control group on the linear combination of the two dependent variables is different at pretest than it is at posttest. Table 10.3 presents the means and standard deviations on the two variables. Examination of the means shows why the interaction is statistically significant; the groups do not differ much on either dependent variable at the time of the pretest, but they do differ, particularly on the first dependent variable, at the time of the posttest. Follow-up ANOVAs reveal that the statistically significant change from pretest to posttest was statistically significant only for the first outcome variable, $F(1,18) = 81.00$, $p < .001$, and that the change in the first outcome variable was different for the two groups, $F(1,18) = 58.78$, $p < .001$. Figure 10.4 displays the interaction effect for this variable. Examination of the means in Table 10.3 suggests that the change in the first outcome variable only held for the intervention group.

Table 10.3

Means and Standard Deviations for Two Outcome Variables at Pretest and Posttest

	Pretest		Posttest	
	M	*SD*	*M*	*SD*
		Outcome 1		
Intervention Grp	5.00	1.83	10.00	1.41
Comparison Grp	5.10	1.37	5.50	1.78
		Outcome 2		
Intervention Grp	20.00	7.45	20.50	6.85
Comparison Grp	20.50	6.85	19.00	8.10

Note. N=10 for each group

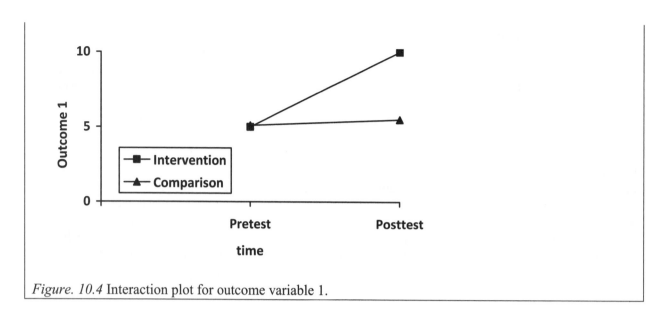

Figure. 10.4 Interaction plot for outcome variable 1.

Problem 10.4: Canonical Correlation

Canonical correlation is similar to MANOVA in that canonical correlation is used when you have two sets of two or more variables each and you want to see how differences in one set relate to differences in the other set of variables. With canonical correlation, however, there is no distinction between independent and dependent variables; they are called by SPSS "Set 1" and "Set 2." Moreover, usually canonical correlation is used when both sets of variables are at least interval level (scale), whereas in MANOVA usually at least some of the independent variables are dummy variables. One would use canonical correlation when the variables in each set can be grouped together conceptually, but you want to see if there are particular subsets of them that relate to subsets in the other variable set, so you do not want to sum each set to make an overall score. Usually, canonical correlation is used as an exploratory technique; it is not commonly used to test specific hypotheses. For example, one might wish to relate a set of child behavior variables to a set of parent behavior variables. One might wish to see which subset parenting variables is associated with which subsets of child behavior variables. Like principal components analysis, canonical correlation enables you to see which variables go together; however, it determines which subset of the "Set 1" variables best relate to which subset of the "Set 2" variables, then which other subset of the "Set 1" variables relate to another subset of the "Set 2" variables, etc. (Note: For those of you using earlier versions of SPSS, it has been reported that SPSS versions below 10.0 tend to have problems running canonical correlations. If you are using an earlier version and have problems, check the Help menu.)

- Retrieve **hsbdataB.sav**. Note: You are to get the **hsbdataB.sav** file, *not the* **MixedMANOVAdata.sav** file from the last lab assignment.

10.4. What is the pattern of relationships between the motivation items and the competence items?

We will need to check the assumptions of linearity, multivariate normality, and homoscedasticity. One way to do this is to graph the canonical variate scores that are generated by the canonical correlation syntax. Because the canonical correlation needs to be computed first, we have done that below, with the matrix scatterplot of the canonical variates afterward. <u>Be sure not to save your data file after running these commands,</u> or you will save the canonical variates.

Canonical correlation must be computed through syntax and requires access to the SPSS file for canonical correlation.

First, go to the website and download the file "Canonical correlation.sps" to your c: drive. If you download it to another location you will need to change the syntax to identify where the file is located. Next, use the following syntax to answer the question above.

```
INCLUDE 'c:\Canonical Correlation.sps'.
CANCORR SET1=item01 item07 item12 item13  /
        SET2=item03 item09 / .
```

Output 10.4a: Canonical Correlation Output

```
include 'c:\canonical correlation.sps'.
1252  0  * Canonical correlation.sps.  This version allows long variable names and uses
datasets.Canonical correlation.sps.
1253  0
1255  0  preserve.
1257  0  set printback=off.
1961  0  RESTORE.
1962  0
1964  0  * End of INSERT and INCLUDE nesting level 01.
CANCORR SET1=item01 item07 item12 item13
/SET2=item03 item09 /.
```

Matrix

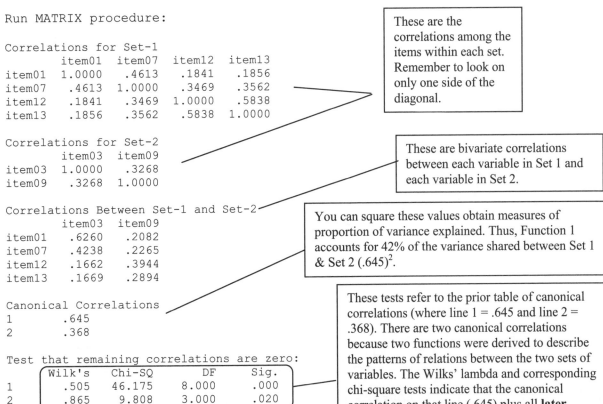

```
Run MATRIX procedure:

Correlations for Set-1
         item01   item07   item12   item13
item01   1.0000    .4613    .1841    .1856
item07    .4613   1.0000    .3469    .3562
item12    .1841    .3469   1.0000    .5838
item13    .1856    .3562    .5838   1.0000


Correlations for Set-2
         item03   item09
item03   1.0000    .3268
item09    .3268   1.0000


Correlations Between Set-1 and Set-2
         item03   item09
item01    .6260    .2082
item07    .4238    .2265
item12    .1662    .3944
item13    .1669    .2894


Canonical Correlations
1         .645
2         .368


Test that remaining correlations are zero:
     Wilk's   Chi-SQ      DF     Sig.
1     .505    46.175    8.000    .000
2     .865     9.808    3.000    .020
```

These are the correlations among the items within each set. Remember to look on only one side of the diagonal.

These are bivariate correlations between each variable in Set 1 and each variable in Set 2.

You can square these values obtain measures of proportion of variance explained. Thus, Function 1 accounts for 42% of the variance shared between Set 1 & Set 2 $(.645)^2$.

These tests refer to the prior table of canonical correlations (where line 1 = .645 and line 2 = .368). There are two canonical correlations because two functions were derived to describe the patterns of relations between the two sets of variables. The Wilks' lambda and corresponding chi-square tests indicate that the canonical correlation on that line (.645) plus all **later** correlations are statistically significantly different from zero. Thus, the first line tests whether both correlations, together, are significantly different from zero. The second line tests whether the second correlation (.368) is statistically significant, even after removing the variance explained by the previous correlation.

```
Standardized Canonical Coefficients for Set-1
                1         2
item01        -.838     -.276
item07        -.259     -.089
item12        -.047      .914
item13        -.011      .190

Raw Canonical Coefficients for Set-1
                1         2
item01        -.919     -.303
item07        -.243     -.083
item12        -.056     1.089
item13        -.013      .236
```

These indicate how much each item in Set 1 is weighted to create the linear combinations used in each of the two canonical correlations (canonical variates).

```
Standardized Canonical Coefficients for Set-2
                1         2
item03        -.972     -.418
item09        -.077     1.055

Raw Canonical Coefficients for Set-2
                1         2
item03       -1.070     -.459
item09        -.100     1.378
```

These indicate how much each item in Set 2 is weighted to create each of the two canonical variates for Set 2.

```
Canonical Loadings for Set-1
                1         2
item01        -.968     -.113
item07        -.665      .169
item12        -.297      .943
item13        -.286      .641
```

These indicate the correlation between each item in Set 1 and each of two canonical variates for Set 1.

```
Cross Loadings for Set-1
                1         2
item01        -.625     -.042
item07        -.429      .062
item12        -.192      .347
item13        -.184      .236
```

```
Canonical Loadings for Set-2
                1         2
item03        -.997     -.073
item09        -.395      .919
```

These indicate the correlation between each item in Set 2 and each of the two canonical variates for Set 2.

```
Cross Loadings for Set-2
                1         2
item03        -.644     -.027
item09        -.255      .338
```

The Redundancy Analysis suggests that the second function does not enable one to explain much of the variance in the other set of variables.

```
                Redundancy Analysis:

Proportion of Variance of Set-1 Explained by Its Own Can. Var.
                Prop Var
CV1-1             .387
CV1-2             .335

Proportion of Variance of Set-1 Explained by Opposite Can.Var.
```

```
               Prop Var
CV2-1             .161
CV2-2             .045

Proportion of Variance of Set-2 Explained by Its Own Can. Var.
               Prop Var
CV2-1             .575
CV2-2             .425

Proportion of Variance of Set-2 Explained by Opposite Can. Var.
               Prop Var
CV1-1             .240
CV1-2             .057

------ END MATRIX -----
```

Output 10.4b: Matrix Scatterplot of Canonical Variates

```
GRAPH
  /SCATTERPLOT(MATRIX)=S1_CV001 S2_CV001 S1_CV002 S2_CV002
  /MISSING=LISTWISE .
```

Graph

The data appear to meet the assumptions of linearity, multivariate normality, and homoscedasticity because there does not appear to be a pattern in the scatterplots, and there are not large differences in how spread out each scatterplot is.

Interpretation of Outputs 10.4a and 10.4b
The first two matrices, **Correlations for Set-1** and **Correlations for Set-2,** are ordinary correlation tables. The first matrix is for the variables in Set 1, and the second matrix is for the variables in Set 2. We can see from these tables that most variables in each set are weakly to moderately correlated with each other.

The next matrix is the **Correlations Between Set-1 and Set-2,** which contains the bivariate correlations between each variable in Set 1 and each variable in Set 2.

The **Canonical Correlations** are the correlations between a linear combination of the Set 1 variables and a linear combination of the Set 2 variables (the canonical variates). Note that there are two different correlations, corresponding to two different pairs of linear combinations. By squaring and summing all canonical correlations, you can calculate a measure of R^2 indicating how much variance in one set of variables is explained by the other set of variables. Thus, $(.645^2 = .416) + (.368^2 = .135) = .551$, so about 55% of the variance is shared.

One important part of the output to check is the **Test that remaining correlations are zero.** These chi-square goodness-of-fit tests indicate whether all correlations from that point on are statistically significant, even after removing variance accounted for by all prior correlations.

The **Standardized Canonical Coefficients** can be interpreted much like regression weights, to show which items are weighted most heavily in the linear combination of variables for each set of variables. These weights are created so as to maximize the correlation between the two sets of variables. For example, the first canonical variate for Set 1 is created by weighting item01 most heavily ($-.838$), followed by item07 ($-.259$), item12 ($-.047$), and item13 ($-.011$). This canonical variate is then correlated with the canonical variate created by weighting item03 by $-.972$ and item09 by $-.077$ (see table of loadings in the output). The set of canonical coefficients in the second column is the set used for the second pair of canonical variates, which are correlated to produce the second canonical correlation. Thus, there are actually two linear combinations for each set of variables. These are derived, much like principal components analysis, by creating the linear combination for each set of variables that maximizes the correlation between the two sets of variables, then doing this again with what remains after the variance associated with the first correlation is removed, and so on. These coefficients are often called pattern coefficients.

Canonical Loadings are the correlations between each item and the linear combinations of variables for that same set (canonical variates). They are often called structure coefficients. These loadings aid in the interpretation of the correlations, much as the loadings in principal components analysis are interpreted to give meaning to the different components.

Cross Loadings for each set indicate the correlation between each item in one variable set and the canonical variate for the other variable set. In the **Cross Loadings for Set-2,** we can see that both items for Set 2 are negatively correlated with the Set 1 canonical variate for the first canonical correlation.

Example of How to Write About Problem 10.4

Results

Canonical correlation analysis was performed to assess the pattern of relationships between the motivation items and the competence items. (The assumptions of linearity, multivariate normality, and homoscedasticity were checked by evaluating a bivariate scatterplot of the canonical variate scores.) The first canonical correlation was .65 (42% overlapping variance); the second was .37 (14% overlapping variance). With both canonical correlations included, $\chi^2(8) = 46.18$, $p < .001$, and with the first removed, $\chi^2(3) = 9.81$, $p = .02$. The correlations and canonical coefficients are included in Table 10.4. Examination of the loadings suggests that the first canonical correlation seems to involve a relation between practicing math a lot, independently, and becoming efficient (quick) at math; whereas, the second seems to capture a relation between persistence and thoroughness and being very competent at math.

Table 10.4

Correlation and Standardized Canonical Coefficients Between Motivation and Competence Variables

Item content	First canonical correlation		Second canonical correlation	
	Loading	Coefficient	Loading	Coefficient
Motivation				
Practice till do well	−.97	−.84	−.11	−.28
Figure out math without help	−.67	−.26	.17	−.09
Complete math even if it takes a long time☐	−.3☐	−.☐5	.94	.91
Explore all solutions	−.29	−.☐1	.64	.19
Competence				
Solve math quickly	−1.00	−.97	−.07	−.42
Very competent in math	−.40	−.08	.92	1.06

Interpretation Questions

10.1   In Output 10.1b: (a) Are the multivariate tests statistically significant? (b) What does this mean? (c) Which individual dependent variables are statistically significant in the univariate ANOVAs? (d) How are the results similar and different from what we would have found if we had done three univariate one-way ANOVAs?

10.2   In Output 10.2: (a) Are the multivariate tests statistically significant? What does this mean? (b) If the interaction effect had been statistically significant, what would that mean? (c) For which individual/univariate dependent variables are the genders statistically significantly different? (d) Write sentences summarizing the multivariate results, being sure to include the F values and degrees of freedom as these would be reported in a journal article.

10.3   In Output 10.3: (a) What makes this a "doubly multivariate" design? (b) What information is provided by the multivariate tests of significance that is not provided by the univariate tests? (c) State in your own words what the interaction between time and group tells you. (d) What implications does this have for understanding the success of the intervention?

10.4   In Output 10.4: (a) What is the difference between canonical coefficients (pattern coefficients) and canonical loadings (structure coefficients)? What information do each of these sets of coefficients tell you? (b) Give an example of a research problem that could be addressed using canonical correlation. (c) What do the canonical correlations tell you? (d) Why is there more than one canonical correlation?

Extra SPSS Problems

10.1   A company is interested in how consumers of different age groups like their DVD players. Open the dvdplayer.sav data file, and conduct a MANOVA using *agegroup* and *sex* (male or female) as fixed factors and *price, ease, support, and func* as dependent variables. Request that descriptives, estimates of effect size, parameters, and tests of homogeneity are printed, and specify that you want a polynomial contrast on *agegroup*.

a. How many participants of each gender are in each group? How might this affect results?

b. Using Wilks' lambda, which results are statistically significant?

c. What are the eta squared values for each effect using Wilks' lambda? What do these mean?

d. Were homogeneity assumptions met?

e. What do the B values listed under Parameter Estimates (and their significance levels) tell you? What are the parameters?

f. Which polynomial contrasts are statistically significant for each dependent variable? Interpret these results.

10.2   Now conduct the same analysis as in Extra SPSS Problems 10.1, but omit *sex* as an independent variable.

a. Why might you choose to omit *sex* as a factor?

b. Was the effect of *agegroup* statistically significant (using Wilks' lambda)? What does this mean?

c. Were the homogeneity assumptions met?

d. Which univariate effects were statistically significant? Interpret this.

e. Which group differences were statistically significant, for which variables?

f. Which polynomial contrasts were statistically significant, for which variables? Describe the results of this MANOVA, making sure to include information about the significance tests.

10.3   Open the World95.sav data file, and conduct a canonical correlation, using *literacy, fertility, gdp_cap*, and *calories* as Set 1 and *birth_rt, lifeexpf, death_rt,* and *aids_rt* as Set 2. Be sure to check your syntax carefully!

a. Which of the canonical correlations were statistically significant? How do you know?

b. Which variables in Set 1 were weighted most heavily for Function 1? Which Set 2 variables were weighted most heavily for Function 1? Which Set 1 and Set 2 variables were weighted most for Function 2?

c. Interpret the meaning of Functions 1 and 2, based on the canonical loadings.

10.4   Using the New drug.sav data file, conduct a canonical correlation using *Respiratory Time1, Respiratory Time2,* and *Respiratory Time3* as Set 1, and *Pulse Time1, Pulse Time2,* and *Pulse Time3* as Set 2.

a. Which of the canonical correlations were statistically significant? How do you know?

b. Which variables in Set 1 were weighted most heavily for Function 1? Which Set 2 variables were weighted most heavily for Function 1? Which Set 1 and Set 2 variables were weighted most for Function 2?

c. Interpret the meaning of Functions 1 and 2, based on the canonical loadings.

CHAPTER 11
Multilevel Linear Modeling/Hierarchical Linear Modeling

In this chapter, we introduce multilevel linear modeling, which is often called Hierarchical Linear Modeling (HLM). Although these two terms can be used interchangeably in most cases, we will use the term "multilevel linear modeling" or "multilevel modeling" in this chapter, because we are not using the HLM software program. Multilevel modeling is a complex statistic in which several levels of nested data are considered in relation to one another. By *nesting*, we mean that several observations are not independent of one another. For example, there may be multiple observations on the same individuals, such that these observations are not independent of one another (observations nested in individuals). Or there may be a set of particular individuals who are found in particular groups or settings (such as schools) so that the individuals are not independent of one another (individuals nested in groups/settings).

An example of the first type of nesting is found in Problems 11.1 and 11.2. In these problems, we will examine data from a longitudinal study of physical growth, in which data at four different ages are measured on the same individuals. This illustrates multiple observations nested in the same individuals. Although this problem could be analyzed using other methods (see Chapter 9), we will explain why you might want to use multilevel modeling.

In Problems 11.3 and 11.4, we will analyze a slightly different HSB dataset, in which students were nested in particular schools and tested on their math achievement. In multilevel models, differences between the entities in which observations are nested (e.g., individuals or schools) often are not the focus of the study but are seen as random differences within a population of individuals or schools. Yet one cannot ignore the fact that the data are nested within those individuals or schools. In other cases, the variability among schools or persons is of interest, in that the researchers believe they can explain this variability using meaningful variables. Even if you are not interested in the systematic variability between individuals or schools, you might want to explain that variability first before you use predictors to explain the variability in which you are truly interested, much as one covaries out "extraneous" variables in regression or ANCOVA (see Chapters 6 and 8).

In many applications in education and the behavioral sciences you need to deal with nested data. For example, you may have a quasi-experimental design, in which different interventions or curricula must be assigned to different sets of existing schools or classrooms, even though students are not assigned randomly to those schools or classrooms. In addition to the effects of the manipulation, you may need to determine whether preexisting characteristics of the classrooms or schools impact the outcome. Multilevel linear modeling enables you to appropriately treat students as nested within particular schools or classrooms and to examine the role of school or classroom-level data, such as class size, gender of teacher, average socioeconomic status of school, or type of school (e.g., Core Knowledge, International Baccalaureate, or traditional) as predictors of the student-level outcome variables. Another common situation is to have many observations on each participant (e.g., in a longitudinal study) and to want to use participant-level data to explain a pattern or growth curve shown in those many observations. It is possible to examine many of these models using the SPSS program **Linear Mixed Models**.

The term **Mixed Models** refers to the fact that some variables are viewed as <u>fixed</u> variables, and some are viewed as <u>random</u>. Typically, the variables that one is construing as predictors are considered fixed, meaning that the levels of the variable that you measured are the levels in which you are interested. In contrast, random variables are viewed as providing a random sample of the levels of the variable to which one wants to generalize. In multilevel or hierarchical linear models, the levels of the nesting variable (e.g., schools or individuals) are viewed as being random. The various schools or individuals are considered to represent a larger population of schools or individuals. As a result, the Level 1 intercepts (*means* of the different levels of the nesting variable) are viewed as random as well.

Typically, when one uses this approach, the first step is to examine an unconditional model, in which the lowest (nested) level of data (Level 1) is modeled without any predictors of the differences between entities at that level. In the unconditional model, only the average level of the outcome variable (the intercept of the model) for each entity, the variance among these intercepts, and the within-entity variability are modeled. The results of this unconditional model analysis inform the researcher about whether to pursue a model with predictors. To the extent that there is significant variance in the unconditional model, it makes sense to think of predictors that may help explain this variance (such as school SES or gender of individuals). The variance among the intercepts for the different entities at Level 1 (variation in the mean level of the outcome variable for, for example, schools or individuals) will be explained by one or more predictors in the conditional model(s), which is tested next. There may be predictors at Level 1, or one might immediately move to a Level 2 model, in which Level 2 predictors are used to explain Level 1 variance. One compares the models to see whether much variability is explained by Level 1 and/or Level 2 predictors.

In this chapter, we will use multilevel linear modeling to model and explain age-related growth and then to model a students-nested-in-schools design. In each case, you will first do an unconditional Level 1 model, followed by conditional models used to explain the variability at Level 1. You will learn how to aggregate and center variables, which often will be useful in doing multilevel linear modeling. Often, you may wish to aggregate data from the nested level of data so that you have data at the level of the independent entities. For example, in the school data set that will be used, we have data on SES for each student, but we want to have data at the level of the schools, which are independent of each other. In the dataset, SES already has been aggregated by schools, by averaging the data for all of the students nested in each school. We will show you how this was achieved.

Centering involves subtracting each entity's (e.g., person's/school's) score on a variable from its mean. Typically, one centers the "covariates," or continuous variable predictor(s), because this makes it easier to interpret the slope of the line predicting the dependent variable in terms of how change in the predictor affects change in the dependent variable. Moreover, centering predictors also is useful if you will want to examine the interaction between continuous predictor variables, as it will make these interactions independent of the main effects of those variables. Because the data sets we will use either have dichotomous predictors (for the repeated-measures design) or have predictors that already have been centered, we will just tell you how to center the variable SES on the mean SES for each school, but you will not actually need to save your results.

Assumptions of Multilevel Linear Modeling

The assumptions of multilevel linear modeling include: (a) independent observations at the level above the nesting, (b) bivariate normality of the intercepts and slopes at Level 1, (c) a linear relation between predictors and outcome variables, and (d) random residuals, with errors distributed normally, with a mean of zero. Normality of the intercepts can be checked by looking at the normality of the distribution of the dependent variable for the different entities at Level 1. Bivariate normality of Level 1 slopes and the linear relation between predictors and the outcome variable(s) can be checked with a scatterplot for a single continuous predictor or matrix scatterplots for more than one predictor. Random residuals can be checked using residual plots, as we did in Chapter 6, using Regression → Linear. You will also need to specify in the models whether you have any assumptions about the covariance matrix; we will elaborate on this in connection with the specific problems.

Retrieve **Growth study.sav**. Note: You are to get **Growth study.sav**, not the **hsbdataB** file from the last lab assignment. In this data set from Potthoff and Roy (1964), children's growth, as indicated by the variable *distance* (mm from center of pituitary to pteryomaxillary fissure) is measured on four occasions: when each participant is 8, 10, 12, and 14. This measurement is useful to orthodontists who wish to track the growth of the jaw. Notice that the data are arranged so that there are four lines for each participant, corresponding to their measurement at each of the four ages. This structure is necessary for the **Linear**

Mixed Models procedure, but if your data are not in this format, one can convert them using **Restructure**, as follows: **Data → Restructure**. Then, follow the directions you will see.

Problem 11.1: Unconditional Level 1 Repeated-Measures Model

Although one can use **GLM** to compute analyses of repeated-measures data, as shown in Chapter 9, multilevel models often are more useful for analyzing repeated-measures data for several reasons. First, it is possible to use multilevel models even if there is some incomplete information on some participants or if their data are from different time points. Second, one can model differently shaped growth curves more readily in multilevel models. Finally, one can select the best variance-covariance structure for the data and specify only the interactions of interest for the analyses. In a repeated-measures design, the Level 1 model describes the repeated measures data for the participants and Level 2 involves variables that measure systematic differences among the participants, in which the repeated measures are nested, that might help explain the pattern of change in the repeated measures. Typically, the first step in undertaking multilevel linear modeling is to determine whether there is sufficient variability at Level 1 to require explanation by Level 2 variables. The unconditional Level 1 model answers this question:

11.1. Is there significant variability among participants in the average *Distance* (in mm from center of pituitary to pteryomaxillary fissure) across ages? Is there a linear relation between the within-subject variable, *Age,* and *Distance*? Is there a quadratic relation between *Age* and *Distance*?

Before we do the analysis to answer these questions, we will calculate descriptive statistics and do a boxplot to help us in answering them.

- First, compute descriptive statistics by clicking on **Analyze → Descriptive Statistics → Explore.**
- Click on *Distance* and move it into **Dependent List:** box (see Fig. 11.1).
- Click on *Age* and move it into the **Factor List**: box.
- Check to be sure **Both** is selected under **Display**.

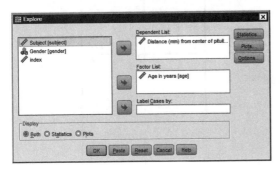

Fig. 11.1. Explore.

- Click on **OK**.

Compare your output and syntax with Output 11.1a.

Output 11.1a: Descriptive Statistics for Distance as a Function of Age

```
EXAMINE VARIABLES=distance BY age
  /PLOT BOXPLOT STEMLEAF
  /COMPARE GROUPS
  /STATISTICS DESCRIPTIVES
  /CINTERVAL 95
  /MISSING LISTWISE
  /NOTOTAL.
```

Explore Age in years

Case Processing Summary

No cases are missing.

There are 27 participants at all ages.

	Age in years	Cases					
		Valid		Missing		Total	
		N	Percent	N	Percent	N	Percent
Distance (mm) from center of pituitary to pteryo-maxillary fissure	8	27	100.0%	0	.0%	27	100.0%
	10	27	100.0%	0	.0%	27	100.0%
	12	27	100.0%	0	.0%	27	100.0%
	14	27	100.0%	0	.0%	27	100.0%

Descriptives

The four means (boxed) steadily increase with age, suggesting a linear trend.

All four skewness values (circled) are lower than 1.0, suggesting normal distributions.

Means and medians for each age are very similar, also suggesting distributions are normal.

	Age in years			Statistic	Std. Error
Distance (mm) from center of pituitary to pteryo-maxillary fissure	8	Mean		22.185	.4685
		95% Confidence Interval for Mean	Lower Bound	21.222	
			Upper Bound	23.148	
		5% Trimmed Mean		22.220	
		Median		22.000	
		Variance		5.926	
		Std. Deviation		2.4343	
		Minimum		16.5	
		Maximum		27.5	
		Range		11.0	
		Interquartile Range		2.5	
		Skewness		-.248	.448
		Kurtosis		.833	.872
	10	Mean		23.167	.4152
		95% Confidence Interval for Mean	Lower Bound	22.313	
			Upper Bound	24.020	
		5% Trimmed Mean		23.122	
		Median		23.000	
		Variance		4.654	
		Std. Deviation		2.1573	
		Minimum		19.0	
		Maximum		28.0	
		Range		9.0	
		Interquartile Range		3.0	
		Skewness		.331	.448
		Kurtosis		.004	.872
	12	Mean		24.648	.5422
		95% Confidence Interval for Mean	Lower Bound	23.534	
			Upper Bound	25.763	
		5% Trimmed Mean		24.580	
		Median		24.000	
		Variance		7.939	
		Std. Deviation		2.8176	
		Minimum		19.0	
		Maximum		31.0	
		Range		12.0	
		Interquartile Range		3.0	
		Skewness		.641	.448
		Kurtosis		.615	.872
	14	Mean		26.093	.5324
		95% Confidence Interval for Mean	Lower Bound	24.998	
			Upper Bound	27.187	
		5% Trimmed Mean		26.137	
		Median		26.000	
		Variance		7.655	
		Std. Deviation		2.7667	
		Minimum		19.5	
		Maximum		31.5	
		Range		12.0	
		Interquartile Range		3.0	
		Skewness		-.163	.448
		Kurtosis		.365	.872

Distance (mm) from center of pituitary to pteryo-maxillary fissure

(Stem and leaf plots omitted)

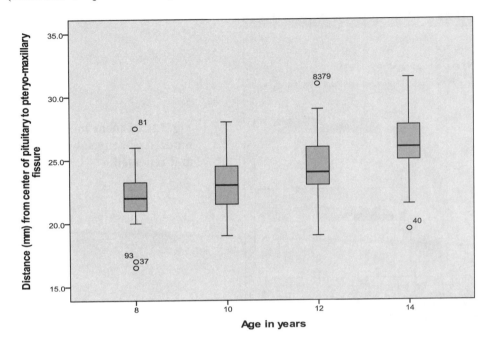

Note that if we connected the medians they would make a nearly straight (linear) line. There are some outliers at 8, 12, and 14 years.

Interpretation of Output 11.1a

First, we examine the output from the **Explore** program, which provides us with descriptive statistics for the *distance* variable at each age period. We have omitted the stem-and-leave plots to conserve space because we can obtain the most pertinent information from the tables and boxplot.

The first table in Output 11.1a shows us that there were 27 children at each age, so there was no attrition over time, and none were missing data on *distance* at any age. The **Descriptives** table shows that at age 8, the average *distance* (mm from the center of the pituitary to the pteryomaxillary fissure) was 22.19 (*SD* = 2.43); at 10, 12, and 14, the mean *distance*s were 23.17, 24.65, and 26.09, respectively, with corresponding standard deviations of 2.16, 2.82, and 2.77. These numbers, along with the boxplots, suggest that distance increases in a linear manner; however, to see if there is one change in direction/rate of change (and to show you how to do polynomial trends), we will also look at a quadratic trend for age.

Now we will answer our research questions: Is there significant variability among participants in the average *Distance* (in mm from center of pituitary to pteryomaxillary fissure) across ages? Is there a linear relation between *Age* and *Distance*? Is there a quadratic relation between *Age* and *Distance*?

- Select **Analyze → Mixed Models → Linear**.
- Highlight *Subject* and move it to the **Subjects:** box (see Fig. 11.2 for help). Note that **Subjects** is a way to specify the lowest independent level of data (the level in which the lowest level of data are nested). In this case, it involves the *Subject* variable, because observations are nested in subjects.
- Highlight *Age* (Age in years) and move it into the **Repeated:** box, specifying the repeated-measures variable. This models within-subject variance, as distinguished from the between-subject variance modeled by the **Random** statement.
- Click on the arrow next to **Repeated covariance type**, and change Diagonal to specify **AR(1)**, as shown in Fig. 11.2. This is an autoregressive covariance structure with homogeneous variances, with

a lag of 1 (one age level in this case). The autoregressive structure indicates that each person's *distance* measurement at one time is correlated with his or her distance measurement at the previous time period, which is typical of a repeated-measures situation.

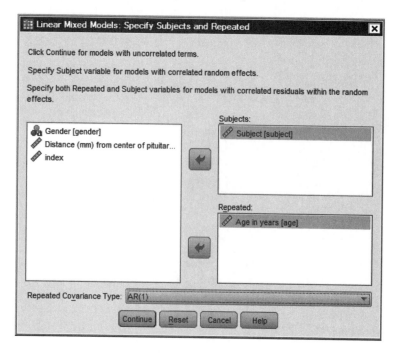

Fig. 11.2. Linear mixed models: Specify subjects and repeated.

- Click on **Continue.** This will open the **Linear Mixed Models** window (Fig. 11.3).
- Click on *Distance* and move it into the **Dependent Variable:** box.
- Click on *Linear* and move it into the **Covariate(s):** box.
- Click on *Quadratic* and move it into the **Covariate(s):** box. We have created these two variables to look at the linear and quadratic effects of age, referenced to the youngest age. Note that these really get at the effects of age, even though they are separate variables, because they correspond to the different levels of *Age* in the dataset. Both consist of weights beginning with 0, which causes SPSS to use the initial age level as the reference. The quadratic weights simply involve squaring the linear weights (see Growth study.sav).

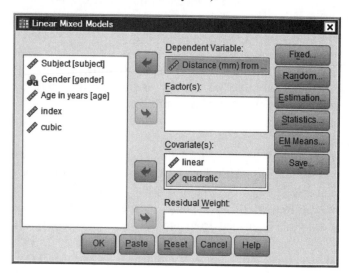

Fig. 11.3. Linear mixed models.

- Next, click on **Fixed** in the upper right-hand corner of Fig. 11.3 to get to Fig. 11.4.
- Click on the arrow next to **Factorial** and change Factorial to **Main Effects.**
- Click on *linear* and then on **Add**; this will move *linear* into the **Model** box. Repeat this for *quadratic*. Leave the defaults for the other options, making sure that **Include intercept** is checked and **Type III sums** of squares is in the box for sums of squares (see Fig. 11.4).

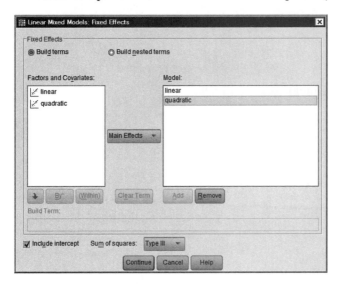

Fig. 11.4. Linear mixed models: Fixed effects.

- Click on **Continue.** This will take you back to Fig. 11.3.
- In the Linear Mixed Models window click on **Random** to get to Fig. 11.5.
- Under **Random Effects** check the box next to **Include intercept**. This will enable us to look at differences between the individual participants in mean level of the dependent variable.
- Leave the **Covariance Type** as **Variance Components**.
- We have already included an auto-regressive, repeated measures structure for the Age variable, and have entered fixed effects for the polynomial trend analysis, so we will not add any independent variables to the **Random Effects**.
- Under **Subject Groupings**, move *Subject* into the **Combinations:** box (see Fig. 11.5).

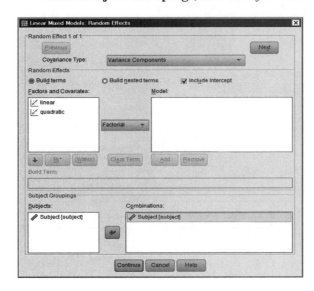

Fig. 11.5. Linear mixed models: Random effects.

- Click on **Continue**. This will take you back to Fig. 11.3.

- Click on **Statistics.** Select **Parameter estimates, Test for covariance parameters, Covariances of random effects,** and **Contrast coefficient matrix** (see Fig. 11.6).

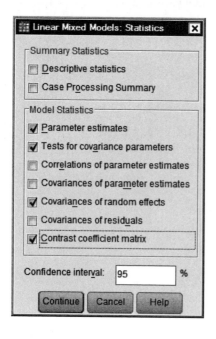

Fig. 11.6. Linear mixed models: Statistics.

- Click on **Continue** to go back to Fig. 11.3.
- Click on **OK**.

Compare your output with Output 11.1b

Output 11.1b Unconditional Model for Age Nested in Subject

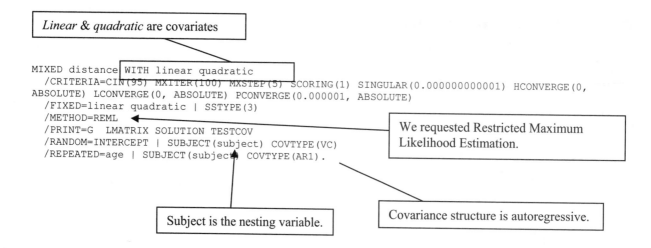

Mixed Model Analysis

Model Dimension[b]

		Number of Levels	Covariance Structure	Number of Parameters	Subject Variables	Number of Subjects
Fixed Effects	Intercept	1		1		
	linear	1		1		
	quadratic	1		1		
Random Effects	Intercept[a]	1	Variance Components	1	subject	
Repeated Effects	age	4	First-Order Autoregressive	2	subject	27
Total		8		6		

a. As of version 11.5, the syntax rules for the RANDOM subcommand have changed. Your command syntax may yield results that differ from those produced by prior versions. If you are using version 11 syntax, please consult the current syntax reference guide for more information.

b. Dependent Variable: Distance (mm) from center of pituitary to pteryo-maxillary fissure.

A total of six parameters are estimated for the unconditional.

Information Criteria[a]

-2 Restricted Log Likelihood	446.960
Akaike's Information Criterion (AIC)	452.960
Hurvich and Tsai's Criterion (AICC)	453.197
Bozdogan's Criterion (CAIC)	463.922
Schwarz's Bayesian Criterion (BIC)	460.922

A measure of the goodness of fit of the model.

The information criteria are displayed in smaller-is-better forms. ———— Lower numbers = better

a.   Dependent Variable: Distance (mm) from center of pituitary to pteryo-maxillary fissure.

Fixed Effects

The linear effect is statistically significant, but the quadratic effect is not.

Estimates of Fixed Effects[a]

Parameter	Estimate	Std. Error	df	t	Sig.	95% Confidence Interval	
						Lower Bound	Upper Bound
Intercept	22.160222	.488661	42.062	45.349	.000	21.174107	23.146337
linear	.971889	.432638	78.554	2.246	.027	.110668	1.833110
quadratic	.115741	.137928	78.973	.839	.404	-.158799	.390281

a. Dependent Variable: Distance (mm) from center of pituitary to pteryo-maxillary fissure.

Covariance Parameters

An estimate of within-age variance.

AR1 diagonal is significant, suggesting a large amount of within-age variance.

Estimates of Covariance Parameters[a]

Parameter		Estimate	Std. Error	Wald Z	Sig.	95% Confidence Interval	
						Lower Bound	Upper Bound
Repeated Measures	AR1 diagonal	2.123323	.408870	5.193	.000	1.455820	3.096881
	AR1 rho	.058434	.175191	.334	.739	-.278490	.382552
Intercept [subject = subject]	Variance	3.198092	1.093986	2.923	.003	1.635749	6.252666

a. Dependent Variable: Distance (mm) from center of pituitary to pteryo-maxillary fissure.

There is little covariation between adjacent ages, once differences between individuals are taken into account.

There are significant differences between individuals in *distance*.

Interpretation of Output 11.1b

First, you see the log file, or syntax, indicating what you did. Note that you used REML (Restricted Maximum Likelihood) as your estimation method. REML adjusts for the fixed effects, usually leading to a reduction in standard error, and is the default approach in SPSS.

In the first table of Output 11.1b, **Model Dimensions**, we can check to make sure that everything is as we intended it and how many parameters are being estimated. We see that the intercept and *Linear* and *Quadratic* are fixed effects, *age* also is a repeated effect with a first-order autoregressive covariance structure, and *Subject* is a nesting variable. The repeated effects of *age* involve estimating two parameters: **AR(1) rho,** an estimate of the covariation between age periods and **AR(1) diagonal**, which is a measure of average within-age variance. Note that since *linear* and *quadratic* were specified as covariates, they only have had one level listed, and dummy variables were not created.

Next, we have information about the goodness of fit of the unconditional model. We can compare this to later models to see how much the goodness of fit is improved when predictors are added. Fit is better if the **Information Criteria** are smaller. The **-2 restricted log likelihood** criterion is a basic measure of goodness of fit of the model. The other four criteria are based on this same criterion, but they make adjustments for the complexity of the model.

In the next table, we see **Fixed Effects**, in this case the intercept for the *Distance* variable (**Intercept)** and *linear* and *quadratic* effects of age. The t test for the intercept is testing whether the average *Distance* from the pituitary to the pteryomaxillary fissure, across individuals, is statistically significantly different from zero, which it is, $t(42.06) = 45.35$, $p < .001$; however, this is not really of interest. The t test for *linear* and *quadratic* are more familiar and more useful, testing whether the *Distance* variable changes statistically significantly in a linear and/or quadratic fashion across the four ages (8, 10, 12, and 14 years). We see that the linear growth curve is significant, $t(78.55) = 2.25$, $p = .027$. On the other hand, the quadratic growth curve is not significant, $t(78.97) = .84$, $p = .40$.

The next tables, **Type III Estimable Functions**, indicate the coefficients used to test the fixed effects. The next table, the **Covariance Parameters,** shows the variance estimates for the random and within-subjects effects, along with a test of statistical significance. The **AR(1) rho** estimate is an intraclass correlation coefficient, indicating the extent to which the age periods are correlated. Adjacent age periods (e.g., 8 and 10 or 10 and 12) are correlated an average of rho; those separated by another age group (e.g., 8 and 12) are rho^2. In this case, rho is low (.047) and is not statistically significant. This means that rho^2 is estimated to be $(.047)^2$ or .0022 for the correlation between age groups that are separated by another group (8 and 12 or 10 and 14), suggesting quite negligible correlations between age groups that are further removed. These results suggest that, at least after taking into account effects of *subjects*, the contribution of autoregression is negligible. Under normal circumstances, we would modify our model of the random covariance based on this, but we will continue using AR1 in the next model so that we can show you how to compare a conditional model to an unconditional model with everything specified the same except for the new predictor. The **AR1 diagonal** estimate is the estimate of the variance within age periods, which in this case is high and significant, suggesting that there is significant variability within age that could be predicted by conditional model predictor(s). The final entry in this table (**Intercept [subject = subject]**) is for the variance component pertaining to variation between participants. It, too, is large and significant, suggesting that there is variability between subjects that could be explained using predictors in a conditional model. The statistical significance tests should be interpreted with caution, however; Wald Z test may be unreliable with small samples, such as those for this study.

Example of How to Write About Output 11.1
Results

The unconditional repeated-measures model revealed that there was significant variability in the *distance* measure, suggesting that it would be worthwhile to examine a conditional model that could potentially explain some of this variability. (The assumptions of independent observations at the level above the nesting, bivariate normality, linear relationships, and random residuals were checked and met.) The linear trend for age was a statistically significant predictor of changes in the *distance* measure, $t(78.55) = 2.25$, $p = .027$. On the other hand, the quadratic trend for age was not significant, indicating that age was related to the distance from center of pituitary to pteryomaxillary fissure measure in a linear manner. Examination of the means for the four age supported this, indicating that there was a steady, linear increase in the measure from age 8 until age 12 periods ($M = 22.19$, 23.17, 24.65, and 26.09; $SD = 2.43$, 2.16, 2.82, and 2.77 for ages 8, 10, 12, and 14, respectively). There also was substantial and statistically significant within-age and between-subject variance (see Table 11.1). In contrast, it appeared unnecessary to model the covariance matrix as a first-order autoregressive matrix; there were small, nonsignificant intraclass correlations among adjacent age levels in the *distance* variable, *rho* $=.047$, Wald $Z = .273$, $p = .785$. Thus, scores for each age level were relatively independent of one another once overall differences between individuals were taken into account.

Table 11.1
Unconditional Growth Model for Distance

			95% Confidence Interval	
Effect	*Estimate*	*SE*	*Lower Bound*	*Upper Bound*
Fixed effects				
Intercept	22.16***	.49	21.17	23.15
Linear effect of age	.97***	.43	.11	1.83
Quadratic effect of age	.12***	.14	-.16	.39
Random effects				
Repeated measures				
Within-age variance	2.12***	.41	1.46	3.10
Between-age covariance (rho)	.06	.18	-.28	.38
Between-subject variance	3.20**	1.09	1.64	6.25

**$p < .01$. ***$p < .001$.

Problem 11.2: Repeated-Measures with Level 2 Predictor

Now that we have determined that there is significant variance to explain, we will test another model with a Level 2 predictor, *gender*. This analysis will enable us to answer the following question:

11.2.   Does knowing a person's *gender* help us in understanding his or her growth from age 8 to age 14, as measured by the *distance* variable?

To answer this question, we will build on the model we just created for Problem 11.1. If you have not yet reset the **Linear Mixed Models** program from the previous problem, you will just need to do the following:

- Select **Analyze → Mixed Models → Linear**.
- Retain the settings for the first window. If you reset already, then repeat the settings for Fig. 11.2.

- Click on **Continue.** This will open the **Linear Mixed Models** window (Fig. 11.3).
- Keep the variables as they were in Fig. 11.3, but also move *Gender* into the **Factors:** box.
- Click on **Fixed** to get Fig. 11.7.
- Click to change **Main Effects** to **Factorial** is in the middle box, then Click on **Build nested terms**. Click on *linear* and click on the curved arrow to add it to the **build terms** box. Click on **By** to add the multiplication symbol to the box, then click on *gender* and click on the curved arrow to move it into the box. You should see *linear*, *quadratic, gender,* and *linear * gender*, as in Fig. 11.7.
- Click on **Add** to move the interaction into the **Model** box.

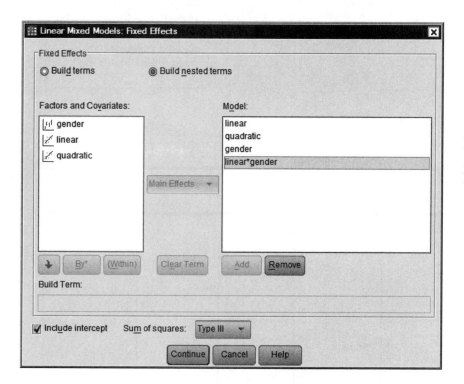

Fig. 11.7. Linear mixed models: Fixed effects.

- Click on **Continue**.
- Leave the settings for **Random** and **Statistics** as they are (or repeat what you did for Problem 11.1).
- Click on **OK.**
- Check to see if your syntax and output are like Output 11.2 below (but with additional outputs for the contrast coefficients, which we are omitting to save space).
- Unfortunately, we can't use **EM Means** to calculate the means for the interaction between *linear* and *gender* because *linear* is a covariate instead of a factor. We can calculate this using **Explore** after first using **Split file** to calculate the means and other statistics separately for boys and girls.
  - Click on **Data→Split File**.
  - Click on **Organize output by groups**.
  - Hit **OK**.
  - Use Explore, as before, to calculate statistics for the dependent variable *distance* with factor *age*.

Output 11.2 Conditional Model With Gender as a Predictor

```
MIXED distance BY gender WITH linear quadratic
  /CRITERIA=CIN(95) MXITER(100) MXSTEP(10) SCORING(1) SINGULAR(0.000000000001) HCONVERGE(0,
ABSOLUTE) LCONVERGE(0, ABSOLUTE) PCONVERGE(0.000001, ABSOLUTE)
  /FIXED=linear quadratic gender linear*gender | SSTYPE(3)
  /METHOD=REML
  /PRINT=G  LMATRIX SOLUTION TESTCOV
  /RANDOM=INTERCEPT | SUBJECT(subject) COVTYPE(VC)
  /REPEATED=age | SUBJECT(subject) COVTYPE(AR1).
```

The *linear* effect of age, the *quadratic* effect of age, *gender,* and the interaction between the *linear* effect of age and *gender* all are fixed effects in this model.

Mixed Model Analysis

Now there are five fixed effects parameters being estimated.

Model Dimension[b]

		Number of Levels	Covariance Structure	Number of Parameters	Subject Variables	Number of Subjects
Fixed Effects	Intercept	1		1		
	linear	1		1		
	quadratic	1		1		
	gender	2		1		
	gender * linear	2		1		
Random Effects	Intercept[a]	1	Variance Components	1	subject	
Repeated Effects	age	4	First-Order Autoregressive	2	subject	27
Total		12		8		

a. As of version 11.5, the syntax rules for the RANDOM subcommand have changed. Your command syntax may yield results that differ from those produced by prior versions. If you are using version 11 syntax, please consult the current syntax reference guide for more information.

b. Dependent Variable: Distance (mm) from center of pituitary to pteryo-maxillary fissure.

Now, there are eight parameters instead of six because we added *gender* and *gender *linear* as predictors.

Information Criteria[a]	
-2 Restricted Log Likelihood	436.587
Akaike's Information Criterion (AIC)	442.587
Hurvich and Tsai's Criterion (AICC)	442.827
Bozdogan's Criterion (CAIC)	453.520
Schwarz's Bayesian Criterion (BIC)	450.520

We will do a χ^2 to see if the fit of this model is significantly better than that of the unconditional model.

All information criteria indicate improved fit of the conditional model (lower numbers than in our output for Problem 11.1).

The information criteria are displayed in smaller-is-better forms.

a. Dependent Variable: Distance (mm) from center of pituitary to pteryo-maxillary fissure.

Fixed Effects

Type III Tests of Fixed Effects[a]

Source	Numerator df	Denominator df	F	Sig.
Intercept	1	43.580	2482.193	.000
linear	1	76.597	4.822	.031
quadratic	1	77.796	.752	.389
gender	1	36.092	2.763	.105
gender * linear	1	35.840	6.592	.015

a. Dependent Variable: Distance (mm) from center of pituitary to pteryo-maxillary fissure.

Estimates of Fixed Effects[b]

Parameter	Estimate	Std. Error	df	t	Sig.	95% Confidence Interval	
						Lower Bound	Upper Bound
Intercept	22.156527	.444407	43.388	49.856	.000	21.260527	23.052527
linear	1.289352	.427006	76.617	3.020	.003	.439005	2.139698
quadratic	.115741	.133695	77.341	.866	.389	-.150462	.381943
[gender=F] * linear	-.773180	.216583	49.794	-3.570	.001	-1.208244	-.338116
[gender=M] * linear	0[a]	0	.	.	.	.	.

a. This parameter is set to zero because it is redundant.

b. Dependent Variable: Distance (mm) from center of pituitary to pteryo-maxillary fissure.

These two variables represent the *gender × linear* age interaction, but only one is needed because the other provides redundant information.

Covariance Parameters

Estimates of Covariance Parameters[a]

Parameter		Estimate	Std. Error	Wald Z	Sig.	95% Confidence Interval	
						Lower Bound	Upper Bound
Repeated	AR1 diagonal	1.891491	.336741	5.617	.000	1.334336	2.681287
Measures	AR1 rho	-.037365	.167334	-.223	.823	-.350321	.283096
Intercept [subject = subject]	Variance	3.333923	1.083152	3.078	.002	1.763642	6.302325

a. Dependent Variable: Distance (mm) from center of pituitary to pteryo-maxillary fissure.

Random Effect Covariance Structure (G)[a]

	Intercept | subject
Intercept | subject	3.333923

Variance Components

a. Dependent Variable: Distance (mm) from center of pituitary to pteryo-maxillary fissure.

Interpretation of Output 11.2

The syntax and **Model Dimension** tables, again, enable you to check to make sure that the program did everything as intended. Note that we have now specified 12 parameters, 4 more than we specified in the unconditional model.

Next, you see the **Information Criteria**, providing goodness-of-fit data for this new model. If you compare the −2 Restricted Log Likelihood, which is a useful measure of goodness of fit, for this model (432.374) and for the unconditional model (437.43), you can see that the goodness of fit has improved by about 5. Again, smaller numbers indicate better fit. We will do a likelihood ratio shortly to see if this is a significant improvement in the model.

The next table provides information about the **Fixed Effects**. Note that *linear* still is a statistically significant predictor, $F(1, 76.6) = 4.82$, $p = .031$. Now, we see that *gender* * *linear* also is a statistically significant predictor, over and above the effect of *linear*, $F(1, 35.84) = 6.59$, $p = .015$. However, the main effect of *gender* is not a statistically significant predictor, $p > .05$.

We are omitting the **Type III Estimable functions** tables from the output reproduced here to save space, but these show you how the computer program contrasted the dummy variables.

The net table provides the parameter estimates for the fixed effects. Notice that two dummy variables were created for the gender × linear age predictor, but only one was needed because the other was redundant with it.

The next table shows that the **diagonal** estimate (now 1.89, but 2.12 in the Level 1 model) has been reduced, suggesting that *gender**linear explained additional variance. However, the between-participants' variability (**Intercept [subject = subject]**) has actually increased slightly (from 3.2 to 3.3). Moreover, the Wald statistics for both these effects suggest that there is still significant variance left to explain if we had additional predictors.

Before we show you how to write about this output, let's calculate a chi-square to determine whether there is a significant improvement in the fit of the model because of the addition of the *gender* variable.

- Click on **Transform → Compute variable**.
- In **Function Group:** box, select **All**.
- In **Functions and Special Variables:** scroll down and highlight **Sig.Chisq**. Move it into the **Numeric expression** box by clicking on the up arrow to the left of the **Function group** box (see Fig. 11.8).
- For **Target variable**, type in *chisqgenderlinear*.

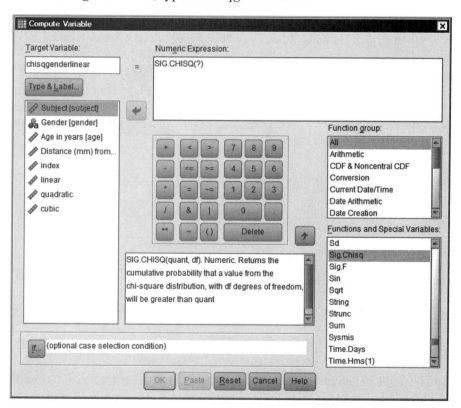

Fig. 11.8. Compute variable.

- Click on **Type and Label** and label this variable as *Likelihood ratio sign for adding* gender *to linear* (see Fig. 11.9).

**Fig. 11.9. Compute variable:
Type and label.**

- Click on **Continue.** This will take you back to Fig. 11.8.
- Notice that in the **Numeric expression** box, **SIG.CHISQ** is followed by a parenthesis with a question mark. Highlight the question mark and type enter 10.37, the rounded difference between the −2 restricted log likelihoods for the conditional and the unconditional models (436.59−446.96). Next, type a comma and enter the degrees of freedom, which is the difference in number of parameters (8-6) or 2 (see Fig. 11.8). It should now look like SIG.CHISQ(10.37,2)
- Click on **OK.**
- If you check your **Data Editor**, you will see a new column on the right side, with the new variable, *chiqgenderlineare.* The value is .01, which means that the difference in models is significant at *p* =.01.Thus, adding *gender* and the interaction between *gender* and the linear effect improves the fit of the model to a statistically significant degree, as suggested by the fact that the *gender x linear* effect was statistically significant.

```
COMPUTE chisqgenderage = SIG.CHISQ(10.37,2).
VARIABLE LABELS chisqgenderage 'Likelihood ratio sign for adding gender to age'.
EXECUTE.
```

Example of How to Write About Output 11.2

(Note that usually one would present the results from Output 11.1 in this results section as well and compare the two models.)

Results

As Tables 11.2 and 11.3 indicate, both the linear effect of age, $F(1,76.6) = 4.82, p = .031$ and the interaction between this linear trend and *gender*, $F (1,35.8) = 6.59, p =.015$ were significant predictors of *distance from pituitary to pteryomaxillary fissure*, a measure of growth of the jaw, but the effect of *gender* was not statistically significant ($p = .105$). As Figure 11.10 shows, size increased steadily from age 8 years to age 14 years for both males and females, but it increased more quickly for males. The model that included *gender* and the linear and quadratic trends of *age* indicated a significant interaction between the linear trend and gender; moreover, it explained statistically significantly more variance than did the unconditional model that included only the linear and quadratic trends of *age*. A likelihood ratio Chi-square indicated that the change in −2 restricted log likelihood of 10.37 ($df = 2$) was significant, $p = .01$. Table 11.4 presents the parameter estimates for both fixed and random effects.

Table 11.2

Means and Standard Deviations for Distance as a Function of Age and Gender

Effect	n	Distance from pituitary to pteryomaxillary fissure	
		M	SD
Girls	11	22.65	2.40
8 years		21.18	2.12
10 years		22.23	1.90
12 years		23.09	2.36
14 years		24.09	2.44
Boys	16	24.97	2.90
8 years		22.88	2.45
10 years		23.81	2.14
12 years		25.72	2.65
14 years		27.47	2.09
Total	27	24.02	2.93
8 years		22.19	2.43
10 years		23.17	2.16
12 years		24.65	2.82
14 years		24.02	2.93

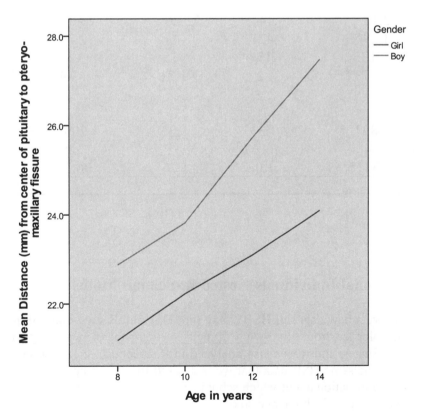

Figure 11.10. Interaction between age and gender in mean distance from pituitary to pteryomaxillary fissure.

Table 11.3

Effects of Age and Gender on Distance (mm) from Pituitary to Pteryomaxillary Fissure[a]

Source	Numerator df	Denominator df	F	p
Age linear	1	76.597	4.822	.031
Age quadratic	1	77.796	.752	.389
Gender	1	36.092	2.763	.105
Gender x linear	1	35.840	6.592	.015

[a] Dependent variable: Distance (mm) from center of pituitary to pteryomaxillary fissure.

Table 11.4

Covariance Parameters for Conditional Growth Model, with Gender as a Level 2 Predictor

Effect	Estimate	SE	95% Confidence Interval	
			Lower Bound	Upper Bound
Fixed effects				
Intercept	22.16	.444	22.26	23.05
Linear effect of age	1.29**	.427	.44	2.14
Quadratic effect of age	.12	.13	− .15	.38
Gender × linear age	−.77 ***	.22	−1.21	− .34
Random effects				
Repeated Measures				
Within-age variance	1.89***	.337	1.33	2.68
Between-age covariance (rho)	− .04	.167	−.35	.28
Between-subject variance	3.33**	1.083	1.76	6.30

* $p < .05$.   ** $p < .01$.   *** $p < .001$.

Problem 11.3: Unconditional Individuals-Nested-in-Schools Model

For this problem, you will need to retrieve a new data set, **HSB12.sav** (not **HSBdataB.sav** or any of the other data sets). This data set was downloaded from http://www.ats.ucla.edu/stat/paperexamples/singer/ with permission of Professor Judith D. Singer, and it was also analyzed in Raudenbush & Bryk (2002) and Singer (1998). It involves much of the same HSB data that we have used in other chapters, except that this version of the dataset includes information about which school students attended, students' SES, average school SES, information about the type of school, and so on.

This data set includes 7185 students whose data are nested within 160 different schools. *Mathach* has a mean of 12.75 and *SD* = 6.88 for the whole sample; however, the mean *mathach* varies across schools from 4.24 to 19.09, and the SD for *mathach* ranges from 3.88 to 8.48. The question we ask in this problem is whether there is sufficient variability within and/or between schools that we might want to try to explain that variability.

Let's answer the following question:

11.3   Is there significant variability within and/or among schools in the average *mathach*?
  - First, click on **Analyze → Mixed Models → Linear**.
  - Next, highlight *school* and move it into the **Subjects:** box to get Fig. 11.11.

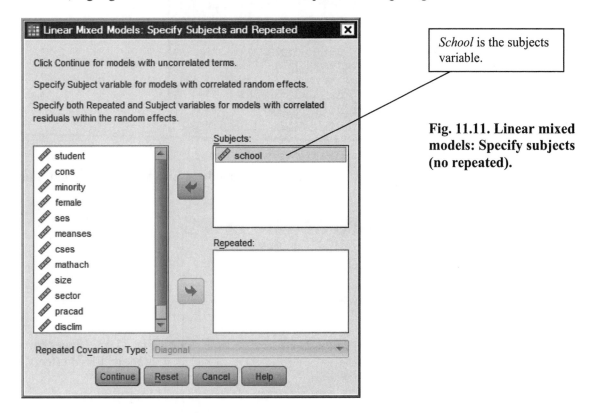

School is the subjects variable.

Fig. 11.11. Linear mixed models: Specify subjects (no repeated).

  - Click on **Continue.**
  - Highlight *mathach* and move it into the **Dependent Variable:** box. Do not put in any factors or covariates for this unconditional model. Your window should look like Fig. 11.12.

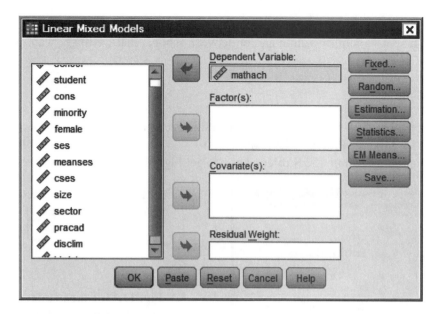

Fig. 11.12. Linear mixed models.

- Click on **Fixed** to get Fig. 11.13.
- In Figure 11.13, leave the defaults. Make sure that **Include intercept** is checked and **Sums of Squares** is **Type III**.

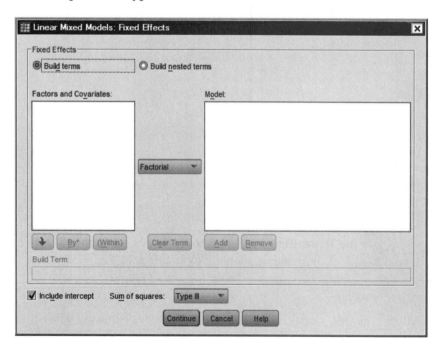

Fig. 11.13. Linear mixed models: Fixed effects.

- Click on **Continue**, which will take you back to Fig. 11.12.
- Click on **Random** to get Fig. 11.14.
- Under **Covariance Type**, click on the arrow next to **Variance Components** and scroll down to select **Unstructured**, which places no constraints on the covariance structure.
- Check **Include intercept.**
- Under Subject Groupings, highlight *school* and move it into the **Combinations:** box. Your window should look like Fig. 11.14.

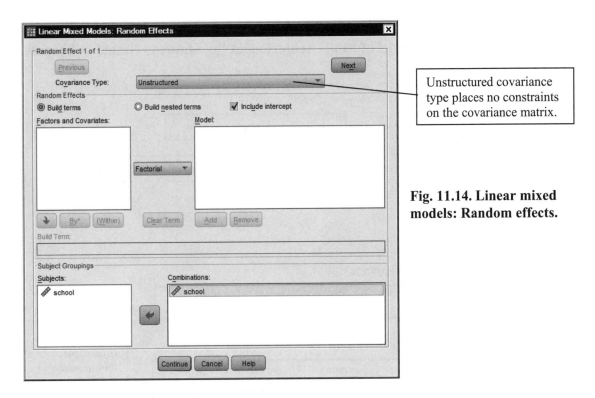

Fig. 11.14. Linear mixed models: Random effects.

Unstructured covariance type places no constraints on the covariance matrix.

- Click on **Continue** to get back to Fig. 11.12.
- Click on **Statistics.**
- Check **Parameter estimates** and **Tests for covariance parameters.** Your window should look like Fig. 11.15.

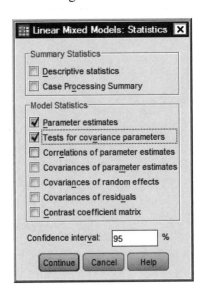

Fig. 11.15. Linear mixed models: Statistics.

- Click **Continue.**
- Click on **OK.**

Compare your output and syntax with Output 11.3.

Output 11.3 Unconditional Model of Math Achievement for Students Nested in Schools

```
MIXED mathach
   /CRITERIA=CIN(95) MXITER(100) MXSTEP(5) SCORING(1) SINGULAR(0.000000000001) HCONVERGE(0,
ABSOLUTE) LCONVERGE(0, ABSOLUTE) PCONVERGE(0.000001, ABSOLUTE)
   /FIXED=| SSTYPE(3)
   /METHOD=REML
   /PRINT=SOLUTION TESTCOV
   /RANDOM=INTERCEPT | SUBJECT(school) COVTYPE(UN).
```

school is the nesting variable.

Unstructured covariance type.

Mixed Model Analysis

Warnings

The covariance structure for random effect with only one level will be changed to Identity.

Two random effects: variability between schools (intercept) and within schools (residual).

Model Dimension[a]

		Number of Levels	Covariance Structure	Number of Parameters	Subject Variables
Fixed Effects	Intercept	1		1	
Random Effects	Intercept	1	Identity	1	school
Residual				1	
Total		2		3	

a. Dependent Variable: mathach.

Three parameters are specified in this model.

Information Criteria[a]

-2 Restricted Log Likelihood	47116.793
Akaike's Information Criterion (AIC)	47120.793
Hurvich and Tsai's Criterion (AICC)	47120.795
Bozdogan's Criterion (CAIC)	47136.553
Schwarz's Bayesian Criterion (BIC)	47134.553

Goodness of fit for unconditional model.

The information criteria are displayed in smaller-is-better forms.

a. Dependent Variable: mathach.

Fixed Effects

Type III Tests of Fixed Effects[a]

Source	Numerator df	Denominator df	F	Sig.
Intercept	1	156.647	2673.663	.000

a. Dependent Variable: mathach.

Estimates of Fixed Effects[a]

Parameter	Estimate	Std. Error	df	t	Sig.	95% Confidence Interval	
						Lower Bound	Upper Bound
Intercept	12.636974	.244394	156.647	51.707	.000	12.154242	13.119706

a. Dependent Variable: mathach.

Covariance Parameters

Within school-variance.

Both effects are significant.

Estimates of Covariance Parameters[a]

Parameter	Estimate	Std. Error	Wald Z	Sig.	95% Confidence Interval	
					Lower Bound	Upper Bound
Residual	39.148322	.660645	59.258	.000	37.874662	40.464813
Intercept [subject Variance	8.614025	1.078804	7.985	.000	6.739122	11.010548

a. Dependent Variable: mathach.

Between-school variance.

Interpretation of Output 11.3

This output is very similar to Output 11.1b, in that it is an unconditional model. This time, there is no repeated-measures variable. Instead, participants are nested in particular schools, which may have their own specific characteristics. The **Model dimension** table shows that there are 3 parameters. One is the estimate for the fixed intercept effect, which, as before, is not of conceptual interest. The other two are for the random school effect (variability between schools) and residual (variability within schools). The **Fixed Effects** and **Covariance Parameters** tables show that all three of these effects are statistically significant ($p < .001$), showing that the *mean* is statistically significantly different from zero, and there is significant variability to explain both within schools and between schools. The main purpose of this unconditional model is to see if there is a significant amount of variability in *math achievement* within schools (the covariance parameter labeled **Residual)** and variability between schools (the covariance parameter labeled **Intercept [subject = Variance school]**), and there is. Note that this is the estimate of the variability among the means of the schools.

Example of How to Write About Output 11.3

Results

The unconditional repeated-measures model revealed that there was significant variability in the *math achievement* measure, suggesting that it would be worthwhile to examine a conditional model that could potentially explain some of this variability. (The assumptions of independent observations at the level above the nesting, and random residuals were checked and met. The assumptions of bivariate normality and linear relationships were not met, thus, results should be viewed with caution.) There was statistically significant variability both between schools, Wald $Z = 7.99$, $p < .001$ and within schools, Wald $Z = 59.26$, $p < .001$. Table 11.5 presents the estimates of the variance components associated with the fixed and random effects.

Table 11.5

Unconditional Model for Math Achievement

Effect	Estimate	SE	95% Confidence Interval	
			Lower Bound	*Upper Bound*
Fixed effects				
Intercept	12.64***	.24	12.15	13.12
Random effects				
Between-school variance	8.61***	1.08	6.74	11.01
Within-school variance	39.15***	.66	37.87	40.46

***p <.001.

Problem 11.4: Conditional Individuals-Nested-in-Schools Model with Level 1 Covariate

In Problem 11.4, we could have looked at *meanses*, which is a variable at the school level (Level 2) and is the average socioeconomic class for the students in a particular school. As part of this problem, we will show you how you might have calculated *meanses* if it were not already available. However, instead we will look at a Level 1 predictor, *cses*, which is students' socioeconomic status measured as a deviation from the school's average SES. Creating such deviation scores is called <u>centering</u> the data, which we will show you how to do prior to actually doing Problem 11.4. We could create a model in which we included both the Level 1 and Level 2 variables, to try to explain both within-school and between-school variability, but we chose not to do so.

Now that we have determined that there is significant variance to explain, we will test another model with a Level 1 predictor, *cses*. This analysis will enable us to answer the following question:

11.4 Does knowing a person's socioeconomic status relative to that of the average student in his/her school (*cses*) help us in understanding his or her *math achievement*, even after the effects of differences among schools in *math achievement* are taken into account?

Before we do the analysis to answer this question, we will calculate a centered Level 1 variable and a Level 2 aggregate (averaged) variable to show you how to do those. Then, we will use the centered variable (which already is a part of the data set) as a Level 1 predictor in the conditional model.

- First, calculate the means for each school for *SES*: Click on **Analyze → Descriptive Statistics → Explore.**
- Highlight *school* and move it into the **Factor List:** box.
- Highlight *ses* and move it into the **Dependent List:** box.
- Under **Display,** click on **Statistics**. Your window should look like Fig. 11.16.

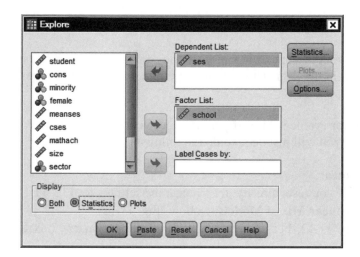

Fig. 11.16. Explore.

- Click on **OK.**

Compare the *mean* for several schools to the values listed for *meanses* in your **Data Editor**. You will see slight rounding differences, but basically the same values for the means. Note that *SES* is already centered on the grand mean for all participants, so some means are negative and some are positive. We are not including the output for this here in order to save space.

Now, we will center SES on each school's *mean.* We'll use *meanses* rather than creating a new variable based on the output we just generated.

- First, click on **Transform → Compute Variable.**
- Type *CSES2* in the box for **Target Variable.**
- Click on **Type and Label.**
- Type in *SES centered on school mean demo* (see earlier example in Fig. 11.9).
- Click on **Continue.**
- Next, highlight and move *ses* into the **Numeric expression** box, and type – (minus sign), then type in *meanses.* Your window should look like Fig. 11.17.

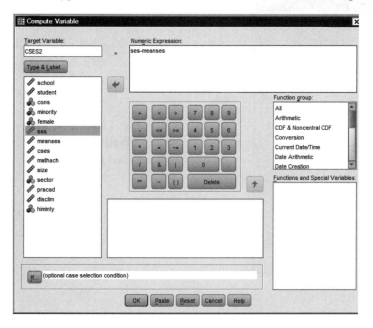

Fig. 11.17. Compute variable.

- Click on **OK.**

  The results will appear as a new column in your data. Compare the results for a few cases to the *cses* variable that is already included in the data. They should be the same. We will use *cses* as a predictor in Problem 11.4.

We will build on the model we just created for Problem 11.3. If you have not yet reset the **Linear Mixed Models** program from the previous problem, you will just need to do the following:

- Select **Analyze → Mixed Models → Linear**.
- Retain the settings for the first window. If you reset already, then repeat the settings for Fig. 11.11.
- Click on **Continue.** This will open the **Linear Mixed Models** window (Fig. 11.12).
- Keep the variables as they were in Fig. 11.12, but also move *cses* into the **Covariate** box to get Figure 11.18.

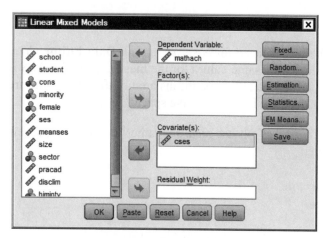

Fig. 11.18. Linear mixed models.

- Click on **Fixed** to get Fig. 11.13.
- Click on *cses*, and **Add** it as a fixed covariate, as in Fig. 11.19.

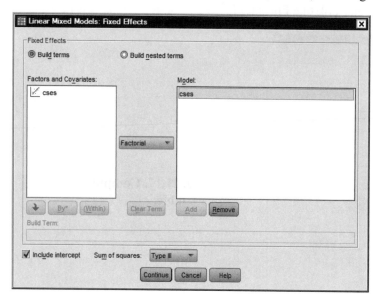

Fig. 11.19. Linear mixed models: Fixed effects.

- Click on **Continue,** to take you back to 11.18.
- Click on **Random**.
- Click on 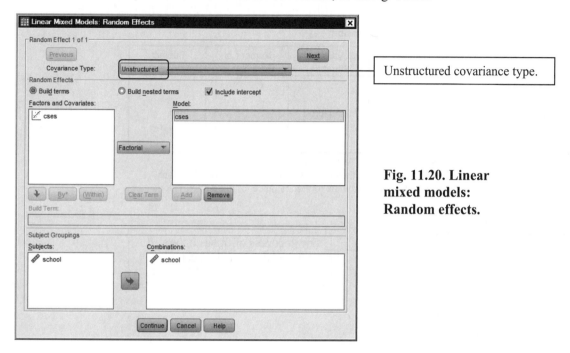 *cses*, and **Add** it as a random covariate, as in Fig. 11.20.

Fig. 11.20. Linear mixed models: Random effects.

- Click on **Continue** to take you back to 11.18.
- Click on **Statistics.**
- Leave the checks for **Parameter estimates** and **Tests for covariance parameters** and also check **Covariances of random effects.**
- Click on **Continue.**
- Click on **OK.**
  Compare your output with Output 11.4.

Output 11.4: Conditional Model Predicting *mathach* From CSES

CSES is a covariate.

```
MIXED mathach WITH cses
  /CRITERIA=CIN(95) MXITER(100) MXSTEP(5) SCORING(1) SINGULAR(0.000000000001) HCONVERGE(0,
ABSOLUTE) LCONVERGE(0, ABSOLUTE) PCONVERGE(0.000001, ABSOLUTE)
  /FIXED=cses | SSTYPE(3)
  /METHOD=REML
  /PRINT=G  SOLUTION TESTCOV
  /RANDOM=INTERCEPT cses | SUBJECT(school) COVTYPE(UN).
```

Mixed Model Analysis

Model Dimension[b]

		Number of Levels	Covariance Structure	Number of Parameters	Subject Variables
Fixed Effects	Intercept	1		1	
	cses	1		1	
Random Effects	Intercept + cses[a]	2	Unstructured	3	school
Residual				1	
Total		4		6	

a. As of version 11.5, the syntax rules for the RANDOM subcommand have changed. Your command syntax may yield results that differ from those produced by prior versions. If you are using SPSS 11 syntax, please consult the current syntax reference guide for more information.

b. Dependent Variable: mathach.

Information Criteria[a]

-2 Restricted Log Likelihood	46714.235
Akaike's Information Criterion (AIC)	46722.235
Hurvich and Tsai's Criterion (AICC)	46722.241
Bozdogan's Criterion (CAIC)	46753.753
Schwarz's Bayesian Criterion (BIC)	46749.753

> The goodness of fit has improved with the conditional model (46714.24 rather than 47116.79)

The information criteria are displayed in smaller-is-better forms.

a. Dependent Variable: mathach.

Fixed Effects

Type III Tests of Fixed Effects[a]

Source	Numerator df	Denominator df	F	Sig.
Intercept	1	156.751	2676.274	.000
cses	1	155.218	292.401	.000

> The effect of *cses* is significant.

a. Dependent Variable: mathach.

Estimates of Fixed Effects[a]

Parameter	Estimate	Std. Error	df	t	Sig.	95% Confidence Interval	
						Lower Bound	Upper Bound
Intercept	12.649339	.244513	156.751	51.733	.000	12.166373	13.132305
cses	2.193192	.128259	155.218	17.100	.000	1.939834	2.446550

a. Dependent Variable: mathach.

> Since *cses* is a covariate (continuous variable), no dummy variables are created.

Covariance Parameters

Estimates of Covariance Parameters[a]

Parameter		Estimate	Std. Error	Wald Z	Sig.	95% Confidence Interval	
						Lower Bound	Upper Bound
Residual		36.700197	.625744	58.650	.000	35.494027	37.947355
Intercept + cses	UN (1,1)	8.681643	1.079626	8.041	.000	6.803757	11.077840
[subject = school]	UN (2,1)	.050747	.406393	.125	.901	-.745768	.847262
	UN (2,2)	.693994	.280786	2.472	.013	.314026	1.533723

a. Dependent Variable: mathach.

Variance of *CSES*.

Variance of *schools* in *mathach*.

Random Effect Covariance Structure (G)[a]

Variability among *schools* in level of *mathach* (variance of intercept/school).

	Intercept | school	cses | school
Intercept | school	8.681643	.050747
cses | school	.050747	.693994

Unstructured

Variance of *cses*.

Covariance between *schools* and *cses*.

a. Dependent Variable: mathach.

Interpretation of Output 11.4

The syntax and **Model Dimension** tables, again, enable you to check to make sure that the program did everything as intended. Note that we have now specified six parameters, three more than we specified in the unconditional model.

Next, you see the **Information Criteria**, providing goodness-of-fit data for this new model. If you compare the −2 restricted log likelihood, which is a useful measure of goodness of fit, for this model (46714.24) and for the unconditional model (47116.80), you can see that the goodness of fit has improved by almost 403. Again, smaller numbers indicate better fit. We will again do a likelihood ratio after we go through Output 11.4, to see if this is a significant improvement in the model.

The next table provides information about the **Fixed Effects**. Note that *cses*, $F (1, 155.22) = 292.4$ is statistically significant at $p < .001$. Moreover, in the **Covariance Parameters** tables, we see that the within schools residual still is statistically significant, $Wald\ Z = 58.65$, $p < .001$, although, as we see by comparing this table with the one in Output 4.3, the variance component estimate has decreased from 39.15 to 36.70. This makes sense, because we are explaining some of this within-school variability by using *cses* as a predictor.

The next entries in this table are less familiar and harder to interpret from the labels that are given, which is why we requested the **Random Effect Covariance Structure**, by checking **Covariances of random effects** in the **Statistics** menu. The line in the **Estimates of Covariance Parameters** table that is labeled **UN (1,1)** is the (unstructured) variance associated with differences between schools. As the **Random Effect Covariance** table indicates, the **(1,1)** indicates that it is the covariation of this effect with itself, or variance. In contrast to the decline in the within-schools variance component, the between-schools variance component actually increased a negligible amount in the conditional model, from 8.61 in Output 11.3 to 8.68 in Output 11.4. The next line in the **Estimates of Covariance Parameters** table, which is labeled **UN (2,1)**, is the covariance between differences due to *cses* and differences between schools, as again made clearer in the **Random Effect Covariance** table. The final line in the **Estimates of Covariance Parameters** table that is labeled **UN (2,2)** is the variance associated with differences within schools that are due to *cses*.

Note that all of these effects are statistically significant except the covariance between *cses* and between-schools variance. Thus, it appears that these two types of variance are relatively independent of one another.

Before we show you how to write about this output, let's again calculate a chi-square to determine whether there is a significant improvement in the fit of the model because of the addition of the *cses* variable.

- First, click on **Transform → Compute Variable**.
- Click **Reset** to clear any previous settings or text.
- In the **Function Group:** box, highlight **All**.
- In the **Functions and Special Variables:** box, scroll down and highlight **Sig.Chisq** and move it into the **Numeric expression:** box by clicking on the up arrow to the left of the **Function group:** box (see Fig. 11.20).
- Notice that in the **Numeric expression:** box **SIG.CHISQ** is followed by a parenthesis with a question mark. Highlight the question mark and enter 402.56, the rounded difference between the −2 restricted log likelihoods for the conditional and the unconditional models (47116.793−46714.235). Then, type a comma and enter the degrees of freedom, which is the difference in number of parameters (6-3) or 3.
- For **Target variable**, type in *chisqcses*. Your window should look like Fig. 11.21.

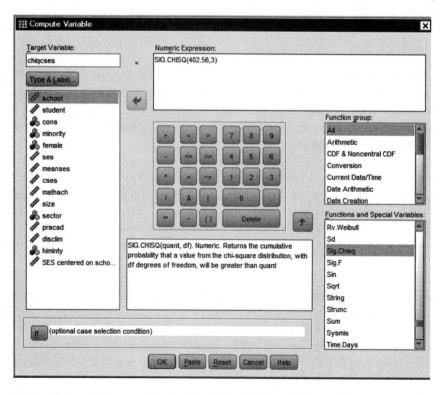

**Fig. 11.21.
Compute variable.**

- Next, click on **Type and Label** and label this variable as *chi square for change in school model with cses*.
- Click on **Continue.** This will take you back to Fig. 11.21.

- Click on **OK**.

If you check your data, you will see a new column with the new variable. The value is .00, which means that the difference in models is significant at $p < .01$.

```
COMPUTE chiqcses=SIG.CHISQ(402.56,3).
VARIABLE LABELS  chiqcses 'chi square for change in school model with cses'.
EXECUTE.
```

Example of How to Write About Output 11.4

(Usually one would present the results from Output 11.3 in this results section and compare the two models.)

Results

As Table 11.6 indicates, *centered socioeconomic status* was a statistically significant predictor of *math achievement* even after the statistically significant remaining within-school and between-school variances were taken into account. The model that included *socioeconomic status* as a predictor explained statistically significantly more variance than did the unconditional model that included only the within-schools residual and between-schools variance. A likelihood ratio chi-square indicated that the change in -2 restricted log likelihood of 402.56 ($df = 3$) was statistically significant, $p < .01$. Table 11.7 presents the parameter estimates for both fixed and random effects.

Table 11.6

Effect of Centered SES on Math Achievement

Source	Numerator df	Denominator df	F	p
Intercept	1	156.75	2676.27	.001
Centered SES	1	155.22	292.40	.001

Table 11.7

Conditional Model for Math Achievement, with Centered SES as a Level 1 Predictor

Effect	Estimate	SE	95% Confidence Interval	
			Lower Bound	Upper Bound
Fixed effects				
Intercept	12.65***	.24	12.17	13.13
Centered SES	2.19***	.13	1.94	2.45
Random effects				
Within-school variance	36.70***	.63	35.49	37.95
Centered SES	.69*	.28	.31	1.53
Between-school variance	8.68***	1.08	6.80	11.08

*$p < .05$.   ***$p < .001$.

Interpretation Questions

11.1   In Output 11.1b: (a) Why did we decide to use the autoregressive covariance structure (AR1)? (b) What did the **AR1 rho** suggest about the need to use the autoregressive covariance structure? (c) If the quadratic trend had been significant, what would that have told us? (d)What do the **Information Criteria** tell you? Why is this important?

11.2   In Output 11.2: (a) What does this analysis tell us that 11.1b did not? (b) the linear *age* × *gender* interaction effect was significant. What does that mean? (c) What did the chi-square tell us? (d) Why would we use multilevel linear modeling to analyze these data rather than using a mixed design (between-subjects and within-subjects IVs) ANOVA?

11.3   In Output 11.3: (a) What do we mean when we say that *school* is a nesting variable? Why does this matter? (b) What is an unstructured covariance structure, and why did we use it? (c) In the **Covariance Parameters** table, what does the intercept variance tell you?

11.4   In Output 11.4: (a) What is *cses* a measure of? Why does one center data? (b) What does the **Covariance Parameters** table tell you? How does it relate to the **Random effect covariance structure** table? (c) Do the results tell us whether it might be reasonable to include additional (e.g., Level 2) predictors? What provides information about this?

Extra SPSS Problems

11.1   Using the HSB12.sav data file, repeat Problem 11.4, but add *sector*, a dummy variable indicating the type of school (0 = public, 1 = Catholic), as a Level 2 factor (not covariate). Only *cses* should be included as a <u>random</u> covariate, but both variables, and their interaction, should be included as fixed predictors.
  a. Do a chi-square to see if this improves the goodness of fit.
  b. Does adding the *sector* variable improve the model significantly?

11.2   Repeat Extra SPSS Problem 11.1, but change the **Covariance Type** to variance components.
  a. Again, do the goodness of fit chi-square to see if this improves the goodness of fit.
  b. Does it do so?
  c. Which variance structure is preferable?

11.3   Repeat Extra SPSS Problem 11.2, but again change the **Covariance Type**. This time, try compound symmetry. Which is the best covariance structure to use?

11.4.   Using the Growth Study.sav data file, repeat Problem 11.2 (the repeated-measures problem), not Extra SPSS Problem 11.2.
  a. Substitute unstructured for AR1 as the **Covariance Type**.
  b. Does this change the results in comparison with Problem 11.2?
  c. If so, how?

APPENDIX A

Getting Started With SPSS and Other Useful Procedures

Don Quick and Sophie Nelson
Colorado State University

This section includes step-by-step instructions for several procedures related to getting started with SPSS as well as other useful procedures. This Appendix includes:
1. Making a working file from the Web site
2. Opening and starting SPSS and getting familiar with the SPSS data editor
3. Setting your computer to print the syntax or log along with each output
4. Importing Data from Excel
5. Defining variables
6. Labeling the levels of variables
7. Printing a dictionary
8. Editing your Output
9. Exporting to Excel, MsWord, HTML, or PDF files
10. Converting variables to standardized variables
11. Selecting cases
12. Splitting files
13. Merging files
14. Using the Means command
15. Using the Graph commands

Two additional resources for students are provided on the Web site: (a) a **Quick Reference Guide (QRG)** to commonly used SPSS procedures and (b) a document, **Making Tables and Figures**, describing how to make tables in APA format.

Copy the Data Files From the Web Site

Copy the files from the Web site, http://www.psypress.com/ibm-spss-intermediate-stats.The files are:

hsbdataB.sav	**dvdplayer.sav**
college student data.sav	**judges.sav**
product data.sav	**satisfy.sav**
mixedMANOVAdata.sav	**Wuensch_logistic.sav**
Anxiety 2.sav	**site.sav**
general social survey.sav	**World95.sav**
DataFemales.sav	**DataMales.sav**
hsb12.sav	**Growth study.sav**
New drug.sav	**Love.sav**

Note: You may not see the file extension .sav depending on your computer setup.

Download these files to a working folder on your personal flash drive or network drive.

Open and Start the SPSS Application

Begin at the **Start** button (bottom left of the Windows Desktop).

- If an **SPSS icon** is available on the desktop, double click on it (see Fig. A.1). If there is no icon, click **Start** → **All Programs** → **SPSS Statistics** → **IBM SPSS Statistics 19** (see Fig. A.1). If **IBM SPSS Inc** is not listed in the **All Programs** menu, it will need to be installed on your computer. It is not part of the Microsoft Windows package or the Web site for this book and must be purchased/rented and loaded separately.

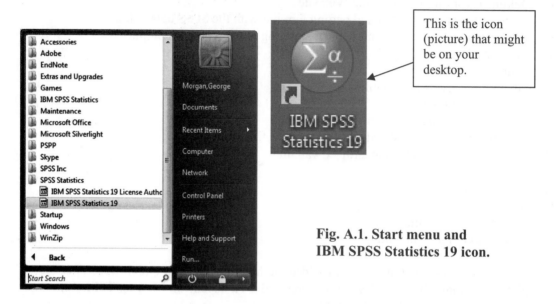

This is the icon (picture) that might be on your desktop.

Fig. A.1. Start menu and
IBM SPSS Statistics 19 icon.

After you start the program, you will see the **SPSS startup screen**. Notice that in the Startup screen, there may be a list of SPSS files available on your computer.

- Click on the SPSS file you wish to use *or* press **Enter** and browse to find the correct file in the correct folder *or* click the **Cancel** button, which will bring up a new SPSS desktop screen, called the **SPSS Data Editor,** as shown later in Figs. A.3 and A.4. If no files are listed, click OK to bring up the **Open File** dialogue box to search for the file you want to open. You can also use the **Open File** dialogue box to open SPSS syntax or output files if you want to open those types of files.

Files also can be opened from the program's **Data Editor** screen. In this screen, there are two tabs at the bottom left side of the screen; the **Data View** tab and the **Variable View** tab (see Fig. A.2). Please refer to your SPSS Help menu for further information on how to do this in earlier versions.

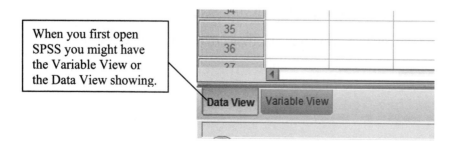

When you first open SPSS you might have the Variable View or the Data View showing.

Fig. A.2. View tabs.

Although the toolbar at the top of the data editor screen is the same for both the Variable and Data View screens, it is important to notice the *subtle* differences in desktop features between these two screens found within the data editor (compare Fig. A.3 and Fig. A.4).

- Click on the **Variable View** tab (see Fig. A.2) in the data editor screen to produce Fig. A.3.

Notice the column headers are those in Fig. A.3 (e.g., Name, Type, Width). One creates (defines and labels) new variables using the **Variable View** (see Chapter 2).

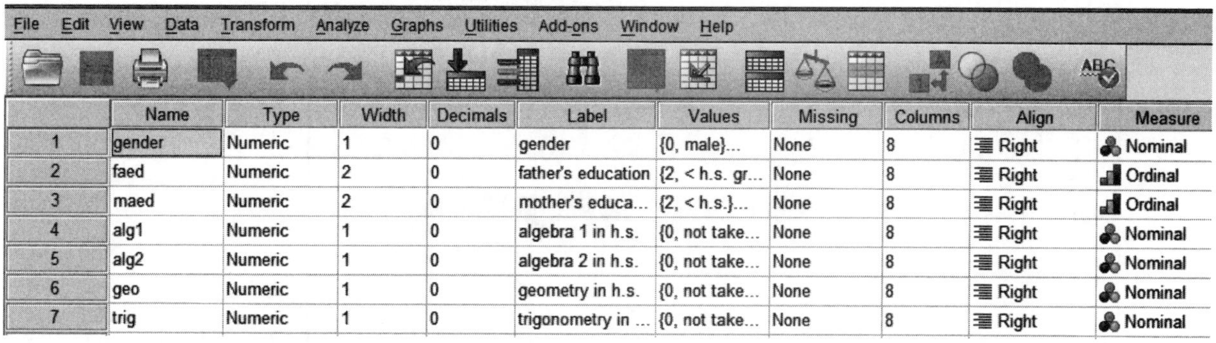

	Name	Type	Width	Decimals	Label	Values	Missing	Columns	Align	Measure
1	gender	Numeric	1	0	gender	{0, male}...	None	8	Right	Nominal
2	faed	Numeric	2	0	father's education	{2, < h.s. gr...	None	8	Right	Ordinal
3	maed	Numeric	2	0	mother's educa...	{2, < h.s.}...	None	8	Right	Ordinal
4	alg1	Numeric	1	0	algebra 1 in h.s.	{0, not take...	None	8	Right	Nominal
5	alg2	Numeric	1	0	algebra 2 in h.s.	{0, not take...	None	8	Right	Nominal
6	geo	Numeric	1	0	geometry in h.s.	{0, not take...	None	8	Right	Nominal
7	trig	Numeric	1	0	trigonometry in ...	{0, not take...	None	8	Right	Nominal

Fig. A.3. SPSS data editor: Variable view.

- Click on the **Data View** tab in the data editor to produce Fig. A.4.

Notice the column headers change to **var** or to the names of your variables if you have already entered them (see Fig. A.4). One enters (inputs) data using the **Data View**.

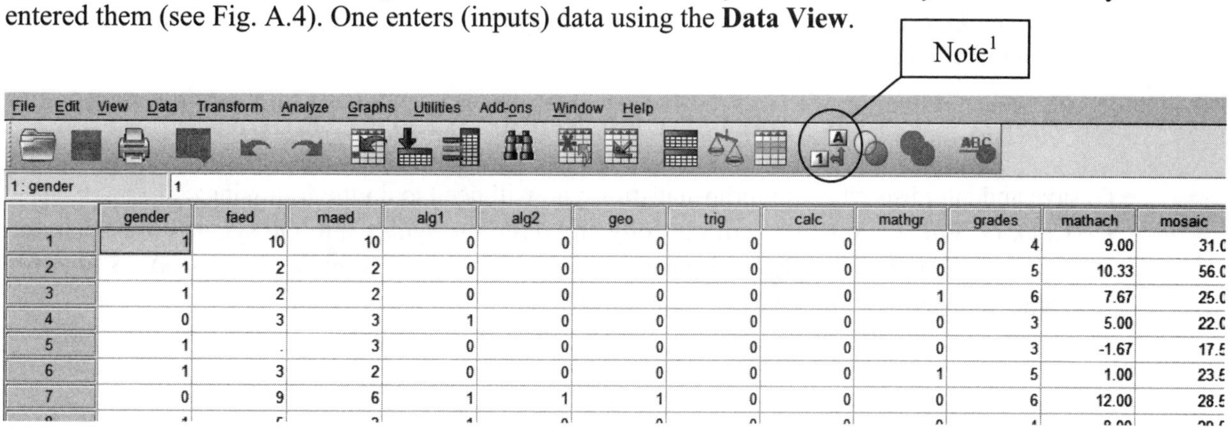

Note[1]

	gender	faed	maed	alg1	alg2	geo	trig	calc	mathgr	grades	mathach	mosaic
1	1	10	10	0	0	0	0	0	0	4	9.00	31.0
2	1	2	2	0	0	0	0	0	0	5	10.33	56.0
3	1	2	2	0	0	0	0	0	1	6	7.67	25.0
4	0	3	3	1	0	0	0	0	0	3	5.00	22.0
5	1	.	3	0	0	0	0	0	0	3	-1.67	17.5
6	1	3	2	0	0	0	0	0	1	5	1.00	23.5
7	0	9	6	1	1	1	0	0	0	6	12.00	28.5

Fig. A.4. SPSS data editor: Data View.

Set Your Computer to Print the SPSS Syntax (Log)

With the current version of the program, your computer will automatically print the SPSS commands on your output, as shown throughout this book. If you are using an earlier version, you may need to turn this function on. To do so, set your computer using the following:

---

[1] If the values for gender are shown as female or male, the value labels rather than the numerals are being displayed. In that case, click on the circled symbol to change the format to show only the numeric values for each variable.

- Click on **Edit → Options.**
- Click on the **Viewer** tab near the top left of the **Options** window to get Fig. A.5 (see the circled tab in Fig. A.5).

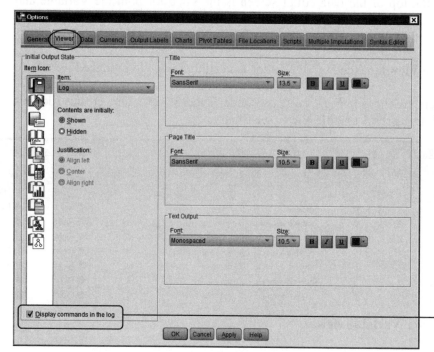

Fig. A.5. Edit: Options.

Check this to display your syntax in the output.

- Check **Display commands in the log** near the lower left of the window (see oval).
- Leave the other defaults as is.
- Click on **OK.** Doing this will always print the syntax on your output on this computer. If you use another computer you may have to set it again.

Save and Later Use Syntax to Rerun Statistics

To save and later use syntax to rerun statistics, you will need to do the following:
- Click on **File → New → Syntax.** Copy and paste the syntax into the syntax editor that you just opened and click **File → Save as.** This will save as a **Syntax File (*.sps) →** type file name in dialog box → **Save** (see Figure A.6.).

To open a saved syntax file, from the menu choose:
- **File → Open → Syntax.**
- Select a syntax file → and click **Open.** Navigate to where you saved the syntax file.
- Once a syntax file is open, from the menu choose **Run → Selection.**

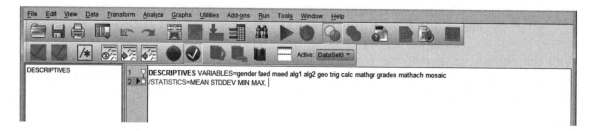

Fig. A.6. SPSS Syntax Editor.

Note: This is a simplified version of how to use the syntax file. The saving and using of the syntax file may be different on your computer depending on whether you have a data file open or not. However, it can be very useful if you need to run the same commands several different times.

Working With Your Output

Resize/Shrink to Print
In order for larger tables in the output to fit onto a single printed page, you will need to do the following:
- From the SPSS Output Viewer, double-click on the table to be resized to enter the editing mode.
- Right click → **Table Properties** → and select the **Printing** tab.
- Check **Rescale Wide Table to Fit Page** and/or **Rescale Long Table to Fit Page.**
- Click on **OK.**

Editing Tables, Charts, and Text
When using the SPSS Output Viewer, editing outputs can be done in a variety of ways by either double-clicking on any item within the table or chart or by choosing **Edit** from the menu and scrolling down to **Options**.

- Double-click on any item within a table or chart. This will allow you to edit the text size, font, color, change the look of a table, or pivot the table. After double-clicking, you can do the following:

To edit text size, font, and color:
- If the Formatting Toolbar is not already there, from the menu choose **View** → **Toolbar**. This will activate the **Formatting Toolbar.**

To customize a table, including text, alignment, shading, footnotes, cell formats, borders, and printing options:
- From the menu choose **Format** → **Table Properties**.

To change the look of a table:
- From the menu choose **Format** → **TableLooks.**
- The **TableLooks** dialog box will appear listing a variety of predefined styles.
- A style can be previewed in the Sample window to the right of the TableLooks dialog box. (See Appendix C on making tables.)

To modify the table layouts and data order:
- From the menu choose **Pivot.**
- The **Pivoting Trays** window will appear which provides a way to move data between columns, rows, and layers.

Most of the table editing procedures can also be completed by choosing **Edit** and then scrolling down to **Options** in the SPSS Output Viewer menu.

Importing Data and Exporting Results

SPSS allows you to import data from Microsoft Access or Excel and export results outputs to Microsoft Excel and Word or other file types.

To import from MS Access or Excel:
- From the SPSS Output Viewer menu choose **File → Open Database → New Query**
- The **Database Wizard** will guide you through the process of importing data.

To export results:
- When the output you wish to export is open, from the SPSS Output Viewer menu choose **File → Export to Database**.
- The **Database Wizard** will guide you through the process of exporting data.

Note: You can also export individual elements of the output by right clicking on the element and selecting **Export.**

Define the Variables

The following section will help you name and label variables. If you still have the hsbdataB data file, you can either use that or bring up a new data screen (**File → New → Data**).

You need to use the **Variable View** screen.

- Click on the **Variable View** tab at the bottom left of your screen (see Fig. A.8).

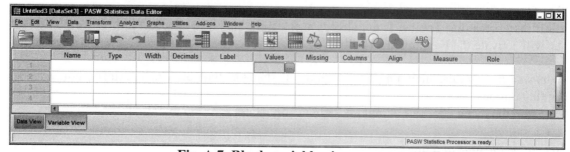

Fig. A.7. Blank variable view screen.

In this window, you will see 11 sections that will allow you to input the variable name, type, width, decimals, label, values, missing (data), columns (width), align (data left or right), measurement type, and role.

To label a variable, follow these commands:
- Click in the blank box directly under **Name** (there may be a variable name there if you have the hsbdataB file open).
- Type the name of the variable in the box directly beneath **Name** (see Fig. A.7.). Notice the number 1 to the left of this box. This indicates that you are entering your first variable. SPSS 11.5 and earlier versions allow only eight letters for the name. SPSS 12 and later versions

allow as many as you wish, although we recommend keeping the name fairly short in order to make the outputs easier to read.
- Press Tab to move to the other attributes of the variable:

Type indicates whether the variable levels are numbers or are letters. Usually, you will use numeric.

Width indicates how wide the columns should be based on the number of characters allowed in the column.

Decimals are the number of decimals that will be shown in the data view window.

Labels gives a longer name for the variable (optional but desirable if the name is unclear).

Values indicates labels for the levels of the variable (optional but needed for nominal variables).

Missing indicates any <u>special</u> values for missing data. The SPSS system missing uses a blank. If only blanks are used for missing, this column will say "none" for no special missing values. We usually use blanks for missing.

Columns defines the number of spaces for the variable in the data view window.

Align indicates how you want the data aligned in the data view window, usually right justified.

Measure shows the type of variable: nominal, ordinal, or scale (i.e., normally distributed).

Role allows the user to assign the term Target to dependent variables, Input for independent variables, and Both for variables that are used as both independent and dependent variables.

Label the Values or Levels of the Variables

For variables that are nominal or dichotomous it is important to label the values or levels so that you will know the group referred to by each number. For example, with the variable of *gender*, the levels are male and female, so you might label males as "1" and females as "2." To do this, follow these commands:

- Under **Values**, click on ▣ (the small blue box with three dots) to get Fig. A.9.
- In the **Value Labels** window, type **1** in the **Value** box, *male* in the **Value Label** box, and then click **Add**. Do the same for 2 = female. The **Value Labels** window should resemble Fig. A.9 just before you click **Add** for the second time.

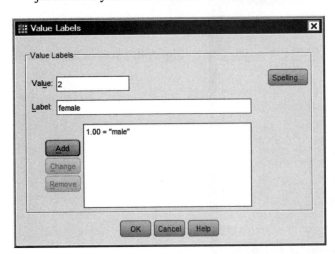

Fig. A.8. Value labels window.

After you define the variables, you are ready to enter data in the **Data View** (Fig. A.5).

Print a Dictionary or Codebook

Now that you have defined and labeled your variables, you can print a codebook or dictionary of your variables. It is a very useful record of what you have done. The dictionary output will be in two tables: one listing each variable, its label, measurement level, etc.; and the other listing values and value labels. Notice that the information in the codebook is essentially the same as that in the variable view (Fig. A.3) so you do not really have to have both, but the codebook makes a more complete printed record of your labels and values.

- Select **File → Display Data File Information → Working File**.
- The Codebook will be in a table in the Output Viewer.

Converting Variables Into Standardized Variables (z Scores)

This procedure transforms the data for one variable to a standard score that has a mean of zero and a standard deviation of one. Standardized scores are used when you want to compute a summated scale score made up of variables with quite different means and standard deviations. They are also used to compare apples and oranges, for example, achievement on a math test and an English test. Next we will make the *math achievement* scores into z scores.

- Click on **Analyze →Descriptive Statistics → Descriptives...**
- Select the variable *math achievement test (mathach)*.
- Click the arrow in the middle of the dialog box to move the variable to the **Variables** box.
- Check the box **Save Standardized Values as Variables.**
- Click **OK.** An output window will appear with the descriptive statistics. The z score for each subject will be included as a new variable (*Zmathach*) in the last column of the SPSS Data Editor. The variable *Zmathach* and the first few z scores are shown in Fig. A.8.

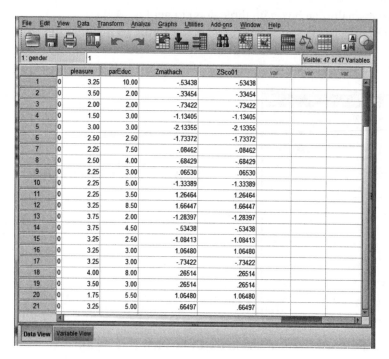

Fig. A.8. z scores for *math achievement*.

Selecting Cases

The select cases command permits the analysis of a specific subset of the data. Once a subset is selected and used for the analysis, the user can either revert back to the entire data set by clicking on reset or delete the unselected cases to create a new data file of the selected cases. If you want to do the same analysis separately on all subsets of data, then **Split File** should be used instead of **Select Cases** (see below). It is advisable to <u>save your work before deleting cases</u>, just in case you change your mind! To select cases:

- Click on **Data → Select Cases.**
- Choose the method of selecting cases you prefer: (a) **If condition is satisfied** (a conditional expression is used to select cases), (b) **Random sample of cases** (cases are selected randomly based on a percent or number of cases), (c) **Based on time or case range** (case selection is based on a range of case numbers or a range of dates/time), or (d) **Use filter variable** (a numeric variable can be used as the filter—any cases with a value other than 0 or missing are selected). **Unselected cases** may be **Filtered** (remain in the data file but are excluded in the analysis) or **Deleted** (removed from the working data file and cannot be recovered if the data file is saved after the deletion) (see Fig. A.9).
- For example, if you wanted to select only males, you would use **If condition is satisfied** and click on the **If...** button.
- Then type gender = 0 and click **Continue.** Your window should look like Fig. A.9.
- Click on **OK.**

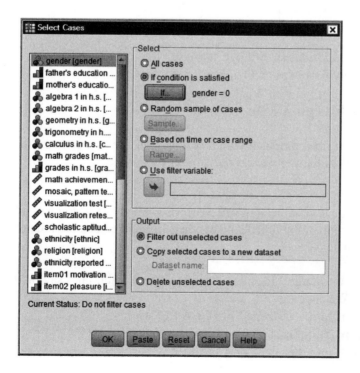

Fig. A.9. Select cases.

Splitting Files

Files splits the data file into separate groups for analysis based on the values of one or more grouping variables. Data can be displayed for group comparisons, or data can be displayed separately for each group (see Fig. A.10). This is a very useful tool, but <u>be sure to reset **Split File** after doing the analyses you want split, or all further analyses will be split in the same way</u>. In this example, we will split the hsbdata.sav file into two files, one with the data for the males and one with the data for the females.

- **Data → Split File**.
- Select the appropriate radio button for the desired display option (**Compare groups** or **Organize output by groups**). Be sure the **Sort the file by grouping variables** is selected. The window should look like Figure A.10.
- Click on **OK.**

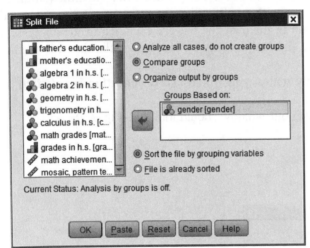

Fig. A.10. Split file.

Note: Now you can do statistics separately for males and females.

Merging Files

Merge files allows the working data file to be combined with a second data file that contains (a) the *same variables but different cases* or (b) the *same cases but different variables*.

To Add Cases
An example of merging files with the same variables but different cases might be if you had all the males for the hsbdata set in one file and all the females in another. In order to compare males and females, these two data files need to be merged.

- Open both data files you want to merge. In this example, open DataMales.sav and DataFemales.sav. (They are on the Web site for this book.)
- In the DataFemales.sav file, click on **Data → Merge Files → Add Cases**.
- The **Add Cases to DataFemales.sav [DataSet2]** window will open (see Fig. A.11).
- Highlight **DataMales.sav [DataSet1]** and then click on **Continue**.

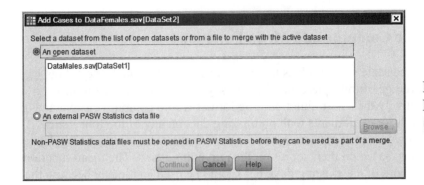

Fig. A.11. Add cases to
DataFemales.sav
[DataSet1].

- The **Add Cases from DataMales.sav [DataSet1]** will open (see Fig. A.12).

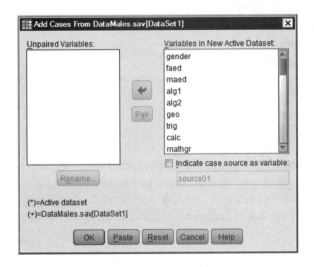

Fig. A.12. Add cases from
DataMales.sav [DataSet1].

- Click on **OK.** The data from the DataMales.sav file will be added to the DataFemales.sav file.

Using a similar procedure, you can merge two files that have the same, or at least overlapping cases but different variables.

To Add Variables
Before you add <u>variables</u> to a file using this method, you should first make sure that each participant who has data in both data sets is identified by the same ID number in both files. Then, you should use **Sort Cases** to sort each file (by itself), sequentially in ascending order, saving each file once it is sorted. You should make sure that you open the data file <u>first</u> that has the correct values of any variables that exist in both data sets. SPSS will save only one copy of each variable, and that will be the one that is in the first (working data) file.

- Click on **Data → Merge Files → Add Variables.**
- In the **Add Variables to…** window (similar to Fig. A.11), select the dataset you want to add a variable from and click **Continue**.
- In the **Add Variables from…** window (similar to Fig. A.12), select **Match cases on key variables in sorted files** to select a key variable. A key variable must be a variable common to both datasets (such as a participant ID) that SPSS will use to match the participants from the two datasets. Choices for a key variable will appear in the **Excluded Variables:** box.
- Click on such a variable and move it into the **Key Variables:** box.
- Click on **OK.**

The Compute and Mean Functions

In order to compute a summated scale score such as the pleasure scale shown in Table 1.2 (as variable #44), which is the average of four questionnaire items, you could use the **Compute Variables** function or alternatively the **Mean** function. The former would compute the average or mean *pleasure* score for only those participants with no missing data on any of the four items. The Mean function would allow you to compute a mean for participants who were missing data on, say, one or two of the items, based on their scores on the remaining items. The mean function enables the researcher to use more of the existing data, but should be used cautiously because the results can be misleading.

To use the **Compute** function to get the average pleasure score:
- Click on **Transform → Compute Variable…**
- In the **Target Variable** box, type *pleasureCompute*.
- Click on **Type & Label** and give it the name *pleasure scale*.
- Click on **Continue**.
- In the **Numeric Expression** box type, or select and add (item*02*+item*06r*+item*10r*+item*14*)/4.
- Finally, click on **OK**.

The above method will not compute an average score for a particular participant if he or she is missing data for any of the questions. This can result in a sizable decrease in subjects who have composite scores if several participants did not answer even one or a few questions. In this circumstance, one might choose to use the **MEAN** function, because it utilizes all of the available data.

- Click on **Transform → Compute Variable…**
- In the **Target Variable box**, type *pleasureMean*.
- Click on **Type & Label**. Label the new variable *pleasure scale Mean function*.
- Click on **Continue**.
- In the **Function Group** box, highlight **Statistical**.
- In the **Functions and Special Variables** box, highlight **Mean**.
- Click the up arrow to move it into the **Numeric Expression Box**.
- Type or select and add *item02,item06r,item10r,item14* in the brackets. Note the comma, but no spaces, between the variables.

SPSS allows you to specify the minimum number of variables that must have valid (nonmissing) values by typing .n after **MEAN**. For example, if you decide that at least three of the pleasure scale items must have data, your command would read MEAN.3{*item02, item06r, item10r, item14*}.

- Click on **OK**.

The Graphs Commands

Recent versions of SPSS have a new **Graphs** commands. If you are working with an older version, you will not have as many choices for creating graphs. Depending on the version of SPSS that you are using, you many see different choices under the Graphs command; for example, you may see **Graphboard Template Chooser**, **Interactive**, **Legacy**, **IGraph**, **Legacy**

Dialogs, or **Chart Builder**. The Interactive subset is similar to IGraph included on earlier versions of SPSS.

In SPSS 19, there are three ways to create graphs with the Graphs command: (a) using the **Chart Builder**, (b) using the **Graphboard Template Chooser,** and (c) using the **Legacy Dialogs** menu. We will present basic information for utilizing these commands.

Chart Builder

If you know the type of graph or chart you wish to create, **Chart Builder** is a good choice. The Chart Builder command is a flexible method to use if you want to customize your charts. To use the Chart Builder follow these commands:

- First, be sure all your variables are labeled correctly as Nominal, Ordinal, or Scale. You can check this on the **Variable View** screen under **Measure**.
- Click on **Graphs → Chart Builder**... There will be a warning about setting the correct measure and then the Chart Builder window will appear.
- Under the **Gallery** tab, in the **Choose from:** box, select the type of chart you wish to create. Then click on the picture of the chart you want and drag it into the **Chart Preview** box.
- Highlight a variable and drag it to where you want it to be added to the chart in the Chart Preview box.
- Repeat this until all variables are in the chart.
- Click on **OK**.

Graphboard Template Chooser

The **Graphboard Template Chooser** is new to SPSS 19. The benefit of using the Graphboard Template Chooser is that one can easily see what types of charts and graphs which are commonly used for each variable in a data set. For example, if a variable is scale (i.e., *math achievement test*) the choices shown would be histogram, histogram with a normal distribution, and a dot plot. To use the Graphboard Template Chooser follow these commands:

- Click on **Graphs → Graphboard Template Chooser...** The Graphboard Template Chooser window will appear.
- Select a variable of interest from the list. If you wish to reorder the list to make variables easier to find you can select **Natural** (this will list your variables in the order they are in the dataset), **Name** (this will list the variables in alphabetical order), or **Type** (this lists all nominal variables, then all ordinal variables, and then the scale variables).
- Once the variable of interest is selected, the types of charts and graphs commonly used with that type of variable will appear in the right side of the window. Click on the chart or graph that you wish to create.
- Click on the **Detailed** tab. Here, you can select the color and transparency of the chart or graph to indicate other values. For example, if you have selected *math achievement* for your variable of interest, then you may want to identify values for males and females in your graph. By clicking on the arrow next to **Color:** a drop down box of all the variables in the data set will appear. You could then click on *gender*.
- Click on the **Titles** tab. Here you can include a title, subtitle, and/or footnote.
- Click on the **Options** tab. Here you can indicate how you want missing values to be included.
- Click on **OK**.

Legacy Dialogs

For users who preferred the commands from earlier versions of SPSS, the **Legacy Dialogs** are a good choice for creating graphs and charts. The Legacy Dialogs subset includes all the same choices as previous SPSS versions. To use the Legacy Dialogs follow these commands:

- Click on **Graphs → Legacy Dialogs**.
- A drop-down box will appear with the following choices of graphs: Bar, 3-D Bar, Line, Area, Pie, High-Low, Box Plot, Error Bar, Population Pyramid, Scatter/Dot, Histogram.
- Click the one you want to make.
- Follow the instructions for the graph.

Our intention here is not to give you step-by-step instructions but to introduce you to the graphing possibilities. You can customize the graph to your preferences in any of the three ways we discussed. Use the help tool for more details on how to accomplish this.

APPENDIX B

Review of Basic Statistics

John M. Cumming and Andrea E. Weinberg
Colorado State University

This Appendix provides the steps, using the SPSS point and click method, to compute most of the basic inferential statistics in Tables 5.1 and 5.2. We also provide the syntax and parts of the output of an example from our *SPSS for Introductory Statistics* book (Morgan et al., 2011). These steps and examples provide our recommendations for computing the statistic, but in many cases other or additional options could be used. We have circled some key statistics in the outputs to help you identify key parts of the results, but we do not attempt a complete interpretation here. The full output and interpretation, along with detailed instructions and screen shots of the SPSS windows used in the point-and-click method, are provided in Morgan et al.

Order of Basic Statistics Presented

Chi-Square
      Phi
      Cramer's *V*
Odds Ratios (and Risk Ratios)
The *t* Tests and Similar Nonparametric Tests
      One-Sample *t* Test
      Independent Samples *t* Test
      Mann-Whitney *U* Test
      Paired Samples *t* Test
      Wilcoxon Signed Ranks Test
ANOVA and a Similar Nonparametric Test
      One-Way ANOVA
      Kruskal-Wallis H Test
Correlation
      Pearson
      Spearman
Regression

You can easily run the example statistics presented in this Appendix and produce the whole output by copying the appropriate syntax files, and selecting **Run → All** from the syntax window menu bar. To run the same statistic with different variables, just type the desired variable names into the syntax in place of the current variable names or use the point-and-click method.

Chi-Square

Chi-square allows the user to determine whether there is a statistically significant relationship between two nominal variables. This test compares the observed and expected frequencies or counts in each cell to test whether the expected values differ significantly from the observed/actual values. The chi-square test does not indicate the strength (effect size) of a statistically significant relationship. The optional **Phi** (for 2 × 2 tables) or **Cramer's V** (for longer tables) tests can be used as a measure of effect size.

- **Analyze[1]** → **Descriptive Statistics** → **Crosstabs** → select the first nominal variable with a left click and move it to the **Row(s)** box by clicking the top arrow in the middle of the dialog box → select the second nominal variable with a left click and move it to the **Column(s)** box by clicking the arrow in the middle of the dialog box → **Statistics** → check **Chi-square** and **Phi and Cramer's V** → **Continue** → **Cells** → check **Observed, Expected** and **Column** → **Continue** → **OK.**

In this example, we have cross-tabulated whether *geometry* was taken and *gender* in order to see if males and females differed on whether they took geometry. The cross-tabulation table shows that 70.6% of the males took geometry, but only 29.3% of the females did so. The chi-square tests table shows that $\chi^2 = 12.71$, and $p < .001$. Phi (because this is a 2 × 2 table) could be used as an effect size measure. It is −.41, a medium to large size "effect."

```
CROSSTABS
  /TABLES=geo  BY gender
  /FORMAT= AVALUE TABLES
  /STATISTIC=CHISQ PHI
  /CELLS= COUNT EXPECTED COLUMN
  /COUNT ROUND CELL .
```

Crosstabs

geometry in h.s. * gender Crosstabulation

			gender male	gender female	Total
geometry in h.s.	not taken	Count	10	29	39
		Expected Count	17.7	21.3	39.0
		% within gender	29.4%	70.7%	52.0%
	taken	Count	24	12	36
		Expected Count	16.3	19.7	36.0
		% within gender	70.6%	29.3%	48.0%
Total		Count	34	41	75
		Expected Count	34.0	41.0	75.0
		% within gender	100.0%	100.0%	100.0%

Observed and expected counts to be compared.

---

[1] This sequence means select the **Analyze** menu, pull down and select **Descriptive Statistics**, and then select **Crosstabs.**

Chi-Square Tests

	Value	df	Asymp. Sig. (2-sided)	Exact Sig. (2-sided)	Exact Sig. (1-sided)
Pearson Chi-Square	12.714[b]	1	.000		
Continuity Correction[a]	11.112	1	.001		
Likelihood Ratio	13.086	1	.000		
Fisher's Exact Test				.000	.000
Linear-by-Linear Association	12.544	1	.000		
N of Valid Cases	75				

> Indicates if relationship is significant.

a. Computed only for a 2x2 table

b. 0 cells (.0%) have expected count less than 5. The minimum expected count is 16.32.

> This is good.

Symmetric Measures

		Value	Approx. Sig.
Nominal by Nominal	Phi	-.412	.000
	Cramer's V	.412	.000
N of Valid Cases		75	

> Strength of relationship (effect size).

a. Not assuming the null hypothesis.

b. Using the asymptotic standard error assuming the null hypothesis.

Odds Ratios (and Risk Ratios)

Odds ratios can be computed when you have two dichotomous (binary) variables that are cross-tabulated. An odds ratio is a ratio of ratios, computed by dividing one risk ratio by the other.

- **Analyze → Descriptive Statistics → Crosstabs →** select the first variable with a left click and move it to the **Rows** box by clicking the top arrow in the middle of the dialog box. → select the second variable and move it to the **Columns** box → **Statistics →** check **Chi-Square** and **Risk → Continue → Cells →** check **Observed** and **Row → Continue → OK.**

In this example, *math grades* (low or high) was cross-tabulated with whether the student took *algebra 2*.

	Math Grades	
Taken Algebra 2	Low	High
No	A	B
Yes	C	D

The odds ration can be calculated using the following equation:

$$\text{Odds ratio} = \frac{A/B}{C/D}$$

SPSS computes the odds ratio from the two risk ratios as follows. Of the 44 students who <u>had not</u> taken *algebra 2*, 70% had low *math grades* (less A-B). This is 1.53 times the proportion (45.7%) of the students with low *math grades* who had taken *algebra 2*. Thus, 1.53 is the risk ratio for low math grades. Similarly, the risk ratio for high math grades is .55 (30% / 54.3%). The odds ratio is 2.77 (1.53/.53). We know that the odds ratio (and both risk ratios) is significantly different from 1.0 (no effect) because the lower and upper bounds of the 95% confidence intervals for each ratio are both more (or less) than 1.0.

```
CROSSTABS
  /TABLES=alg2  BY mathgr
  /FORMAT= AVALUE TABLES
  /STATISTIC=CHISQ RISK
  /CELLS= COUNT ROW
  /COUNT ROUND CELL .
```

Crosstabs

algebra 2 in h.s. * math grades Crosstabulation

			math grades		Total
			less A-B	most A-B	
algebra 2 in h.s.	not taken	Count	28	12	40
		% within algebra 2 in h.s.	70.0%	30.0%	100.0%
	taken	Count	16	19	35
		% within algebra 2 in h.s.	45.7%	54.3%	100.0%
Total		Count	44	31	75
		% within algebra 2 in h.s.	58.7%	41.3%	100.0%

(Table Omitted)

Risk Estimate

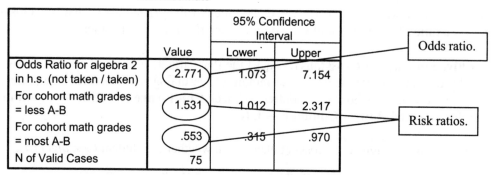

	Value	95% Confidence Interval	
		Lower	Upper
Odds Ratio for algebra 2 in h.s. (not taken / taken)	2.771	1.073	7.154
For cohort math grades = less A-B	1.531	1.012	2.317
For cohort math grades = most A-B	.553	.315	.970
N of Valid Cases	75		

Odds ratio.

Risk ratios.

The *t* Tests and Similar Nonparametric Tests

The *t* test is a procedure that is used to compare sample means to determine if there is evidence that the means of the corresponding populations differ. Three types of *t* tests are available (one-sample, independent samples, and paired samples). If the assumptions for the *t* test are markedly violated (unequal variances and/or non-normally distributed dependent variable), then it is appropriate to compute a nonparametric test rather than a *t* test. The nonparametric equivalent of an independent samples *t* is the Mann-Whitney *U* test, and the nonparametric equivalent of a paired samples *t* is the Wilcoxon signed ranks test.

➤ **One-Sample *t* Test** allows the mean of a sample to be compared to a hypothesized population mean.

● **Analyze → Compare Means → One-Sample T Test →** select the dependent variable with a left click and move it to the **Test Variable(s)** box by clicking the arrow in the middle of the dialog box → type the hypothesized population mean in the **Test Value** box → **OK.**

This example compares the average SAT math test score (490.53) for this sample of 75 students with the presumed national mean of 500. The *t* is .87, which is not significantly different (*p* = .389) from the national mean.

```
T-TEST
  /TESTVAL = 500
  /MISSING = ANALYSIS
  /VARIABLES = satm
  /CRITERIA = CI(.95) .
```

T-Test

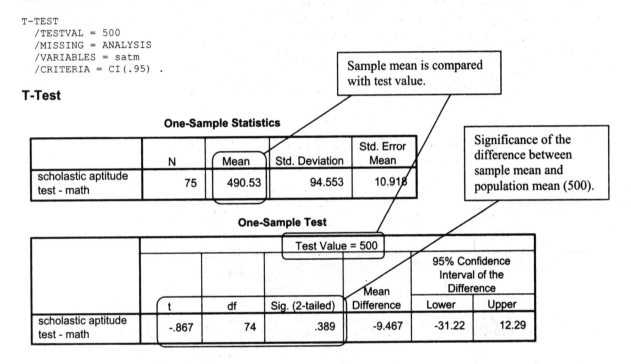

One-Sample Statistics

	N	Mean	Std. Deviation	Std. Error Mean
scholastic aptitude test - math	75	490.53	94.553	10.918

Sample mean is compared with test value.

One-Sample Test

	Test Value = 500				95% Confidence Interval of the Difference	
	t	df	Sig. (2-tailed)	Mean Difference	Lower	Upper
scholastic aptitude test - math	-.867	74	.389	-9.467	-31.22	12.29

Significance of the difference between sample mean and population mean (500).

➤ **Independent Samples *t* Test** is used to compare two independent or unrelated groups (between-groups design) on an approximately normal dependent variable.

● **Analyze → Compare Means → Independent Samples T Test →** select one or more dependent variables with a left click and move them to the **Test Variable(s)** box by clicking the top arrow in the middle of the dialog box → select a dichotomous independent variable with a left click and move it to the **Grouping Variable** box by clicking the bottom arrow in the middle of the dialog box → **Define Groups** → select **Use specified values** → type the values of the independent variable that will designate **Group 1** and **Group 2** → **Continue** → **OK.**

See Chapter 5 and Output 5.1 for an example of the syntax, output, and interpretation of an independent samples *t* test.

➤ **Mann-Whitney** *U* **Test** is a nonparametric test similar to the independent samples *t* test, which assesses whether the mean ranks of two groups are equivalent in the population. The M-W test is appropriate if the dependent variable is ordinal or if the assumptions for the independent samples *t* test are markedly violated.

• **Analyze → Nonparametric Tests → 2 Independent Samples →** select dependent variable(s) with a left click and move to the **Test Variable List** box by clicking the top arrow in the middle of the dialog box → select the independent variable with a left click and move it to the **Grouping Variable** box by clicking the bottom arrow in the middle of the dialog box → check the **Mann-Whitney U** box in the **Test Type** box → **OK.**

In this example, the mean ranks of male and female student on three dependent variables are compared. (Again, high ranks are given for high scores.) Males and females differ significantly on *visualization* (*p* = .048) and *math achievement* (*p* = .010) but not on *grades in h.s.* (*p* = .413). You can see from the ranks table that males had higher mean ranks than females on *visualization* and *math achievement*. An effect size can be computed by converting the *z* to *r* ($r = z / \sqrt{N}$). This effect size for math achievement is *r* = .30, a medium-size effect.

```
NPAR TESTS
  /M-W= visual mathach grades   BY gender(0 1)
  /MISSING ANALYSIS.
```

NPar Tests
Mann-Whitney Test

Ranks

	gender	N	Mean Rank	Sum of Ranks
visualization test	male	34	43.65	1484.00
	female	41	33.32	1366.00
	Total	75		
math achievement test	male	34	45.10	1533.50
	female	41	32.11	1316.50
	Total	75		
grades in h.s.	male	34	35.78	1216.50
	female	41	39.84	1633.50
	Total	75		

Mean ranks to be compared.

Test Statistics[a]

	visualization test	math achievement test	grades in h.s.
Mann-Whitney U	505.000	455.500	621.500
Wilcoxon W	1366.000	1316.500	1216.500
Z	-2.052	-2.575	-.818
Asymp. Sig. (2-tailed)	.040	.010	.413

Tests of significance.

a. Grouping Variable: gender

➢ **Paired Sample *t* Test** is used when the two scores being compared are paired or matched in some way (they are not independent of one another) or if the two scores are repeated measures.

● **Analyze → Compare Means → Paired Samples T Test →** select the two variables that make up the pair and move them simultaneously to the **Paired Variable** box by clicking the arrow in the middle of the dialog box → **OK.**

In this example, we compared the average *father's education* with the average *mother's education* for the 73 students with education measures for both parents. These means and other descriptive statistics are shown in the first table. The third table provides the paired *t* (2.40), *df* = 72, and *p* = .019. Thus, there is a significant difference between father's mean education (it is higher) and mother's. The middle table is <u>not</u> the *t* test; it shows the correlation between father's and mother's education (*r* = .68), which indicates that, in general, children of highly educated fathers also have highly educated mothers and vice versa. However, the *t* test shows that these mothers are on average somewhat less educated than the corresponding fathers.

```
T-TEST
  PAIRS = faed  WITH maed (PAIRED)
  /CRITERIA = CI(.95)
  /MISSING = ANALYSIS.
```

T-Test

Paired Samples Statistics

Means to be compared.

		Mean	N	Std. Deviation	Std. Error Mean
Pair 1	father's education	4.73	73	2.830	.331
	mother's education	4.14	73	2.263	.265

Paired Samples Correlations

		N	Correlation	Sig.
Pair 1	father's education & mother's education	73	.681	.000

Test of statistical significance of difference between the means.

Paired Samples Test

		Paired Differences					t	df	Sig. (2-tailed)
		Mean	Std. Deviation	Std. Error Mean	95% Confidence Interval of the Difference Lower	Upper			
Pair 1	father's education mother's educatio	.589	2.101	.246	.099	1.079	2.396	72	.019

➢ **Wilcoxon Signed Ranks Test** is a nonparametric test that is similar to the paired samples *t* and tests whether two related samples have equivalent mean ranks in the population. This test should be used for a repeated-measures or within-subjects design when the dependent variable is ordinal or if the assumptions for the paired samples *t* test are markedly violated.

• **Analyze → Nonparametric Tests → 2 Related Samples →** select the two variables that make up the pair with left clicks and move them simultaneously to the **Test Pair(s) List** box by clicking the arrow in the middle of the dialog box → check the **Wilcoxon** box in the **Test Type** box → **OK**.

In this example, two Wilcoxon tests were computed. The first compares each set or pair of parents in regard to how they ranked on educational level. Notice that there were somewhat more cases (27) where the father had more education than the mother than cases (21) where the mother had more education than the father. This difference is significant ($z = 2.09$, $p = .037$). The second Wilcoxon compares visualization test and retest scores for each of the 75 students who had both scores. Note that many (55) students had higher visualization test scores than retest scores and that this is significant ($z = 3.98$, $p < .001$). An effect size can be computed by converting the z to r ($r = z / \sqrt{N}$). For parents' education, $r = -.24$, a small to medium effect.

```
NPAR TEST
  /WILCOXON=faed visual  WITH maed visual2 (PAIRED)
  /MISSING ANALYSIS.
```

NPar Tests
Wilcoxon Signed Ranks Test

Number of cases that fit in each of the footnoted categories.

Ranks

		N	Mean Rank	Sum of Ranks
mother's education - father's education	Negative Ranks	27[a]	29.20	788.50
	Positive Ranks	21[b]	18.45	387.50
	Ties	25[c]		
	Total	73		
visualization retest - visualization test	Negative Ranks	55[d]	34.02	1871.00
	Positive Ranks	14[e]	38.86	544.00
	Ties	6[f]		
	Total	75		

a. mother's education < father's education

b. mother's education > father's education

c. mother's education = father's education

d. visualization retest < visualization test

e. visualization retest > visualization test

f. visualization retest = visualization test

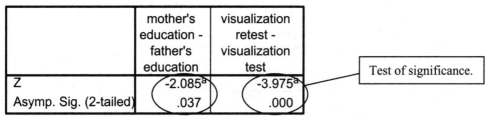

Test Statistics[b]

	mother's education - father's education	visualization retest - visualization test
Z	-2.085[a]	-3.975[a]
Asymp. Sig. (2-tailed)	.037	.000

Test of significance.

a. Based on positive ranks.

b. Wilcoxon Signed Ranks Test

ANOVA and a Similar Nonparametric Test

➢ **One-Way ANOVA**, also called single-factor analysis of variance, is used when you have one independent variable with a few, often nominal, levels and one normally distributed dependent variable.

• **Analyze → Compare Means → One-Way ANOVA →** select one or more dependent variables with a left click and move them into the **Dependent List** box by clicking the top arrow in the middle of the dialog box. Then select the independent variable and move it into the **Factor** (independent variable) box by clicking the bottom arrow in the middle of the dialog box → **Options →** choose **Descriptives** and **Homogeneity of variance test → Continue → OK**.

The following example provides the syntax and output for three one-way ANOVAs comparing the three levels of *father's education* (HS grad or less, some college, and BS or more) on the average scores for each of three dependent variables: *grades in h.s.*, *visualization score*, and *math achievement*. The first output table provides the three means (plus an overall average, called "total") to be compared and other descriptive statistics.

The middle table provides the Levene test of the important assumption that the variances are approximately equal. Note that the assumption is not violated for *grades* and *visualization* but is violated (i.e., significant) for *math achievement*.

The third table provides the one-way ANOVA Fs and ps (Sig.) for each of the dependent variables. Note that there are some differences among *father's education* groups on *grades in h.s.* ($F = 4.09$, $p = .021$) and on *math achievement* ($F = 7.88$, $p = .001$) but not on *visualization test* score ($F = 0.76$, $p = .47$). Post hoc test will tell us which *pairs* of means were different.

```
ONEWAY
  grades visual mathach BY faedRevis
  /STATISTICS DESCRIPTIVES HOMOGENEITY
  /MISSING ANALYSIS .
```

Oneway

Means to be compared

Descriptives

		N	Mean	Std. Deviation	Std. Error	95% Confidence Interval for Mean		Minimum	Maximum
						Lower Bound	Upper Bound		
grades in h.s.	HS grad or less	38	5.34	1.475	.239	4.86	5.83	3	8
	Some College	16	5.56	1.788	.447	4.61	6.52	2	8
	BS or More	19	6.53	1.219	.280	5.94	7.11	4	8
	Total	73	5.70	1.552	.182	5.34	6.06	2	8
visualization test	HS grad or less	38	4.6711	3.96058	.64249	3.3692	5.9729	-.25	14.8
	Some College	16	6.0156	4.56022	1.14005	3.5857	8.4456	-.25	14.8
	BS or More	19	5.4605	2.79044	.64017	4.1156	6.8055	-.25	9.75
	Total	73	5.1712	3.82787	.44802	4.2781	6.0643	-.25	14.8
math achievement test	HS grad or less	38	10.0877	5.61297	.91054	8.2428	11.9326	1.00	22.7
	Some College	16	14.3958	4.66544	1.16636	11.9098	16.8819	5.00	23.7
	BS or More	19	16.3509	7.40918	1.69978	12.7798	19.9221	1.00	23.7
	Total	73	12.6621	6.49659	.76037	11.1463	14.1779	1.00	23.7

Test of Homogeneity of Variances

Tests the assumption of equal variances.

	Levene Statistic	df1	df2	Sig.
grades in h.s.	1.546	2	70	.220
visualization test	1.926	2	70	.153
math achievement test	3.157	2	70	.049

F and p for between-groups differences.

ANOVA

		Sum of Squares	df	Mean Square	F	Sig.
grades in h.s.	Between Groups	18.143	2	9.071	4.091	.021
	Within Groups	155.227	70	2.218		
	Total	173.370	72			
visualization test	Between Groups	22.505	2	11.252	.763	.470
	Within Groups	1032.480	70	14.750		
	Total	1054.985	72			
math achievement test	Between Groups	558.481	2	279.240	7.881	.001
	Within Groups	2480.324	70	35.433		
	Total	3038.804	72			

We know from the ANOVA output that there are significant differences among the three *father's education* groups on *grades in h.s.* and on *math achievement*, but we do not know which pairs of *father's education* groups were different. In order to find out which pairs were different, we do a post hoc multiple comparisons test. Which such test we choose depends on the Levene's test of homogeneity of variances. Because Levene's test for *grades in h.s.* was not significant (p = .220), the assumption of equal or homogenous variances was <u>not</u> violated. So we can use one of the post hoc tests provided by SPSS to use when "equal variances are assumed." In this case we chose the Tukey HSD. You can see the output by running the following syntax. The Tukey HSD output shows that the children of fathers with the most education had significantly higher grades than children of fathers who were high school graduates or less.

```
ONEWAY
  grades BY faedRevis
  /MISSING ANALYSIS
  /POSTHOC = TUKEY ALPHA(.05).
```

(Output not included)

Because the Levene test for *math achievement* was significant (p = .049), the assumption of homogeneity of variances was violated. So we used one of the post hoc tests for "equal variances not assumed." In this case, we chose the Games-Howell (GH) test. This post hoc test indicated that students whose fathers had some college and also those whose fathers had a BS or more scored higher on *math achievement* than students whose fathers were high school grads or less.

```
ONEWAY
  mathach BY faedRevis
  /MISSING ANALYSIS
  /POSTHOC = GH ALPHA(.05).
```

(Output not included)

We do not compute post hoc tests for visualization because the ANOVA was not significant, indicating that we cannot be confident that there were any differences among the *father's education* groups in the population on *visualization test* scores.

> **Kruskal-Wallis H Test** is the nonparametric equivalent of a one-way analysis of variance (ANOVA) and tests whether several independent samples (groups) are from the same population. The K-W test is more appropriate than a one-way ANOVA if the data are ordinal or if the homogeneity of variance assumption is seriously violated and group sizes differ markedly.

• **Analyze → Nonparametric Tests → K Independent Samples →** select the dependent variable(s) with a left click and move them to the **Test Variable List** box by clicking the top arrow in the middle of the dialog box. Then select the independent variable with a left click and move it to the **Grouping Variable** box by clicking the bottom arrow in the middle of the dialog box → **Define Range** → type in the **Minimum** and **Maximum** values of the independent variable → **Continue** → check **Kruskal-Wallis H** in the **Test Type** box → **OK.**

This example is similar to the one-way ANOVA example. The test statistics table shows that the three *father's education* groups differ significantly on *math achievement* ($p = .001$) but not on the *competence scale*. The ranks table shows that students whose fathers were high school grads or less had low average ranks (28.43) on *math achievement*. (The highest math score was ranked 73 and the lowest was ranked 1.) The Kruskal-Wallis test does not provide post hoc tests. To find out which pairs of *father's education* groups were different, one could compute Mann-Whitney tests.

```
NPAR TESTS
 /K-W=mathach competence    BY faedRevis(1 3)
 /MISSING ANALYSIS.
```

NPar Tests
Kruskal-Wallis Test

Ranks

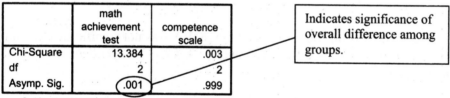

	father's educ revised	N	Mean Rank
math achievement test	HS grad or less	38	28.43
	Some college	16	43.78
	BS or more	19	48.42
	Total	73	
competence scale	HS grad or less	37	36.04
	Some college	16	35.78
	BS or more	18	36.11
	Total	71	

Mean ranks to be compared.

Test Statistics[a,b]

	math achievement test	competence scale
Chi-Square	13.384	.003
df	2	2
Asymp. Sig.	.001	.999

Indicates significance of overall difference among groups.

a. Kruskal Wallis Test

b. Grouping Variable: father's educ revised

Correlations

Correlations are statistics that are used to assess the association or relationship between two variables. A parametric correlation (Pearson product moment correlation) is computed by using the sums and standard deviations of the two variables, while a nonparametric correlation (Spearman Rho) is calculated by ranking/ordering the pairs of scores.

➤ **Pearson Product Moment Correlation (r)**, also known as the Pearson correlation coefficient, is a bivariate parametric statistic used when both variables are approximately normally distributed.

- **Analyze → Correlate → Bivariate →** select two or more normally distributed or scale variables to be correlated with a left click and move them to the **Variables** box by clicking the arrow in the middle of the dialog box → check the **Pearson** box → select the **two-tailed** radio button → check the **Flag significant correlations** box → **Options** → check the **Means and standard deviations** box → select the **Exclude cases listwise** radio button → **Continue → OK.**

This matrix provides the correlation of each of the four requested variables with each of the other three (and itself shown as 1). Each correlation is shown twice, above and below the diagonal (the 1s) so we have crossed out duplicates. Thus, there are six different correlations. The asterisks (**) and Sig., or *p*, values indicate that five of these six coefficients are statistically significant. We have circled the three correlations in the right-hand column, which are the correlations of the other variables with *math achievement*. For example, *grades in h.s.* is significantly correlated with *math achievement*, r (73) = .50, p < .001.

```
CORRELATIONS
  /VARIABLES=visual satm grades mathach
  /PRINT=TWOTAIL NOSIG
  /STATISTICS DESCRIPTIVES
  /MISSING=LISTWISE .
```

> Correlations of other variables with *math achievement*.

Correlations[a]

		visualization test	scholastic aptitude test - math	grades in h.s.	math achievement test
visualization test	Pearson Correlation	1	.356**	.127	.423**
	Sig. (2-tailed)		.002	.279	.000
scholastic aptitude test - math	Pearson Correlation	.356**	1	.371**	.788**
	Sig. (2-tailed)	.002		.001	.000
grades in h.s.	Pearson Correlation	.127	.371**	1	.504**
	Sig. (2-tailed)	.279	.001		.000
math achievement test	Pearson Correlation	.423**	.788**	.504**	1
	Sig. (2-tailed)	.000	.000	.000	

**. Correlation is significant at the 0.01 level (2-tailed).

a. Listwise N=75

> **Spearman Rho (r_s)** or Spearman rank order correlation is the nonparametric equivalent of the Pearson correlation coefficient. This statistic would be selected when the data are ordinal or when the assumptions for the Pearson correlation coefficient are markedly violated. Spearman correlations *can* be used when one or even both the variables are normally distributed.

- **Analyze → Correlate → Bivariate →** select the variables to be correlated with a left click and move them to the **Variables** box by clicking the arrow in the middle of the dialog box → check the **Spearman** box → select the **two-tailed** radio button → check the **Flag significant correlations** box → **Options** → select the **Exclude cases listwise** radio button → **Continue → OK.**

In this example, we have correlated *mother's education* and *math achievement*. The Spearman correlation is .32, which is statistically significant. The result would be written as r_s (73) = .32, p = .006. The 73 indicates the degrees of freedom, which is $N-2$. This medium effect size correlation indicates that, in general, students whose mother's rank near the top for amount of education rank near the top in math achievement and vice versa. Because SPSS correlation outputs are in matrix format, all correlations are presented twice. Ignore the duplicate correlations below (or above) the diagonal (1.000), which is the variable correlated with itself.

```
NONPAR CORR
  /VARIABLES=mathach maed
  /PRINT=SPEARMAN TWOTAIL NOSIG
  /MISSING=PAIRWISE .
```

Nonparametric Correlations

> Association between *math achievement test* and *mother's education*.

Correlations

			math achievement test	mother's education
Spearman's rho	math achievement test	Correlation Coefficient	1.000	.315**
		Sig. (2-tailed)	.	.006
		N	75	75
	mother's education	Correlation Coefficient	.315**	1.000
		Sig. (2-tailed)	.006	.
		N	75	75

**. Correlation is significant at the 0.01 level (2-tailed).

Regression

Bivariate or simple linear regression is used to *predict* scores of a normal/scale dependent variable from one normal/scale independent variable.

- **Analyze → Regression → Linear →** select the dependent variable with a left click and move to the **Dependent** box by clicking the top arrow in the middle of the dialog box → select the independent variable with a left click and move to the **Independent(s)** box → use the drop-down arrow to select **Enter** as the **Method → OK**.

See Chapter 5 and Output 5.2 for the syntax, outputs, and interpretation of a bivariate or simple regression.

APPENDIX C

Answers to Odd Interpretation Questions

1.1 **What is the difference between the independent variable and the dependent variable?** Independent variables are predictors, antecedents, or *presumed* causes or influences being studied. Differences in the independent variable are hypothesized to affect, predict, or explain differences in the dependent or outcome variable. So independent variables are predictor variables, whereas dependent variables are the variables being predicted, or outcome variables.

1.3 **What kind of independent variable is necessary to infer cause? Can one <u>always</u> infer cause from this type of independent variable? If so, why? If not, when can one clearly infer cause and when might causal inferences be more questionable?** A variable must be an *active* independent variable in order for the possibility to exist of one's inferring that it caused the observed changes in the dependent variable. However, even if the independent variable is active, one cannot attribute cause to it in many cases. The strongest inferences about causality can be made when one randomly assigns participants to experimentally manipulated conditions and there are no preexisting differences between the groups that could explain the results. Causal inferences are much more questionable when manipulations are given to preexisting groups, especially when there is no pretest of the dependent variable prior to the manipulation, and/or the control group receives no intervention at all, and/or there is no control group.

1.5 **Write three research questions and a corresponding hypothesis regarding variables of interest to you but not in the HSB data set (one associational, one difference, and one descriptive question).** Associational research question: What is the relation between guilt and shame in 10-year-old children? Associational hypothesis: Guilt and shame are moderately to highly related in 10-year-old children. Difference question: Are there differences between Asian-Americans and European-Americans in reported self-esteem? Difference hypothesis: Asian-Americans, on the average, report lower self-esteem than do European-Americans. Descriptive question: What is the incidence of themes of violence in popular songs, folk songs, and children's songs? Descriptive hypothesis: There will be more violent themes in popular songs than in folk songs or children's songs.

1.7 **If you have categorical, ordered data (such as low income, middle income, high income), what type of measurement would you have? Why?** Categorical, ordered data would typically be considered ordinal data because one cannot assume equal intervals between levels of the variable, there are few levels of the variable, and data are unlikely to be normally distributed, but there is a meaningful order (from low to high) to the levels of the variable.

1.9 **What percent of the area under the standard normal curve is between the mean and one standard deviation above the mean?** Thirty-four percent of the normal distribution is within one standard deviation *above* the mean. Sixty-eight percent is within one standard deviation above and below the mean.

2.1 **Using Output 2.1a and 2.1b: (a) What is the mean *visualization test* score?** 5.24; **(b) What is the range for *grades in h.s.*?** 6; **(c) What is the minimum score for *mosaic pattern test*?** −4. **How does this compare to the values for that variable as indicated in**

Chapter 1? It is the lowest possible score. **Why could the minimum be a negative number?** This is the lowest score anyone made; it may be due to a penalty for guessing incorrectly on many questions.

2.3   **Using Output 2.4: (a) Can you interpret the means? Explain.** Yes, the means indicate the percentage of participants who were coded as "1" on the measure; **(b) How many participants are there all together?** 75; **(c) How many have complete data (nothing missing)?** 75; **(d) What percent are** *male (if male=0)***?** 45; **(e) What percent took** *algebra 1***?** 79

2.5   **In Output 2.8a: (a) Why are matrix scatterplots useful? What assumptions are tested by them?** They help you check the assumption of linearity and check for possible difficulties with multicollinearity.

3.1   **Using Output 3.1 to 3.3, make a table indicating the number of items, the mean inter-item correlation, and the alpha coefficient for each of the scales.   Discuss the relationship between mean inter-item correlation and alpha, and how this is affected by the number of items.**

Scale	Number of items	Alpha	Mean inter-item correlation
Motivation	6	.791	.385
Competence	4	.796	.488
Pleasure	4	.688	.373

The alpha is based on the inter-item correlations, but the number of items is important as well. If there are a large number of items, alpha will be higher, and if there are only a few items, then alpha will be lower, even given the same average inter-item correlation. In this table, the fact that both number of items and magnitude of inter-item correlations are important is apparent. Motivation, which has the largest number of items (six), has an alpha of .791, even though the average inter-item correlation is only .385. Even though the average inter-item correlation of competence is much higher (.488), the alpha is quite similar to that for motivation because there are only four items instead of six. Pleasure has the lowest alpha because it has a relatively low average inter-item correlation (.373) and a relatively small number of items (4).

3.3   **For the pleasure scale (Output 3.3), what item has the highest item-total correlation? Comment on how alpha would change if that item were deleted.** Item 14 (.649). The alpha would decline markedly if Item 14 were deleted, because it is the item that is most highly correlated with the other items and there were only four items to begin with.

3.5   **Using Output 3.5: What is the interrater reliability of the ethnicity codes? What does this mean?** The interrater reliability is .858. This is a high kappa, indicating that the school records seem to be reasonably accurate with respect to their information about students' ethnicity, assuming that students accurately report their ethnicity (i.e., the school records are in high agreement with students' reports). Kappa is not perfect, however (1.0 would be perfect), indicating that there are some discrepancies between school records and students' own reports of their ethnicity.

4.1   **Using Output 4.1: (a) Are the factors in Output 4.1 close to the conceptual composites (motivation, pleasure, competence) indicated in Chapter 1?** Yes, they are close to the conceptual composites. The first factor seems to be a competence factor, the second factor a motivation factor, and the third a (low) pleasure factor. However, item01 (I practice math skills until I can do them well) was originally conceptualized as a motivation question, but it had its strongest loading from the first factor (the competence factor), and there was a strong cross-loading for item02 (I feel happy after solving a hard problem) on the competence factor. **(b) How might you name the three factors in Output 4.1?** Competence, motivation, and (low) mastery pleasure. **(c) Why did we use factor analysis, rather than principal components analysis for this exercise?** We used factor analysis because we had beliefs about underlying constructs that the items represented, and we wished to determine whether these constructs were the best way of understanding the manifest variables (observed questionnaire items). Factor analysis is suited to determining which latent variables seem to explain the observed variables. In contrast, principal components analysis is designed simply to determine which linear combinations of variables best explain the variance and covariation of the variables so that a relatively large set of variables can be summarized by a smaller set of variables.

4.3   **What does the plot in Output 4.2 tell us about the relation of *mosaic* to the other variables and to component 1?** *Mosaic* seems not to be related highly to the other variables nor to component 1. **How does this plot relate to the rotated component matrix?** The plot illustrates how the items are located in space in relation to the components in the rotated component matrix.

5.1   **(a) Is there only one appropriate statistic to use for each research design?** No.
(b) Explain your answer. There may be more than one appropriate statistical analysis to use with each design. Interval (normal/scale) data can always use statistics designed for use with nominal or ordinal data, but you lose some power by doing this. Also see Fig. 5.2 and discussion of the general linear model.

5.3   **Interpret the following related to effect size:**
(a) $d = .25$ small   (c) $R = .53$ large   (e) $d = 1.15$ very large
(b) $r = .35$ medium/typical   (d) $r = .13$ small   (f) $\eta = .38$ large

5.5   **What statistic would you use if you had two independent variables, income group (<\$10,000, \$10,000 – \$30,000, >\$30,000) and ethnic group (Hispanic, Caucasian, African-American), and one normally distributed dependent variable (self-efficacy at work). Explain.** Factorial ANOVA, because there are two (or more) between-groups independent variables and one normally distributed dependent variable. According to Table 5.3, column 2, first cell, you should use factorial ANOVA or ANCOVA. In this case, both independent variables are nominal, so use factorial ANOVA.

5.7   **What statistic would you use if you had three normally distributed (scale) independent variables and one dichotomous independent variable (weight of participants, age of participants, height of participants and gender) and one dependent variable (positive self-image), which is normally distributed. Explain.** Use multiple regression, because all predictors are either scale or dichotomous and the dependent variable is normally distributed. This information is in Table 5.4 (third column).

5.9   **What statistic would you use if you had one, repeated-measures, independent variable with two levels and one ordinal dependent variable?** Wilcoxon because the independent variable is repeated and the dependent is nominal. This is in the fourth column of Table 5.1.

5.11 **What statistic would you use if you had three normally distributed and one dichotomous independent variable, and one dichotomous dependent variable?** Use logistic regression, according to Table 5.4, third column.

6.1. **In Output 6.1: (a) What information suggests that we might have a problem of collinearity?** High intercorrelations among some predictor variables and some low tolerances ($< 1-R^2$); **(b) How does multicollinearity affect results?** It can make it so that a predictor that has a high bivariate (zero-order) correlation with the dependent variable is found to have little or no relation to the dependent variable when the other predictors are included. This can be misleading, in that it may appear that one of the highly correlated predictors is a strong predictor of the dependent variable and the other is not a predictor of the dependent variable; **(c) What is the adjusted R^2 and what does it mean?** The adjusted R^2 indicates the percentage of variance in the dependent variable explained by the independent variables, after taking into account such factors as the number of predictors, the sample size, and the effect size.

6.3 **In Output 6.3. (a) Compare the adjusted R^2 for model 1 and model 2. What does this tell you?** It is much larger for Model 2 than for Model 1, indicating that *grades in high school*, *motivation*, and *parent education* explain additional variance, over and above that explained by *gender*; **(b) Why would one enter *gender* first?** One might enter gender first because it was known that there were gender differences in math achievement, and one wanted to determine whether the other variables contributed to prediction of math achievement scores, over and above the "effect" of gender.

7.1 **Using Output 7.1: (a) When all four predictors are included, which variables make significant contributions to predicting who took algebra 2?** Parents' education and visualization; **(b) How accurate is the overall prediction?** 77.3% of participants are correctly classified, overall; **(c) How well do the variables predict who actually *took* algebra 2?** 71.4% (25 out of 35) of those who took algebra 2 were correctly classified by this equation; **(d) How about the prediction of who *didn't* take it?** 82.5% of those who didn't take algebra 2 were correctly classified.

7.3 **In Output 7.3: (a) What do the discriminant function coefficients and the structure coefficients tell us about how the predictor variables combine to predict who took algebra 2?** The function coefficients tell us how the variables are weighted to create the discriminant function. In this case, *parents' education* and *visual* are weighted most highly. The structure coefficients indicate the correlation between the variable and the discriminant function. As expected, *parents' education* and *visual* are correlated most highly; however, gender (negative) also has a substantial correlation with the discriminant function; **(b) How accurate is the prediction/classification overall and for who would not take algebra 2?** 76% were correctly classified overall. 80% of those who did not take algebra 2 were correctly classified; whereas 71.4% of those who took *algebra 2* were correctly classified; **(c) How do the results in Output 7.3 compare with those in Output 7.1, in terms of success at classifying and contribution of different variables to the equation?** For those who took algebra 2, the discriminant function and the logistic regression yield the same rate of success; however, the rate of success is slightly lower for the discriminative function than the logistic regression for those who did not take *algebra 2* (and, therefore, for the overall successful classification rate).

7.5 **In Output 7.2: Why might one want to do a hierarchical logistic regression?** One might want to do a hierarchical logistic regression if one wished to see how well one predictor successfully distinguishes groups, over and above the effectiveness of other predictors such as gender and other demographics.

8.1   **In Output 8.1: (a) Is the interaction significant?** Yes; **(b) Examine the profile plot of the cell means that illustrates the interaction. Describe it in words.** The profile plot indicates that the "effect" of math grades on math achievement is different for students whose fathers have relatively little education, as compared to those with more education. Specifically, for students whose fathers have only a high school education (or less), there is virtually no difference in math achievement between those who had high and low math grades, whereas for those whose fathers have a bachelor's degree or more, those with higher math grades obtain higher math achievement scores, and those with lower math grades obtain relatively lower math achievement scores; **(c) Is the main effect of *father's education* significant? Yes. Interpret the eta squared.** The eta squared of .243 (eta = .496) for father's education indicates that this is, according to Cohen's criteria, a large effect. This indicates that the "effect" of the level of fathers' education is larger than typical for behavioral science research. However, it is important to realize that this main effect is qualified by the interaction between *father's education* and *math grades*; **(d) Is the "effect" of *math grades* significant?** The "effect" of *math grades* also is significant. Eta squared is .139 for this effect (eta = .37), which is also a large effect, again indicating an effect that is larger than typical in behavioral research; **(e) Why did we put the word effect in quotes?** The word, "effect" is in quotes because this is not a true experiment but rather is a comparative design that relies on attribute independent variables. Thus, one should not impute causality to the independent variable; **(f) How might focusing on the main effects be misleading?** Focusing on the main effects is misleading because of the significant interaction. In actuality, for students whose fathers have less education, math grades do not seem to "affect" math achievement, whereas students whose fathers are highly educated have higher achievement if they made better math grades. Thus, to say that math grades do or do not "affect" math achievement is only partially true. Similarly, fathers' education really seems to make a difference only for students with high math grades.

8.3   **In Output 8.3: (a) Is the adjusted main effect of *gender* significant?** No; **(b) What are the adjusted *math achievement* means (marginal means) for males and females?** They are 12.89 for males and 12.29 for females; **(c) Is the effect of the covariate (*mathcrs*) significant?** Yes; **(d) What do (a) and (c) tell us about *gender* differences in *math achievement* scores?** Once one takes into account differences between the genders in math courses taken, the differences between genders in math achievement disappear.

9.1   **In Output 9.2a: Explain the results in nontechnical terms.** Output 9.2a indicates that the ratings that participants made of one or more products were higher than the ratings they made of one or more other products. Output 9.2b indicates that most participants rated product 1 more highly than product 2 and product 3 more highly than product 4, but there was no clear difference in ratings of products 2 versus 3.

9.3   **In Output 9.3: (a) Is the assumption of sphericity violated?** Yes. **If it is violated, what can you do?** One can either correct degrees of freedom using epsilon or one can use a MANOVA (the multivariate approach) to examine the within-subjects variable; **(b) How would you interpret the *F* for *product* (within subjects)?** This is significant, indicating that participants rated different products differently. However, this effect is qualified by a significant interaction between product and gender; **(c) Is the interaction between product and gender significant?** Yes. **How would you describe it in nontechnical** terms? Males rated different products differently, in comparison to females. Males rated some products (i.e., 1 and 2) much higher but others (i.e., 3 and 4) are rated only somewhat higher than females; **(d) Is there a significant difference between the genders?** No, but this could be due to low power related to the fact that there are only six males and six females in the sample. **Is a post hoc multiple comparison test needed? Explain.** A post hoc test is not needed for gender, both because the effect is not significant and because there are only two groups, so one can tell from the means which group is higher. Because *product* was significant and had four levels, one could do post hoc tests. In this case, because the products had an order to them, linear, quadratic, and cubic trends were examined rather than paired comparisons among means.

10.1 **In Output 10.1b: (a) Are the multivariate tests statistically significant?** Yes; **(b) What does this mean?** This means that students whose fathers had different levels of education differed on a linear combination of *grades in high school*, *math achievement*, and *visualization* scores; **(c) Which individual dependent variables are significant in the univariate ANOVAs?** Both *grades in h.s.*, $F(2, 70) = 4.09$, $p = .021$ and *math achievement*, $F(2, 70) = 7.88$, $p = .001$ are significant; **(d) How are the results similar and different from what we would have found if we had done three univariate one-way ANOVAs?** Included in the Tests of Between-Subjects Effects table of the output are the very same three univariate one-way ANOVAs that we would have done. However, in addition, we have information about how the *father's education* groups differ on the three dependent variables, taken together. If the multivariate tests had not been significant, we would not have looked at the univariate tests; thus, some protection for Type I error is provided. Moreover, the multivariate test provides information about how each of the dependent variables, over and above the other dependent variables, distinguishes between the *father's education* groups. The **parameter estimates** table provides information about how much each variable was weighted in distinguishing particular *father's education* groups.

10.3 **In Output 10.3: (a) What makes this a "doubly multivariate" design?** This is a doubly multivariate design because it involves more than one dependent variable, each of which is measured more than one time; **(b) What information is provided by the multivariate tests of significance that is not provided by the univariate tests?** The multivariate tests indicate how the two dependent variables, taken together, distinguish the intervention from the comparison group, the pretest from the posttest, and the interaction between these two variables. It indicates how each outcome variable contributes, over and above the other outcome variable, to our understanding of the effects of the intervention; **(c) State in your own words what the interaction between time and group tells you.** This significant interaction indicates that the change from pretest to posttest is different for the intervention group than for the comparison group. Examination of the means indicates that this is due to a much greater change from pretest to posttest in Outcome 1 (DV1) for the intervention group than the comparison group; **(d) What implications does this have for understanding the success of the intervention?** This suggests that the intervention was successful in changing Outcome 1. If the intervention group and the comparison group had changed to the same degree from pretest to posttest on DV1, this would have indicated that some other factor was most likely responsible for the change in Outcome 1 from pretest to posttest. Moreover, if there had been no change from pretest to posttest in either group, then any difference between groups would probably not be due to the intervention. This interaction demonstrates exactly what was predicted: that the intervention affected the intervention group but not the group that did not get the intervention (the comparison group) on DV1.

11.1 **In Output 11.1b: (a) Why did we decide to use the autoregressive covariance structure (AR1)?** We decided to use the autoregressive covariance structure because in a repeated-measures design, frequently participants' scores at one time point are correlated with their scores at the following time points, with adjacent scores being most highly correlated. The autoregressive covariance structure takes this into account; **(b) What did the AR1 rho suggest about the need to use the autoregressive covariance structure?** The AR1 rho was very low, suggesting that an autoregressive covariance structure was not needed because the correlation between scores at adjacent time points was very low; **(c) What do the Information Criteria tell you? Why is this important?** The Information Criteria tell us about the goodness of fit of the model to the data. Smaller numbers in the table indicate better fit. The −2 restricted log likelihood is the basic measure of goodness of fit, with the other criteria including adjustments for the complexity of the model. It is important to determine goodness of fit because one is trying to devise a model of appropriate complexity that explains the data. To the extent that additional predictors do not significantly improve the fit, then it is undesirable to include them in the model because it would be more parsimonious to have a simpler model.

11.3 **In Output 11.3: (a) What do we mean when we say that *school* is a nesting variable? Why does this matter?** When we say that *school* is a nesting variable, we mean that data for individual students are not independent of data from other individuals within that school. There is reason to believe that students within a particular school share certain characteristics and experiences (including school experiences), such that they are likely to be more similar to other students in their school than to students in other schools. The nesting variable enables us to take this into account in our model. This is important because most statistical tests make the assumption that all individuals are independent of all other individuals; **(b) What is an unstructured covariance structure, and why did we use it?** An unstructured covariance structure places no constraints on the nature of the covariation among variables. It is useful if one does not have sufficient information to enable one to specify the characteristics of the covariance structure; **(c) In the Covariance Parameters table, what does the intercept variance tell you?** The intercept variance tells us how much schools vary with respect to the dependent variable, in this case *mathach*. Since there is significant variability between schools, one might want to use a school-level (Level 2) predictor to explain this variability (although we did not do so in this book so as not to make the problem overly complex).

For Further Reading

American Educational Research Association (2006). Standards for reporting on empirical social science research in AERA publications. *Educational Researcher, 35*(6), 33-40.

American Psychological Association (APA). (2010). *Publication manual of the American Psychological Association* (6th ed.). Washington, DC: Author.

Cohen, J. (1965). Some statistical issues in psychological research. In B. B. Wolman (Ed.), *Handbook of clinical psychology* (pp. 95–121). New York, NY: McGraw-Hill.

Cohen, J. (1988). *Statistical power and analysis for the behavioral sciences* (2nd ed.). Hillsdale, NJ: Lawrence Erlbaum.

Gliner, J. A., Morgan, G. A., & Leech, N. A. (2009). *Research methods in applied settings: An integrated approach to design and analysis* (2nd ed.). New York, NY: Routledge/Taylor & Francis.

Hair, J. F., Black, B., Babin, B., Anderson, R. E., & Tatham, R.L. (2010). *Multivariate data analysis* (7th ed.). Englewood Cliffs, NJ: Prentice Hall.

Hopkins, K. D. (1998). *Educational and psychological measurement and evaluation* (8th ed.). Needham Heights, MA: Allyn & Bacon.

Huck, S. J. (2007). *Reading statistics and research* (5th ed.). Boston, MA: Allyn & Bacon.

Morgan, G. A., Leech, N. L., Gloeckner, G. W., & Barrett, K. C. (2011). *SPSS for introductory statistics: Use and interpretation* (4th ed.). New York, NY: Routledge/Taylor & Francis.

Morgan, G. A., Gliner, J. A., & Harmon, R. J. (2006). *Understanding and evaluating research in applied and clinical setting.* Mahwah, NJ: Lawrence Erlbaum.

Morgan, S. E., Reichart, T., & Harrison T. R. (2002). *From numbers to words: Reporting statistical results for the social sciences.* Boston, MA: Allyn & Bacon.

Newton R. R., & Rudestam K. E. (1999). *Your statistical consultant: Answers to your data analysis questions.* Thousand Oaks, CA: Sage.

Nicol, A. A. M., & Pexman, P. M. (2010 a). *Displaying your findings: A practical guide for creating figures, posters, and presentations.* Washington, DC: American Psychological Association.

Nicol, A. A. M., & Pexman, P. M. (2010 b). *Presenting your findings: A practical guide for creating tables.* Washington, DC: American Psychological Association.

Raudenbush, S. W., & Bryk, A. S. (2002). *Hierarchical linear models: Applications and data analysis methods* (2nd ed.).Thousand Oaks, CA: Sage.

Rudestam, K. E., & Newton, R. R. (2007). *Surviving your dissertation: A comprehensive guide to content and process* (3rd ed.). Newbury Park, CA: Sage.

Singer, J. D. (1998). Using SAS PROC MIXED to fit multilevel models, hierarchical models, and individual growth models. *Journal of Educational and Behavioral Statistics, 23,* 323–355.

Tabachnick, B. G., & Fidell, L. S. (2007). *Using multivariate statistics* (5th ed.). Boston, MA: Allyn & Bacon.

Thompson, B. (2004). *Exploratory and confirmatory factor analyses: Understanding concepts and applications.* Washington, D.C.: American Psychological Association.

Thompson, B. (Ed.). (2003). *Score reliability: Contemporary thinking on reliability issues.* Thousand Oaks, CA: Sage.

Vaske, J. J., Gliner, J. A., & Morgan, G. A. (2002). Communicating judgments about practical significance: Effect size, confidence intervals and odds ratios. *Human Dimensions of Wildlife, 7,* 287-300.

Vogt, W. P. (2005). *Dictionary of statistics and methodology* (3rd ed.). Newbury Park, CA: Sage.

Wainer, H. (1992). Understanding graphs and tables. *Educational Researcher, 21*(1), 14–23.

Wilkinson, L., & The APA Task Force on Statistical Inference. (1999). Statistical methods in psychology journals: Guidelines and explanations. *American Psychologist, 54,* 594–604.

Index[1]

---

[1] Commands used primarily by SPSS are in bold.